iQ BRAIN TWISTER

Kandour Ltd

Kandour Ltd
1-3 Colebrooke Place, London N1 8HZ
UNITED KINGDOM

First published 2006

10 9 8 7 6 5 4 3 2 1

Managing Editor: James Jackson
Production: Carol Titchener
Author: G. Newton
Jacket Design: Alexander Rose Publishing Limited
Puzzle Layout: Domex e-Data Pvt Ltd

Printed and bound in China

ISBN-10: 0-681-57126-8

ISBN-13: 978-0-681-57126-6

CONTENTS

We have split each section into:

- **E for Easy**
- **M for Medium**
- **D for Difficult**

Once you find the difficult puzzles easy you will know you are an IQ Master!

NUMERICAL

• **Find the missing number.**

1.

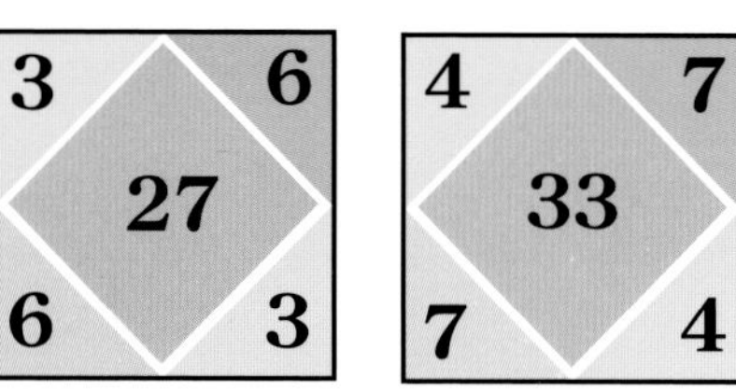

5 8
?
8 5

39	45	89	80
A	B	C	D

2.

5
14
23
9
18
?
36
4
13

19	27	37	1
A	B	C	D

3.

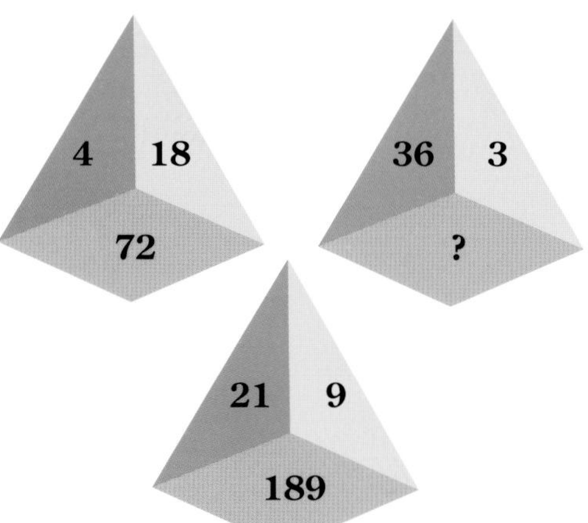

118	138	108	128
A	B	C	D

4.

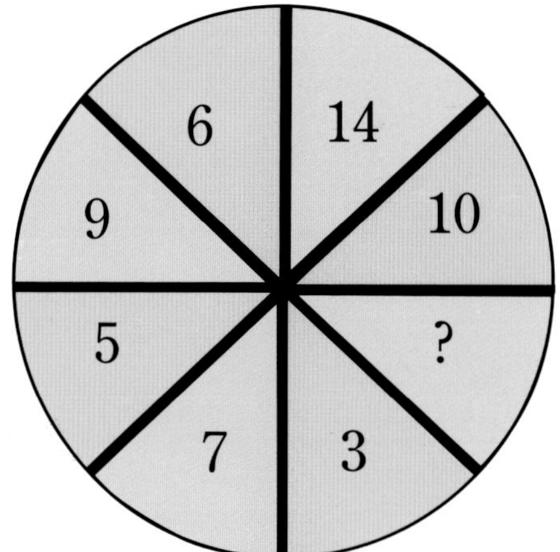

27	3	18	21
A	B	C	D

5.

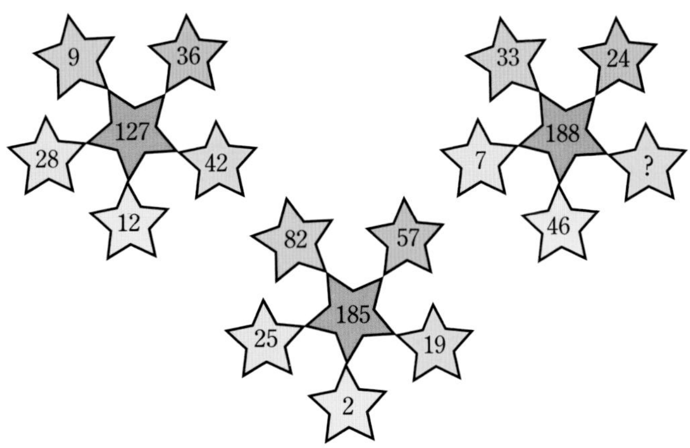

76	75	78	77
A	B	C	D

6.

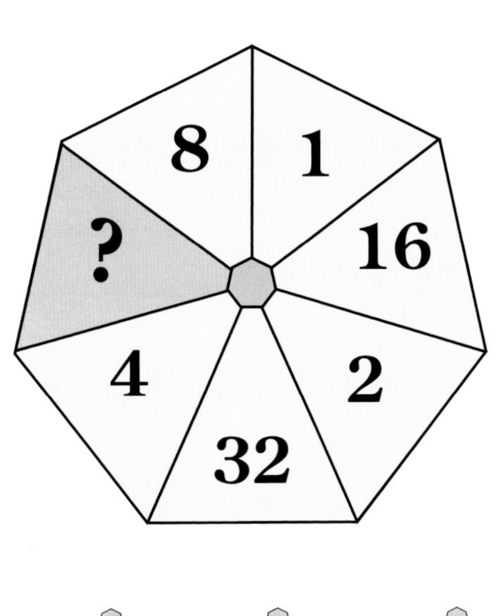

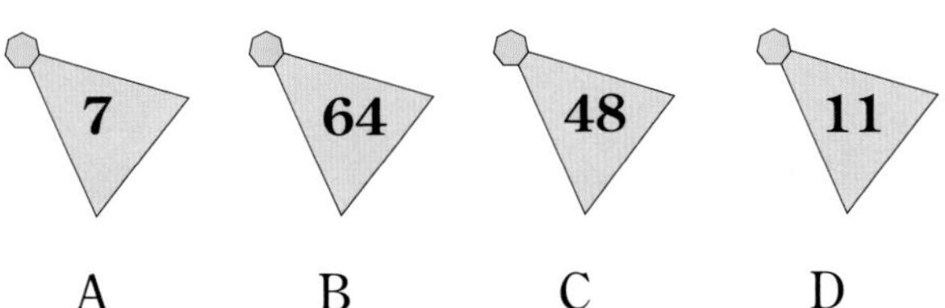

A B C D

7.

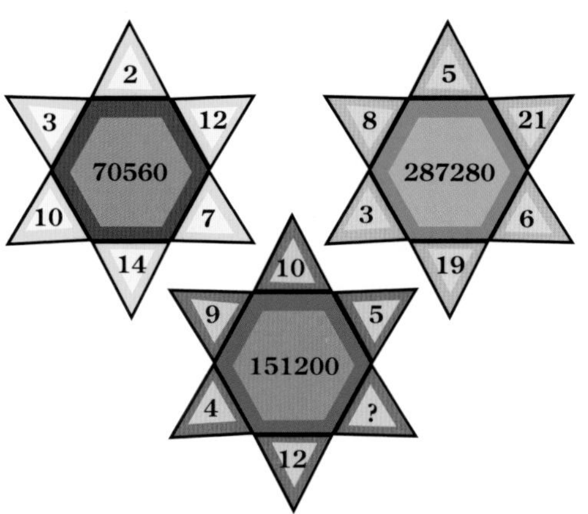

14	5	10	7
A	B	C	D

8.

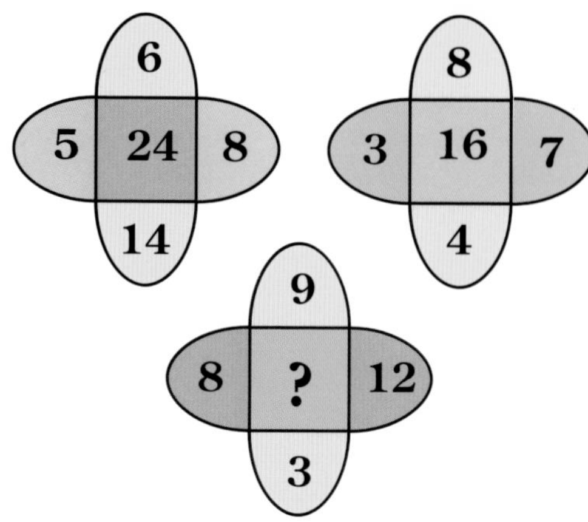

48	28	24	93
A	B	C	D

9.

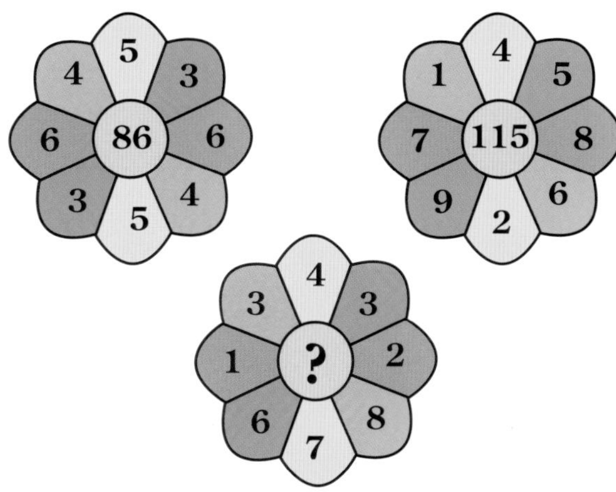

42	72	98	58
A	B	C	D

10.

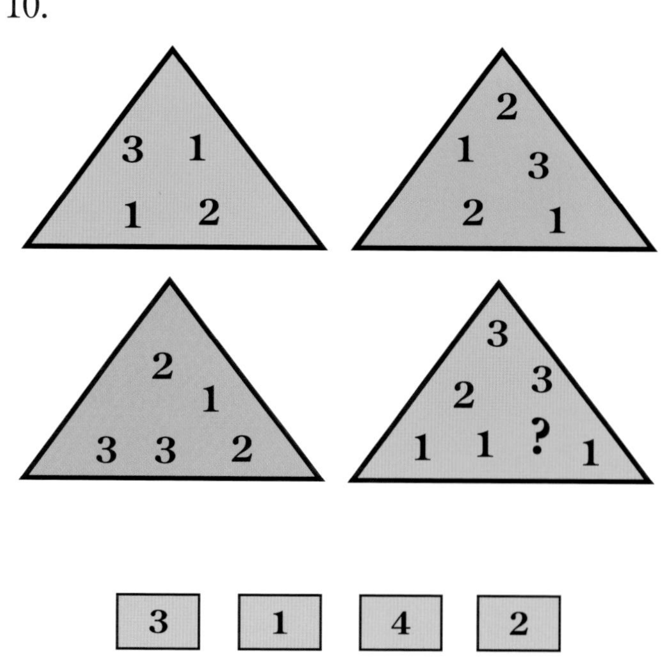

3	1	4	2
A	B	C	D

11.

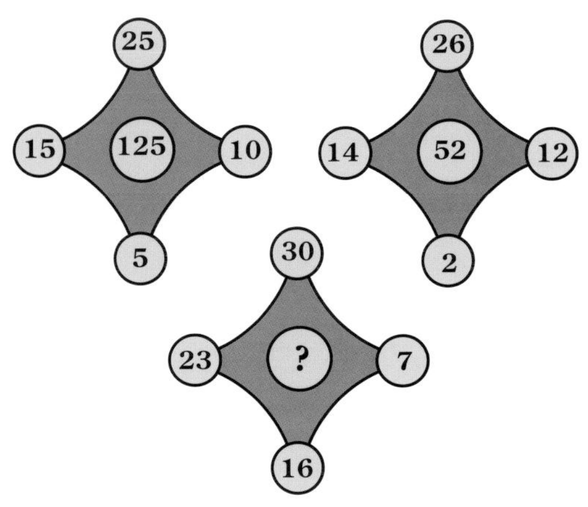

47	481	480	490
A	B	C	D

12.

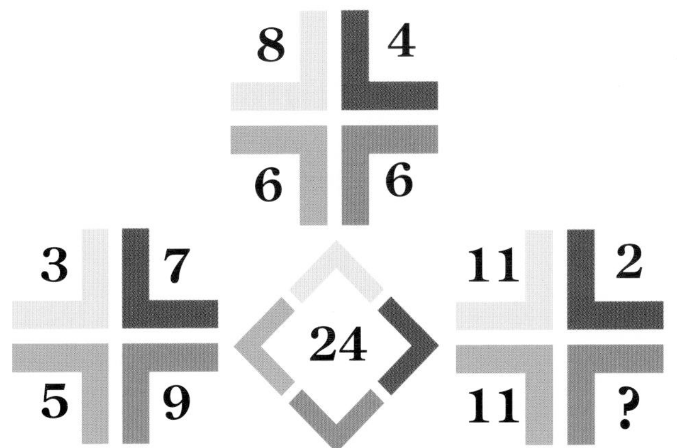

4	9	0	5
A	B	C	D

13.

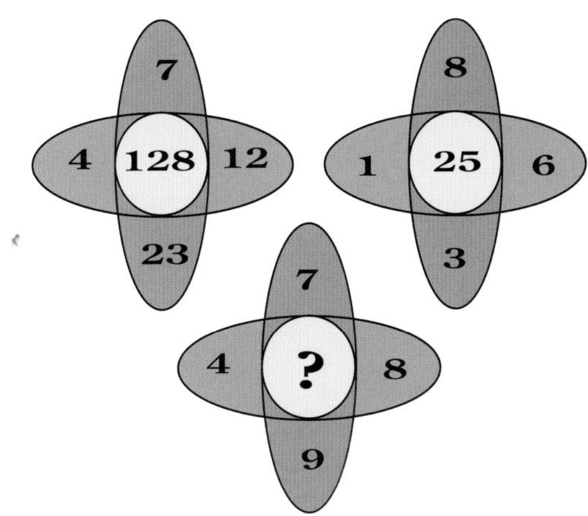

45	8	104	95
A	B	C	D

14.

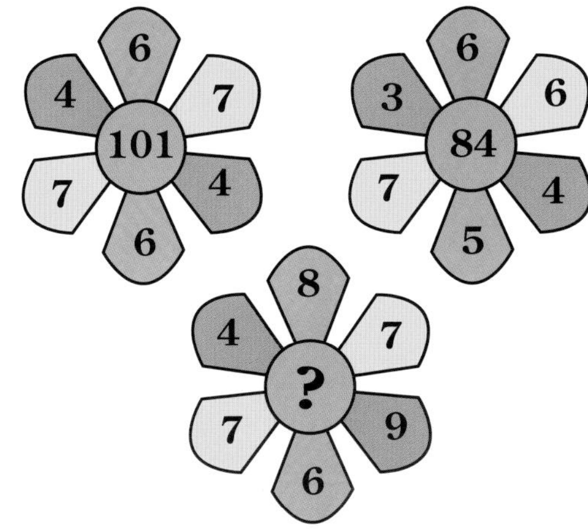

41	133	124	144
A	B	C	D

15.

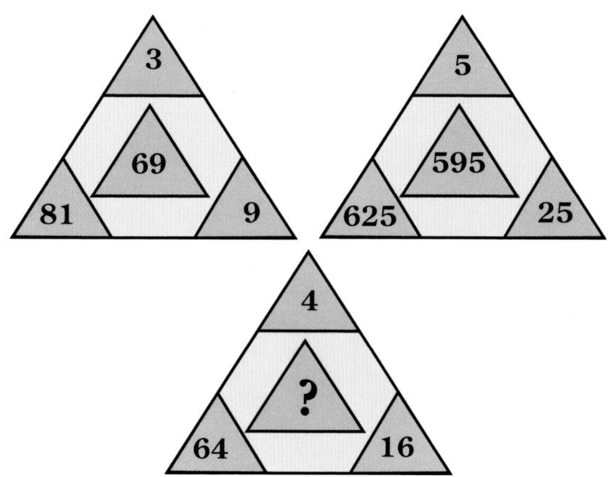

44	43	14	65
A	B	C	D

16.

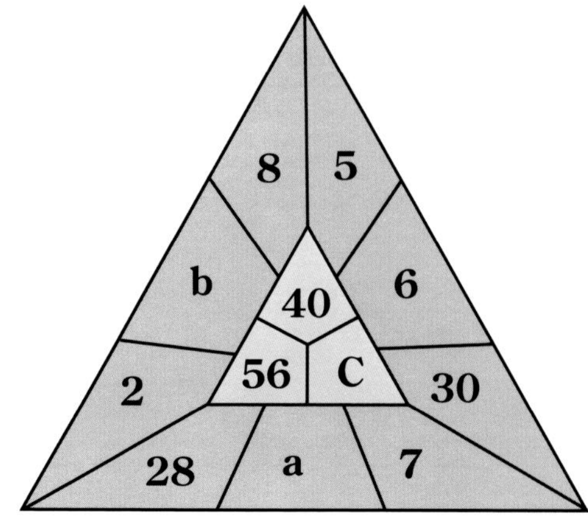

Find the value of a, b & c.

4, 4, 210	3, 4, 210	4, 4, 220	4, 8, 210
A	B	C	D

17.

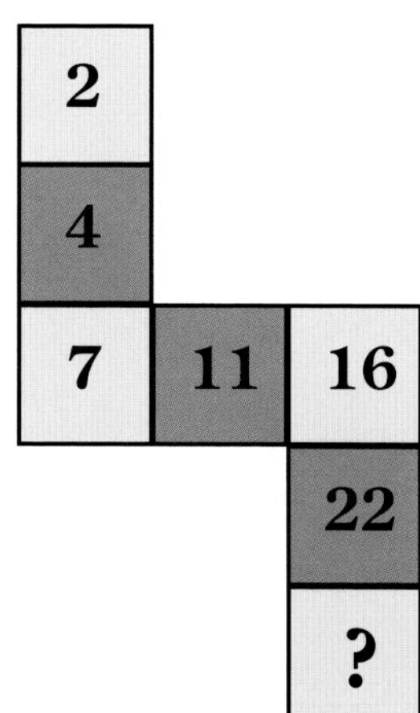

23	28	27	29
A	B	C	D

18.

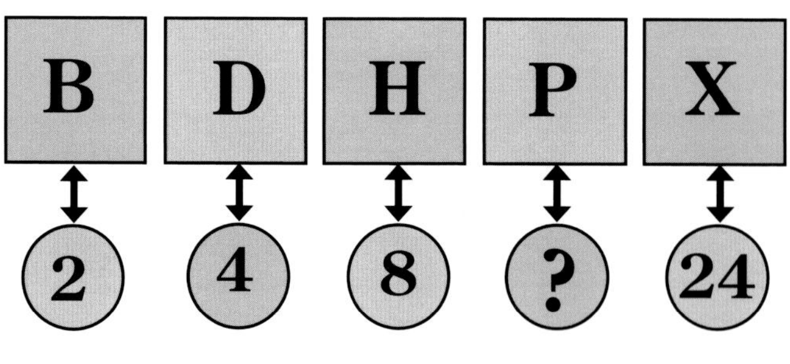

24	8	32	16
A	B	C	D

19.

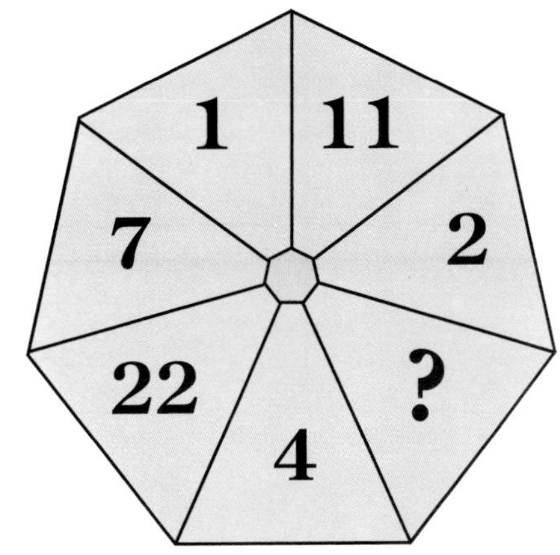

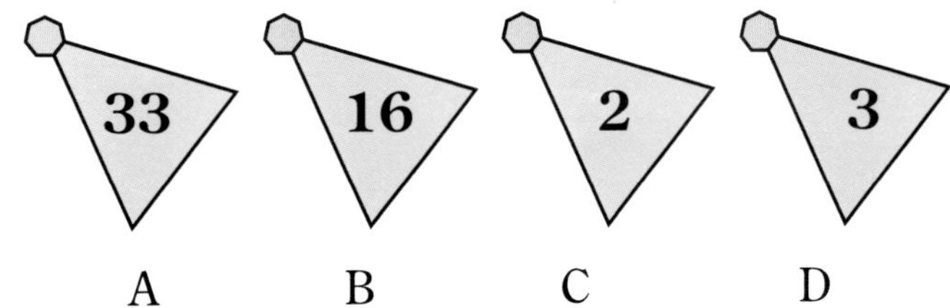

20.

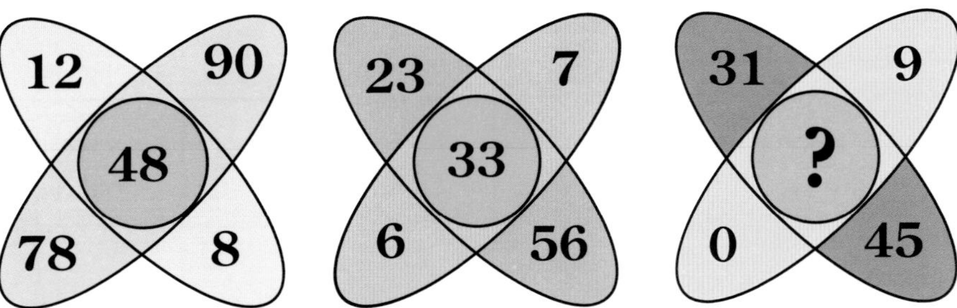

436	85	126	62
A	B	C	D

21.

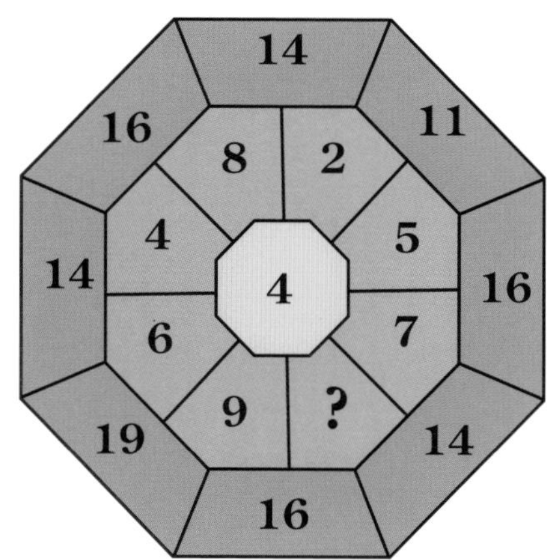

4	6	7	3
A	B	C	D

22.

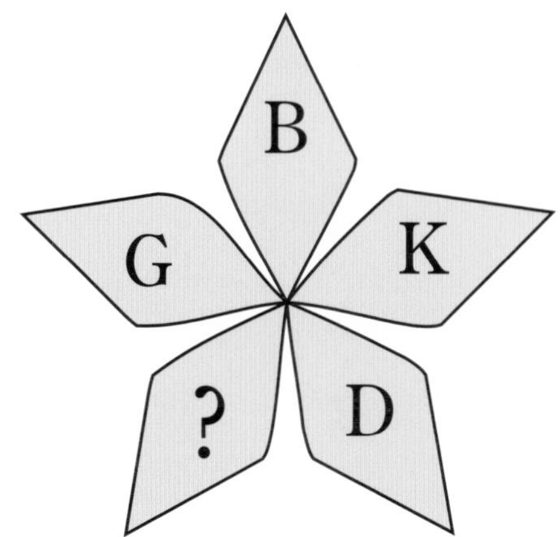

P	B	H	Z
A	B	C	D

23.

10	5	4	3
7	2	9	8
17	7	13	?
34	14	?	22
68	28	52	?

26,11,44	25,11,44	26,12,44	26,12,45
A	B	C	D

24.

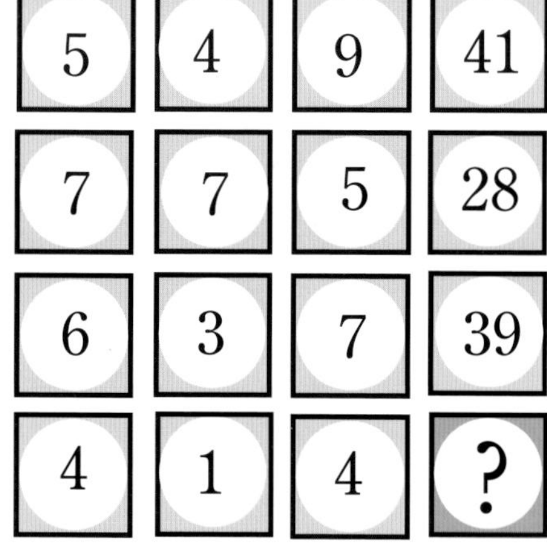

9	108	15	7
A	B	C	D

25.

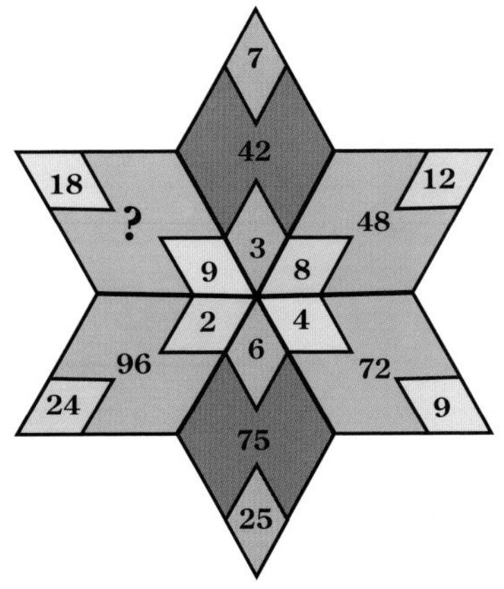

163 A

165 B

324 C

81 D

26.

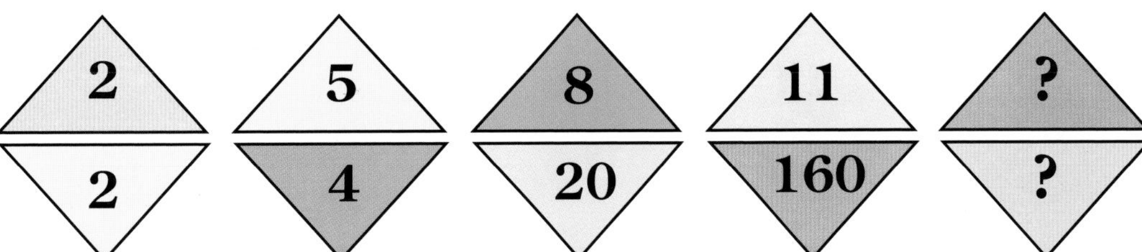

A

B

C

D

OBSERVATION

- In each of the puzzles given, there is a missing letter/number.
- You have to first identify the missing letter/ number.
- There is also a number(s) with a plus or minus sign given.
- Do not count the missing letter/number. To arrive at the solution, you have to count ahead from the missing letter/number (in case of '+') or backwards from the missing letter/number (in case of '-').
- Try solving puzzles in the easy and medium category in two minutes, and puzzles in the difficult category in one minute.

1.

A B C E F G H I J K L M N O P Q R S T U V W X Y Z

+ 4

Z K W H

2.

I J K L M N P Q R S T U V W X Y Z A B C D E F G H

+ 9
- 2

Z U V N

3.

A B C D E F G H I J K L M N O P Q R S T U V W X Z A B

- 3
+ 9

G V D F

4.

A B C D E F G H I J K L M N O Q R S T U V W X Y Z

- 17

T D G Y

5.

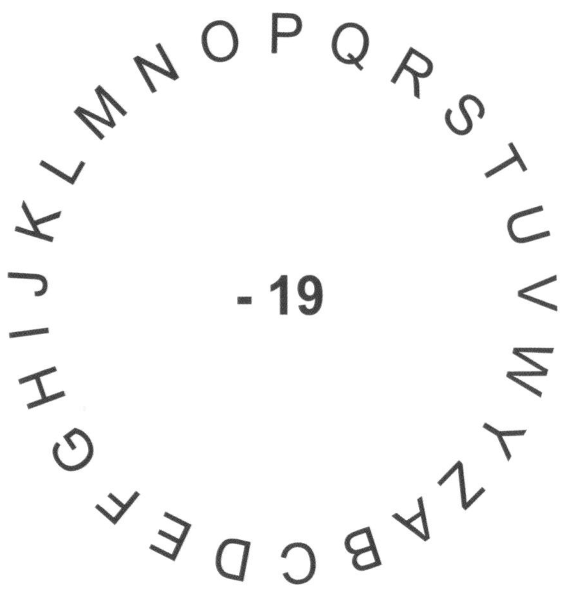
A B C D E F G H I J K L M N O P Q R S T U V W Y Z
- 19

E W Q A

6.

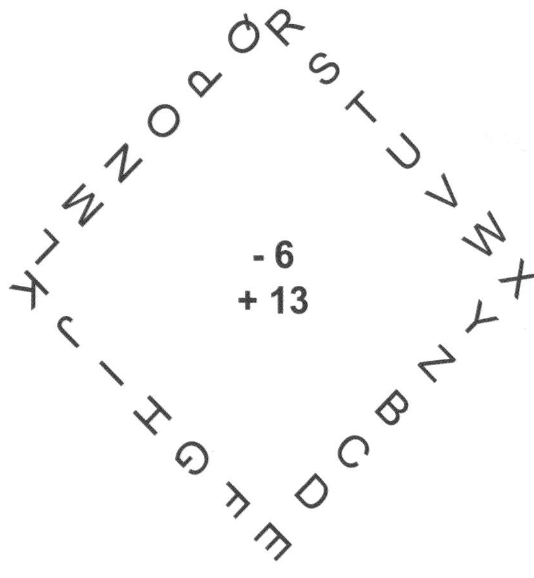
B C D E F G H I J K L M N O P Q R S T U V W X Y Z
- 6
+ 13

G U S I

7.

D C Z B

8.

+ 5
- 12

I T F H

9.

+ 12
- 7
+ 11

F U A E

10.

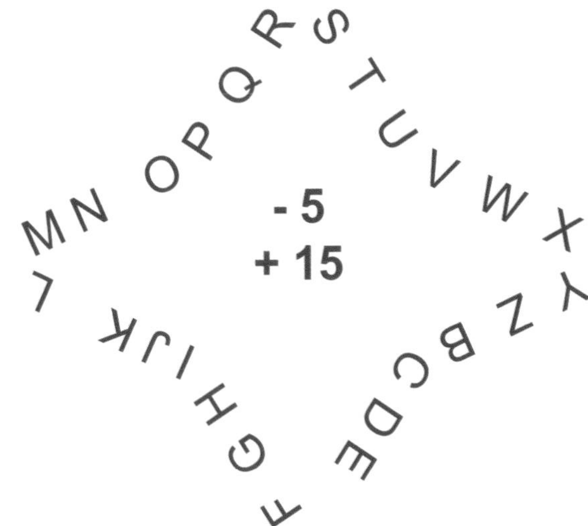

M L V A

11.

X Y Z A B C D
W E
V F
U G
T H
S I
R J
Q P O N M K

- 3
+ 9
- 7

K R I M

12.

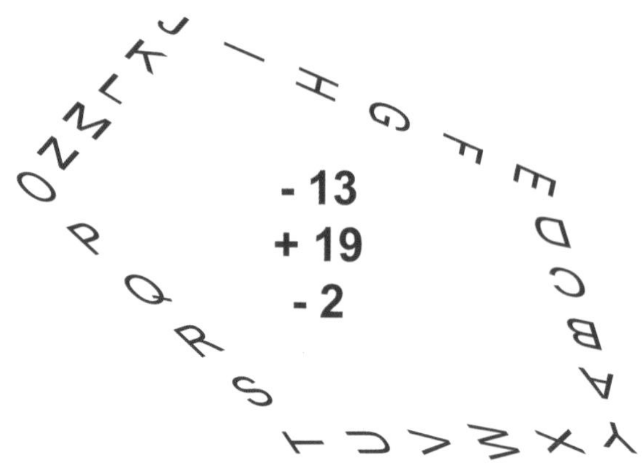

- 13
+ 19
- 2

A D G E

13.

A Z Y X W V U T S R Q P O N L K J I H G F E D C B

- 5
+ 11

S F T U

14.

X Y Z A B C D
W E
V F
U G
T H
S I
Q J
P O N M L K

+ 3
- 4

M T S P

15.

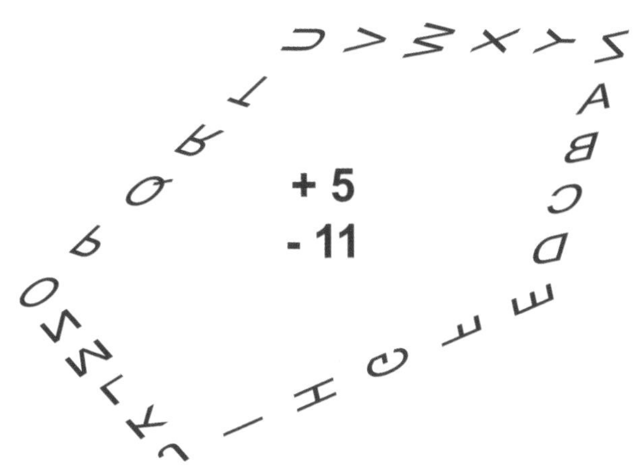

+ 5
- 11

K C L S

16.

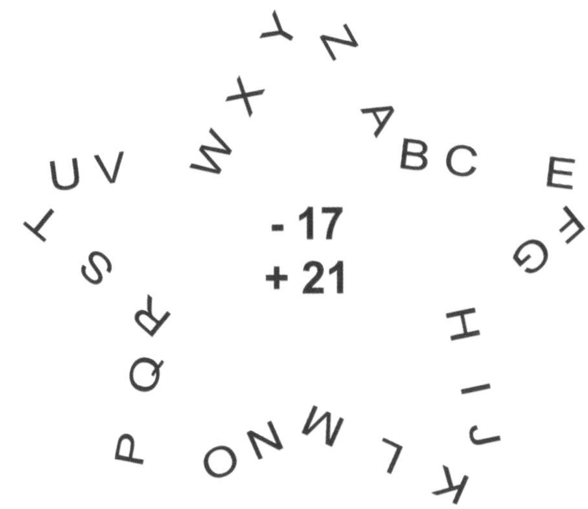

- 17
+ 21

K I F U

17.

A B C E F G H I J K L M N O P Q R S T U V W X Y Z

+ 8
- 11

I T Z H

18.

A B C D E F G H I J K L M N O P Q R S T U V X Y Z

- 13
+ 27
- 19

B J F R

19.

A B C D E F G H I J K L M N O P Q R S T U V W X Y Z a b c d e f g h i j l m n o p q r s t u v w x y z

+ 4
- 19

W U c V

20.

a b c d f g h i j k l m n o p q r s t u v w x y z A B C D E F G H I J K L M N O P Q R S T U V W X Y Z

- 4
+ 24

z A x C

21.

- 9 + 42 - 15

L v S K

22.

+ 5 - 18 + 22

r v S m

23.

+ 25 - 17 + 3

P J 18 Q

24.

- 7 + 36 - 3

o 14 O P

25.

B C F H A I J K D L M E N G O P R S T Q V W X U Y Z Z z x w v t u y s r q p o m l k j i n h g f d c b e a Z X W V Y U T R Q P O B N S M L J I H K G E D C F A a d e f h i j l m n g o p c q r t u k v s w y z x

+ 12
- 31
+ 19

A e C a

26.

A B C D E F G H I J K L M N O P R S T U V W X Y Z A B C D E F G H I J K L M N O P Q R S T U V W X Y Z A B C D E

+ 8
- 12
+ 3
- 4
+ 6

Q R O J

B C D E F G H I J K L M N O P Q R S T U V W X Y Z

ANALOGIES

- The first figure is related to the second one. Similarly, which figure is related to the third figure?

1.

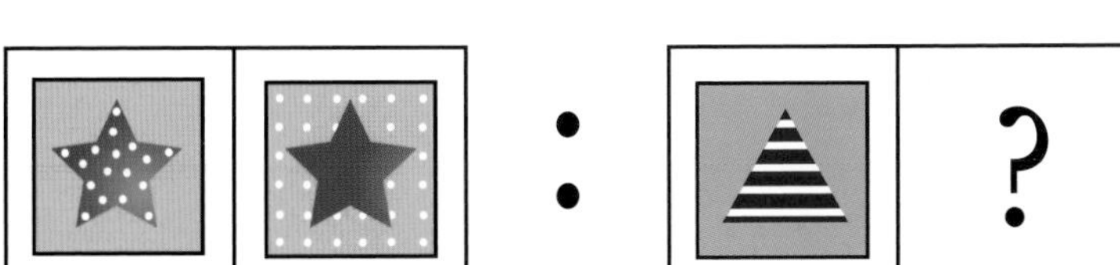

A B C D

2.

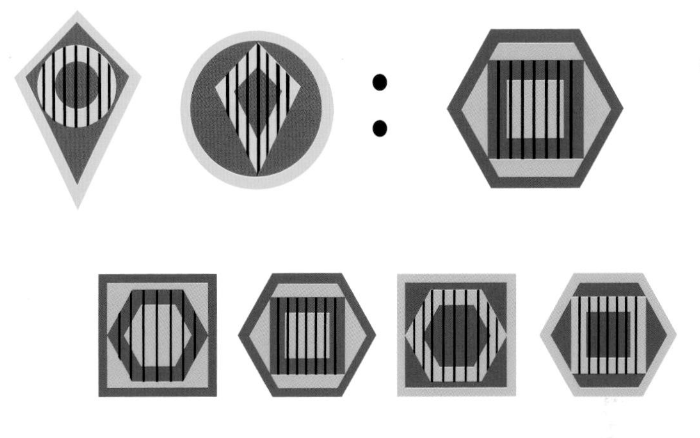

A B C D

3.

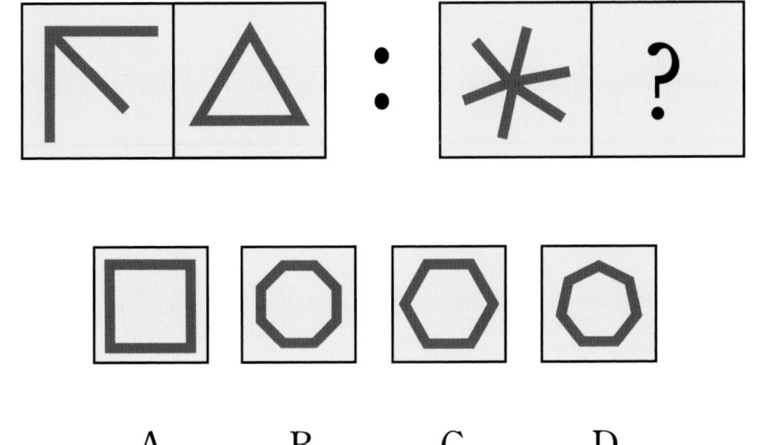

4.

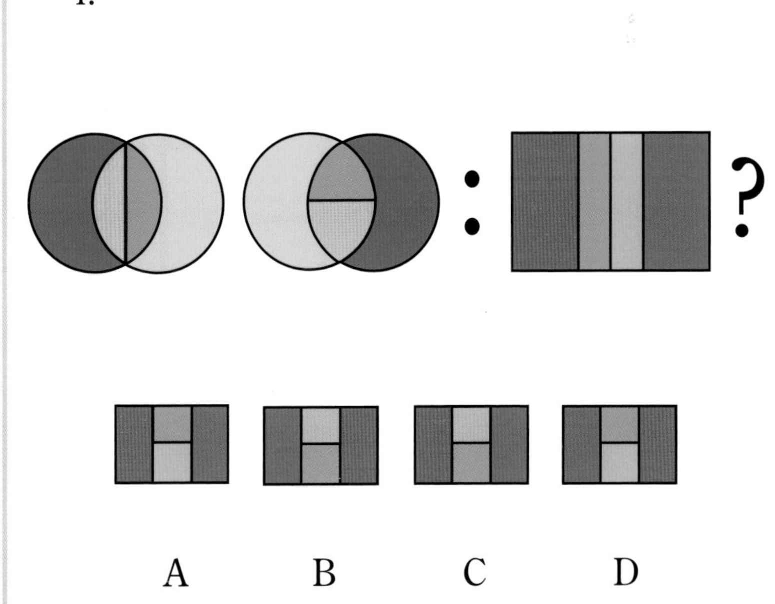

5.

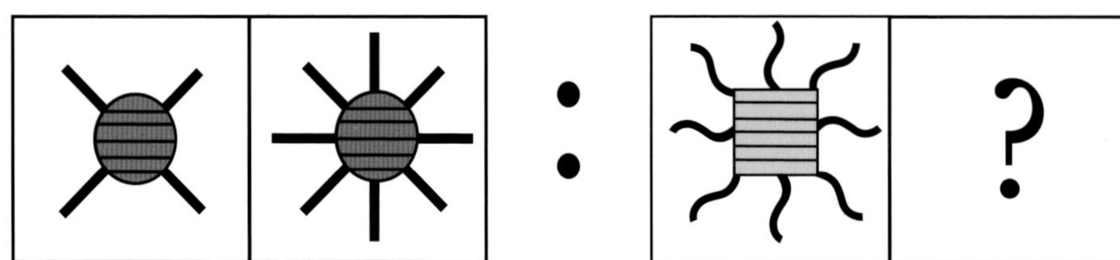

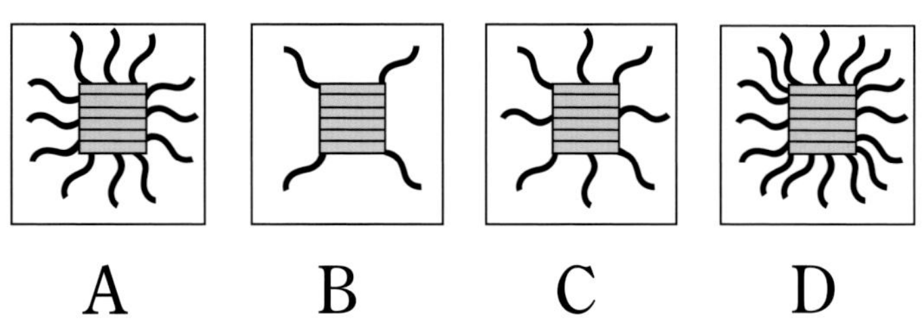

A B C D

6.

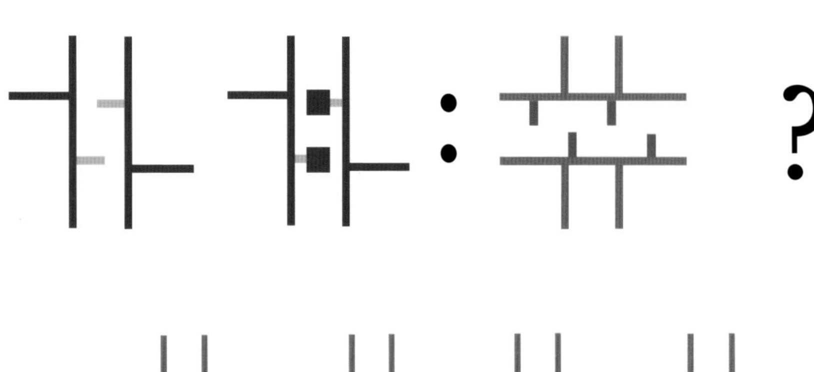

A B C D

7.

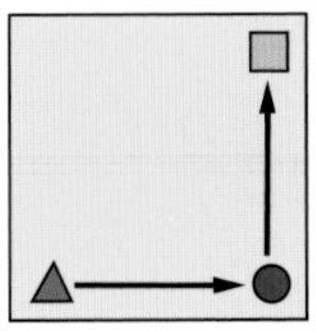
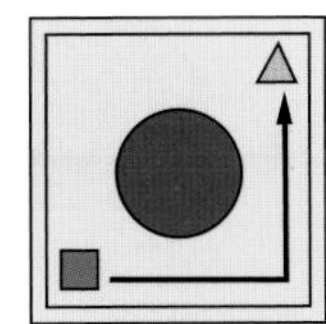
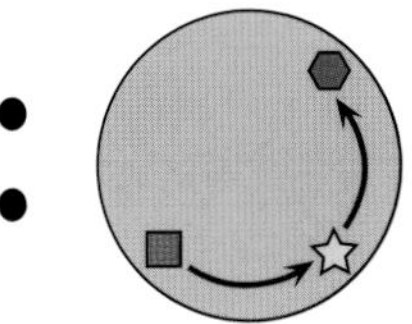
?

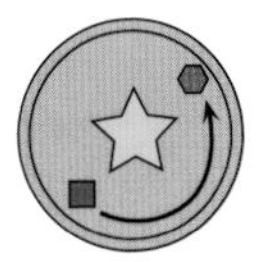
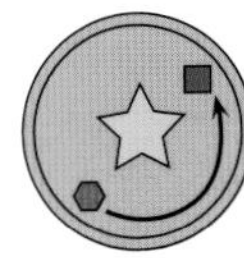

A B C D

8.

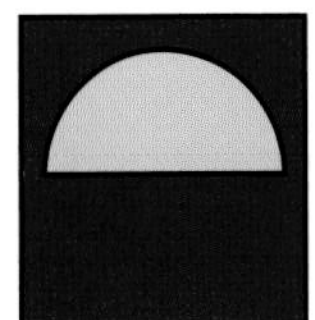
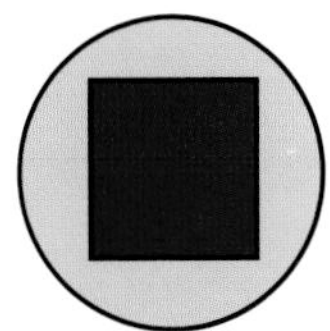

?

A B C D

9.

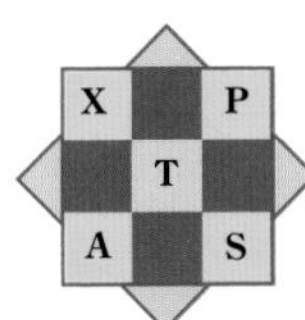

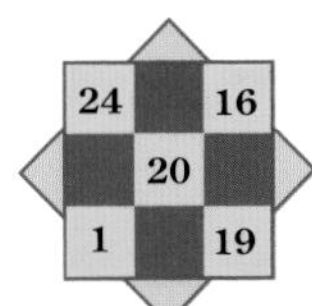

?

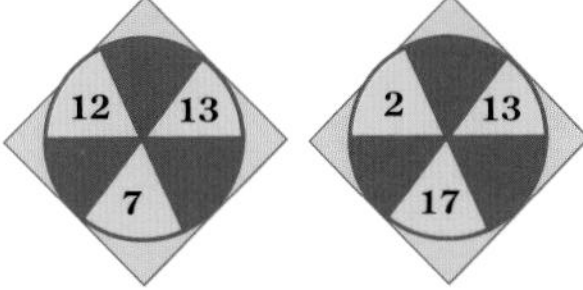
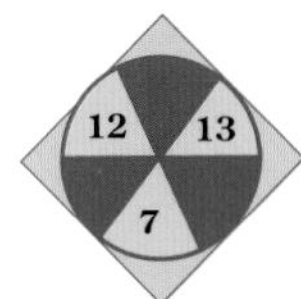

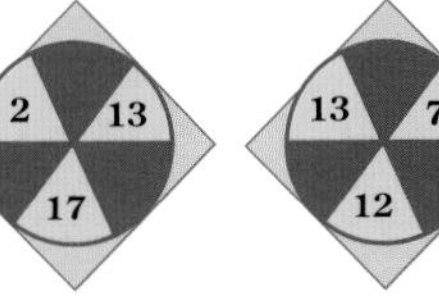

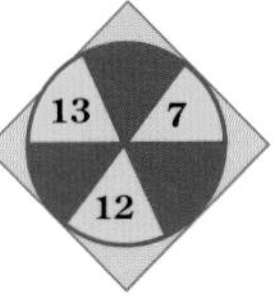

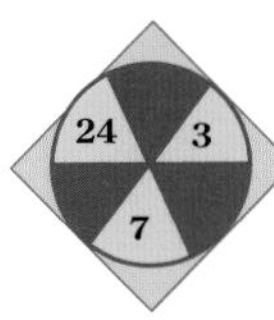

A B C D

10.

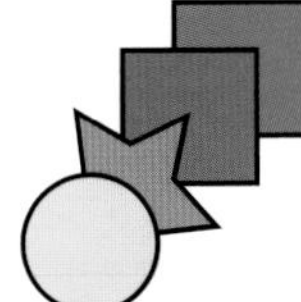
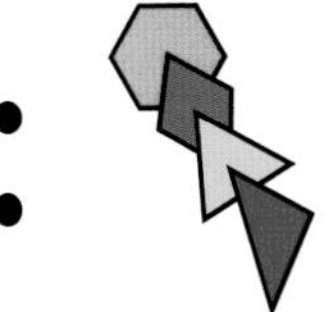

?

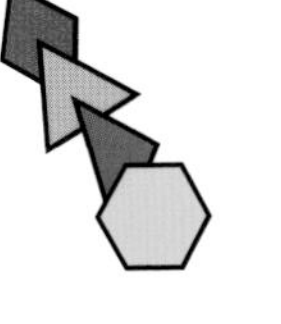

A B C D

11.

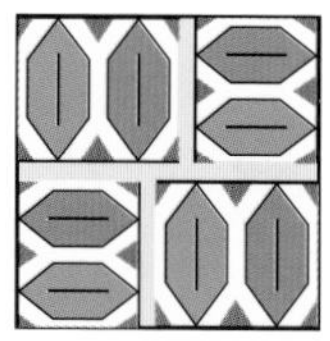
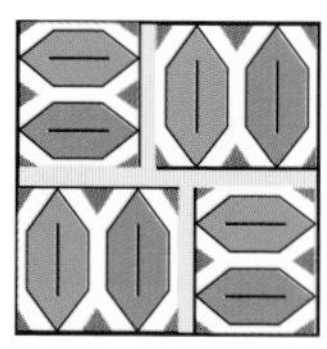
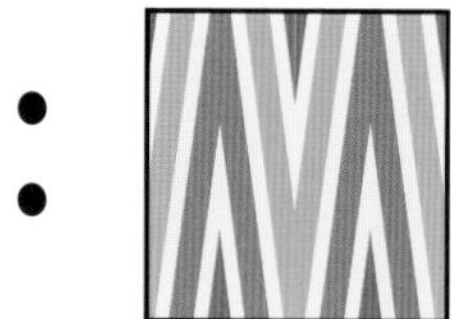

A B C D

12.

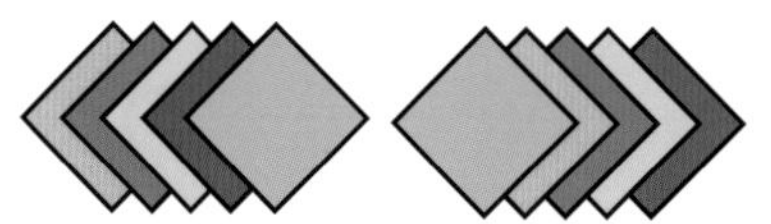

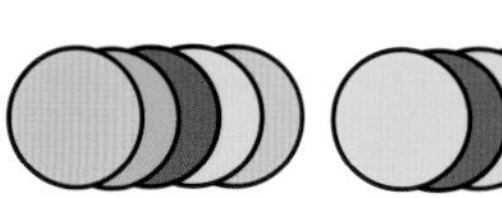

A B C D

13.

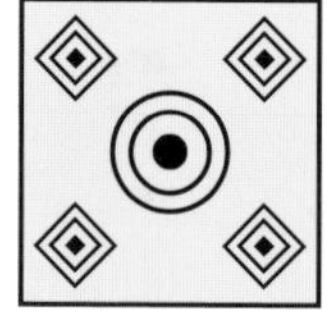
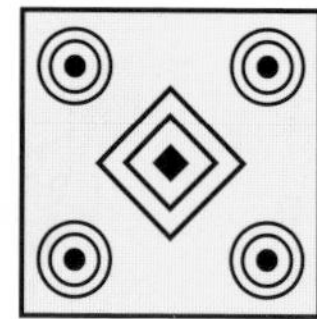
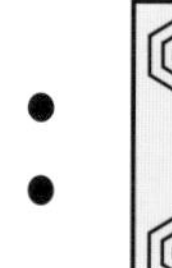
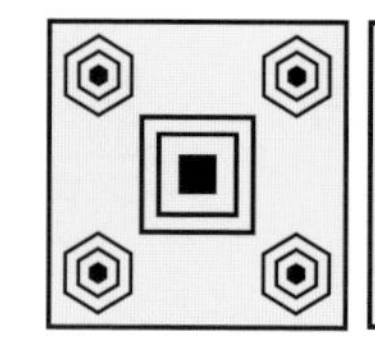

A B C D

14.

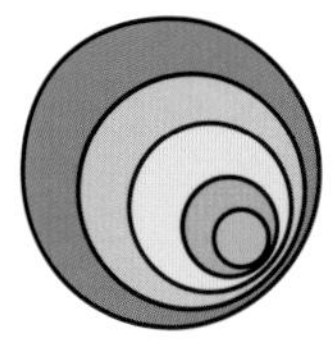
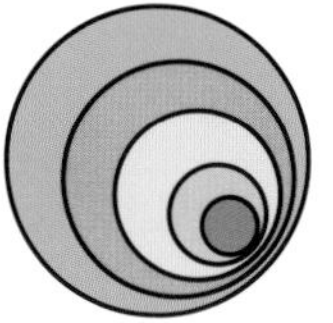

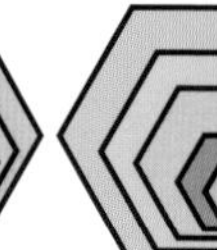

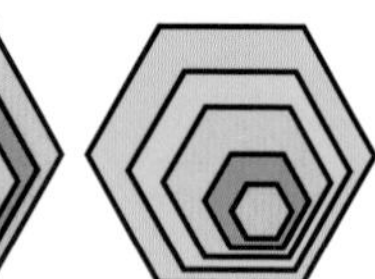

A B C D

15.

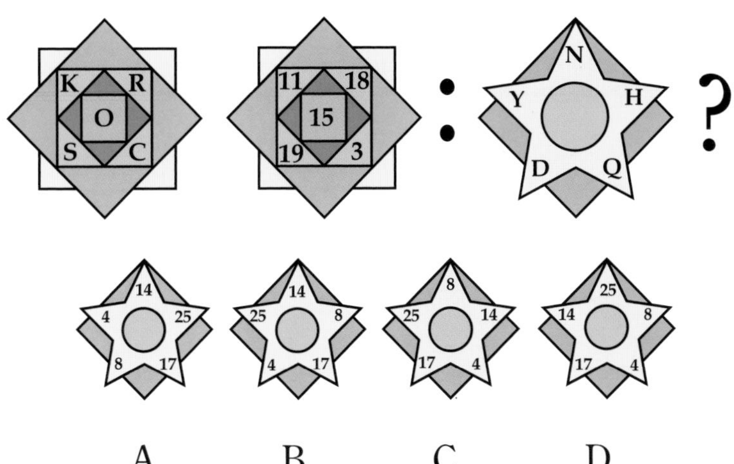

A B C D

16.

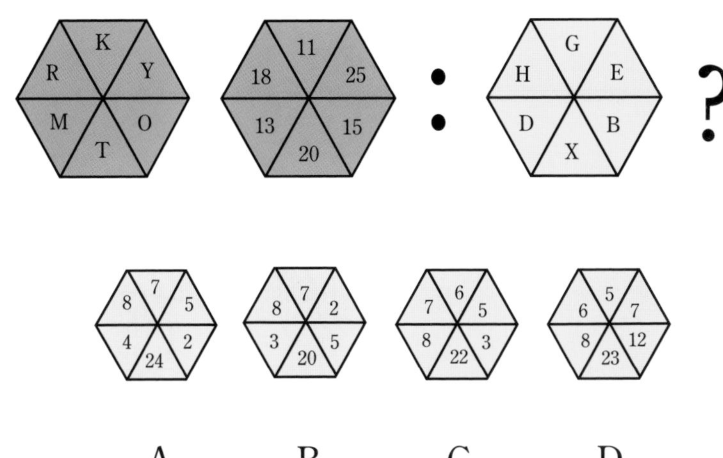

A B C D

17.

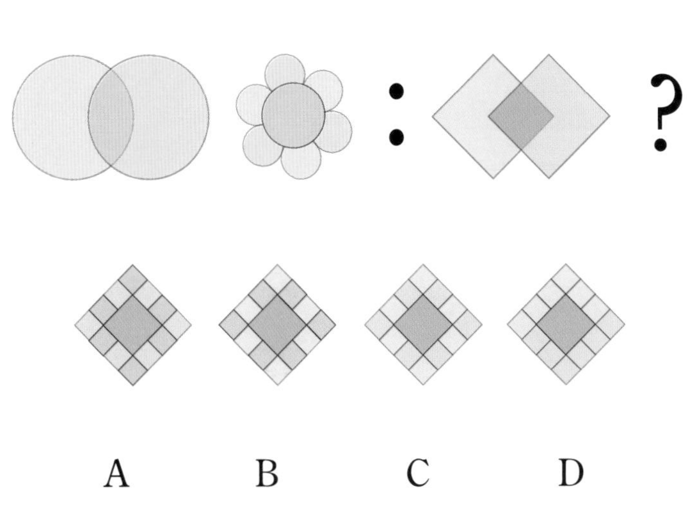

A B C D

18.

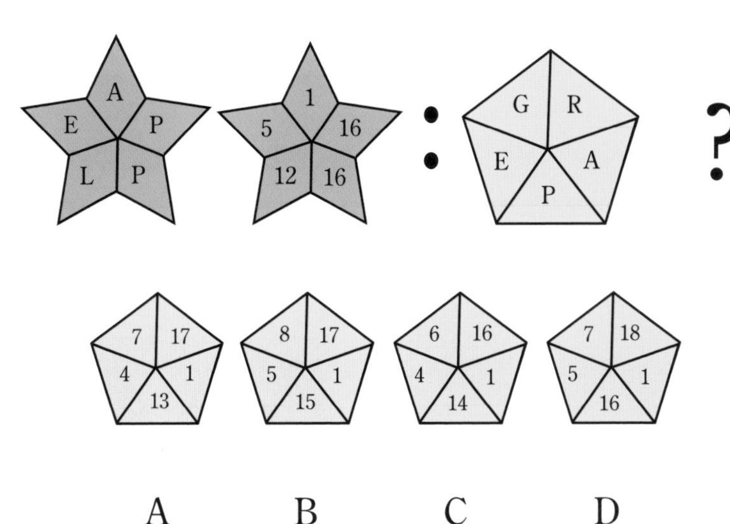

A B C D

19.

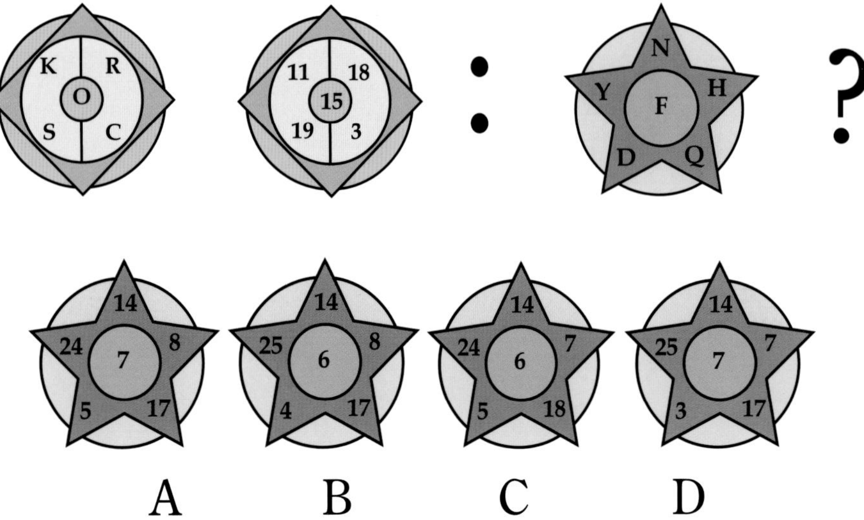
K R O S C
11 18 15 19 3
N Y H F D Q
?
14 24 8 7 5 17
14 25 8 6 4 17
14 24 7 6 5 18
14 25 7 7 3 17
A B C D

20.

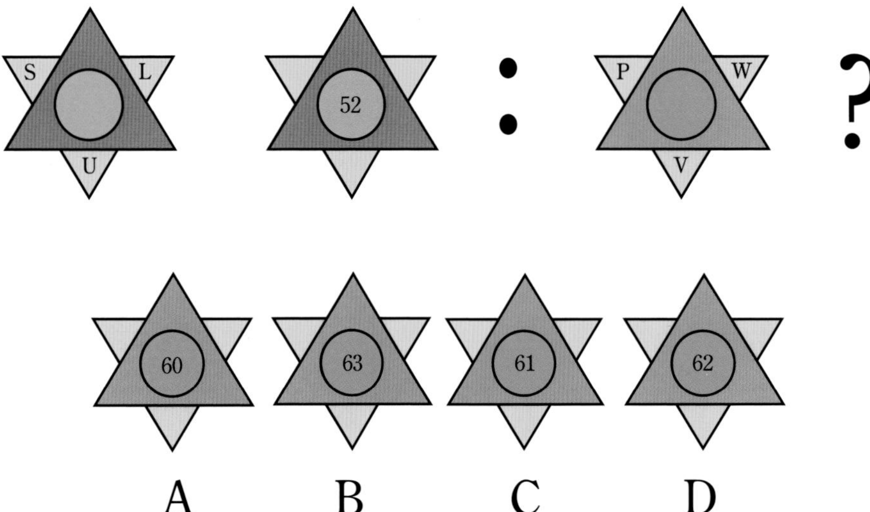
S L U
52
P W V
?
60 63 61 62
A B C D

21.

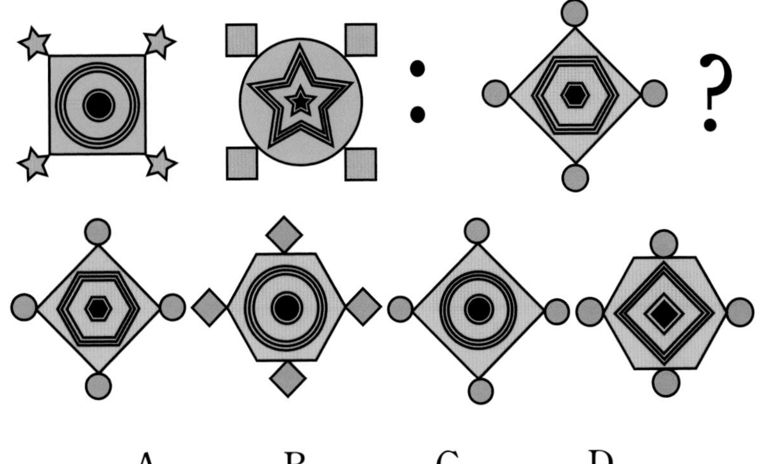
A
B
C
D

22.

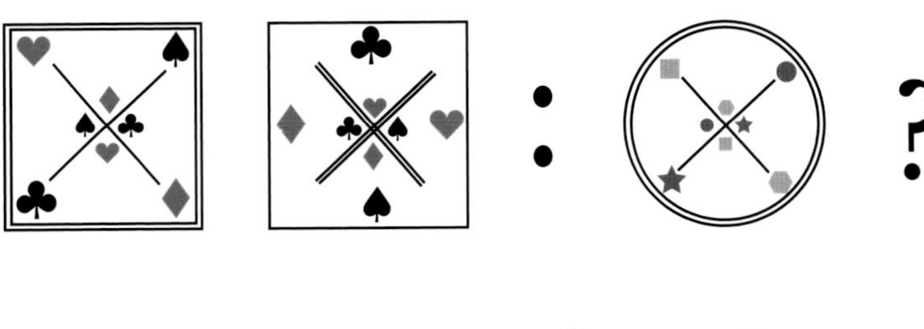

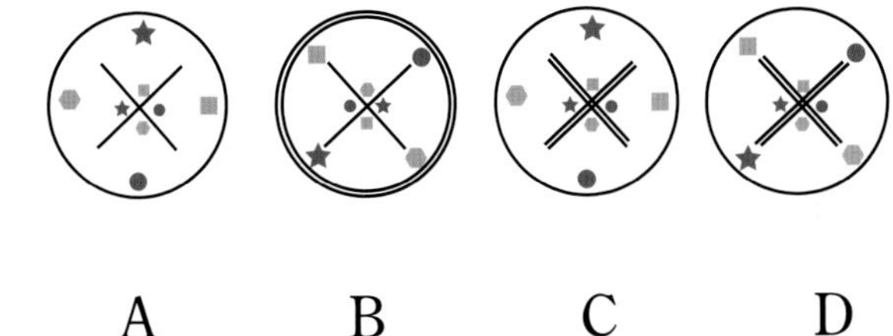
A
B
C
D

23.

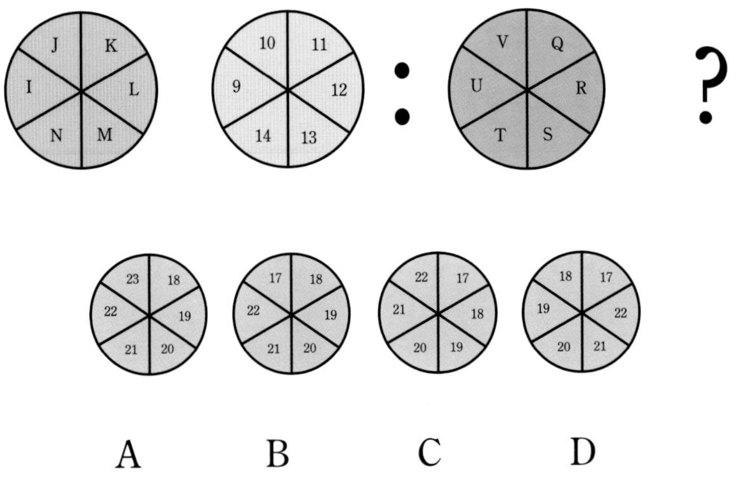
J K L M N I
10 11 12 13 14 9
V Q R S T U
23 18 19 20 21 22
17 18 19 20 21 22
22 17 18 19 20 21
18 17 22 21 20 19
A
B
C
D

24.

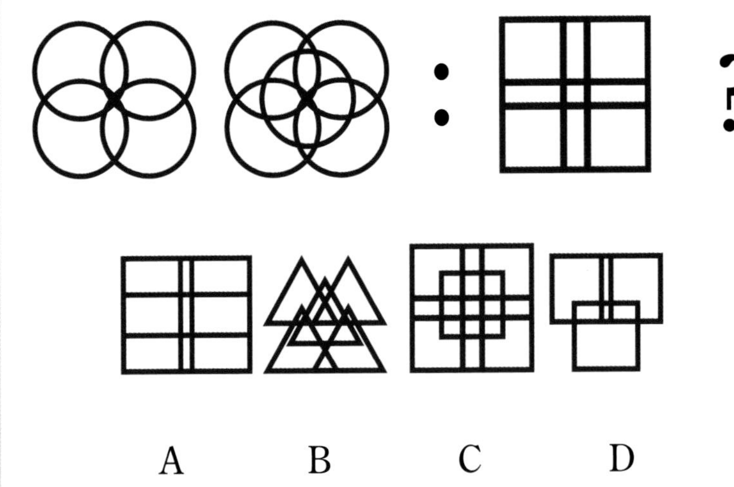
A
B
C
D

25.

CAPITAL=62 : ANIMAL= ?

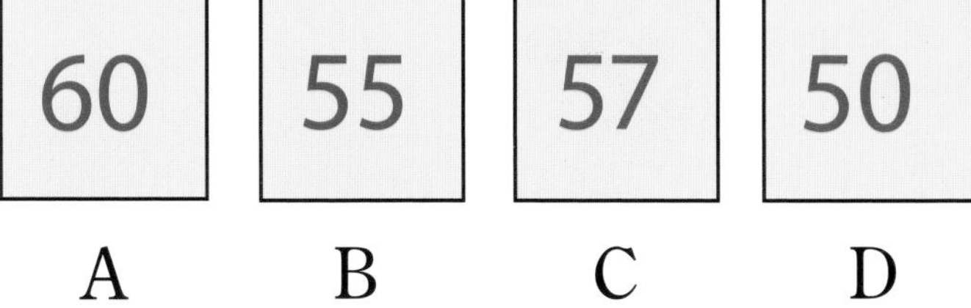

A B C D

26.

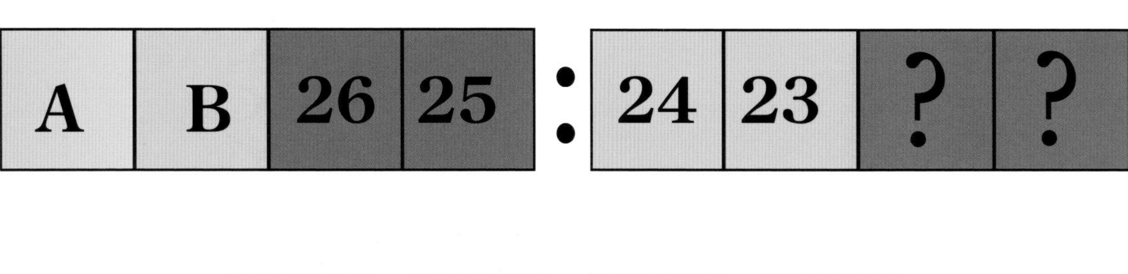

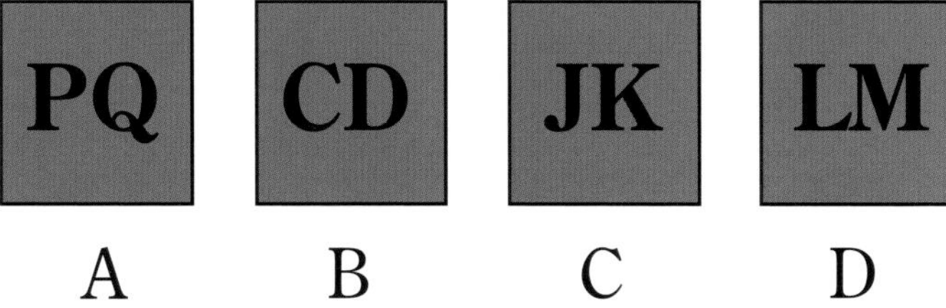

A B C D

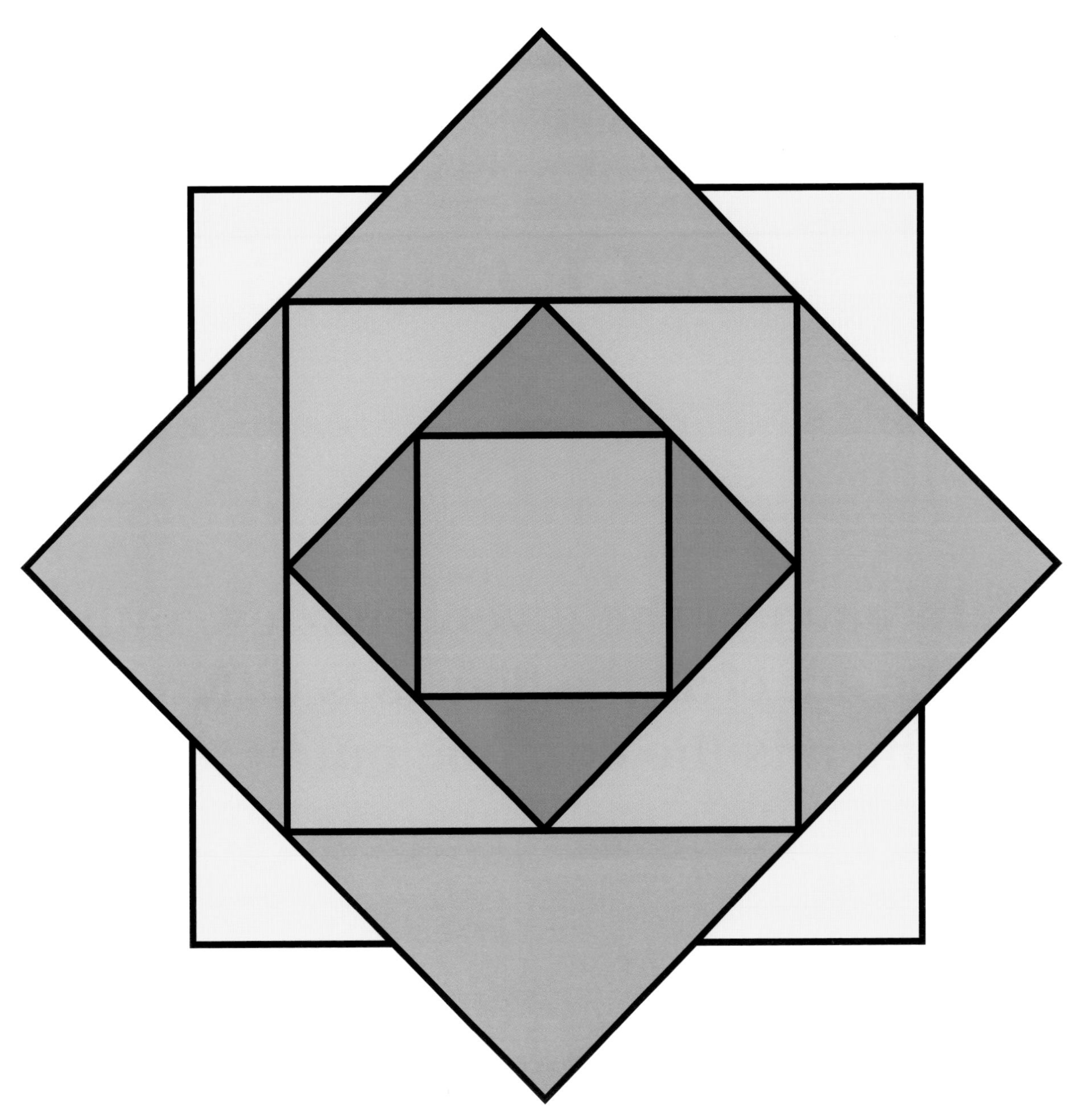

CATEGORY

- **In each of the given puzzles, only one out of all the figures is different.**
- **Which is the odd one out?**

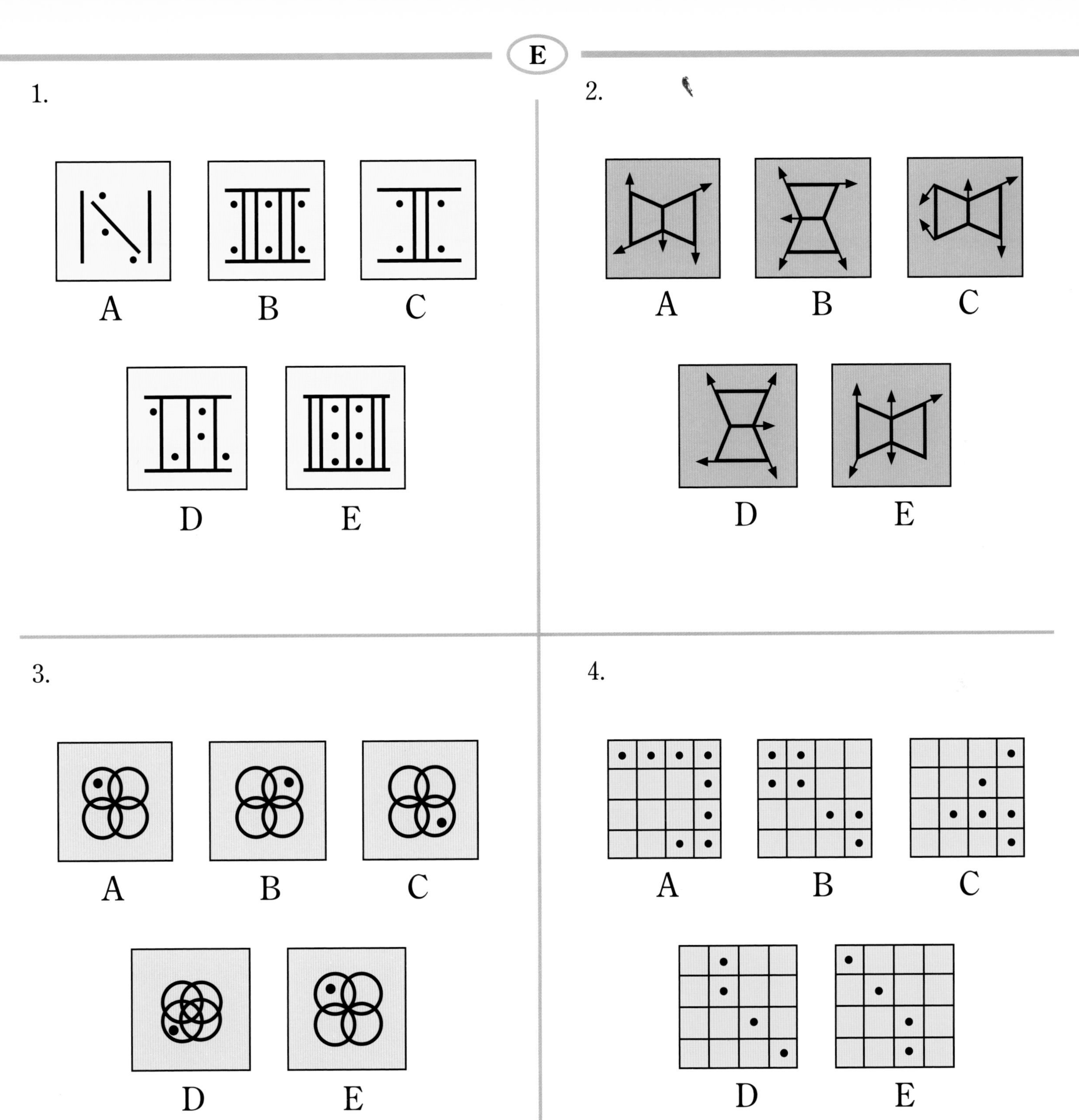
1.
A
B
C
D
E
2.
A
B
C
D
E
3.
A
B
C
D
E
4.
A
B
C
D
E

5.

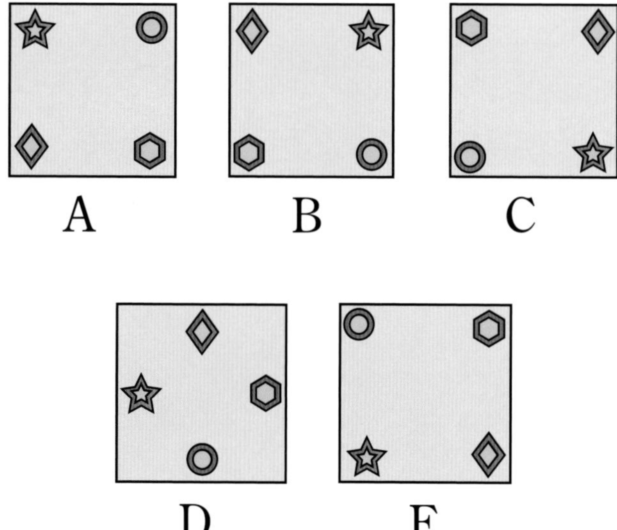

6.

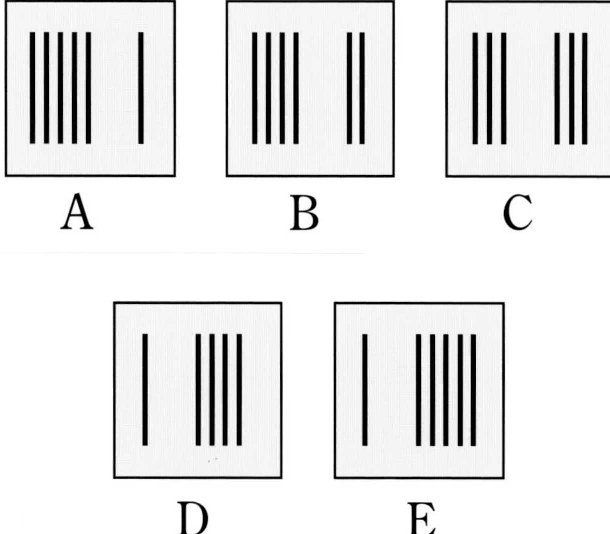

7.

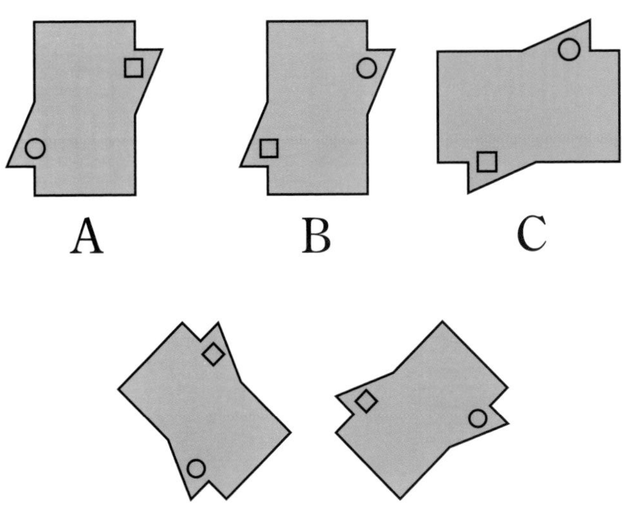

8.

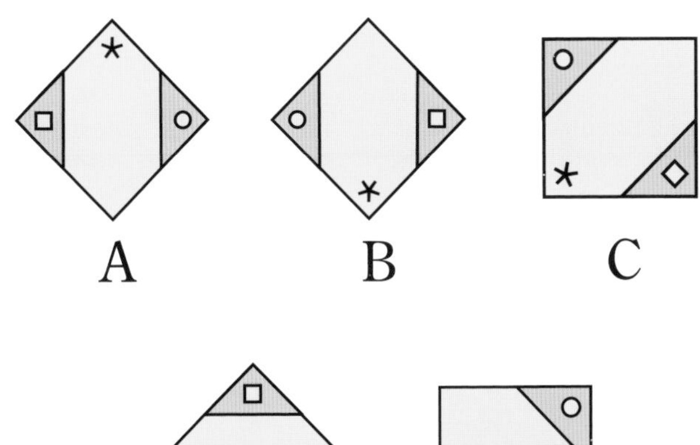

9.

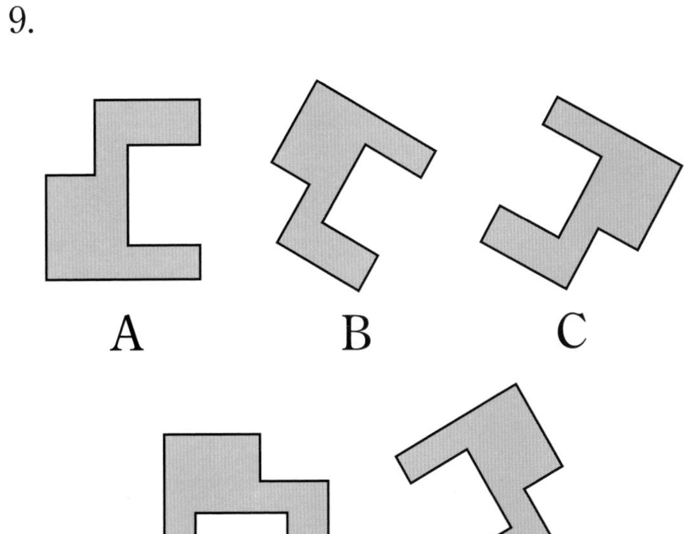

10.

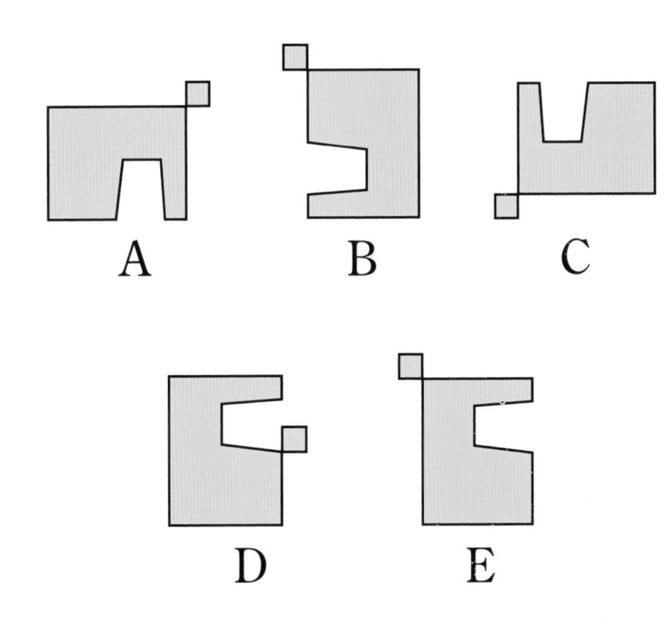

11.

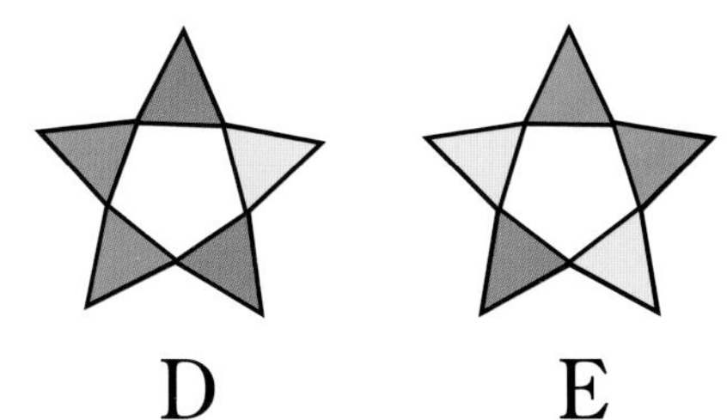

12.

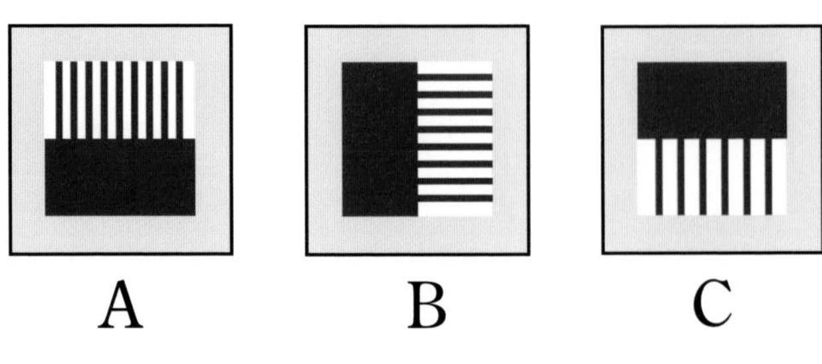

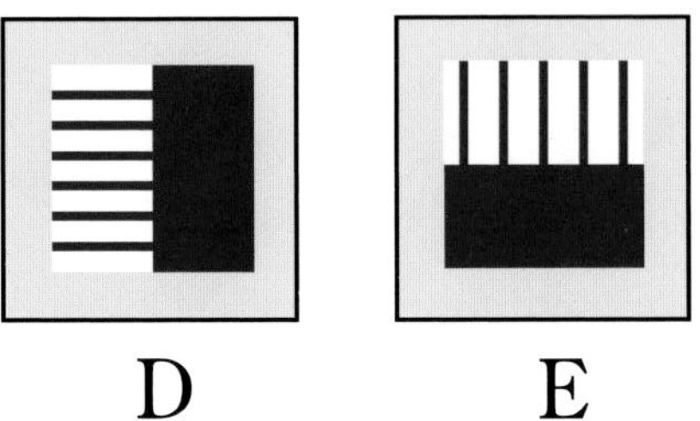

13.

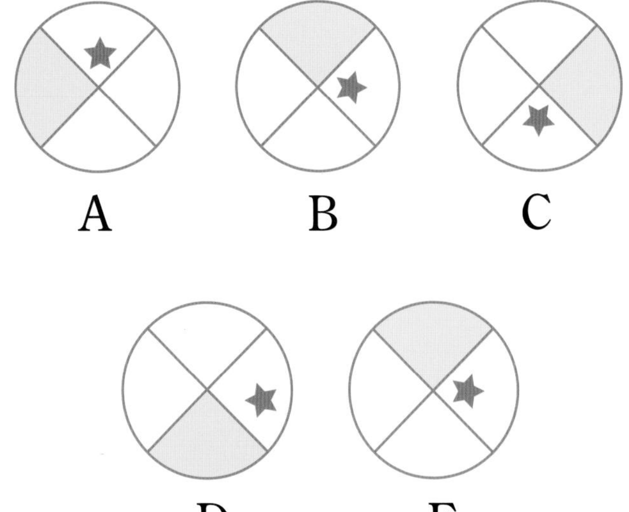

14.

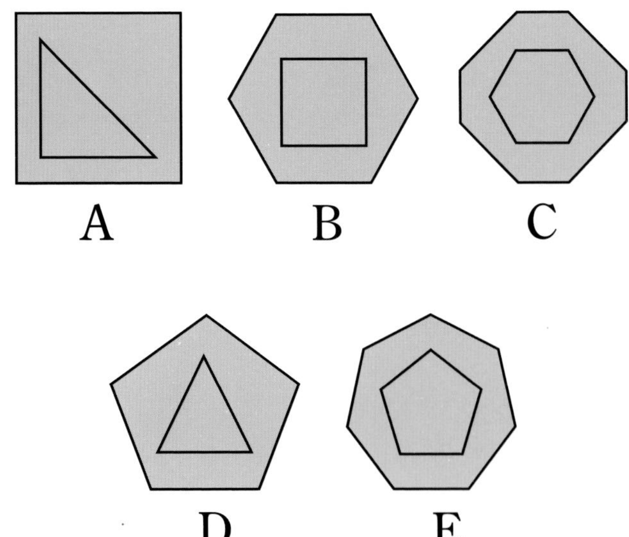

15.

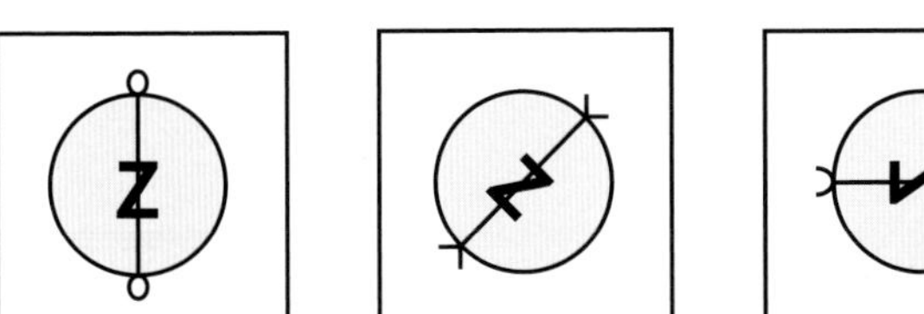

A B

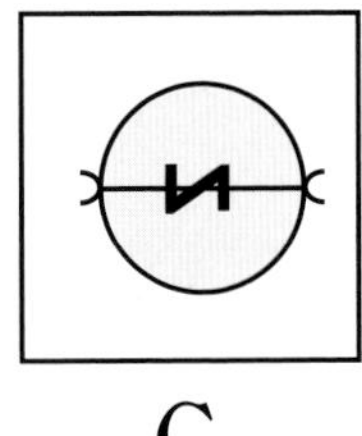

C

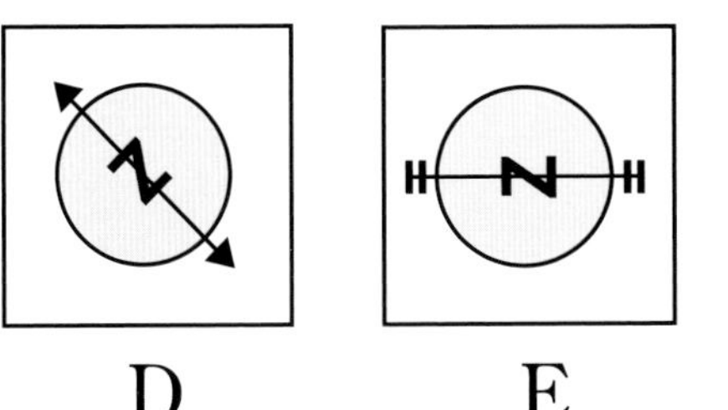

D E

16.

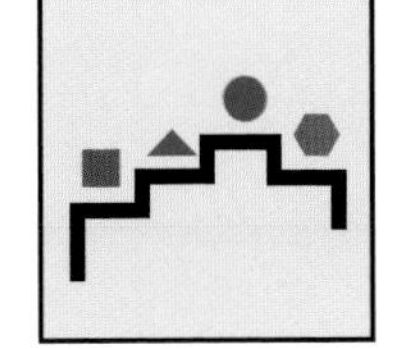

A

B

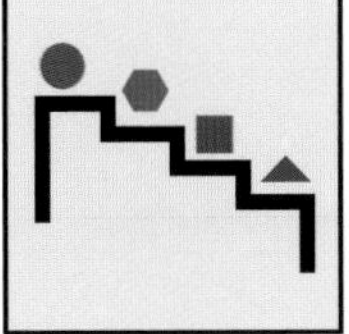

C

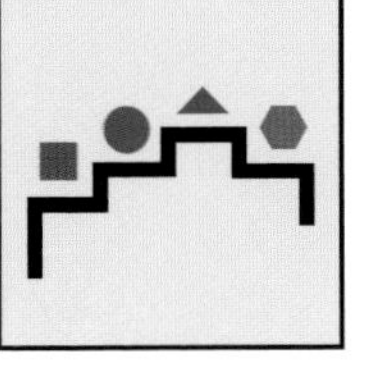

D

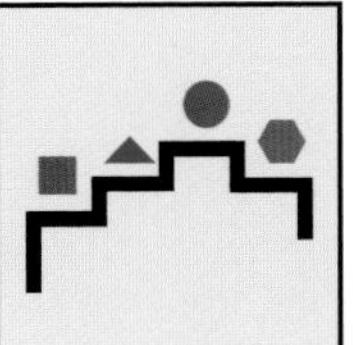

E

17.

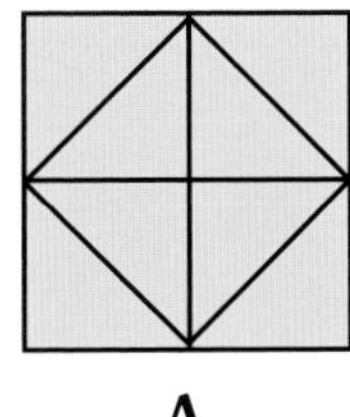

A

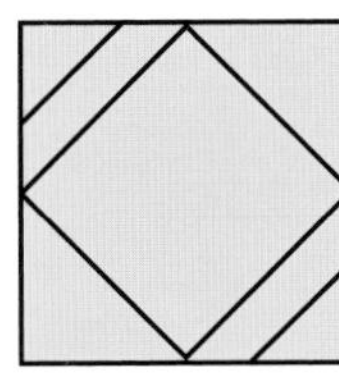

B

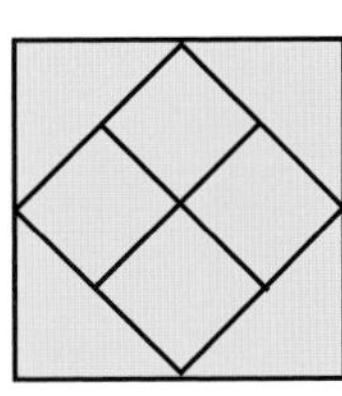

C

D

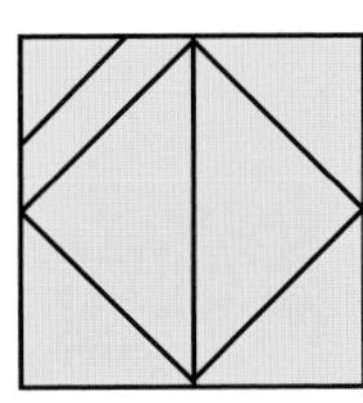

E

18.

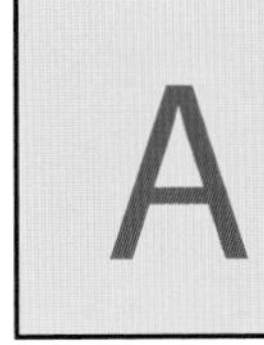

A

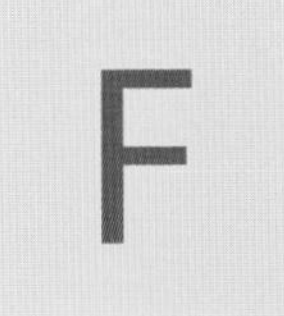

B

C

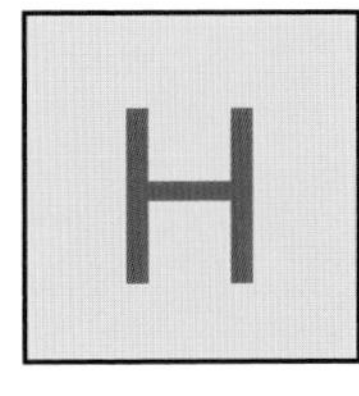

D

E

19.

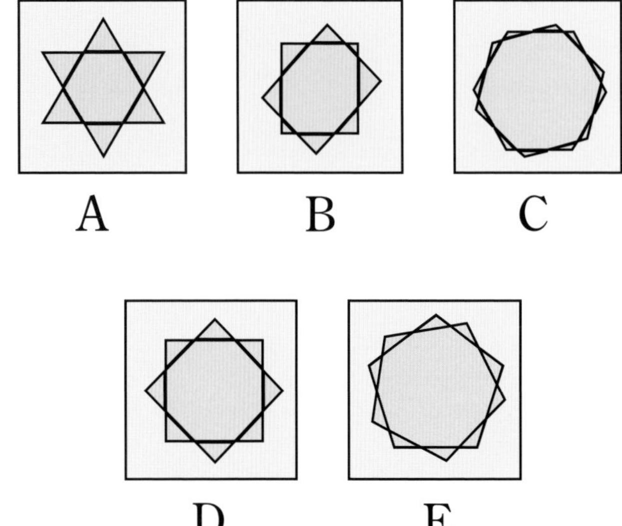

20.

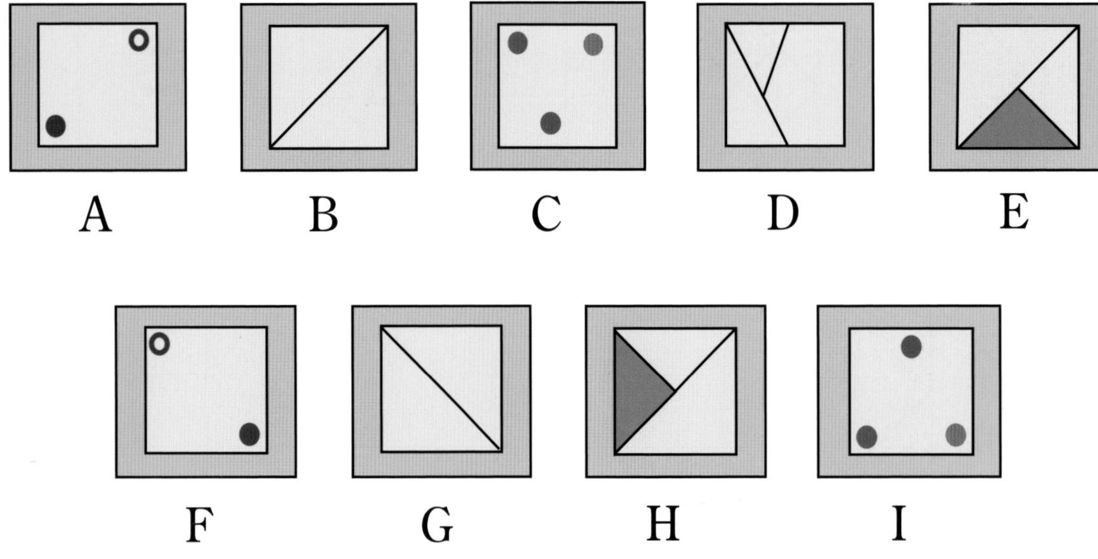

21.

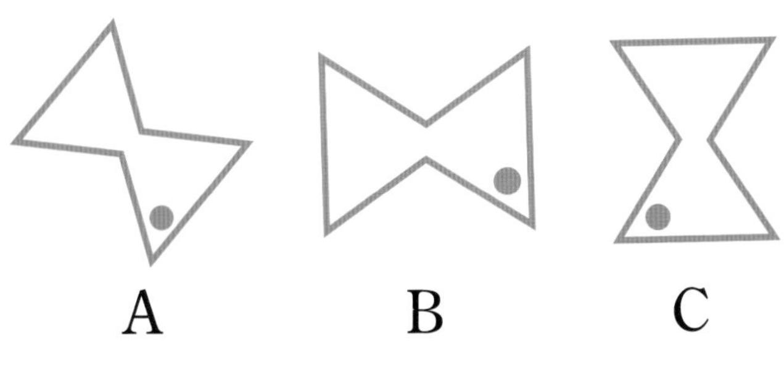

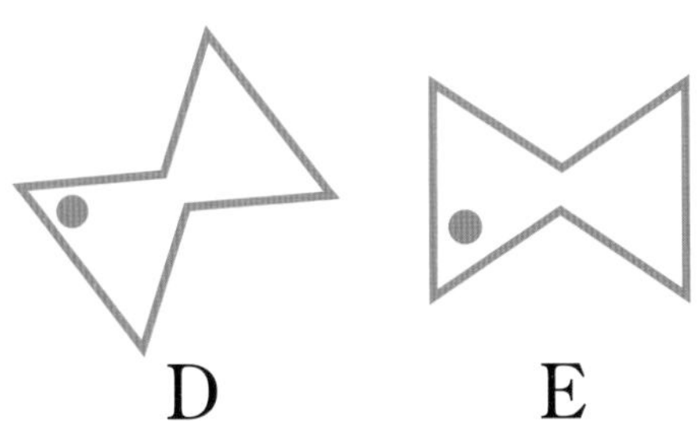

22.

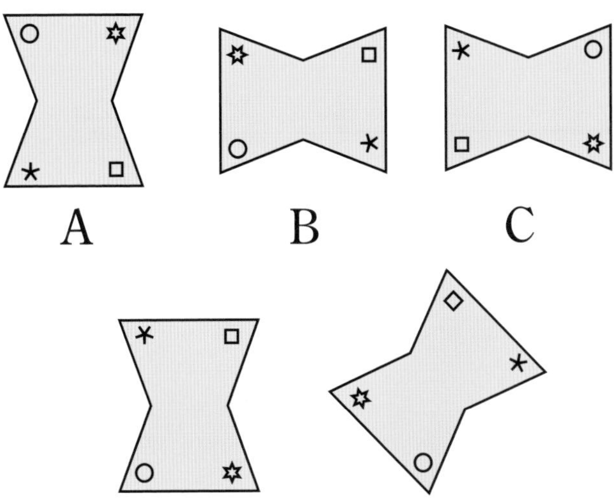

23.

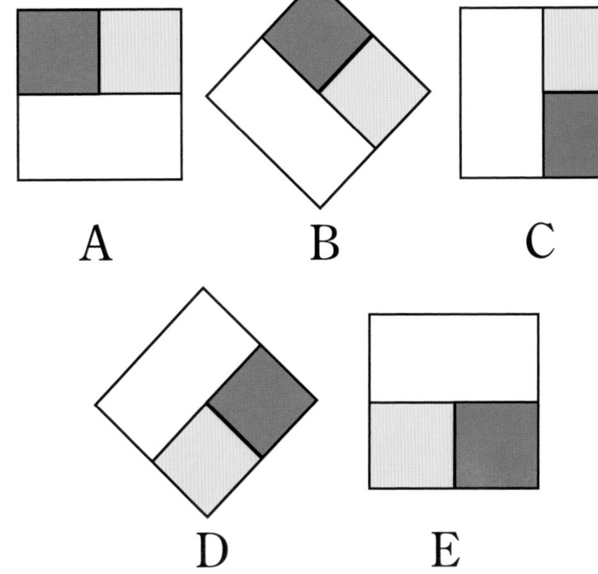

24.

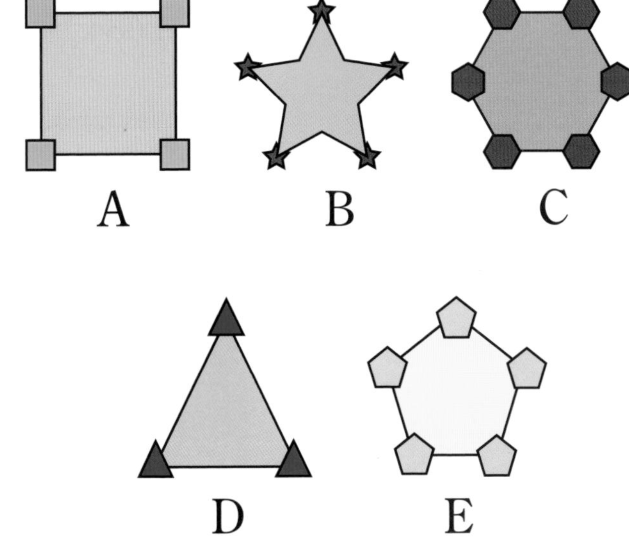

25.

248
329
176
A
B
C

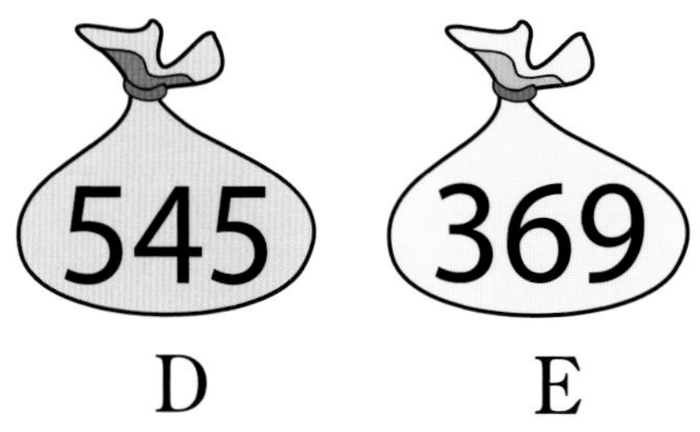
545
369
D
E

26.

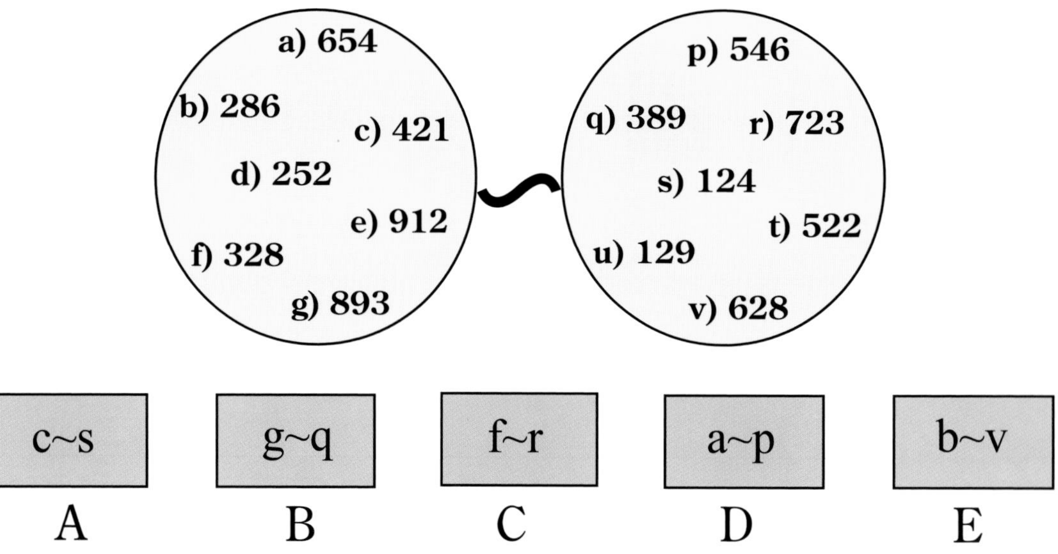
a) 654
b) 286
c) 421
d) 252
e) 912
f) 328
g) 893
p) 546
q) 389
r) 723
s) 124
t) 522
u) 129
v) 628
c~s
g~q
f~r
a~p
b~v
A
B
C
D
E

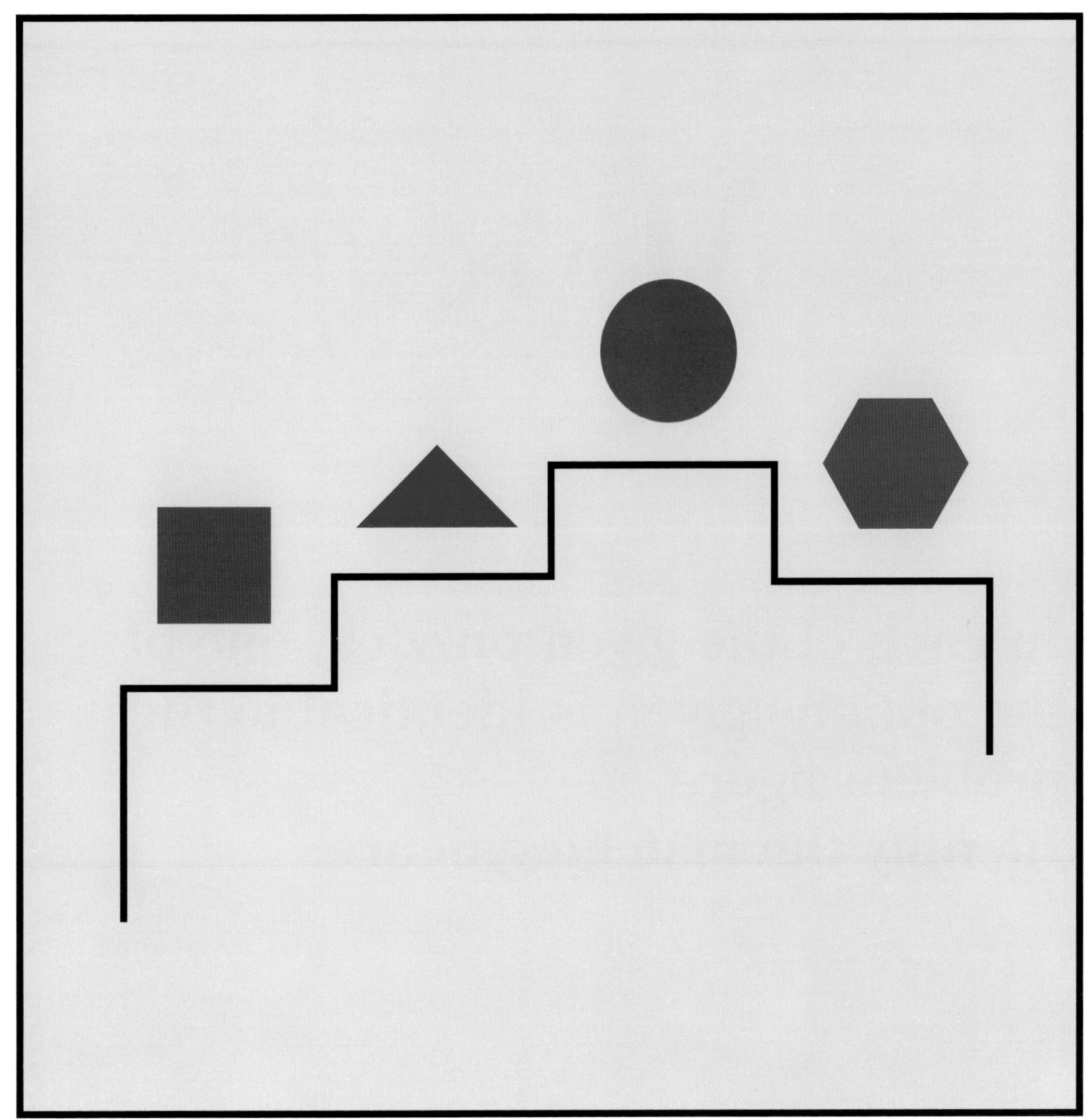

MATCH

- In each of the given puzzles, one of the options given is identical to the problem figure.
- Identify the matching figure.

1.

A

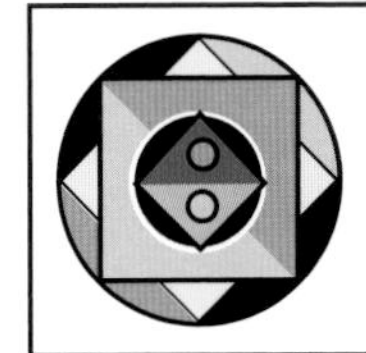

B

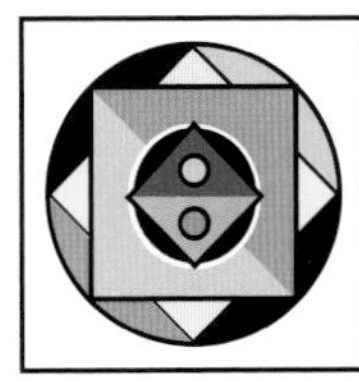

C

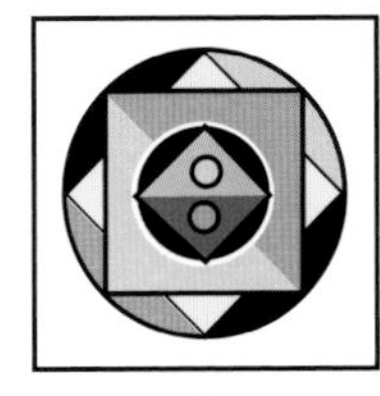

D

2.

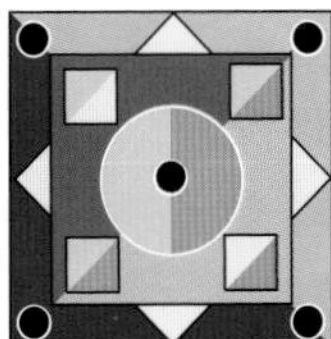

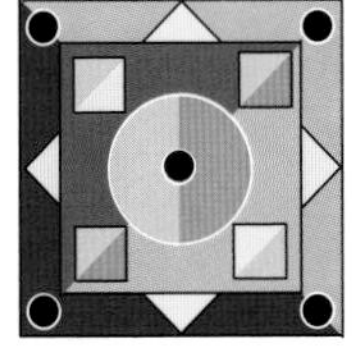

A

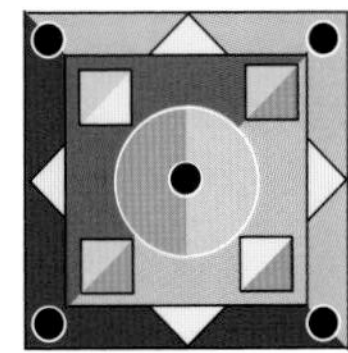

B

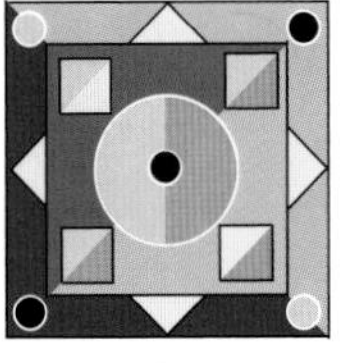

C

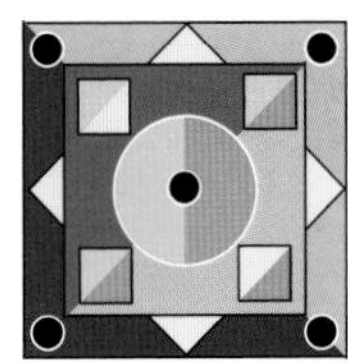

D

3.

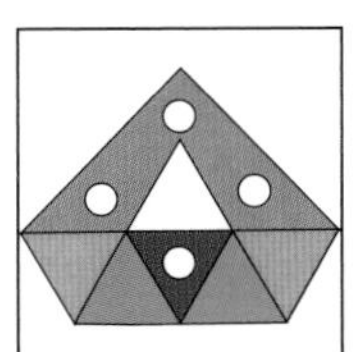

A

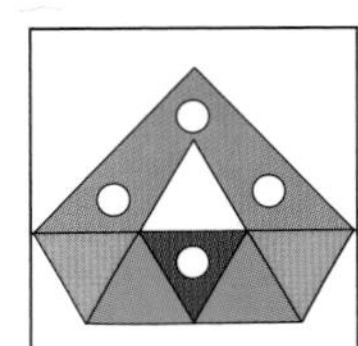

B

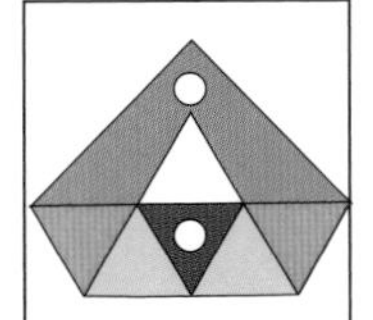

C

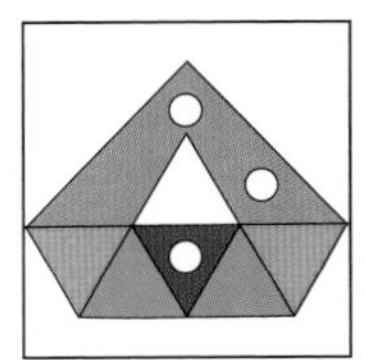

D

4.

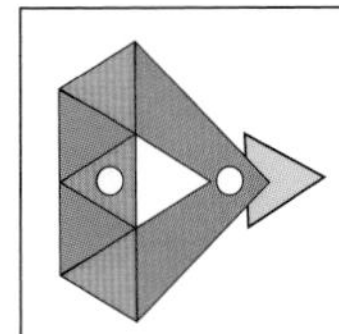

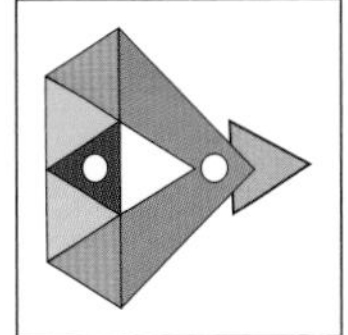

A

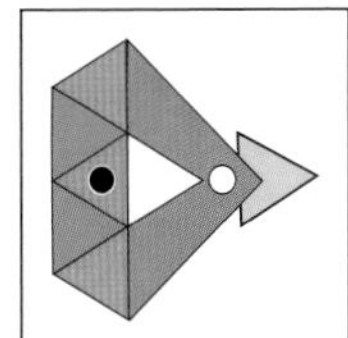

B

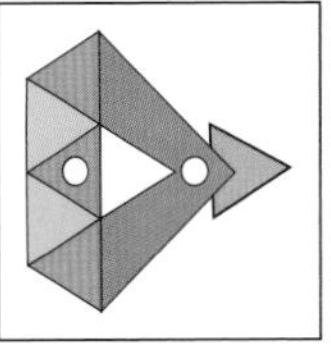

C

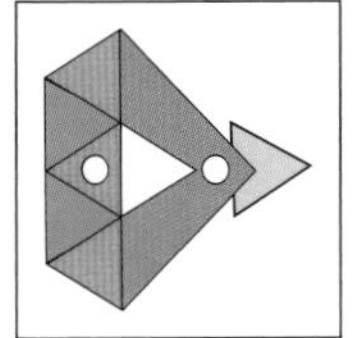

D

5.

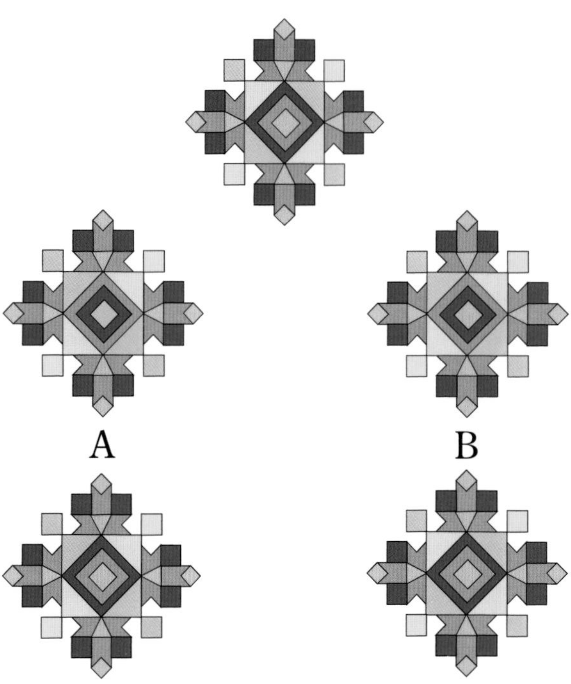

6.

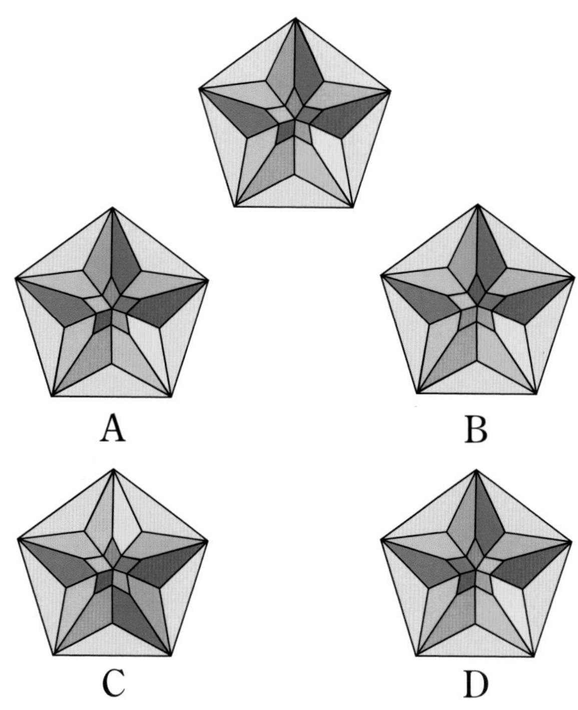

7.

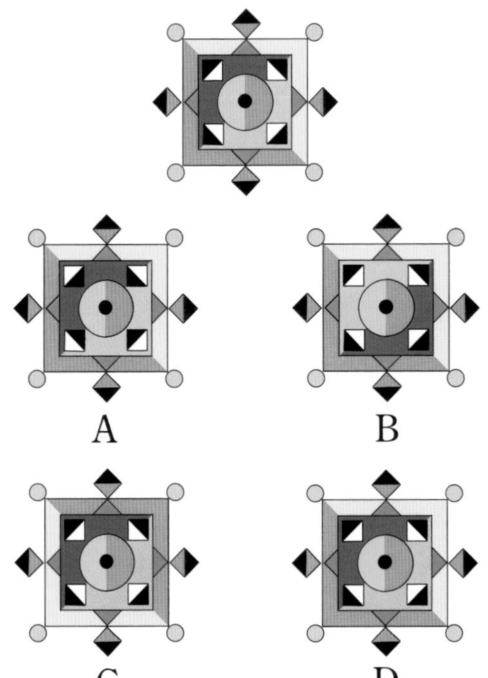

8.

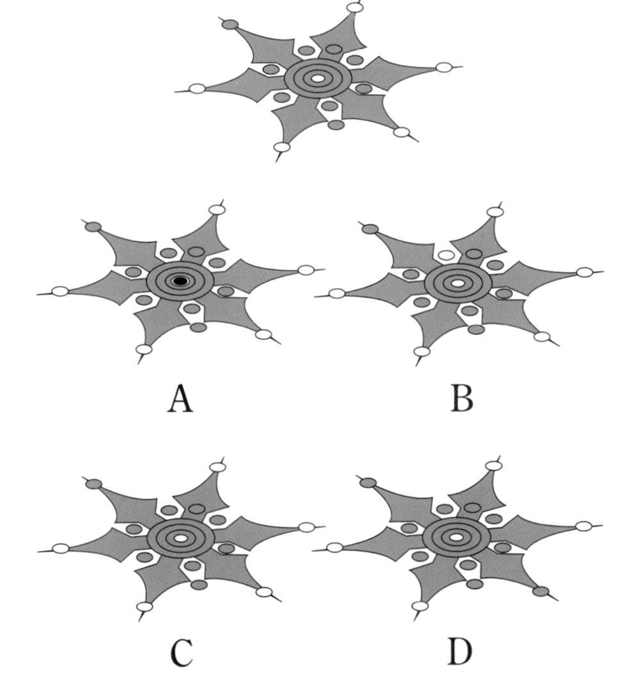

9.

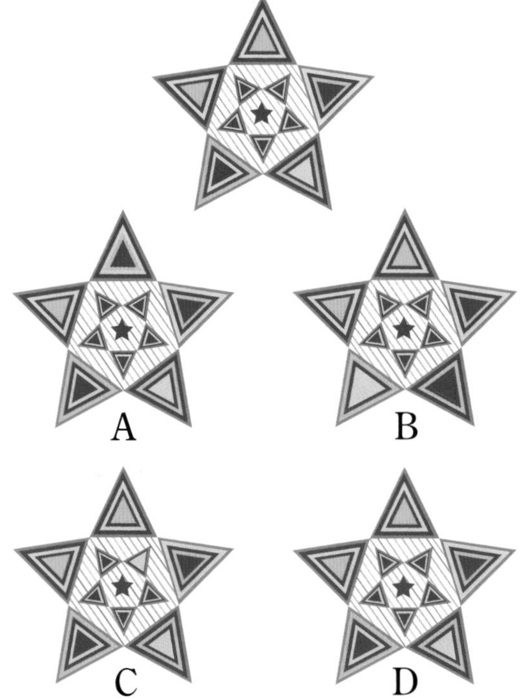

10.

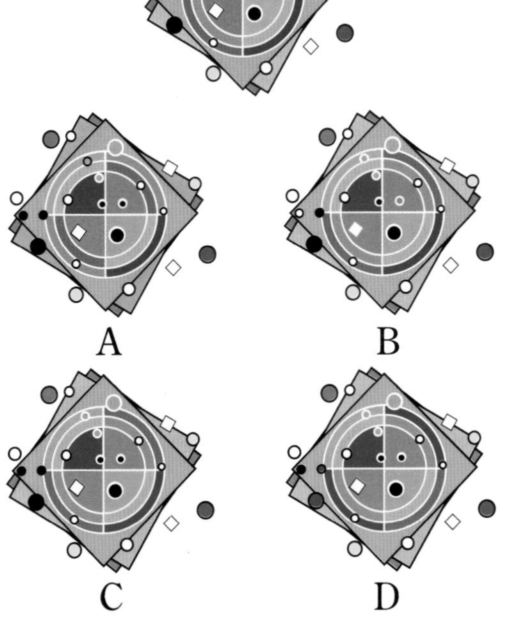

11.

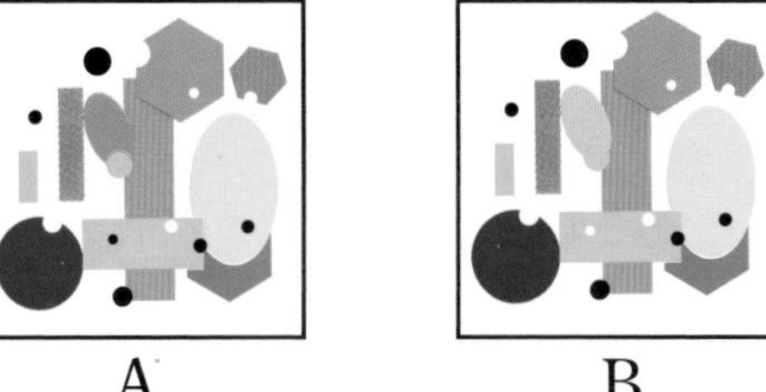

A B

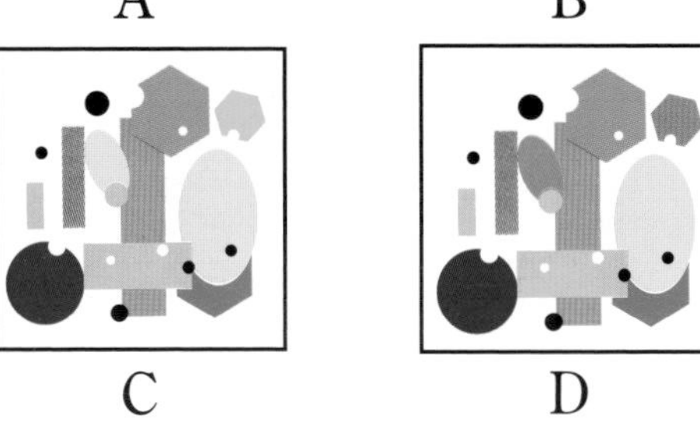

C D

12.

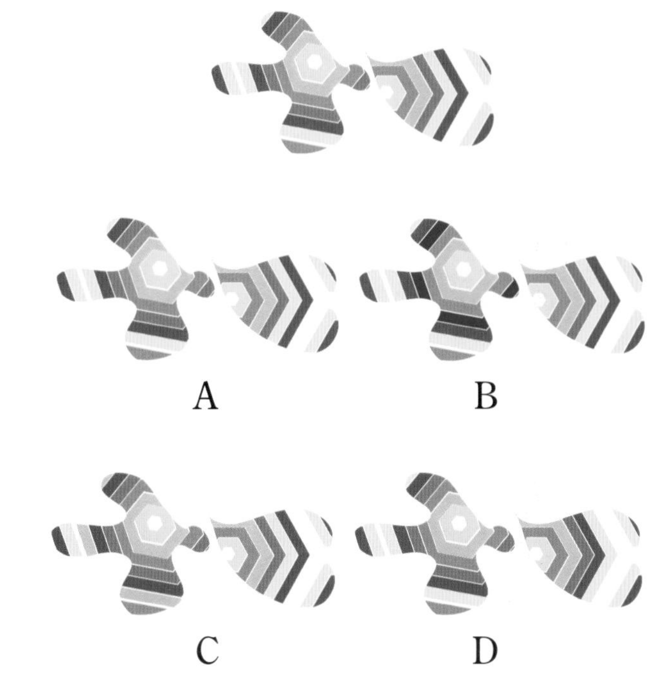

A B

C D

13.

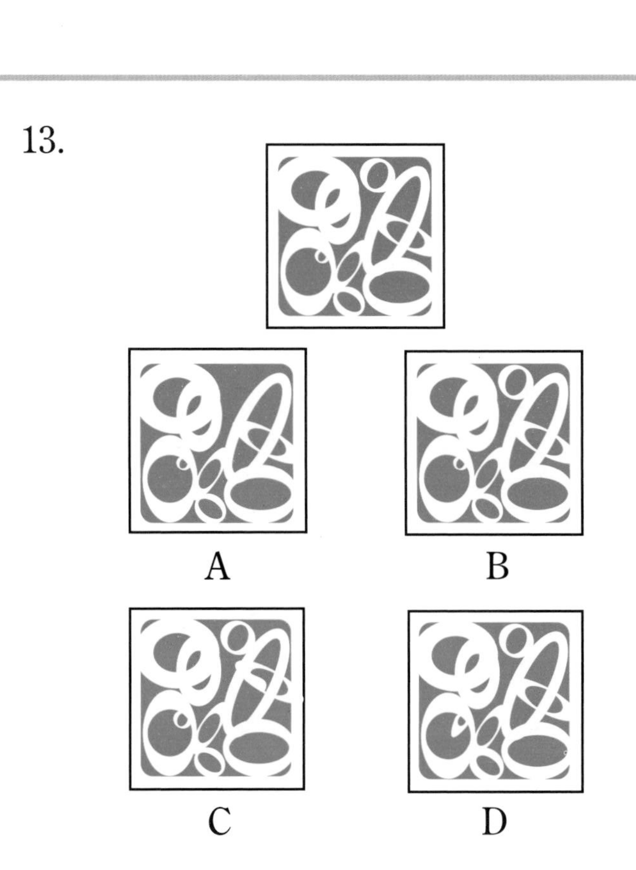

A B

C D

14.

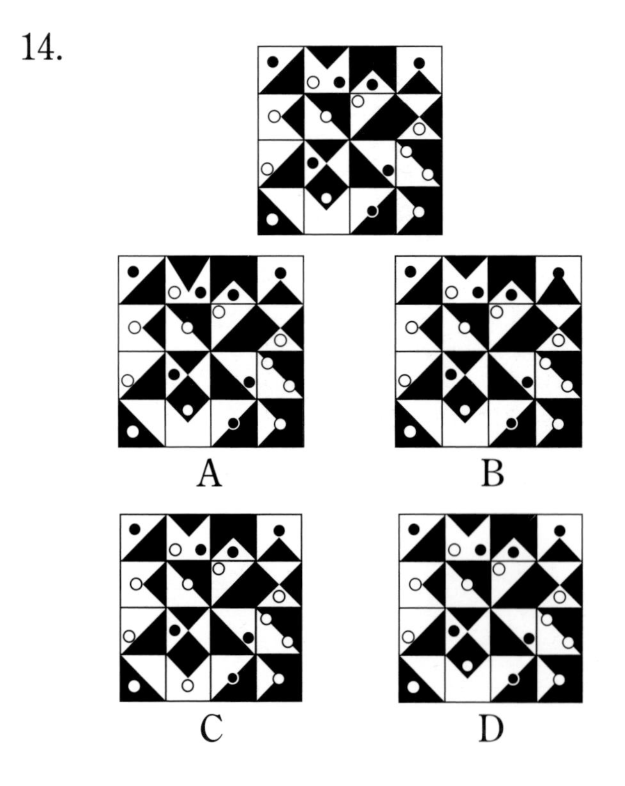

A B

C D

15.

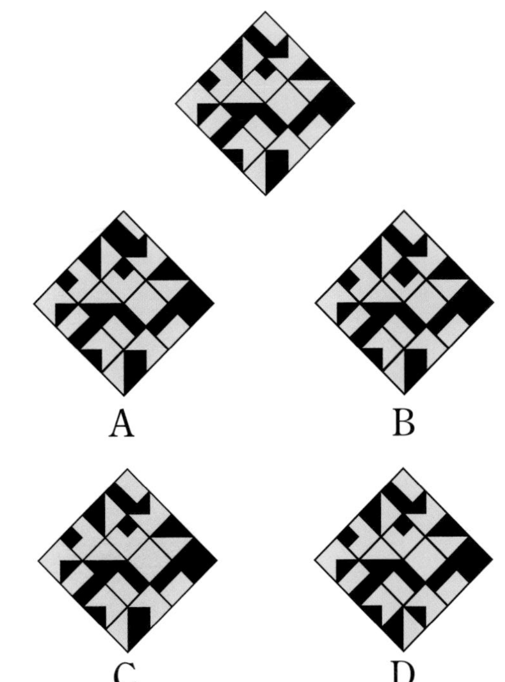

A B C D

16.

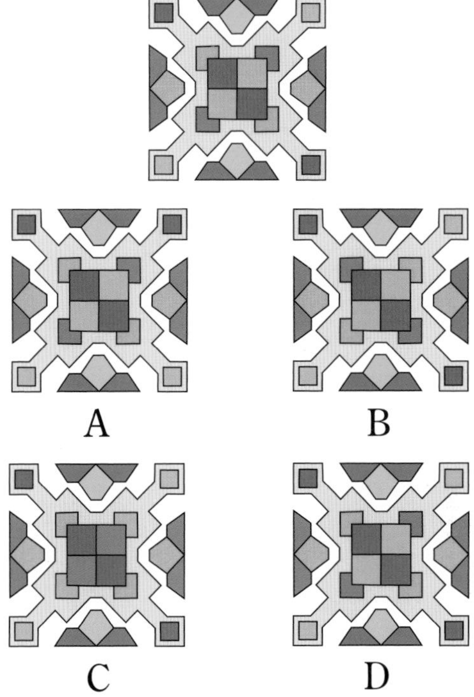

A B C D

17.

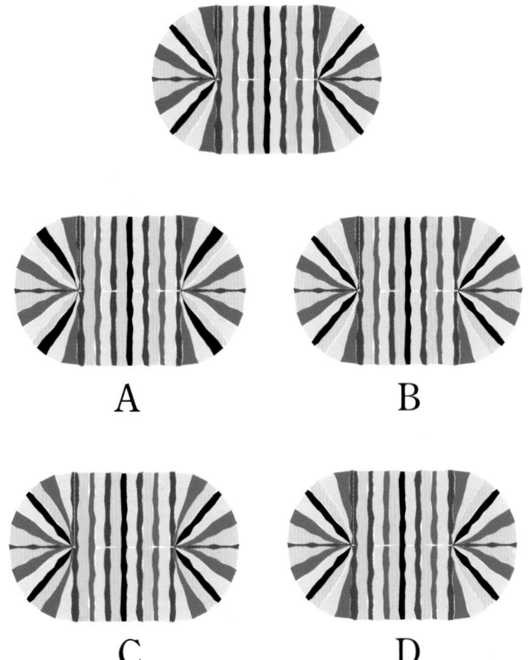

A B C D

18.

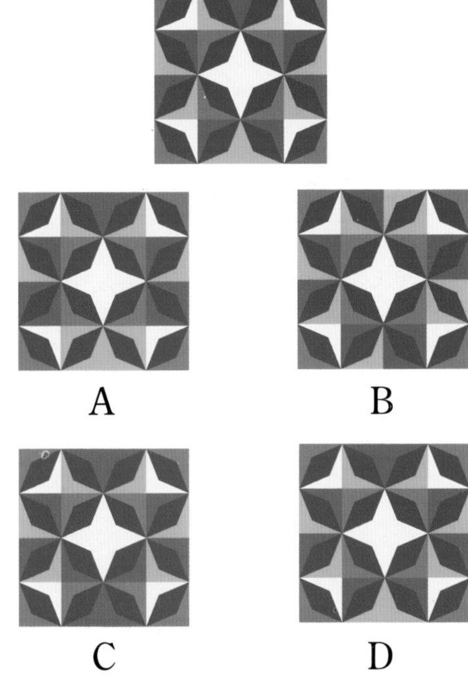

A B C D

19.

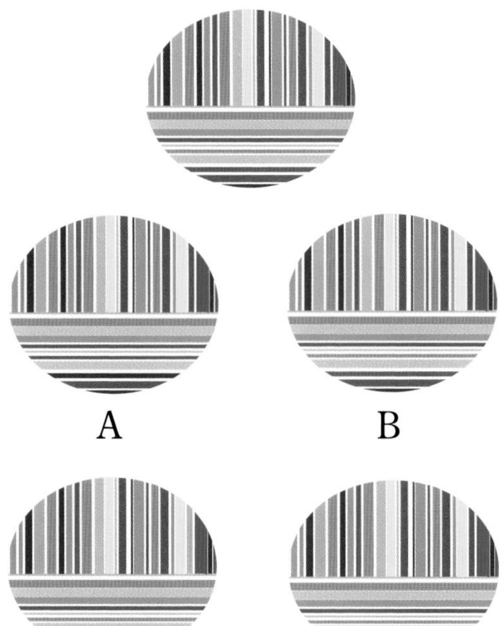

20.

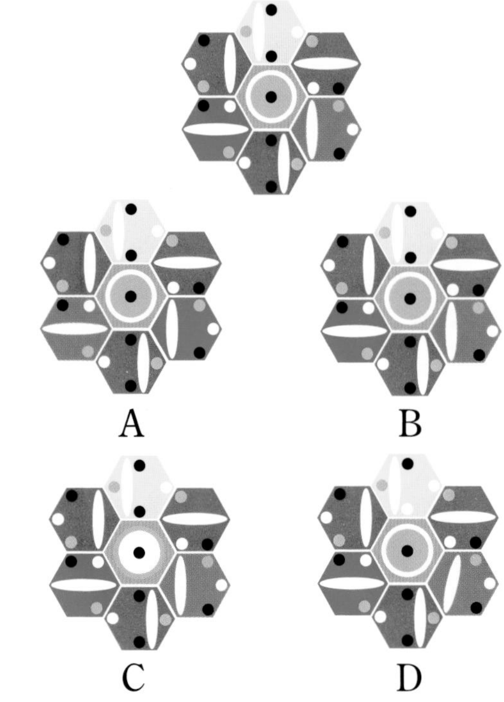

21.

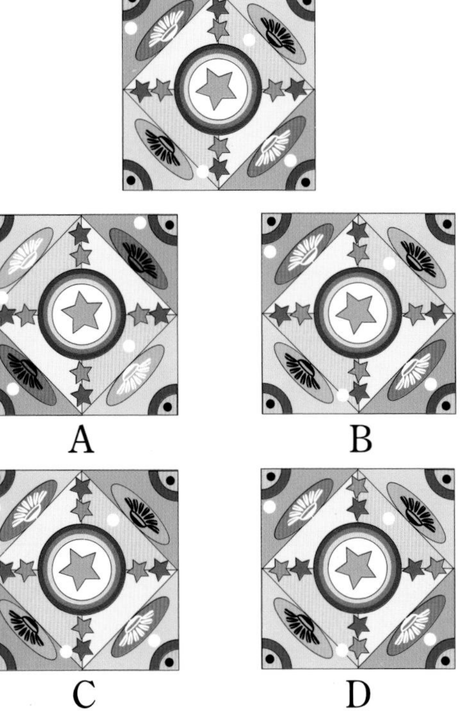

22.

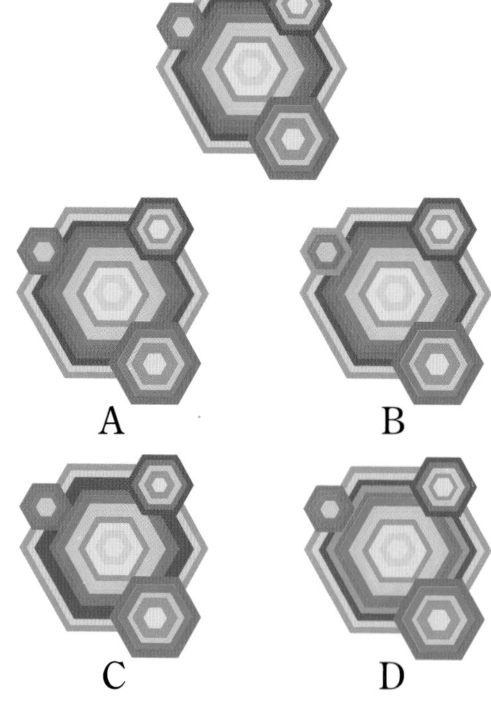

23.

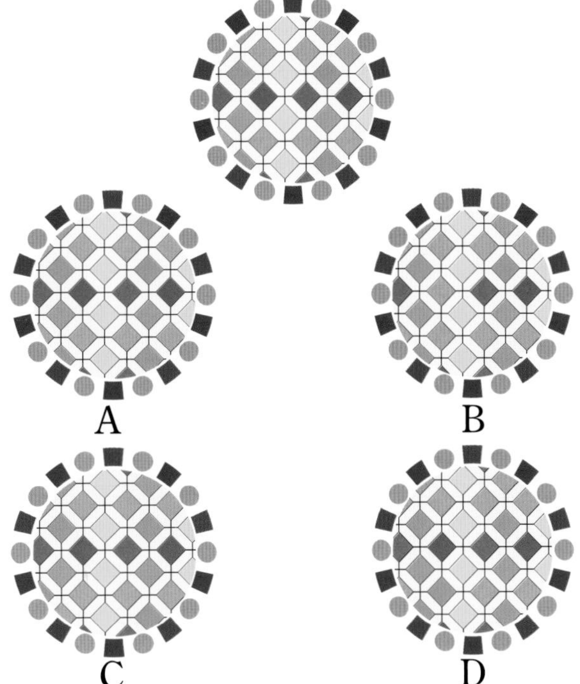

24.

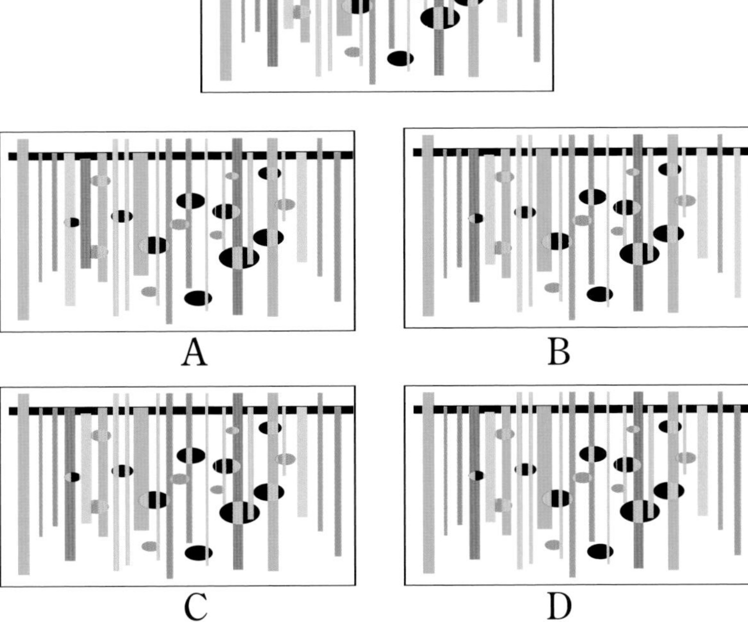

WATER REFLECTION

- **In each of the puzzles which of the options is the water reflection of the problem image?**

1.

A

B

C

D

2.

A

B

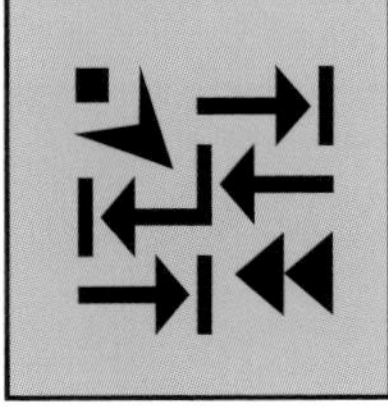

C

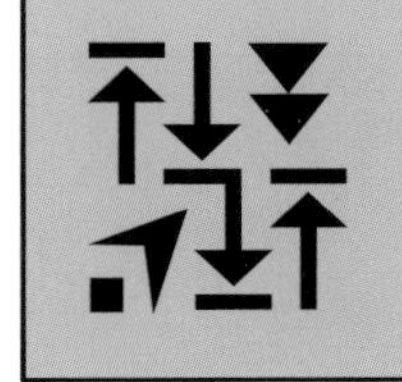

D

3.

A

B

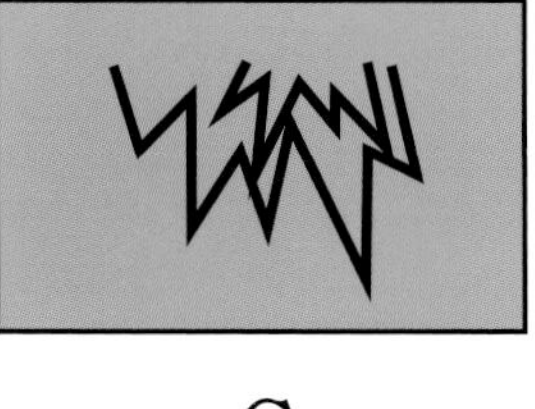

C

D

4.

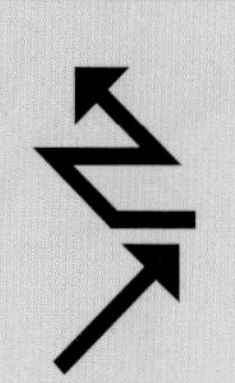

A

B

C

D

5.

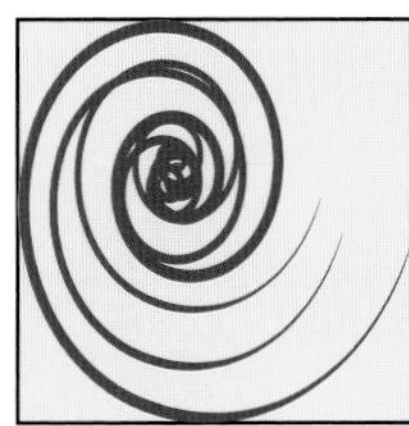

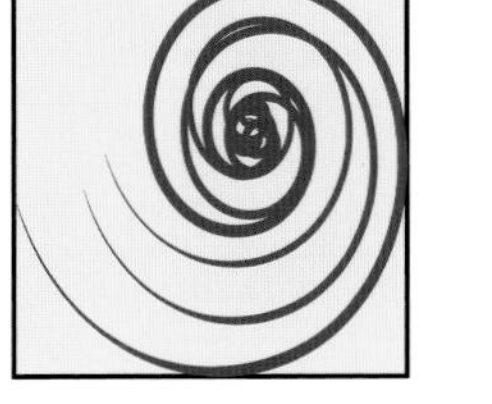

A

B

C

D

6.

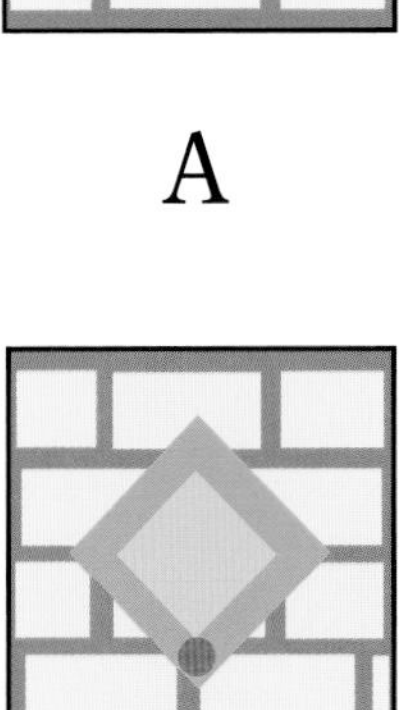

A

B

C

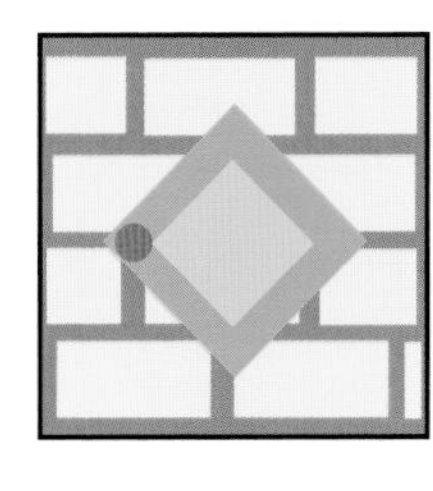

D

7.

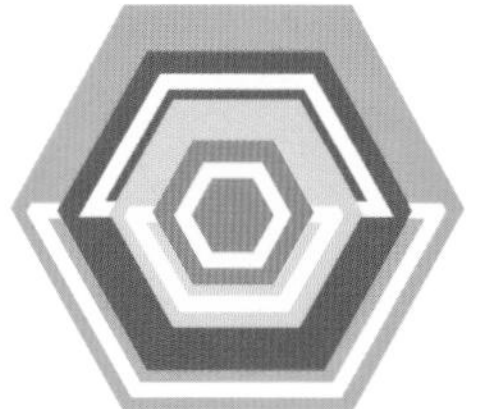

A

B

C

D

8.

A

B

C

D

9.

A

B

C

D

10.

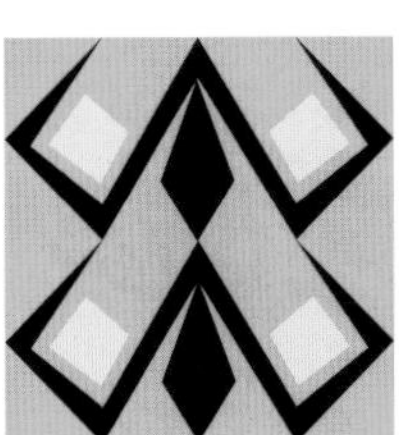

A

B

C

D

11.

A B

C D

12.

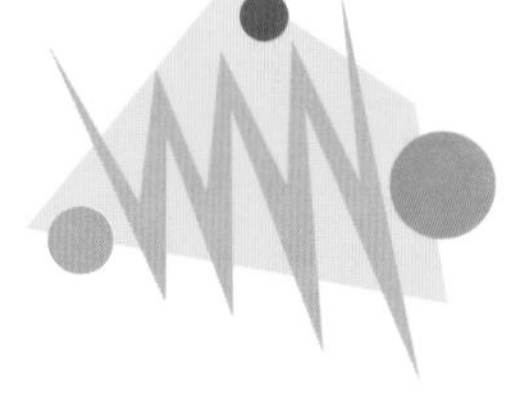

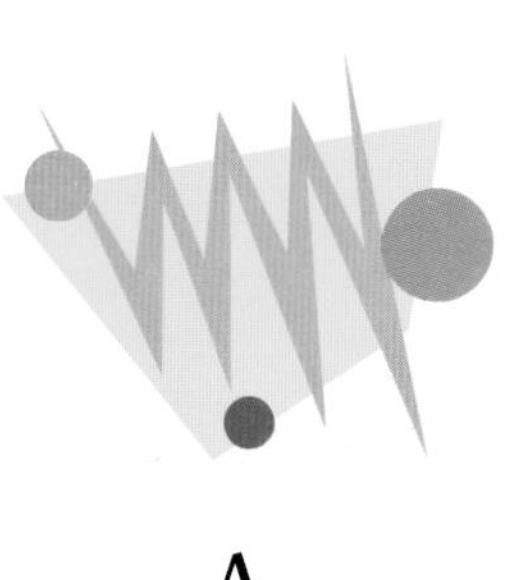

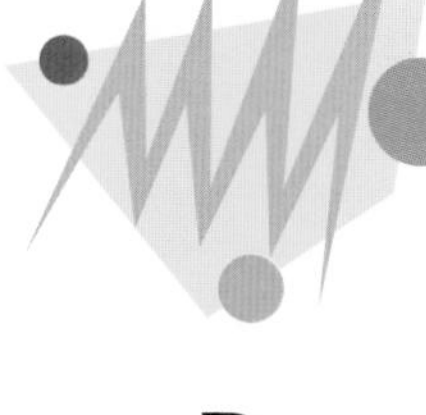

A B

C D

13.

A

B

C

D

14.

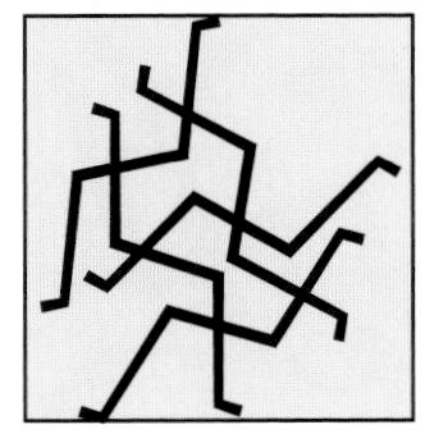

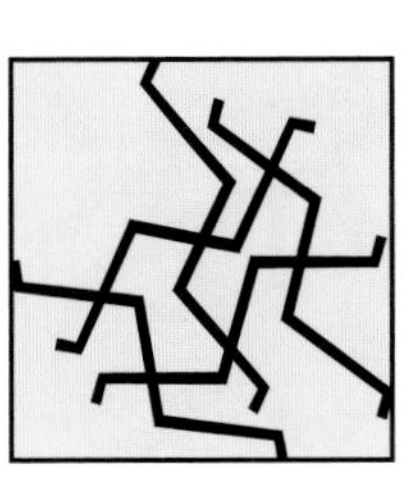

A

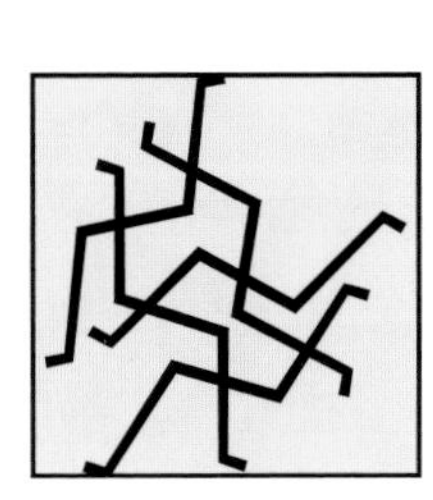

B

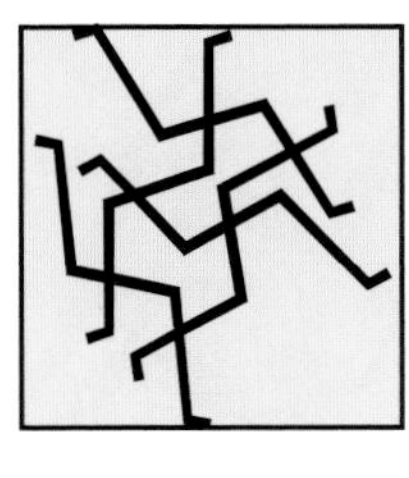

C

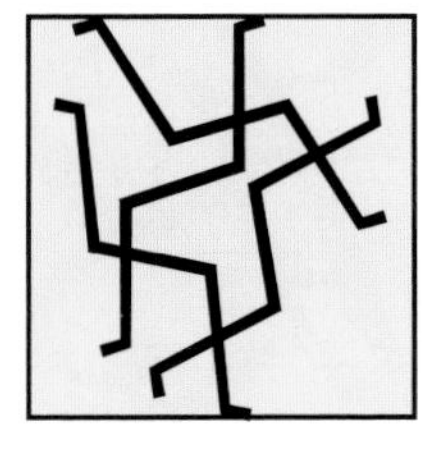

D

15.

A

B

C

D

16.

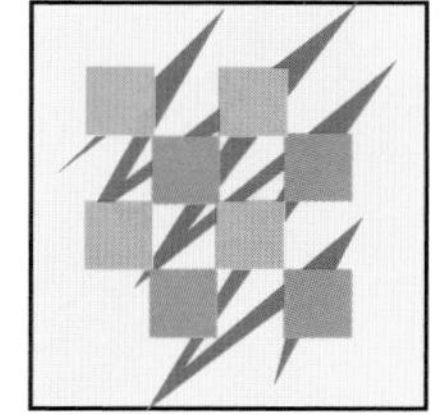

A

B

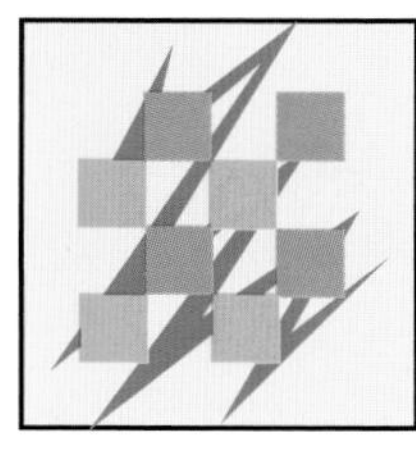

C

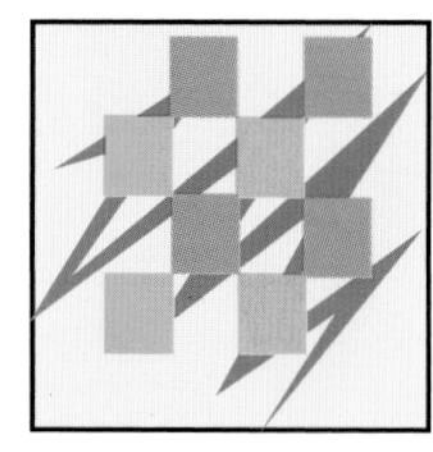

D

17.

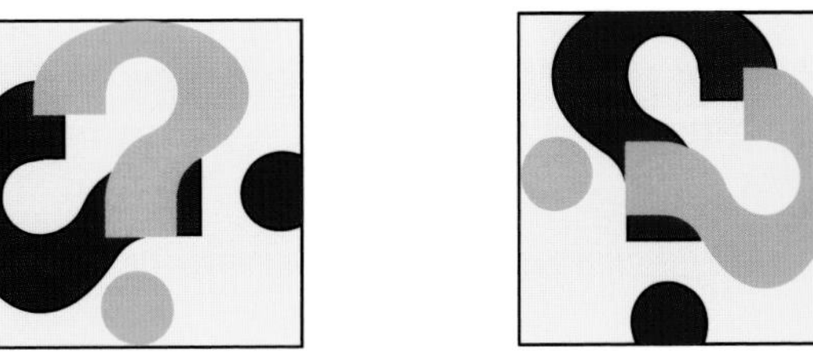

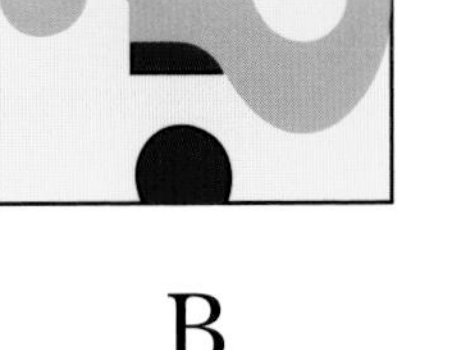

A B

C D

18.

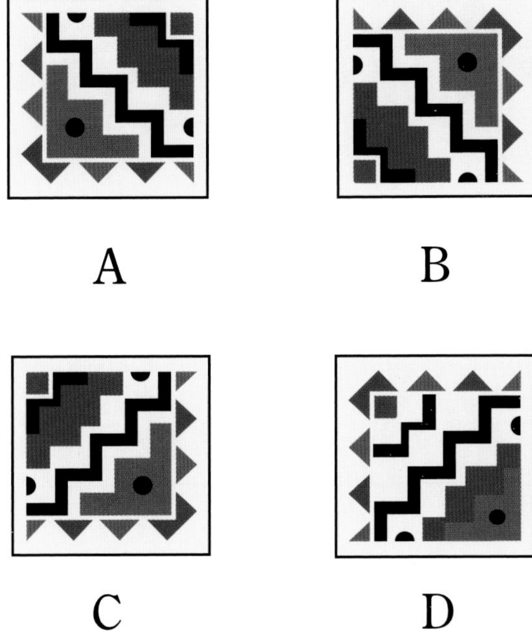

A B

C D

19.

20.

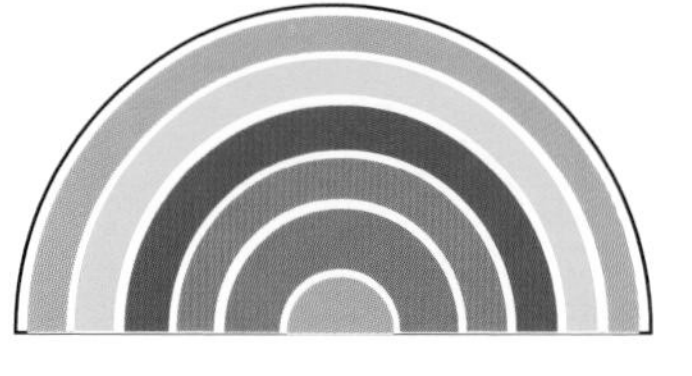

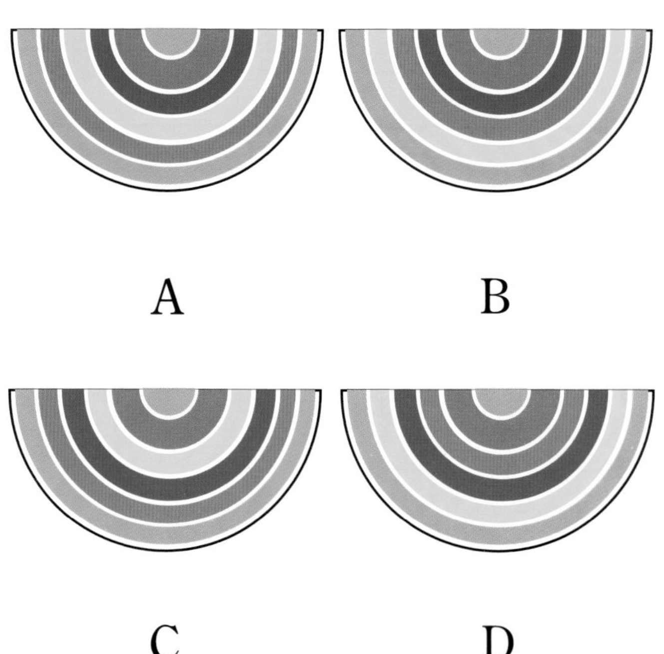

21.

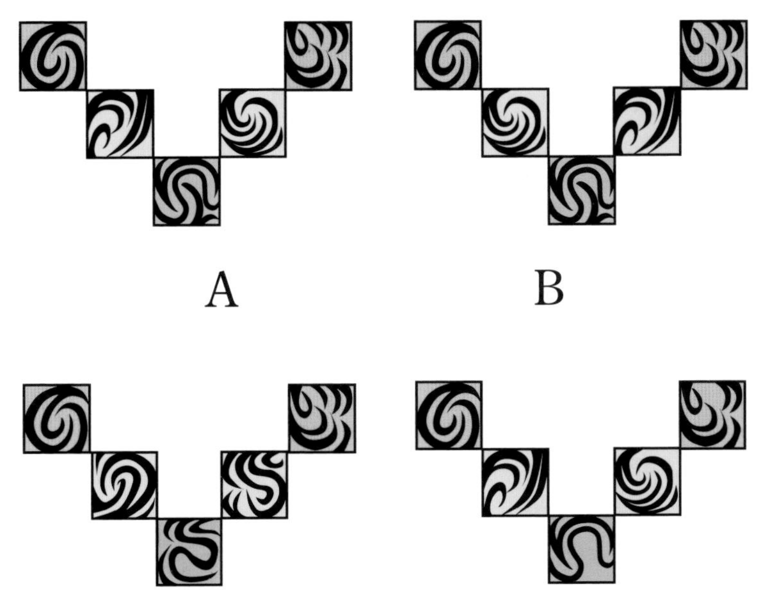

22.

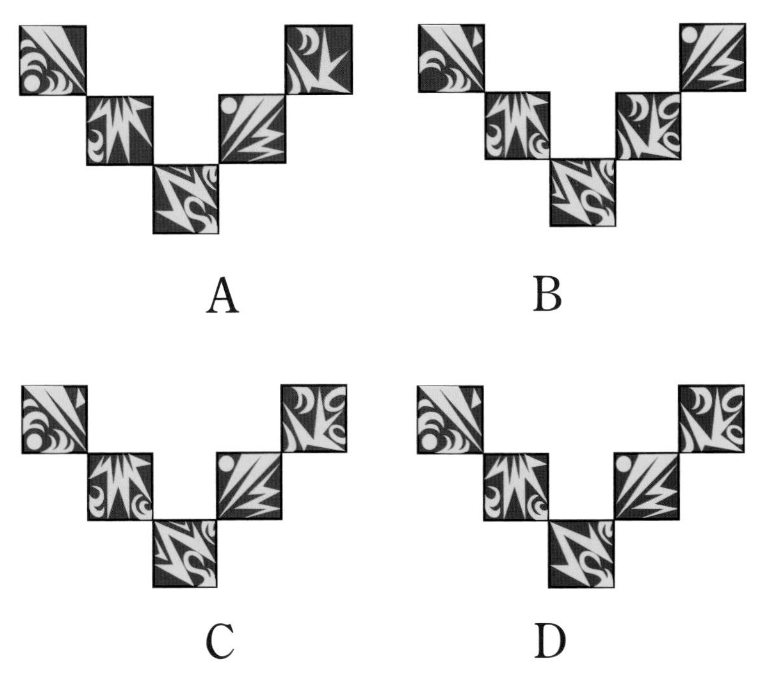

23.

A B

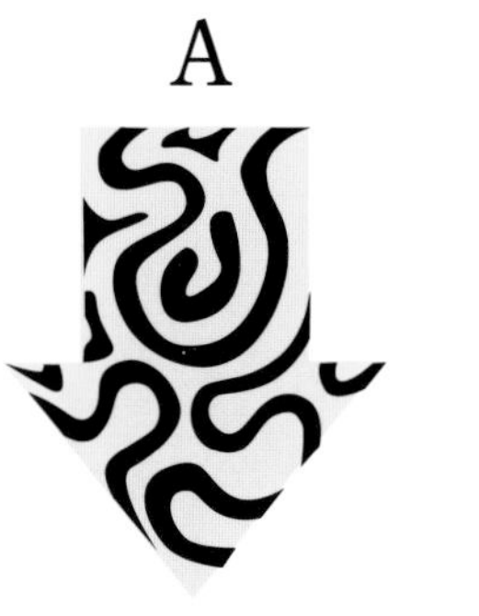

C D

24.

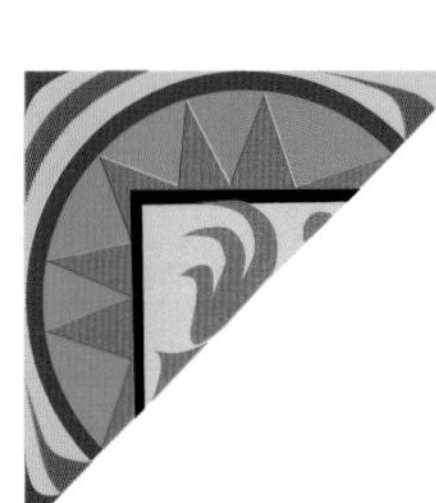

A B

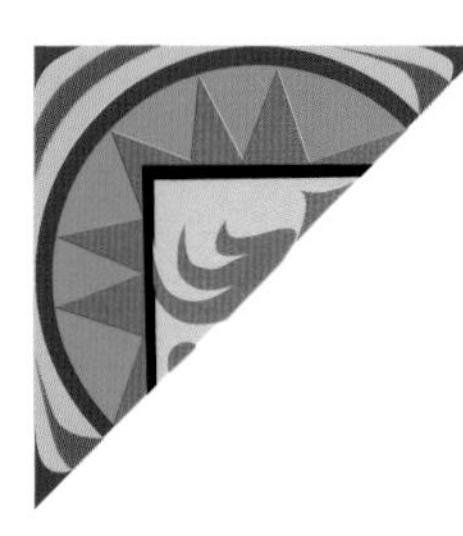

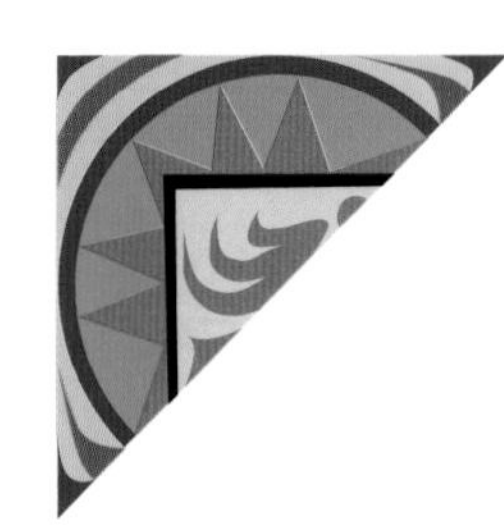

C D

25.

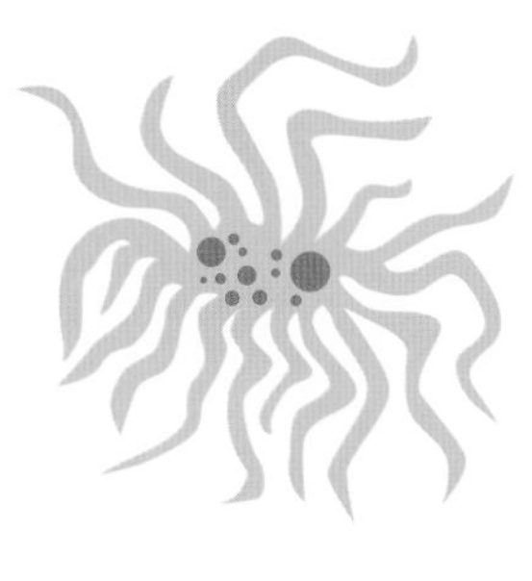

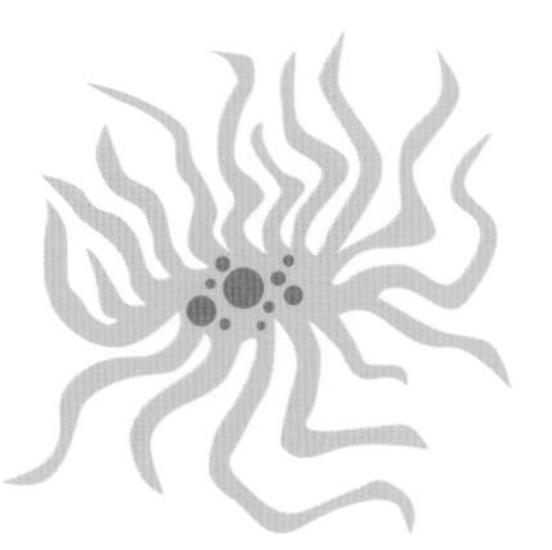

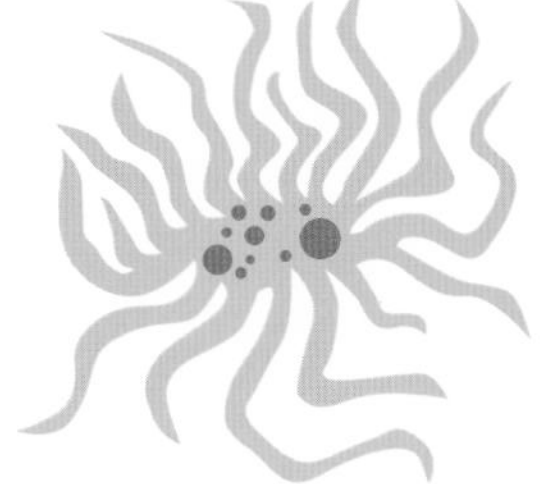

A

B

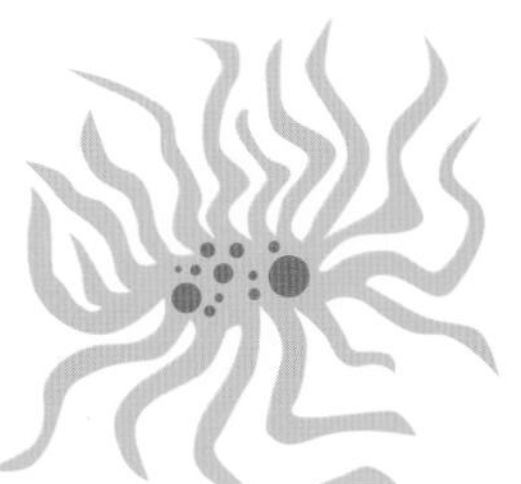

C

D

26.

A

B

C

D

Sequence

- **The presented problem figures follow a certain sequence.**
- **Think logically to find the answer that would be the next in the sequence.**

1.

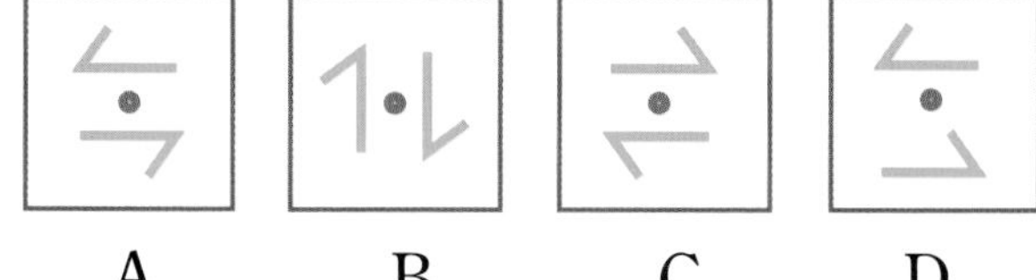

A B C D

2.

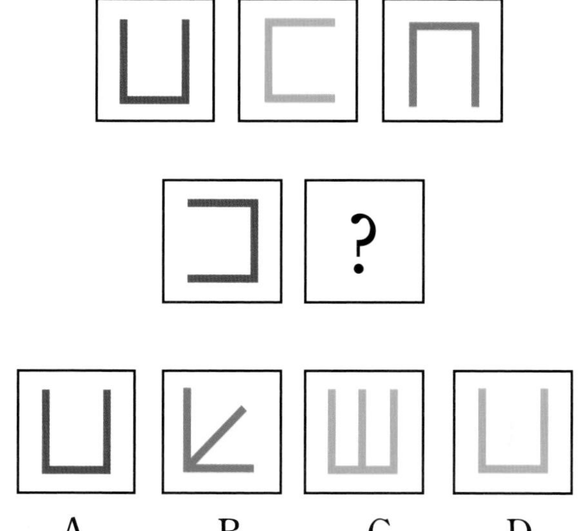

A B C D

3.

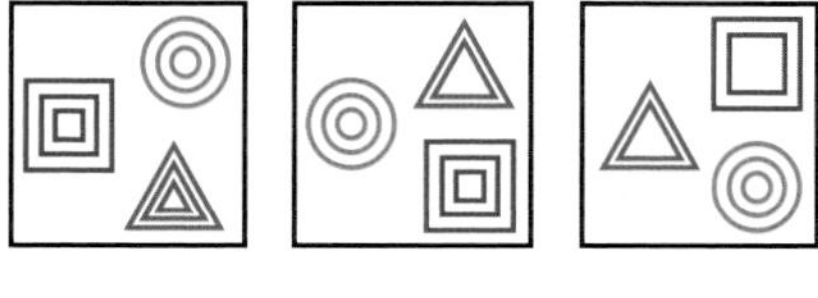

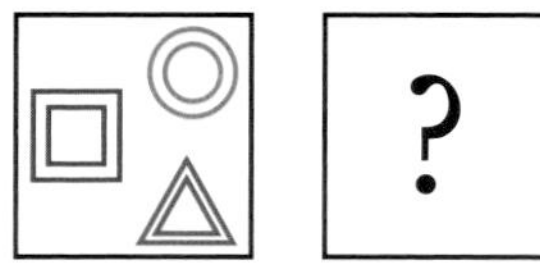

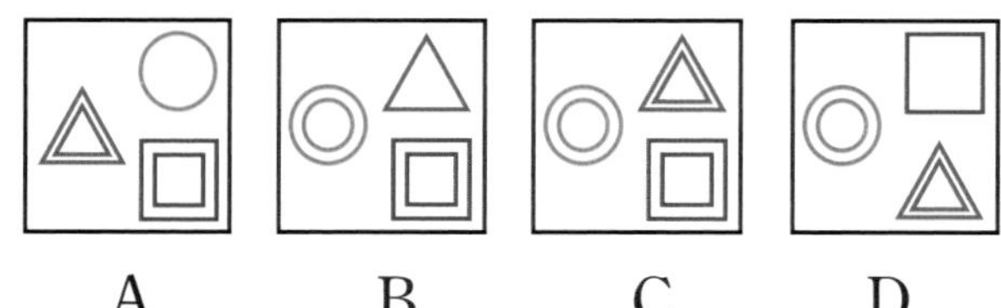

A B C D

4.

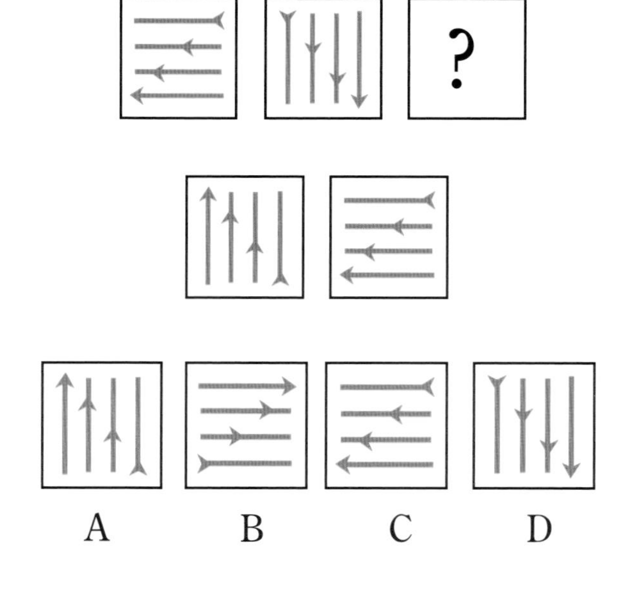

A B C D

5.

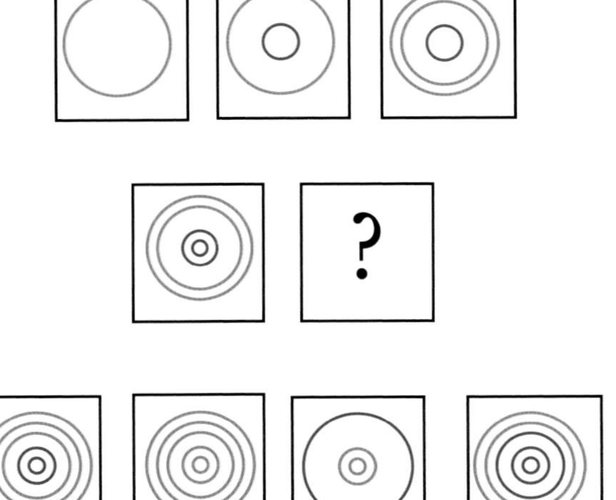

6.

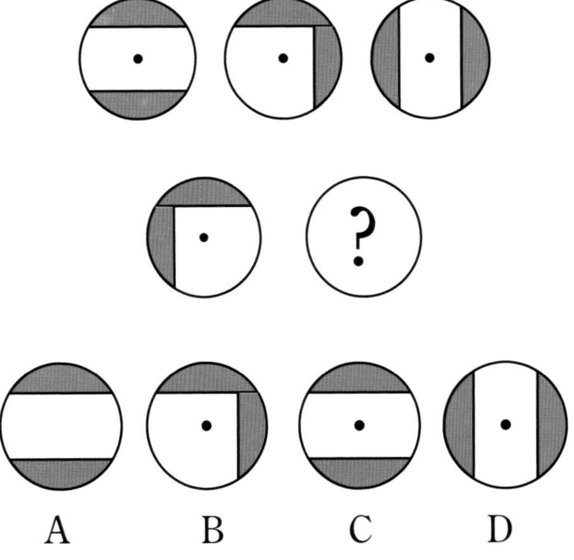

7.

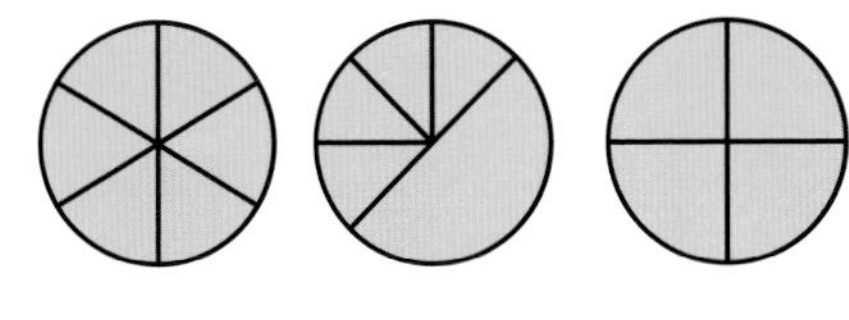

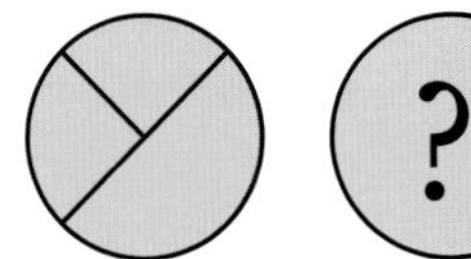

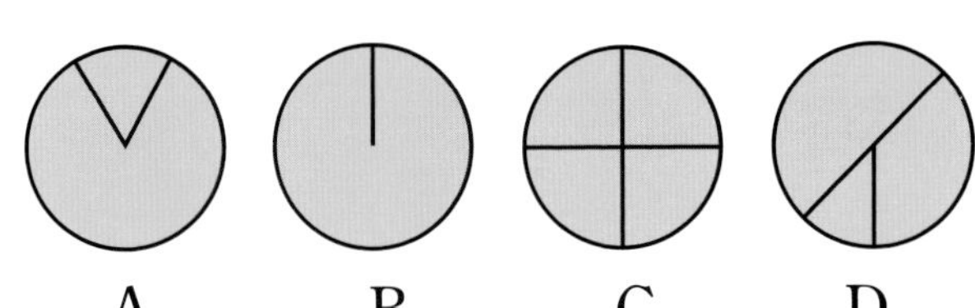

8.

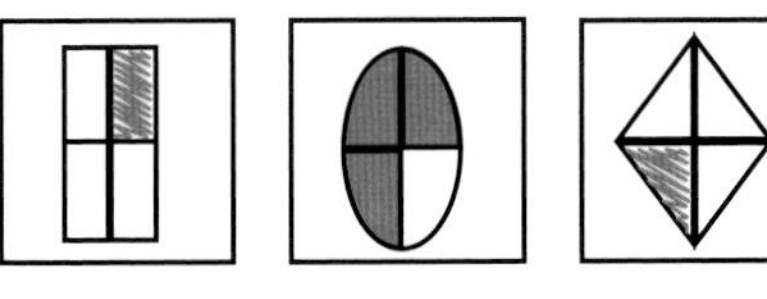

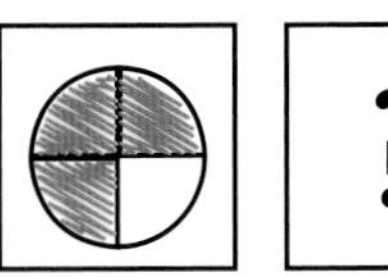

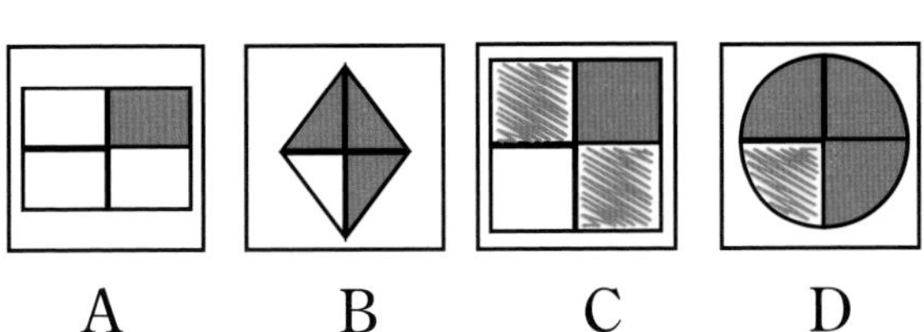

9.

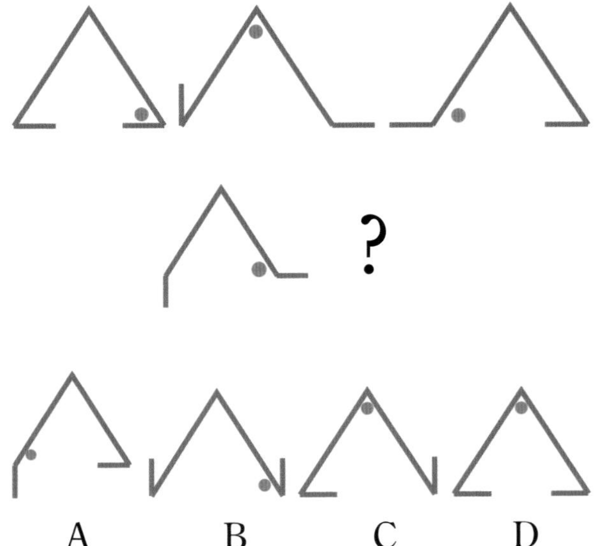

10.

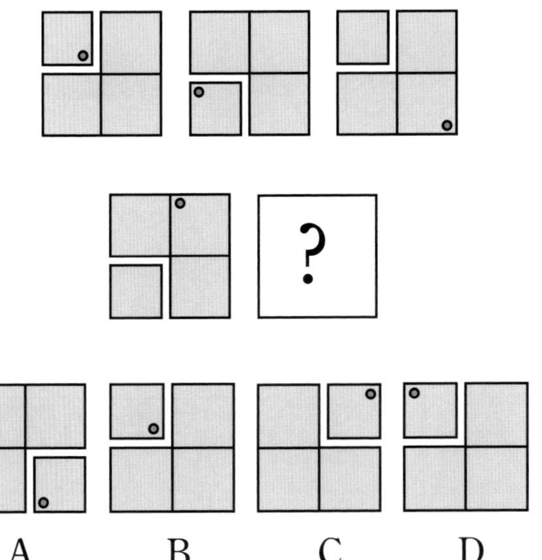

11.

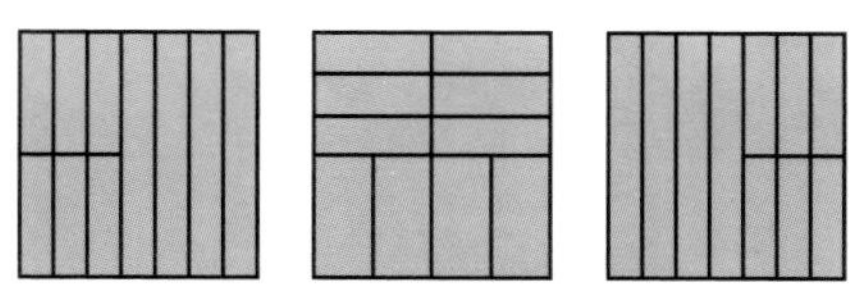

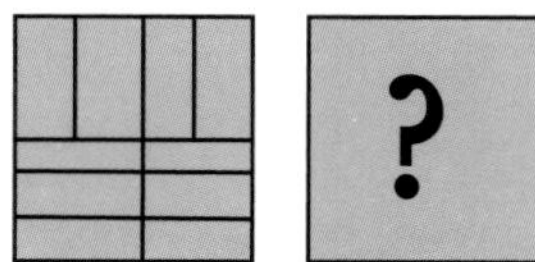

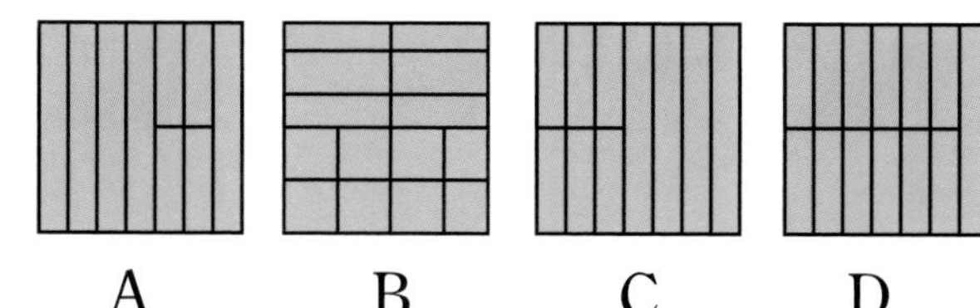

A B C D

12.

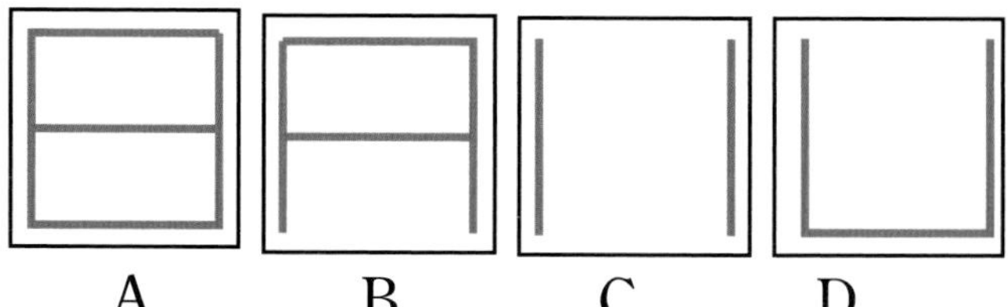

A B C D

13.

?

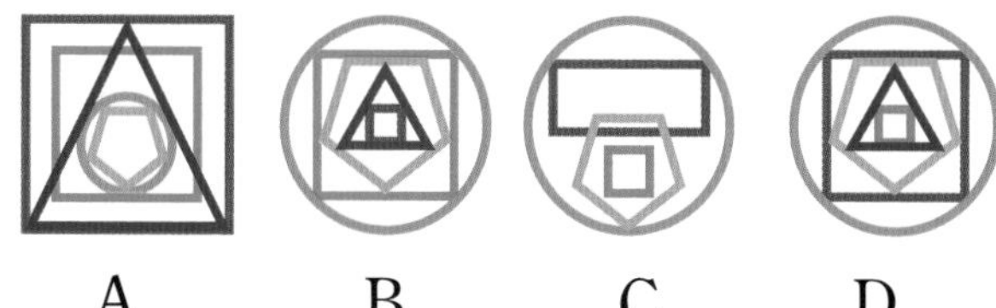

A B C D

14.

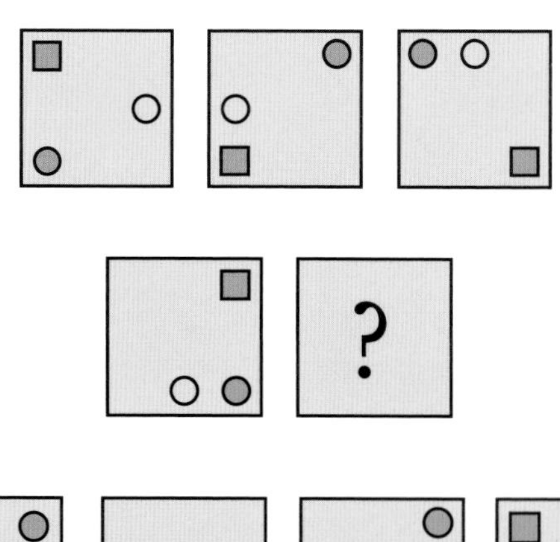

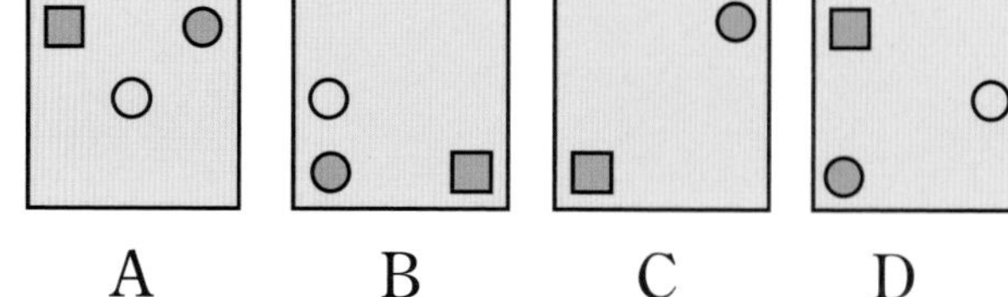

A B C D

15.

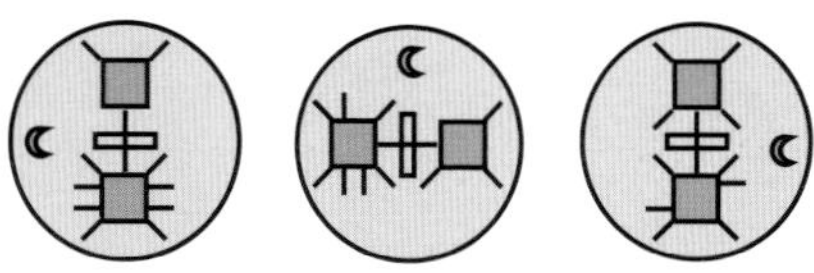

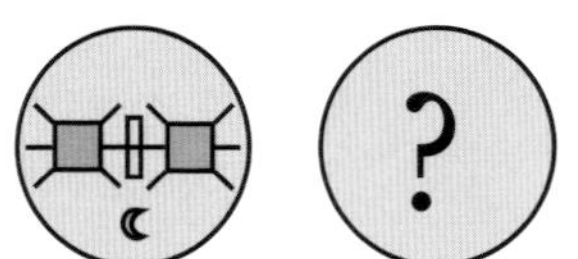

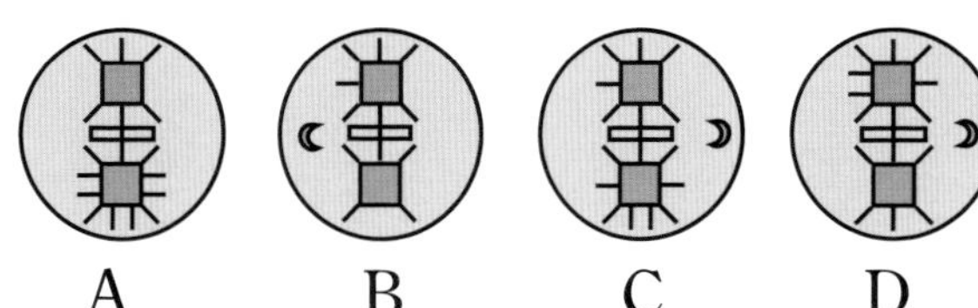

A B C D

16.

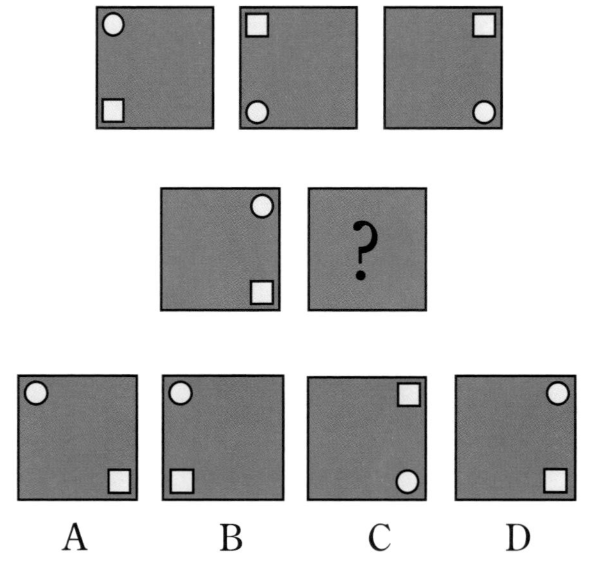

17.

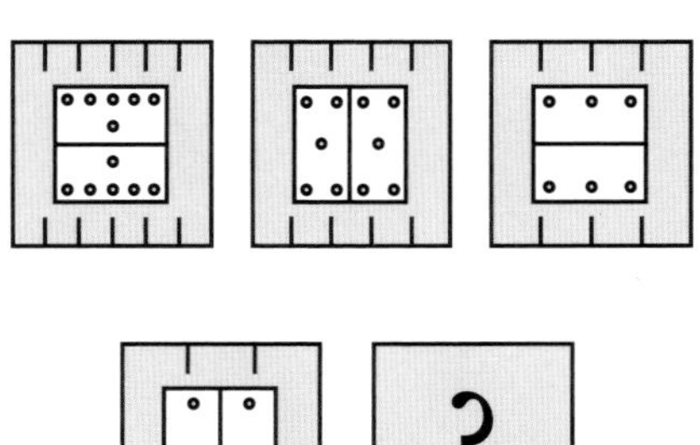

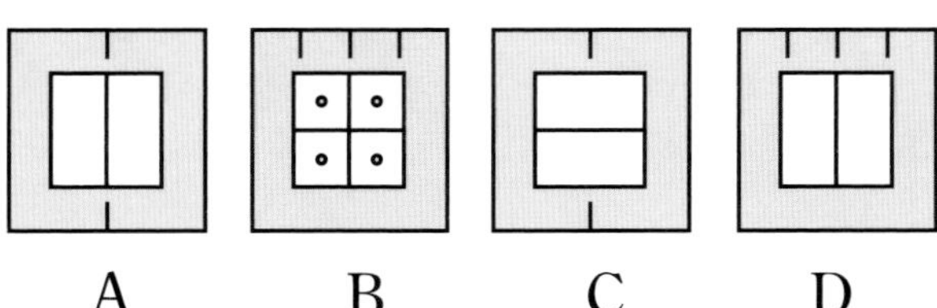

A B C D

18.

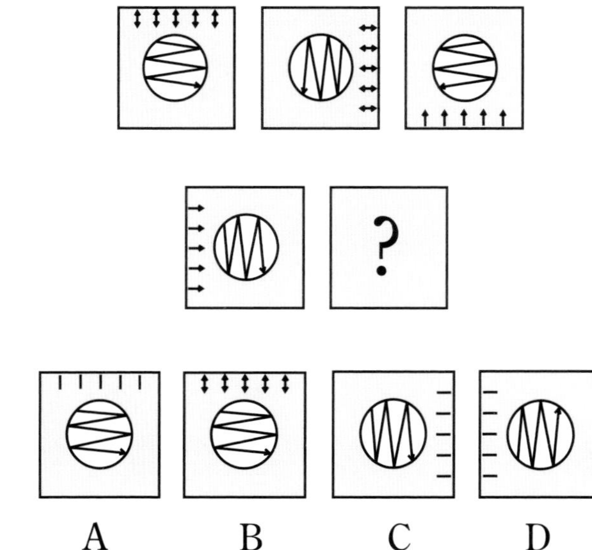

19.

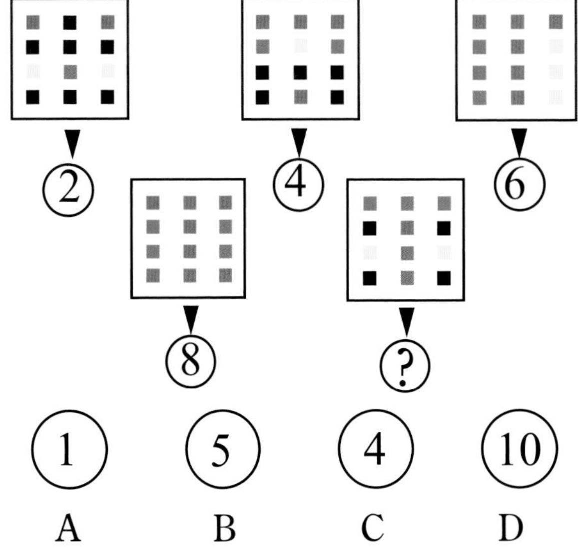

20.

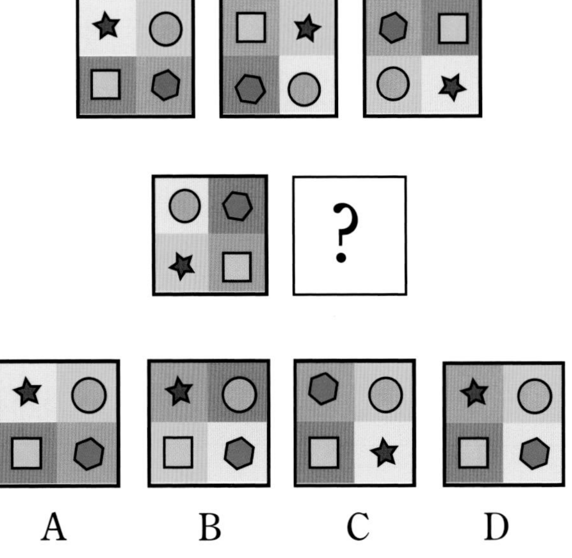

21.

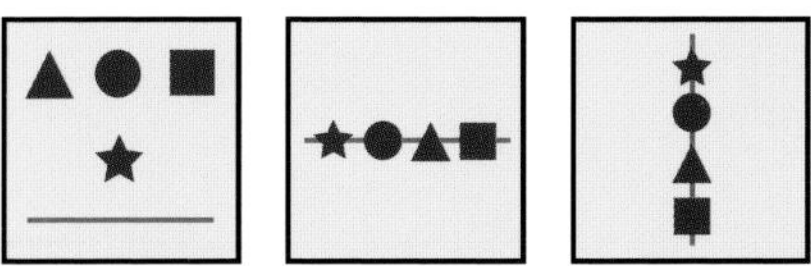

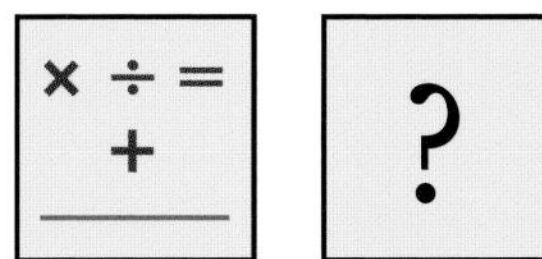

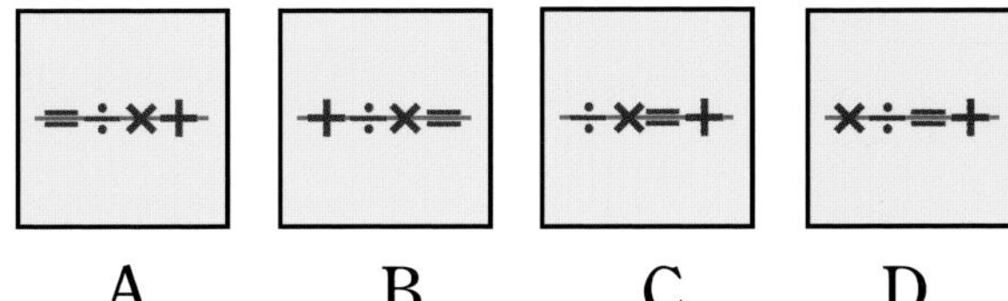

A B C D

22.

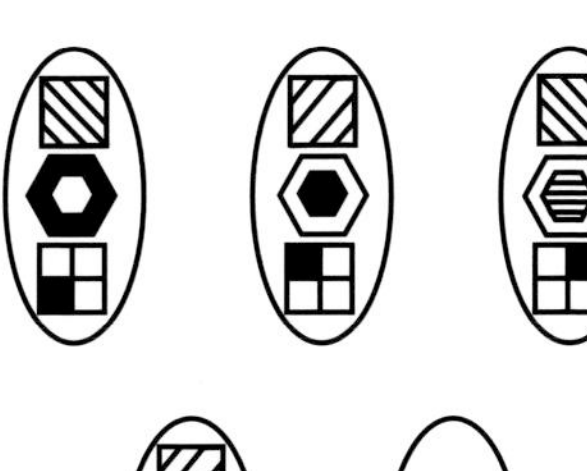

A B C D

23.

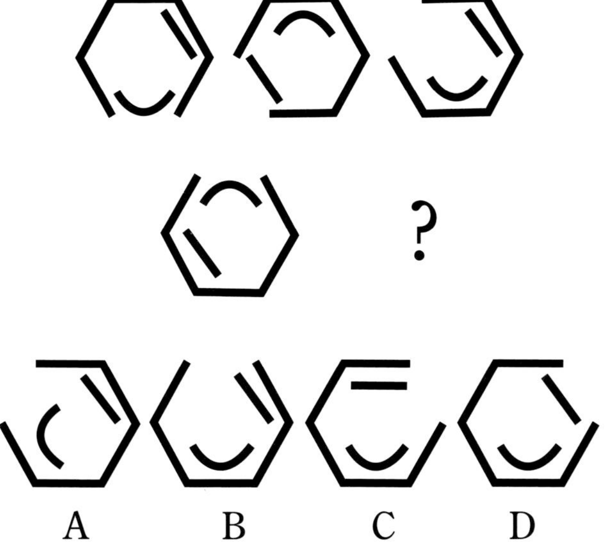

24.

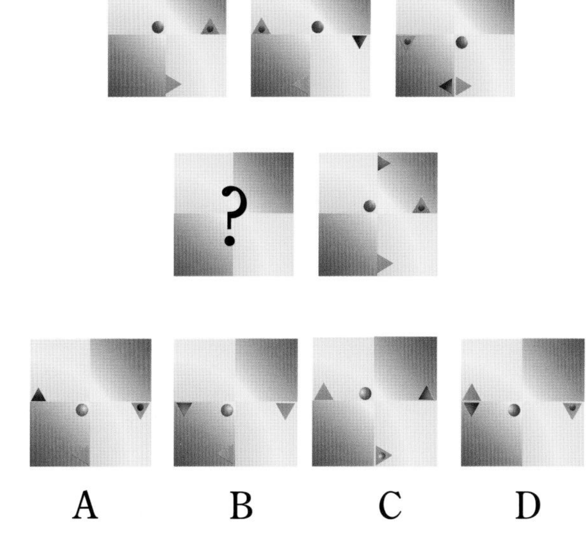

25.

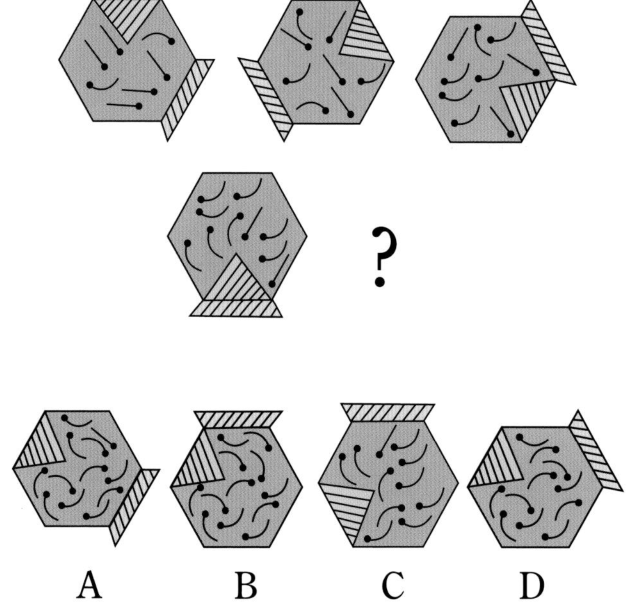

26.

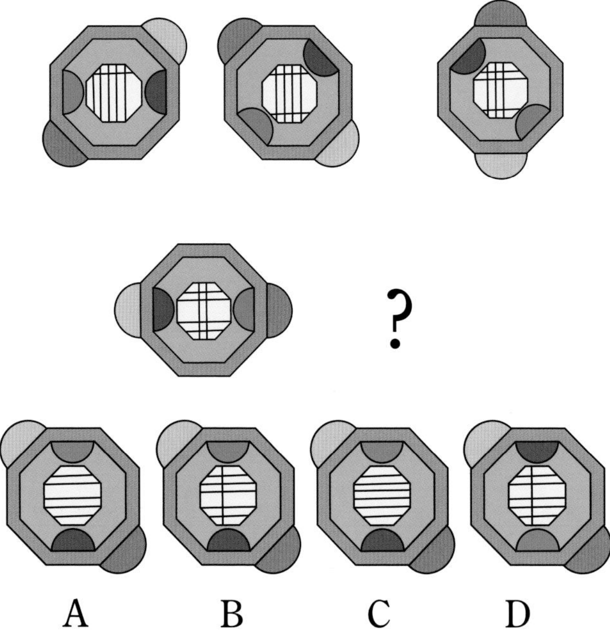

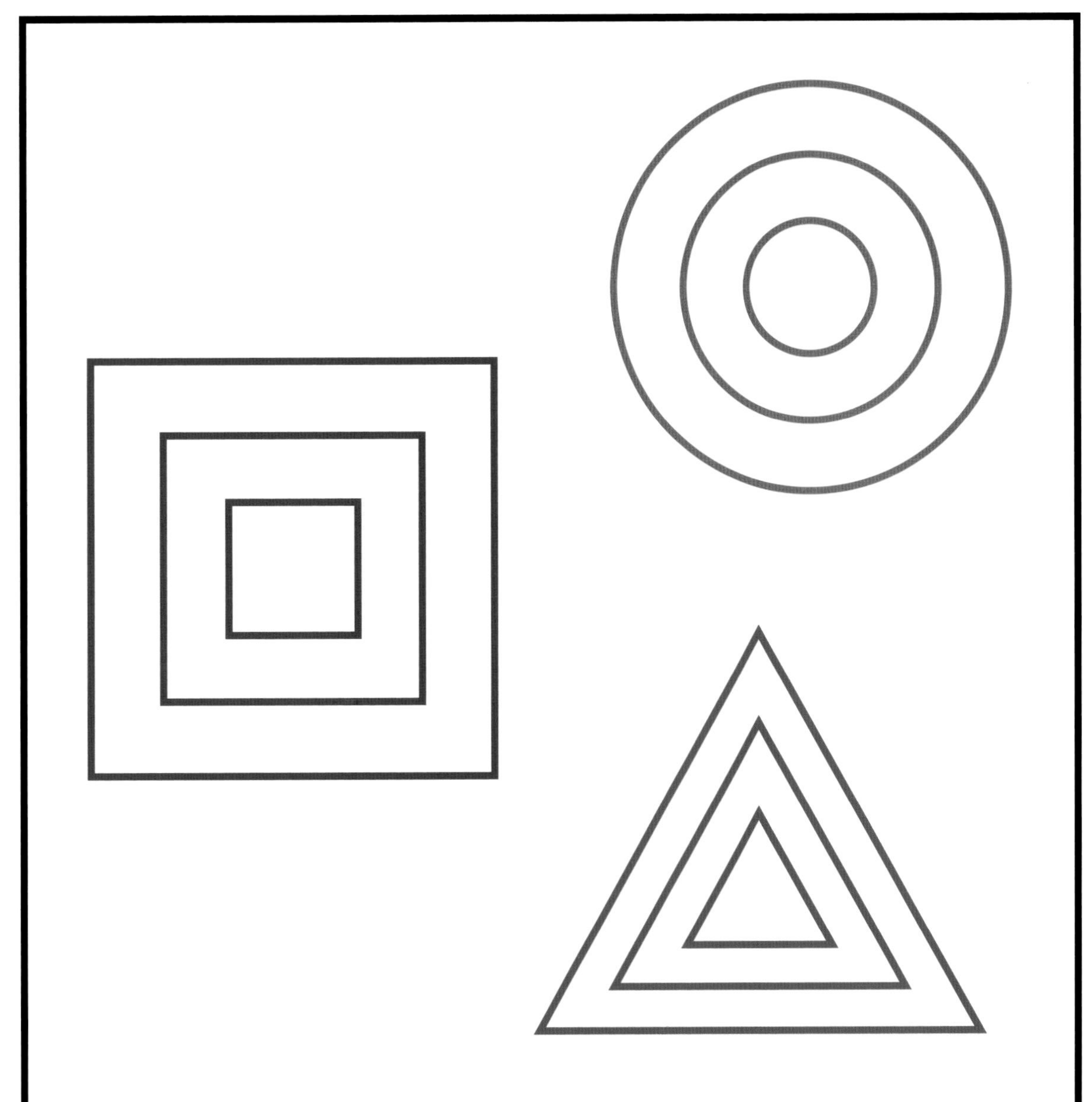

SERIES

- **In each of the puzzles given, find the missing figure that will complete the series.**

1.

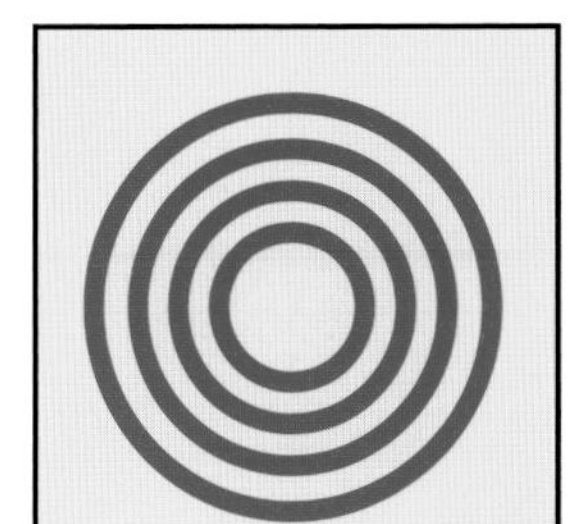
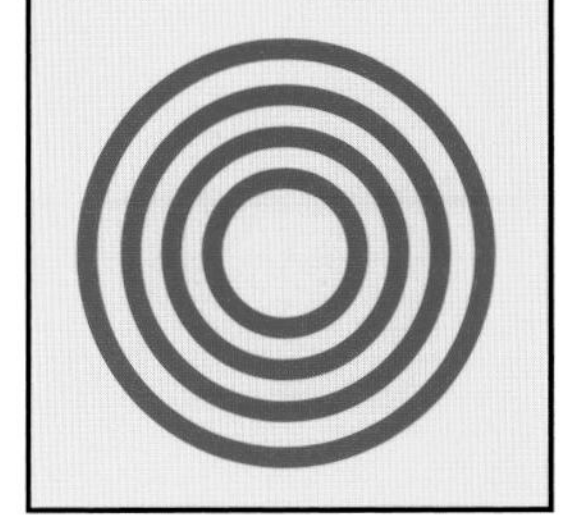

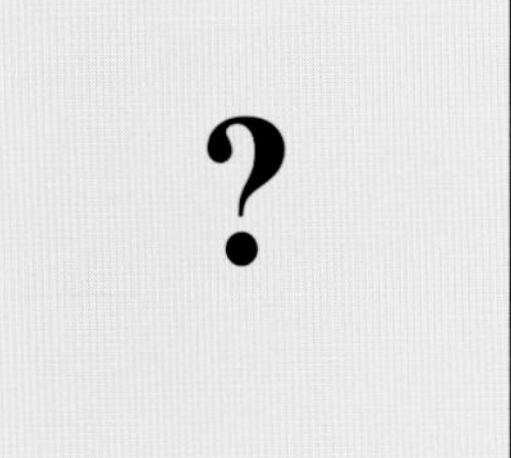
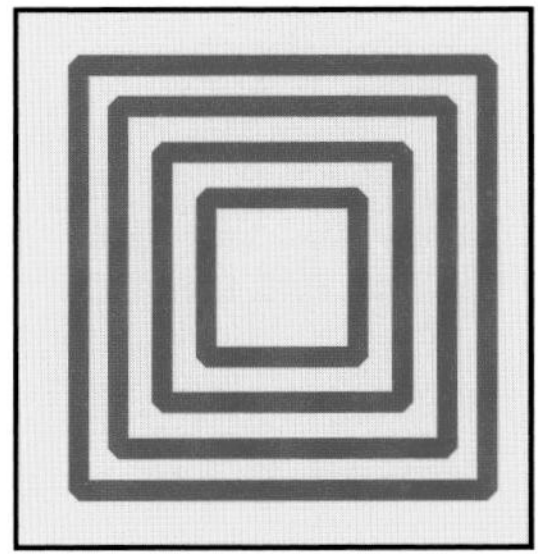

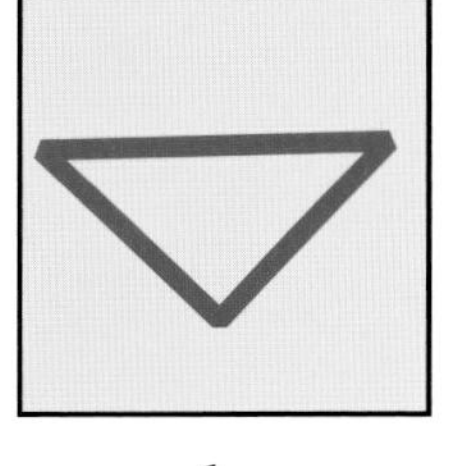
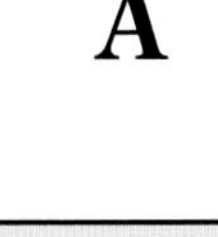
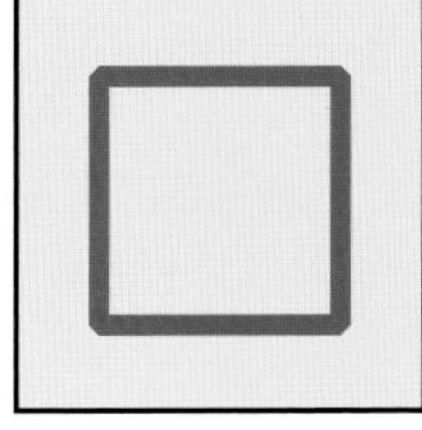

A **B**

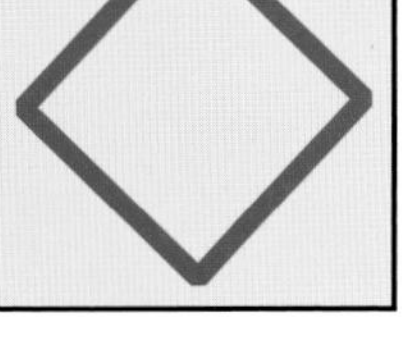
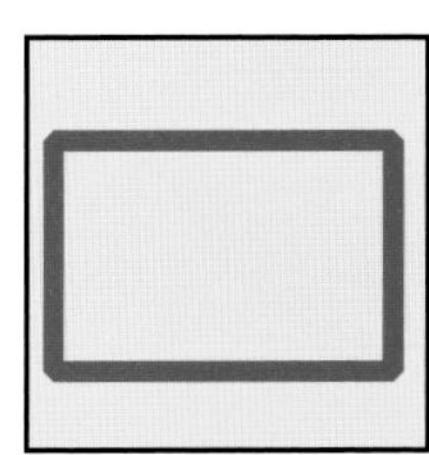

C **D**

2.

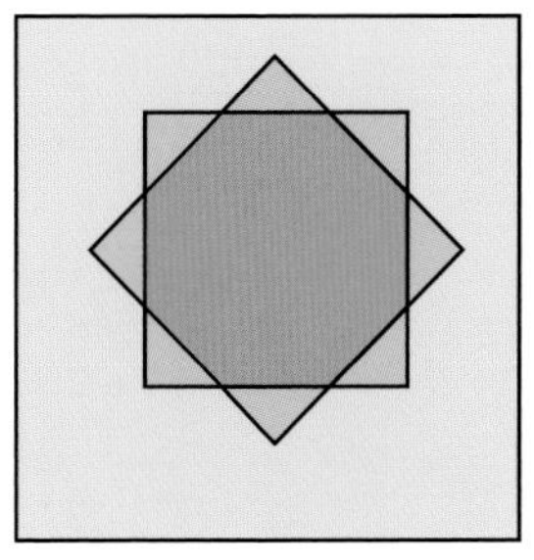

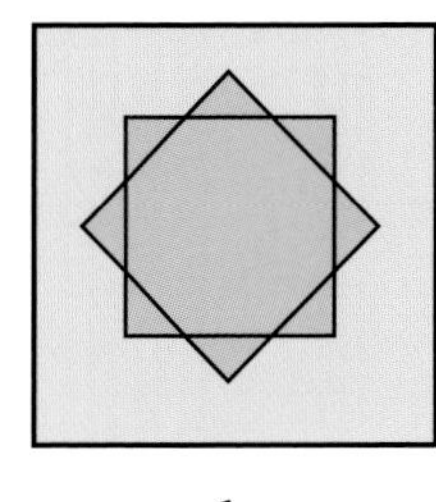
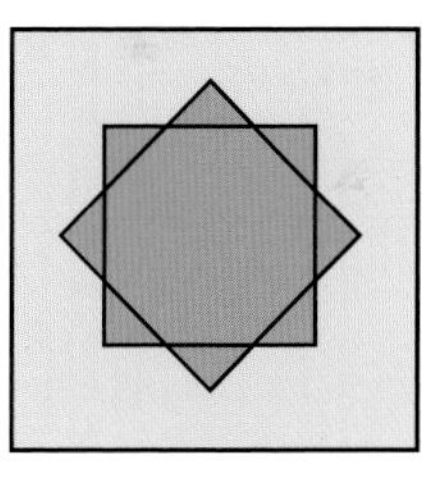

A **B**

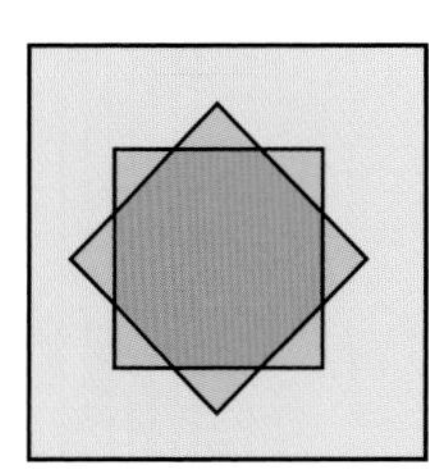
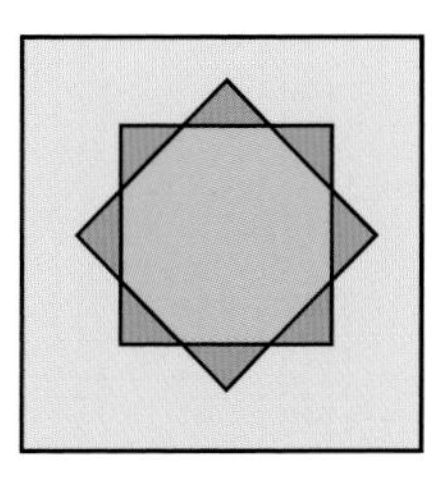

C **D**

3.

4.

5.

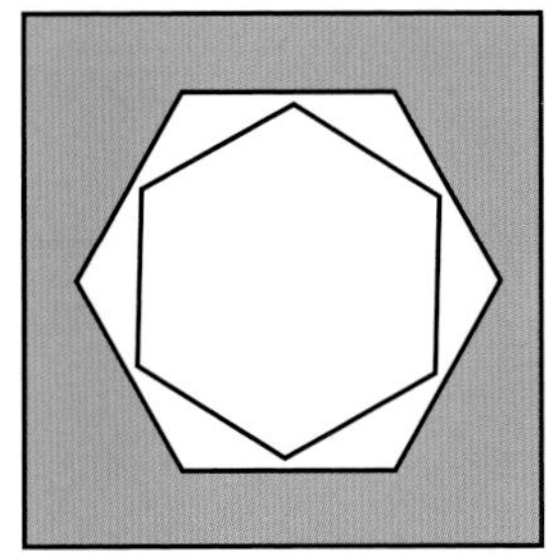
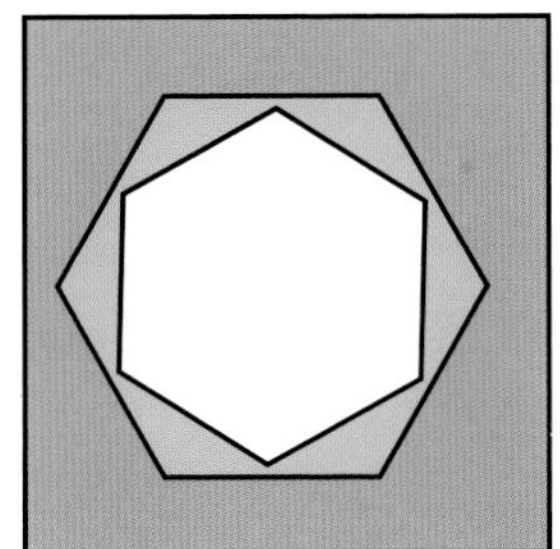
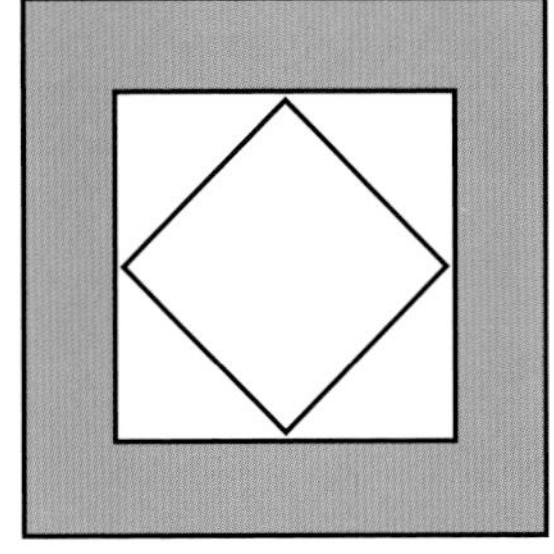

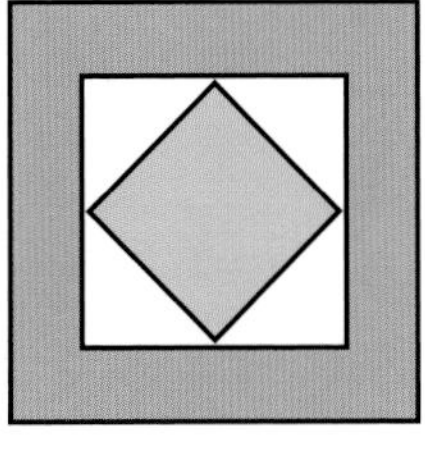
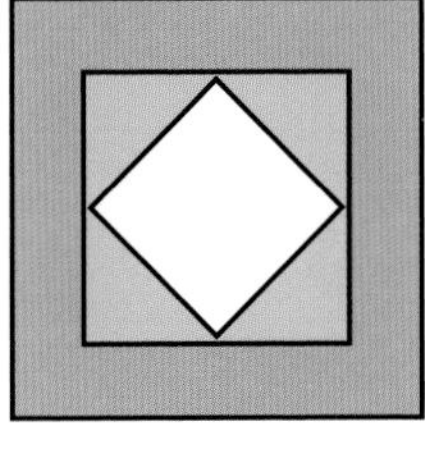

A **B**

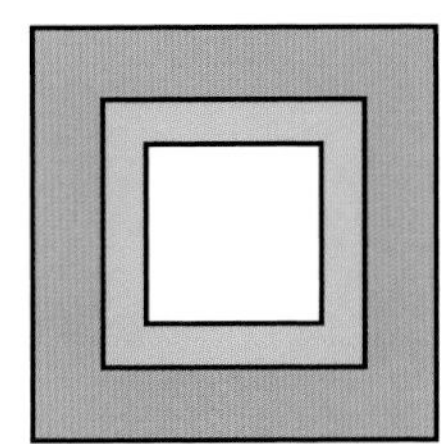

C **D**

6.

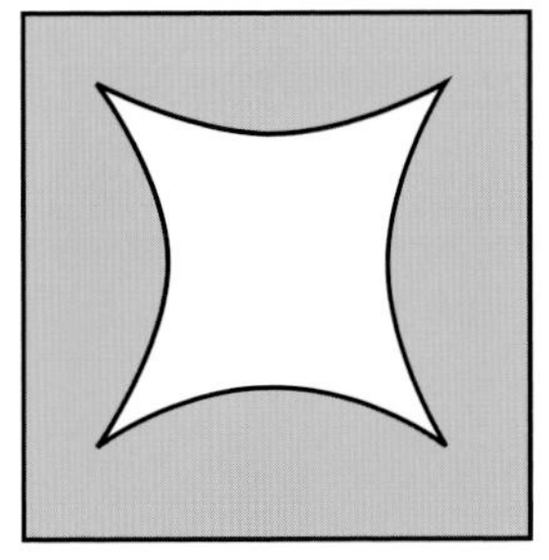
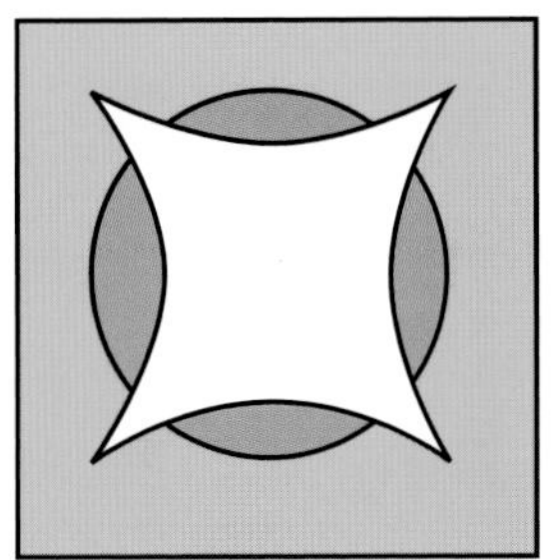
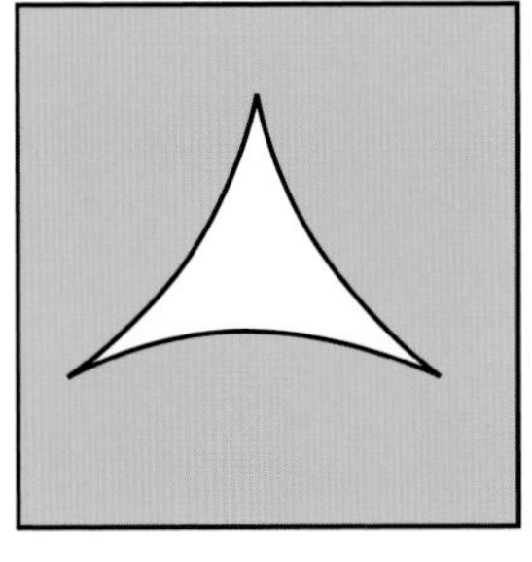

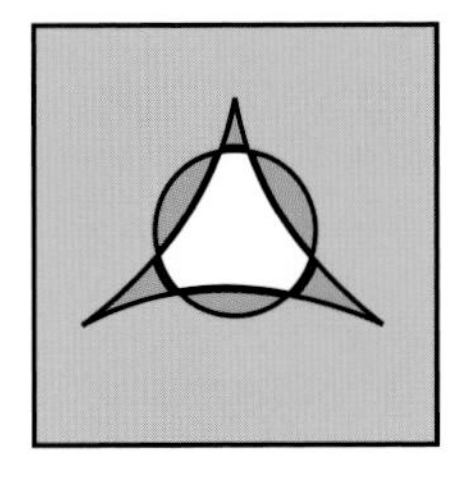
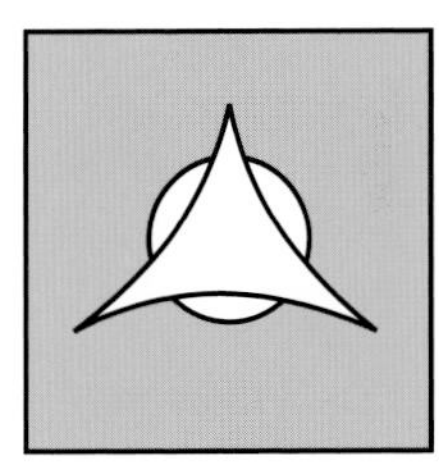

A **B**

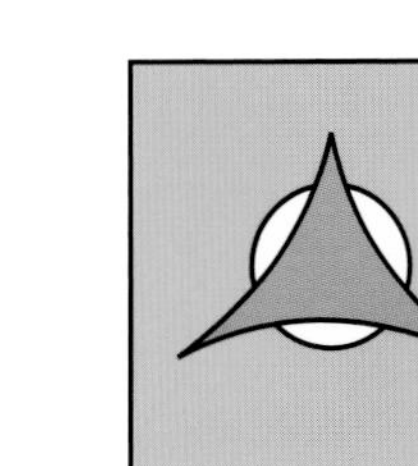
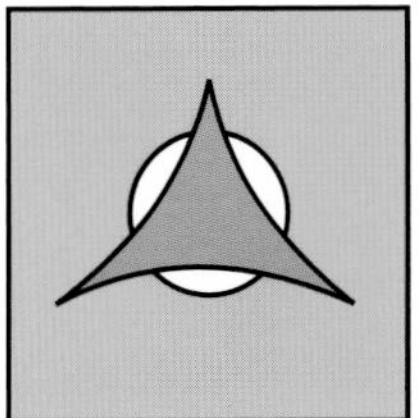

C **D**

7.

8.

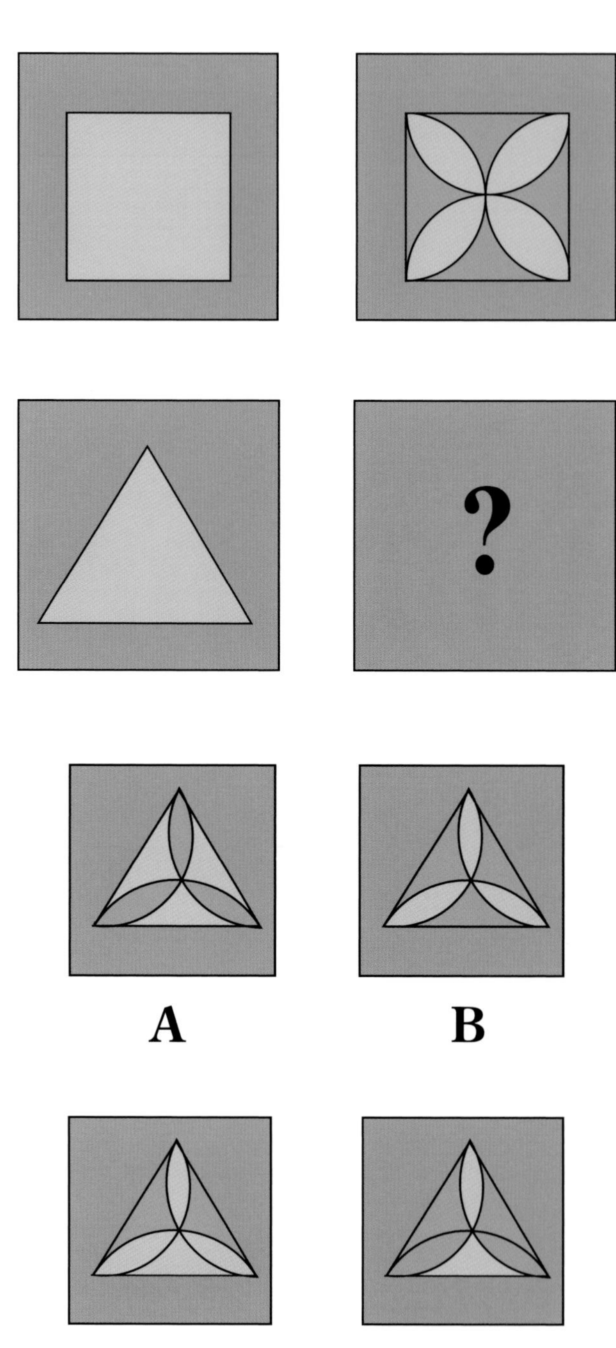

9.

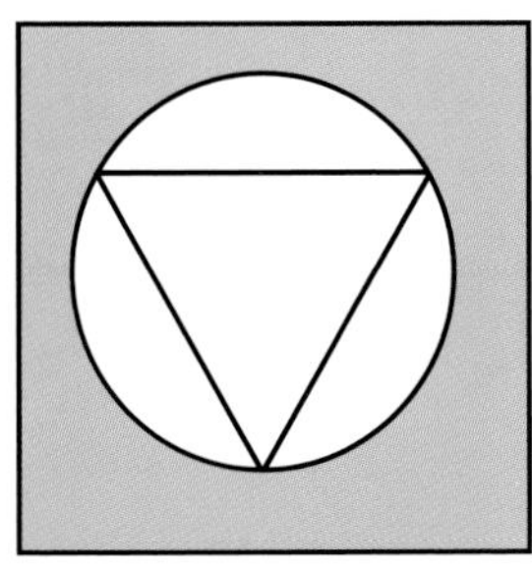
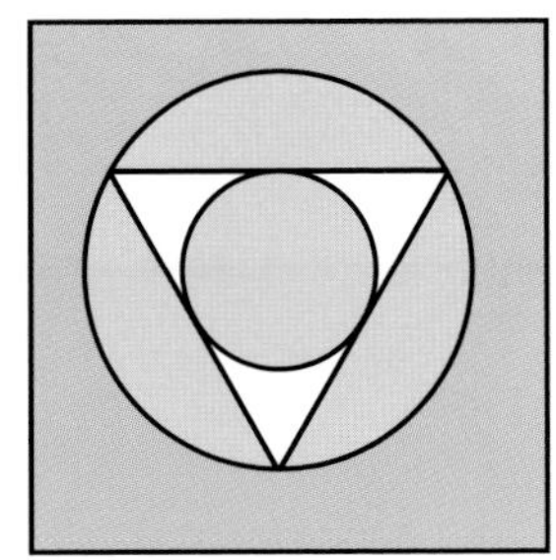
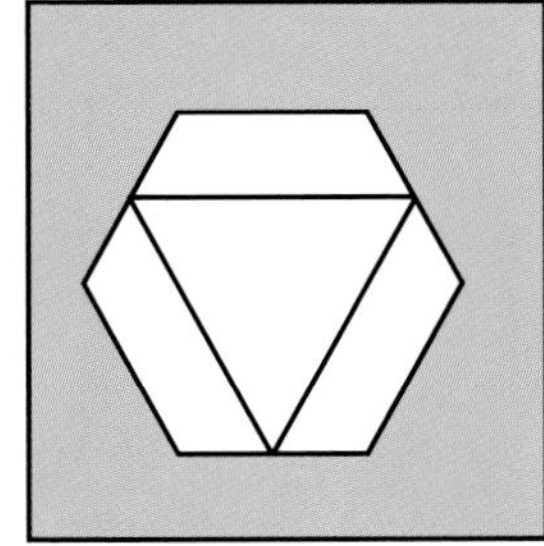
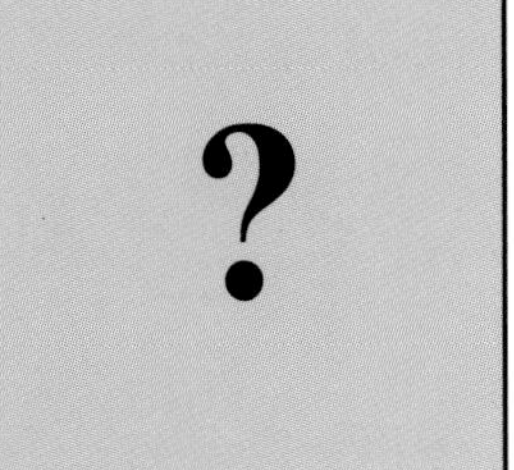

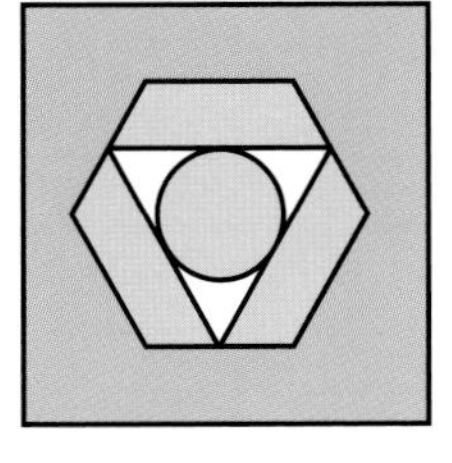

A

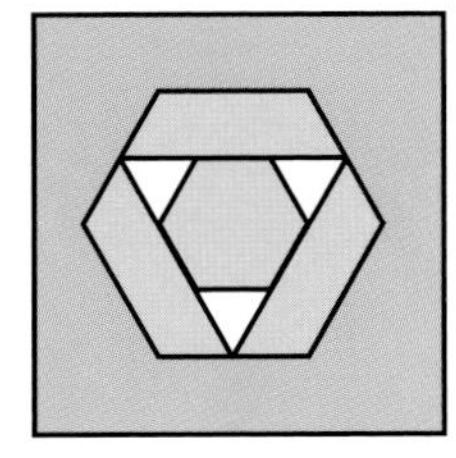

B

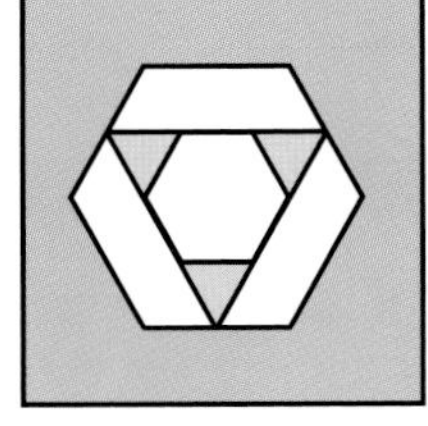

C

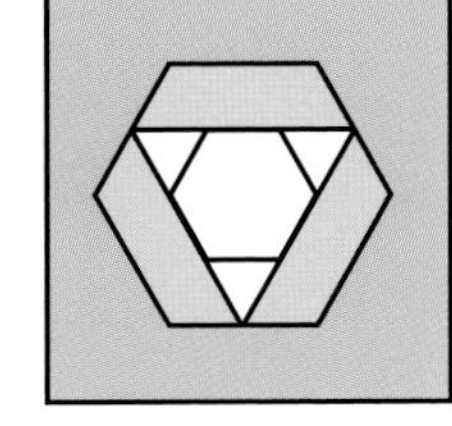

D

10.

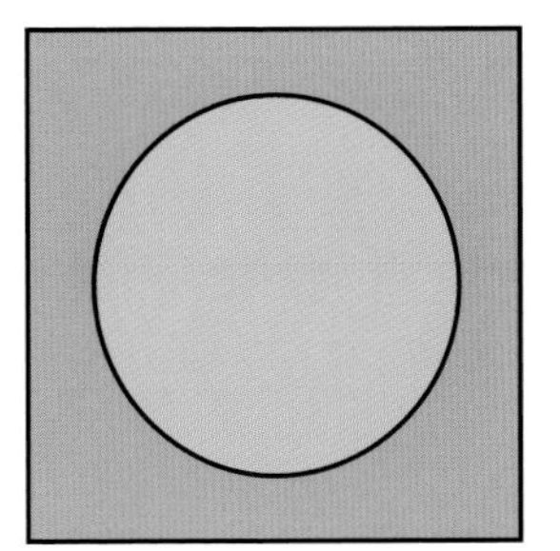
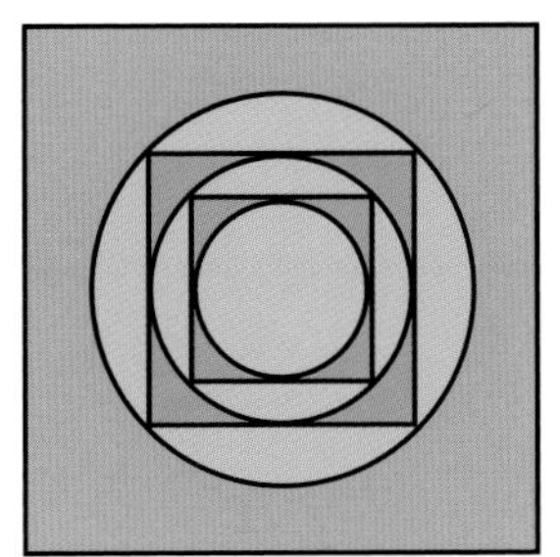

A

B

C

D

11.

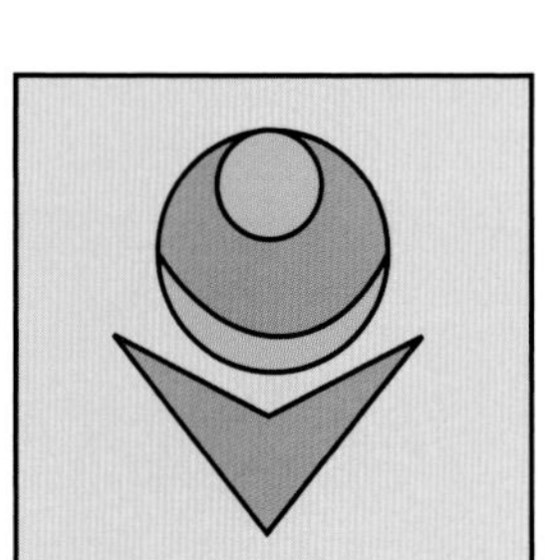

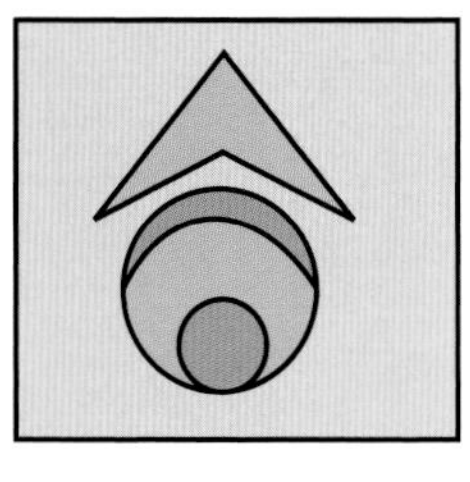

A

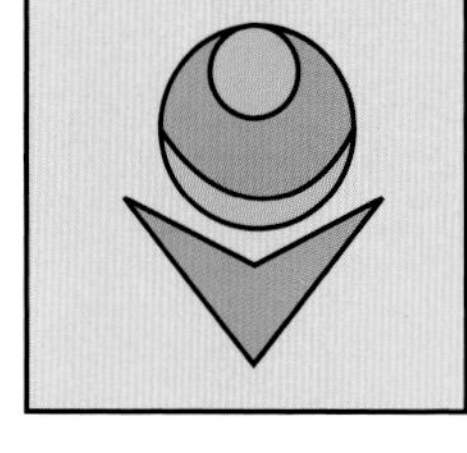

B

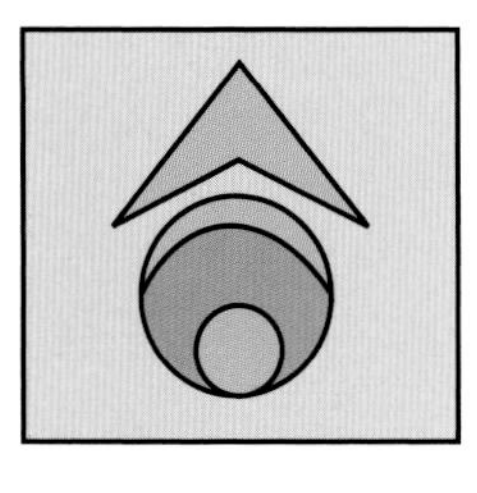

C

D

12.

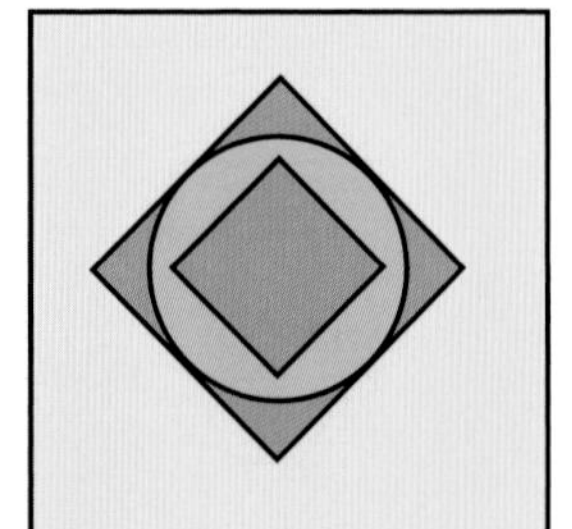
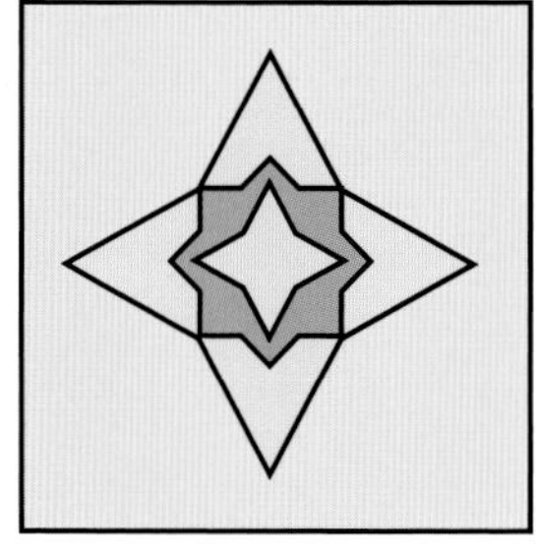

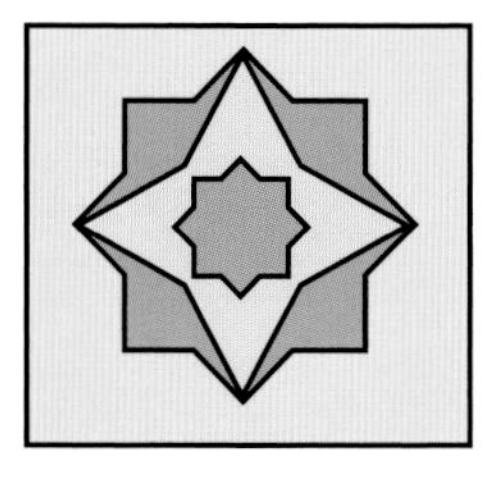

A

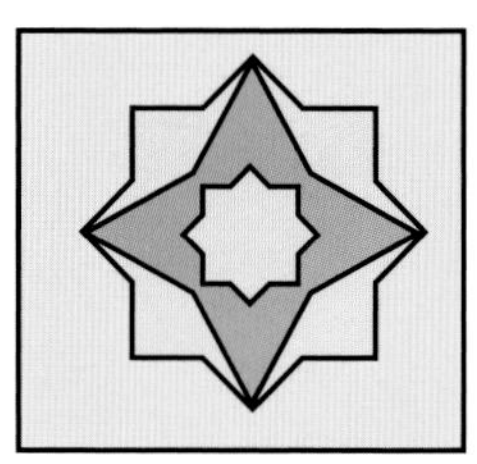

B

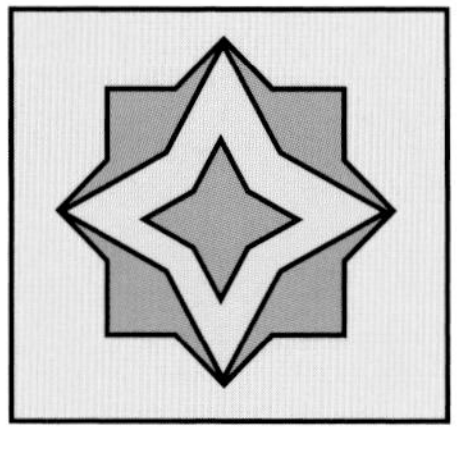

C

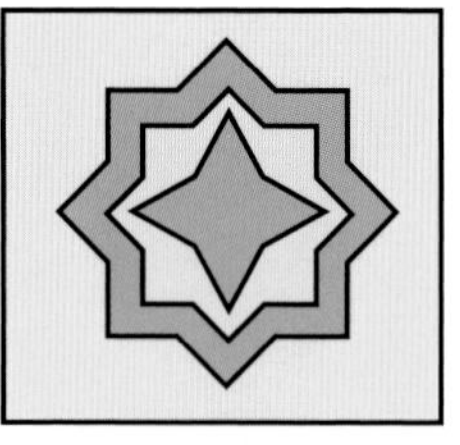

D

13.

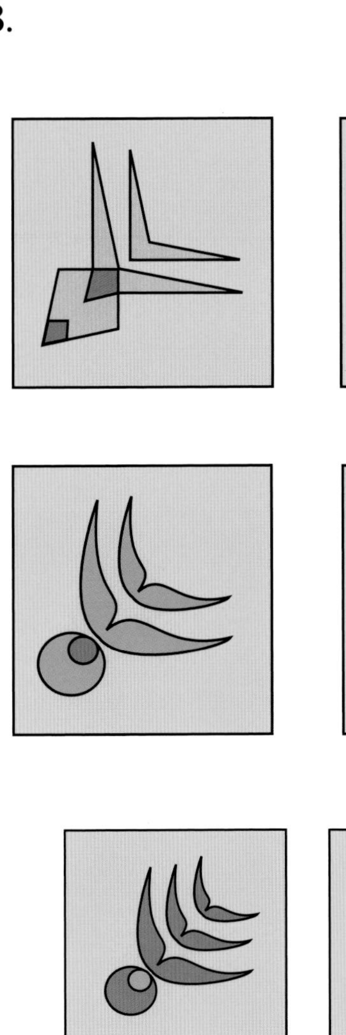

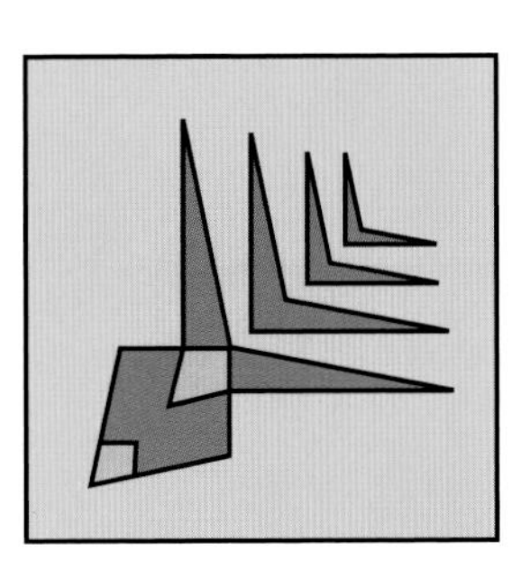

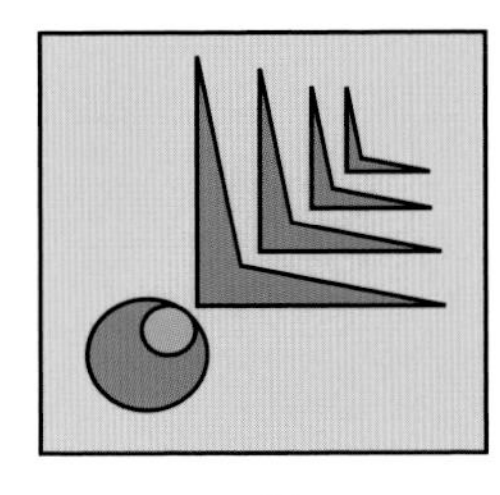

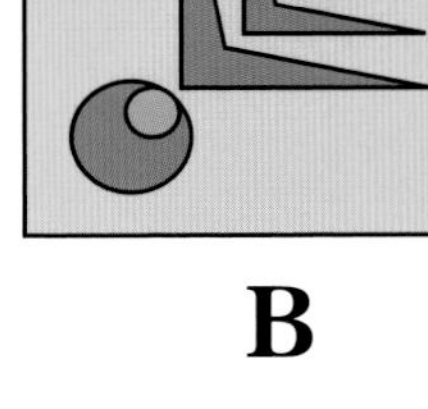

A **B**

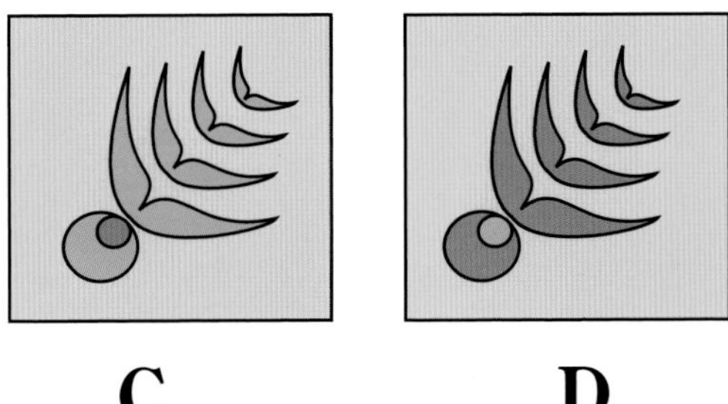

C **D**

14.

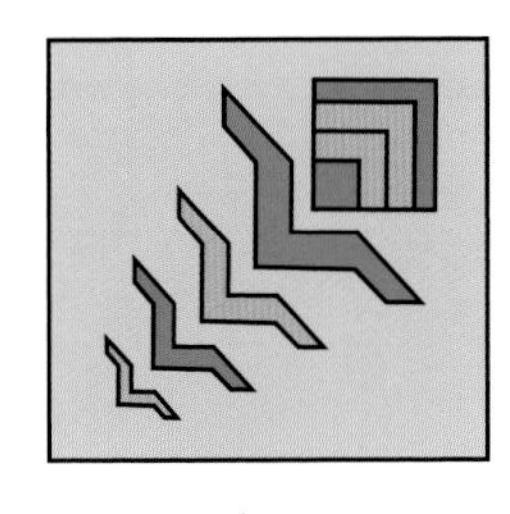

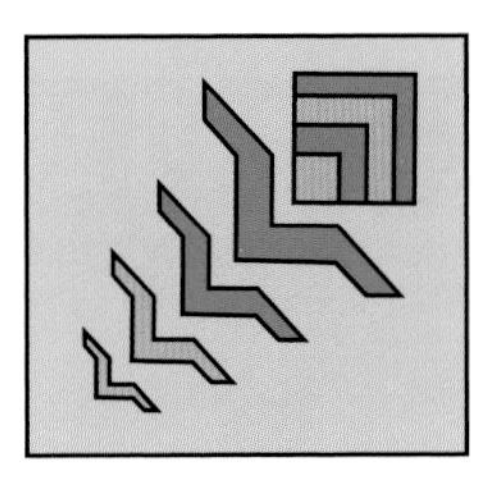

A **B**

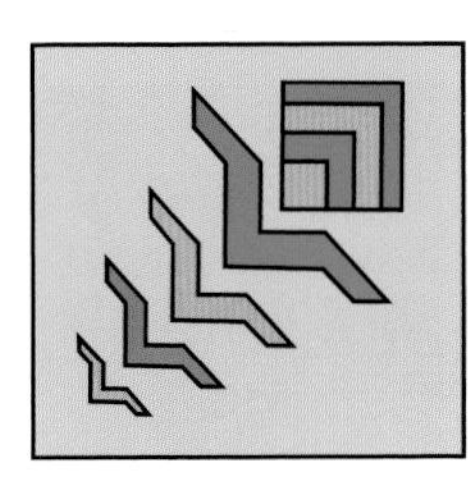

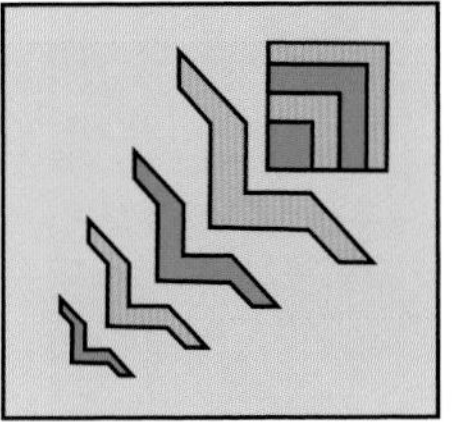

C **D**

15.

?

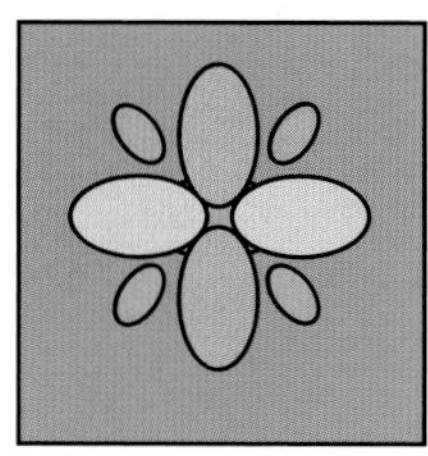

A **B**

C **D**

16.

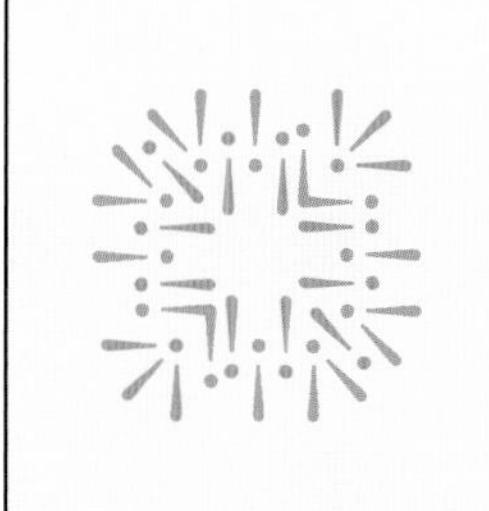

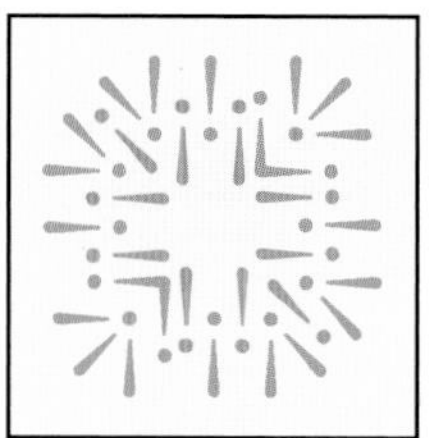

A **B**

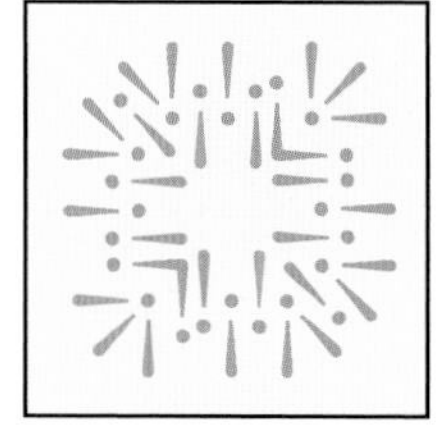

C **D**

17.

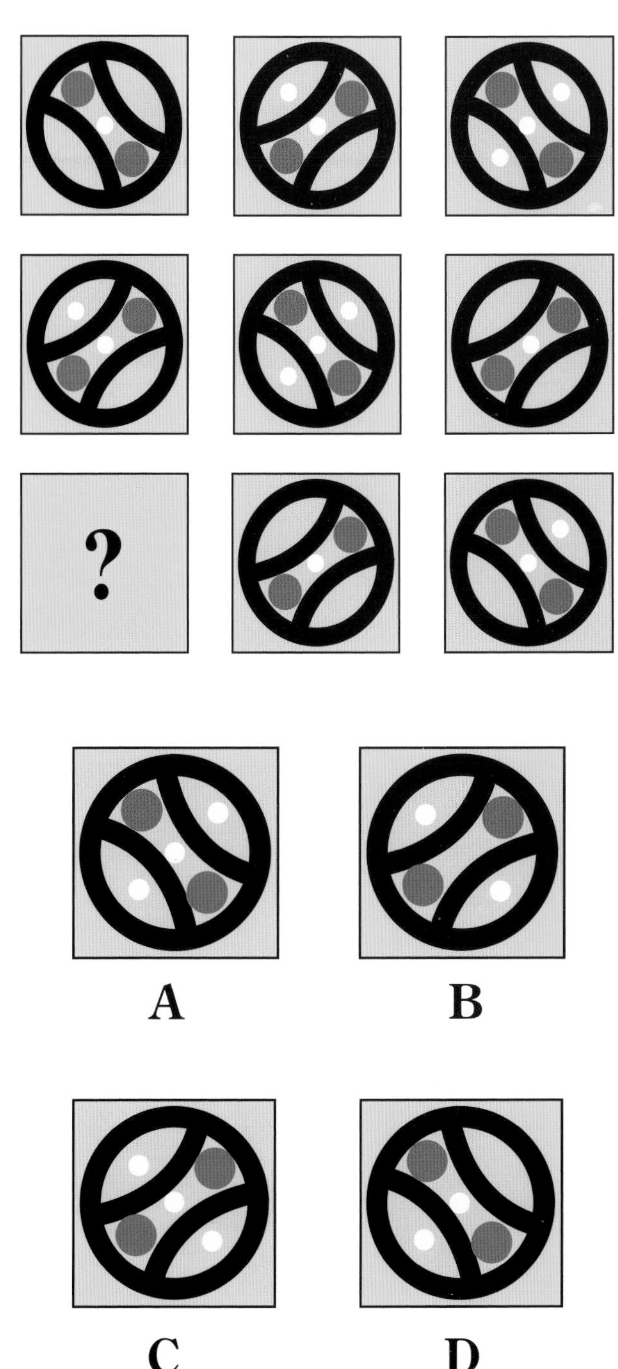

18.

19.

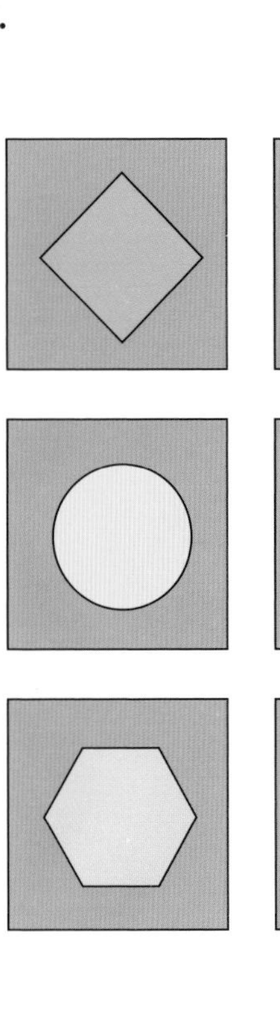
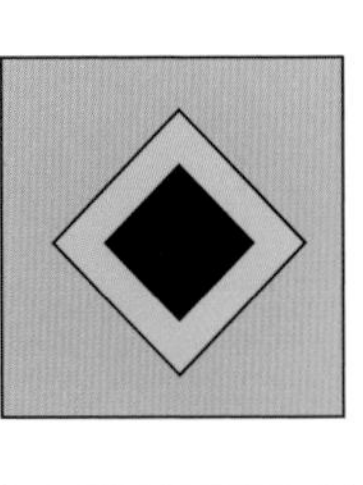

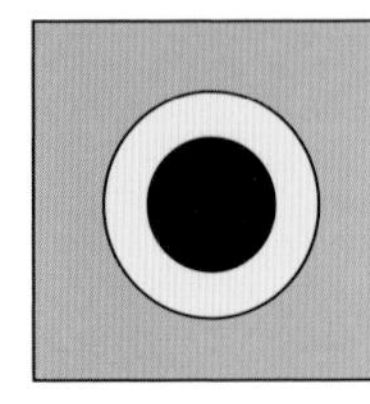
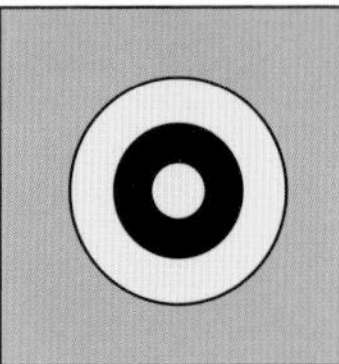
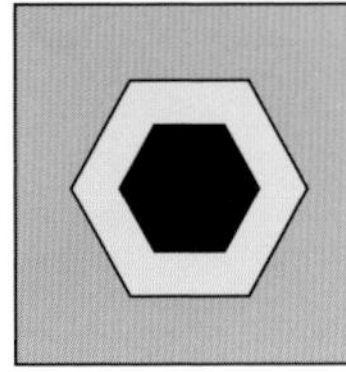

?

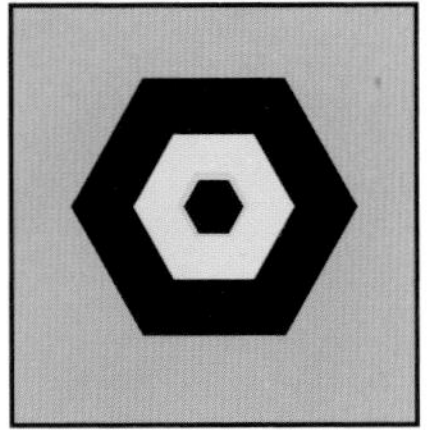

A

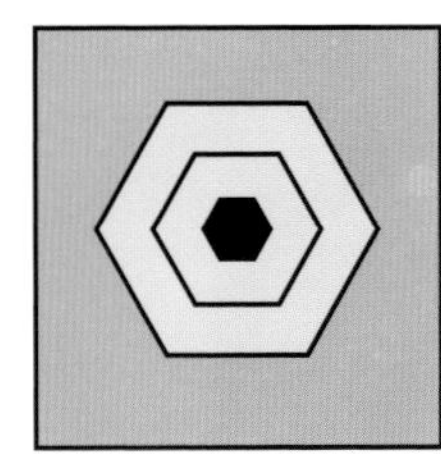

B

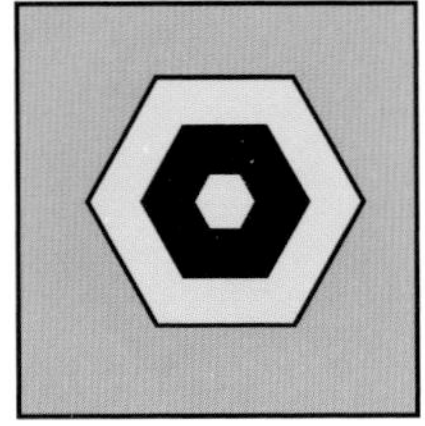

C

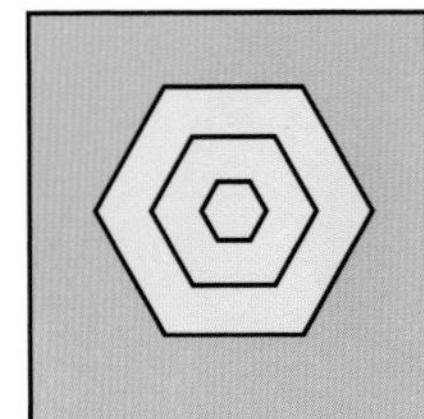

D

20.

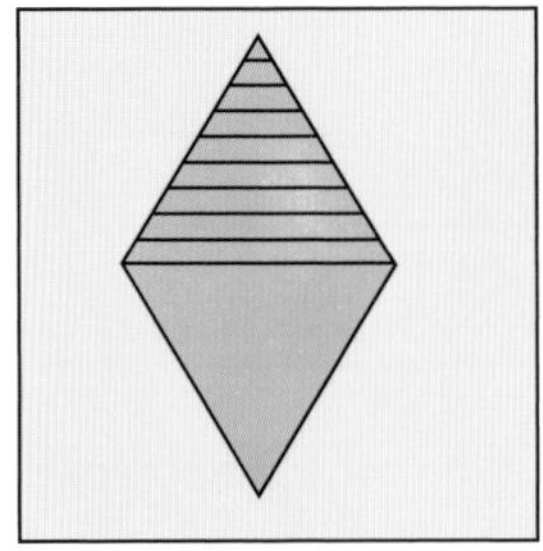
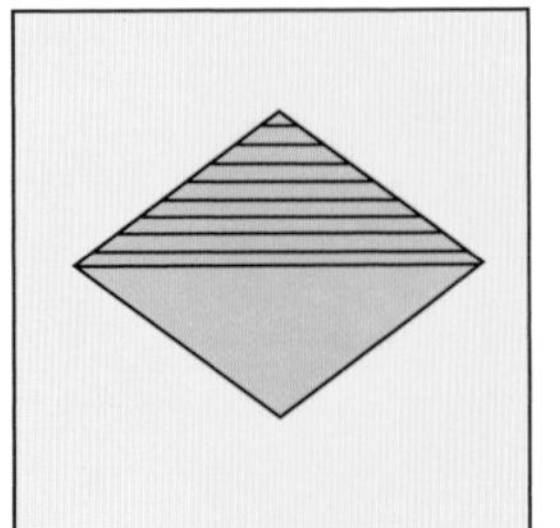
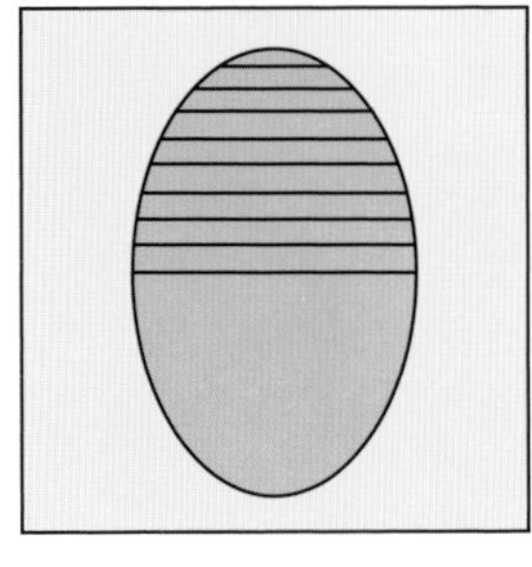

?

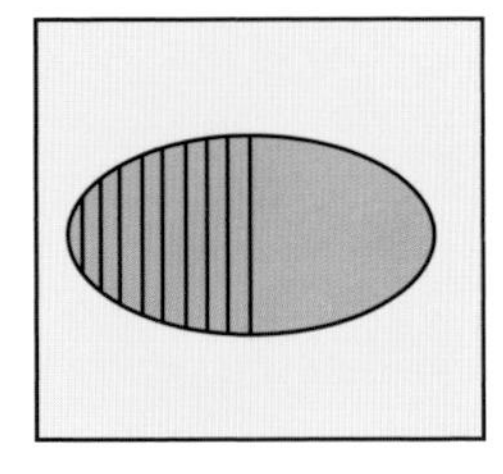

A

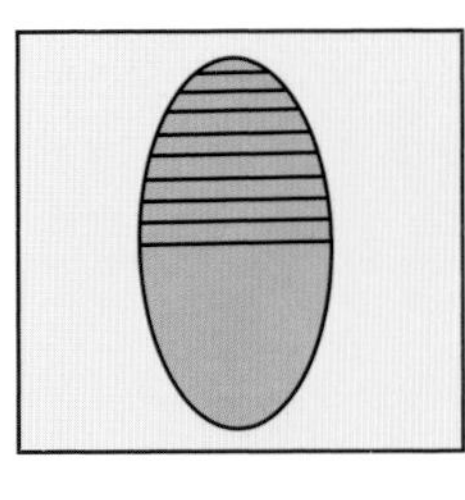

B

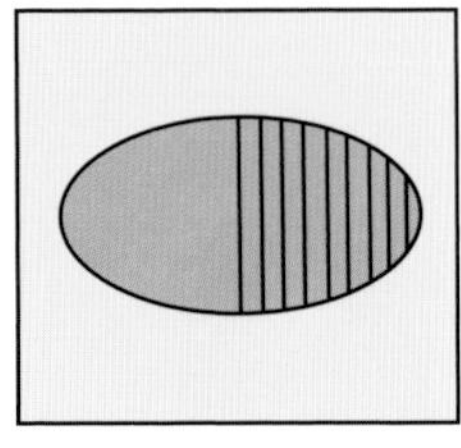

C

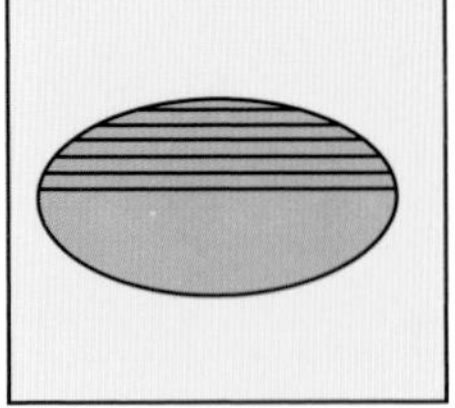

D

21.

22.

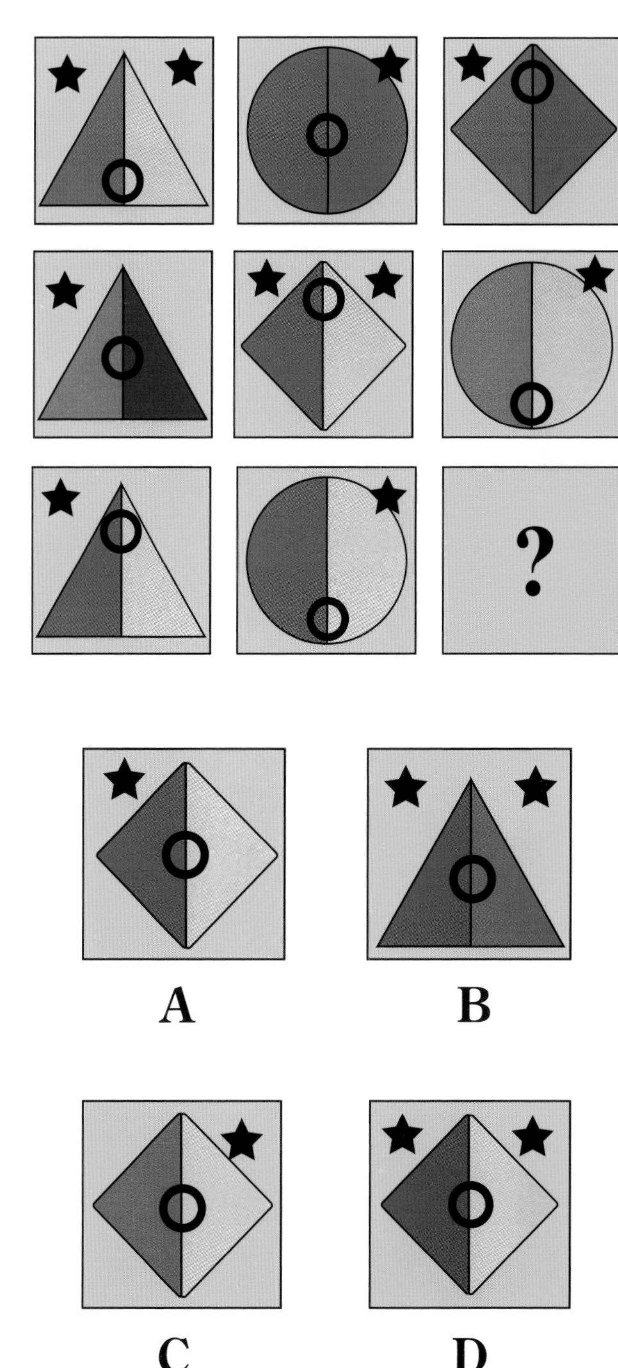

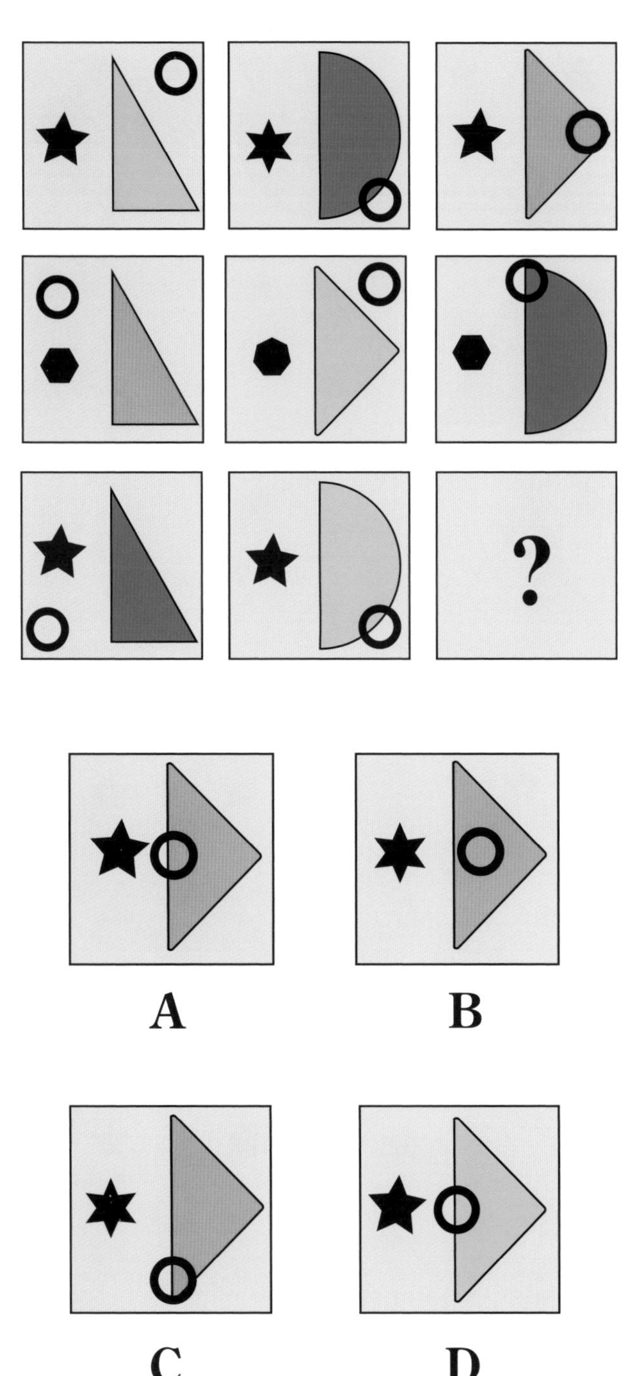
23.
?
A
B
C
D

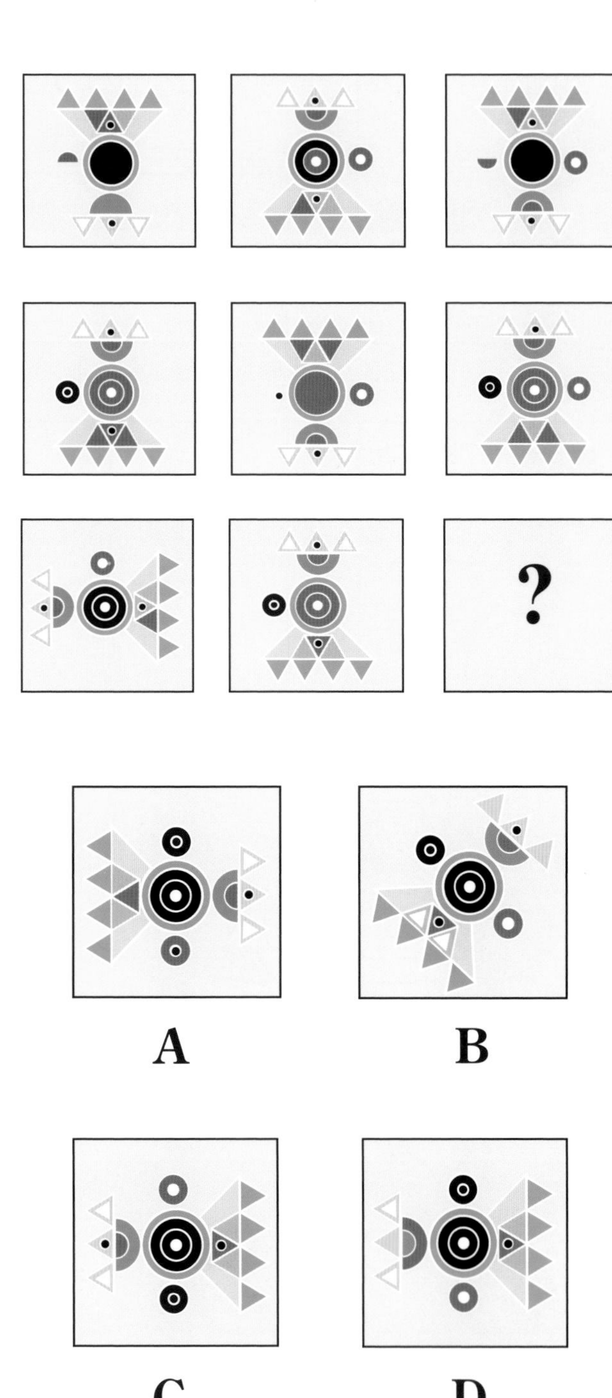
24.
?
A
B
C
D

25.

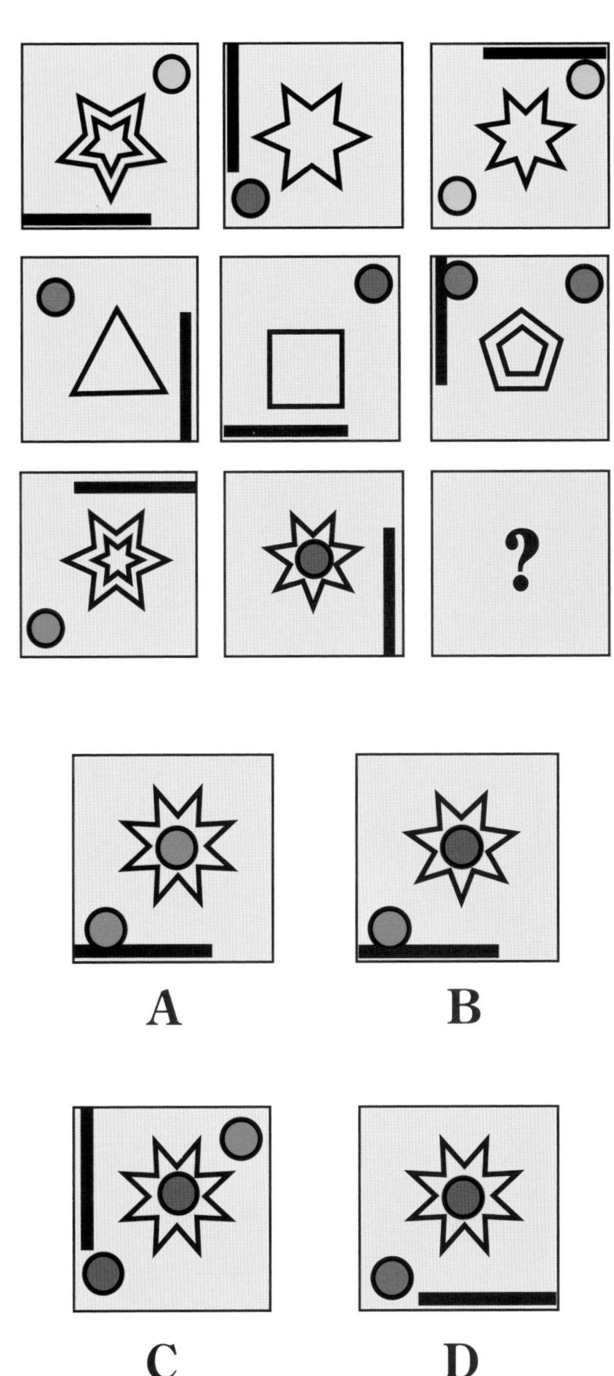

26.

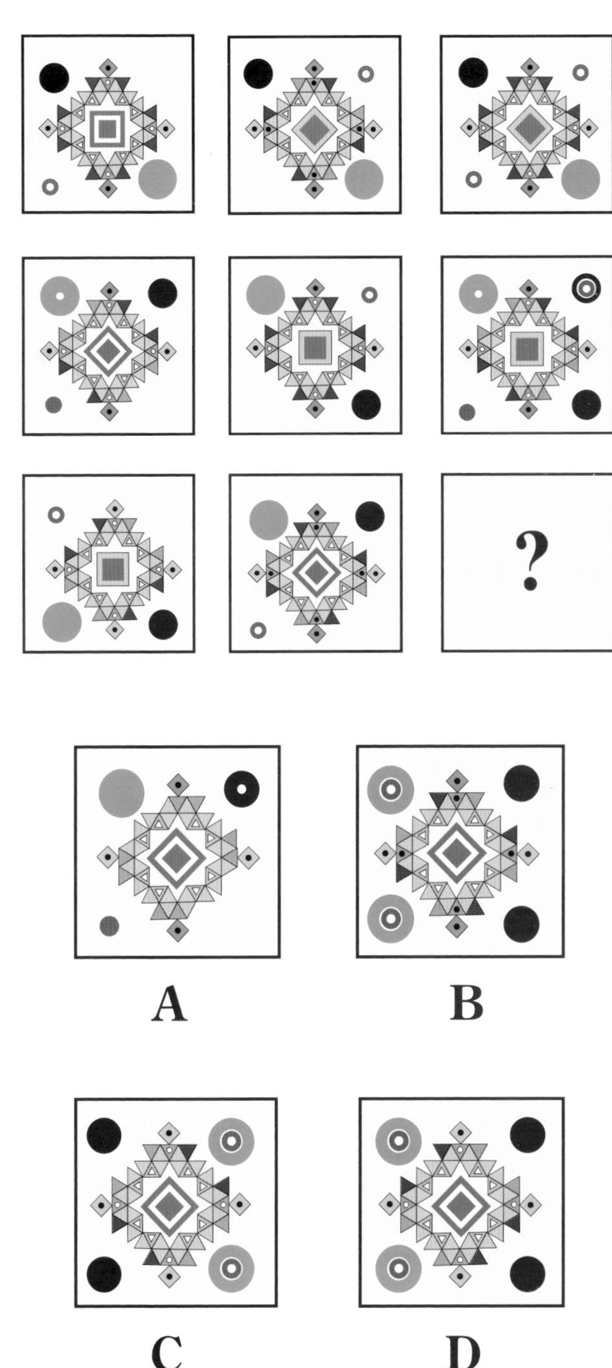

PATTERN

- In the given puzzles, think of the pattern that the cut pieces, if put together, will make.
- There can be only one right answer.

1.

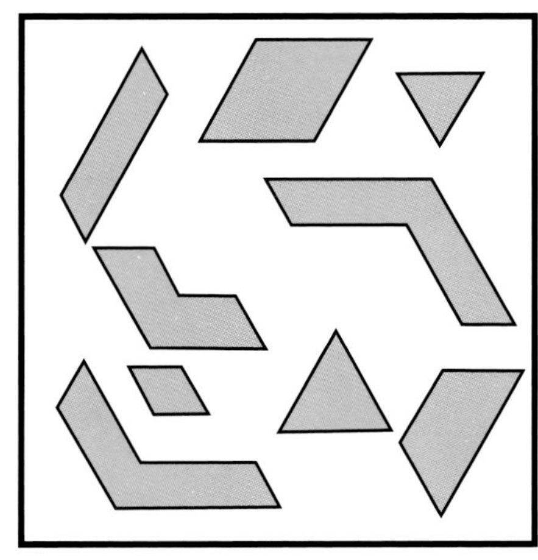

A

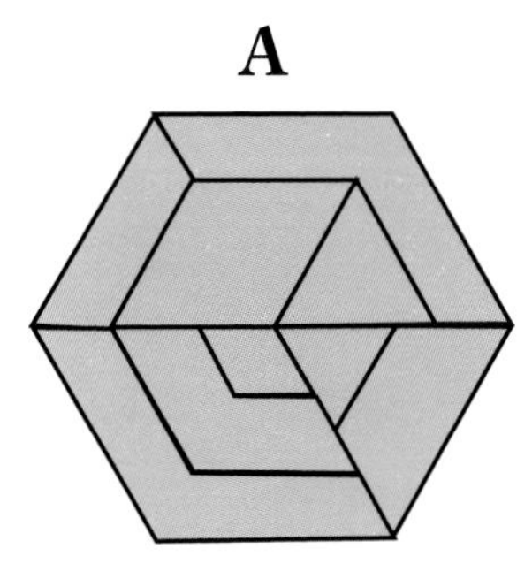

B

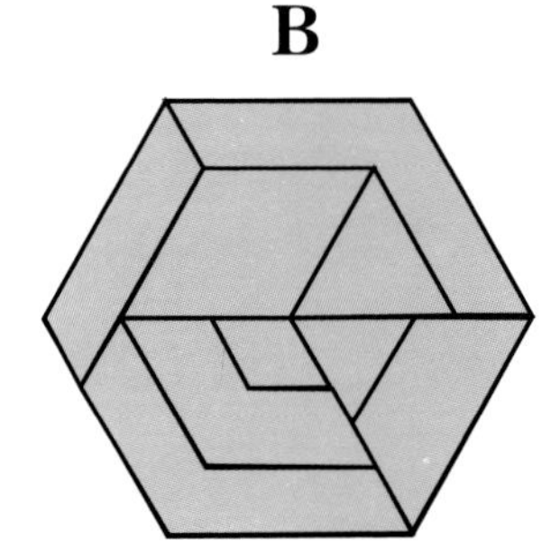

C

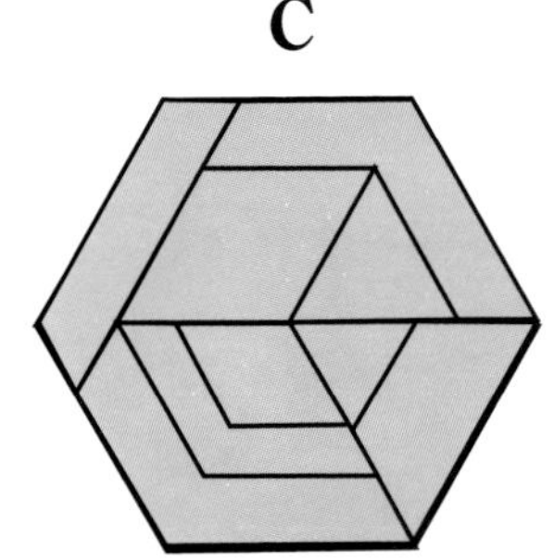

D

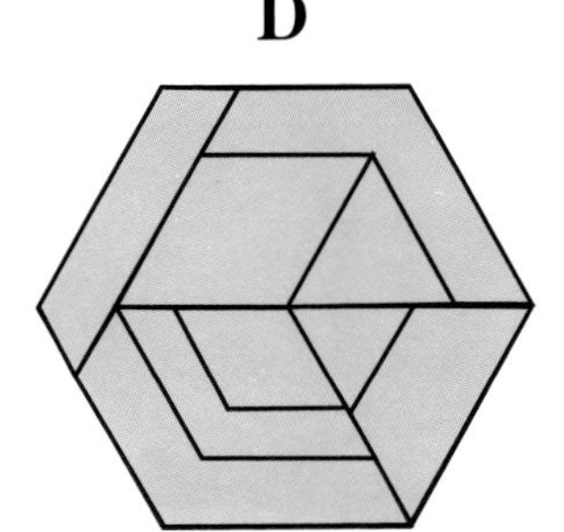

2.

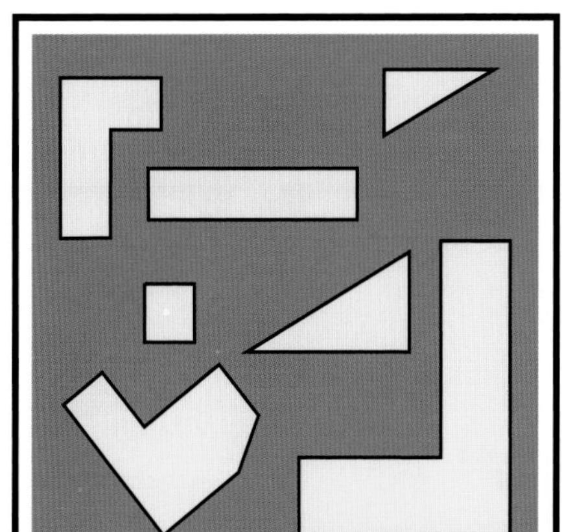

A B

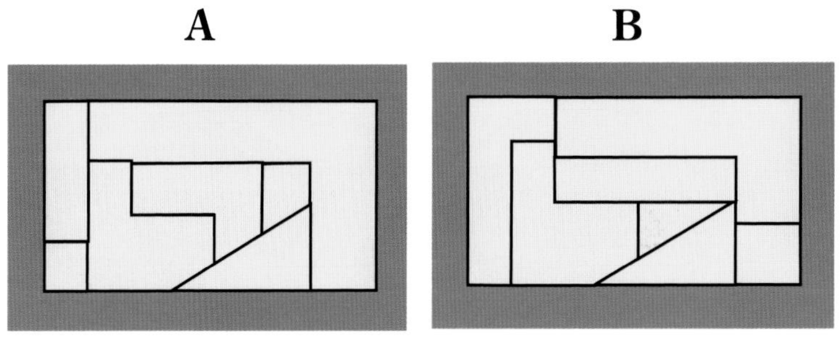

C D

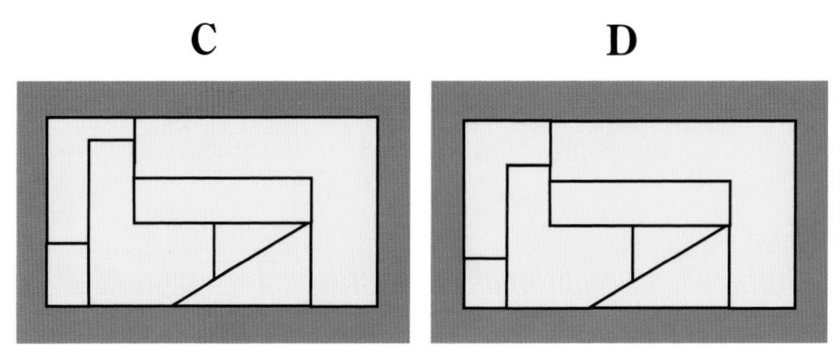

3.

A **B**

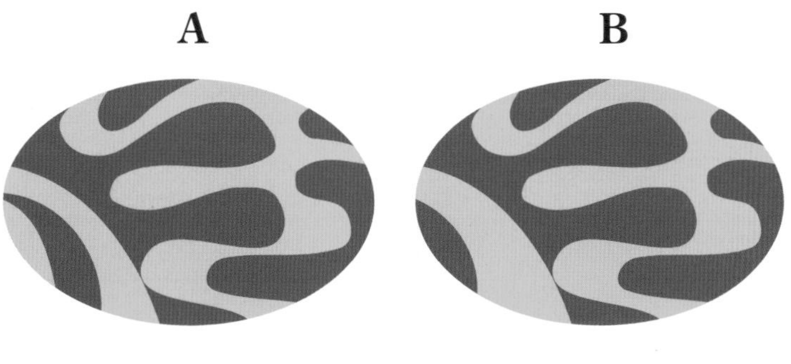

C **D**

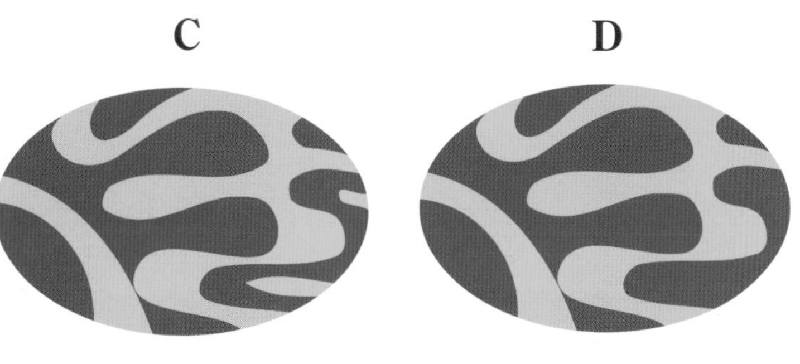

4.

A

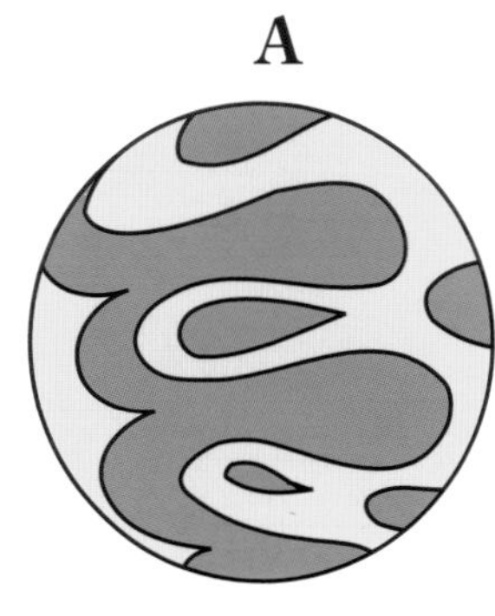

B

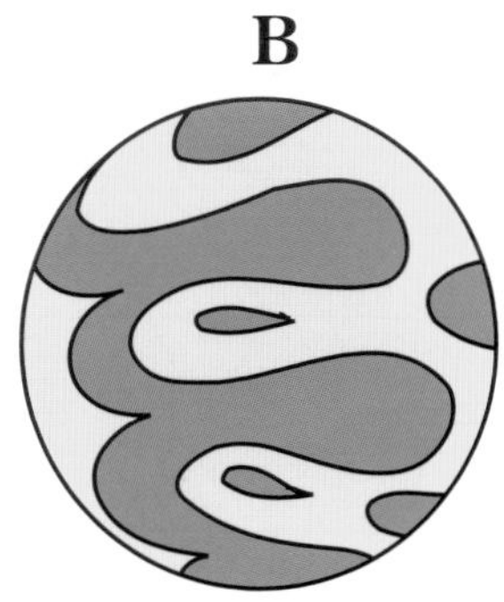

C

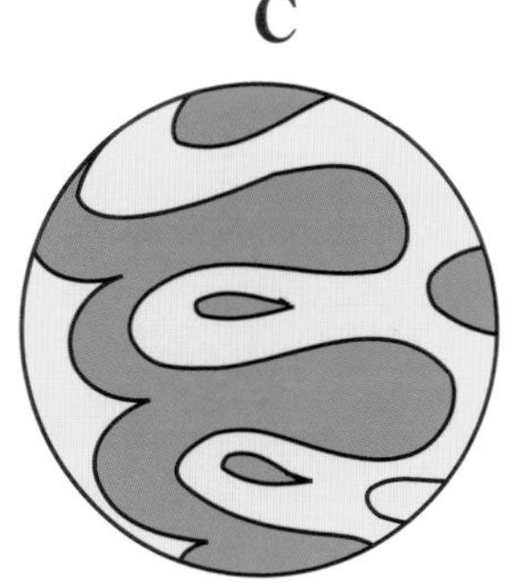

D

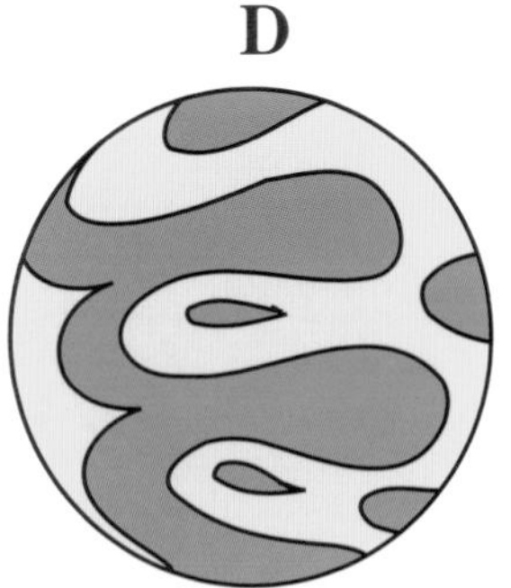

5.

A

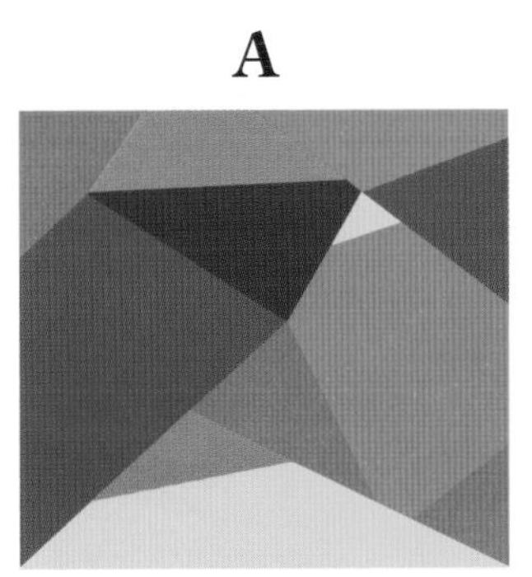

B

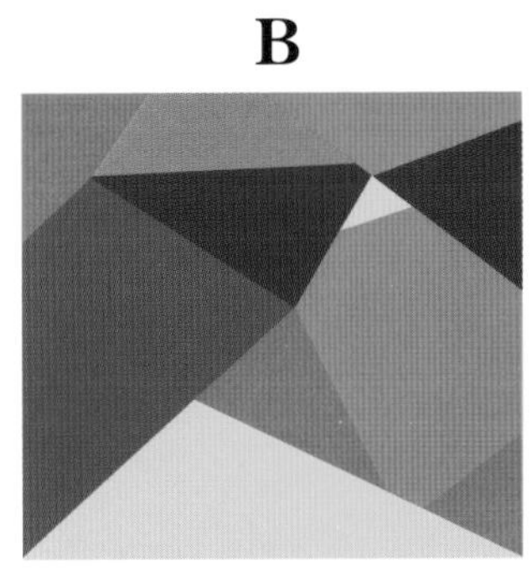

C

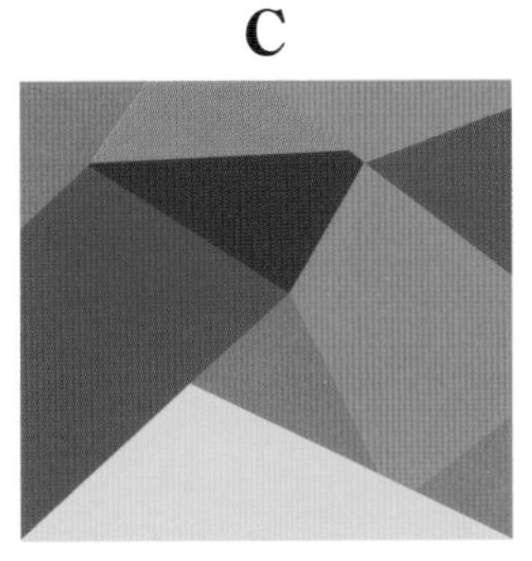

D

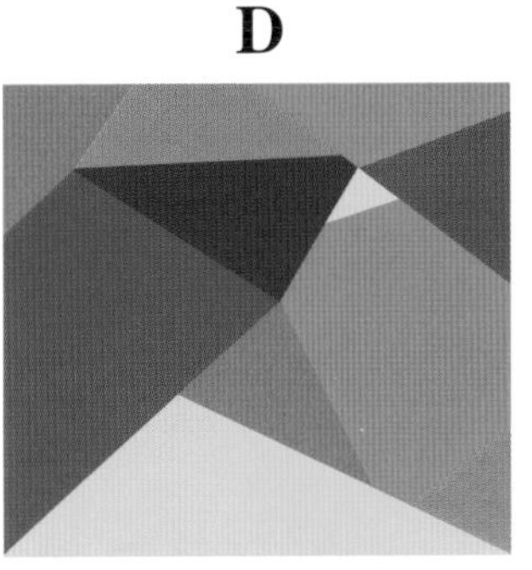

6.

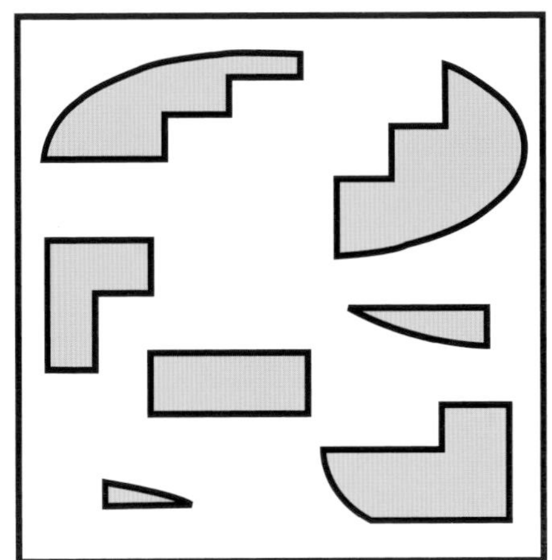

A B

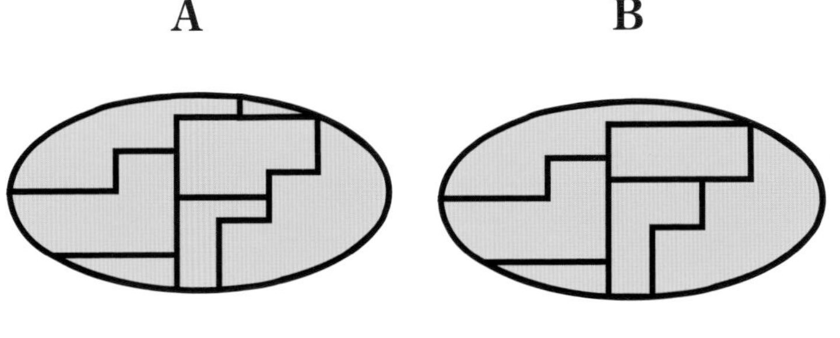

C D

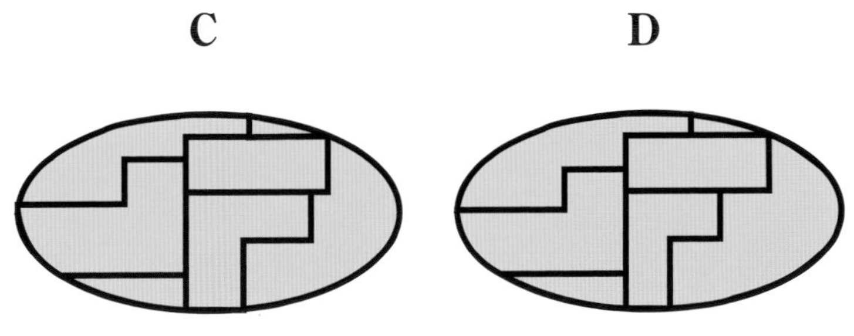

7.

A

B

C D

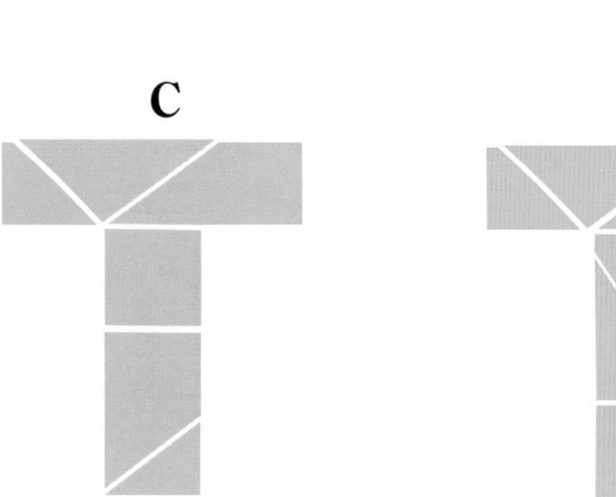

8.

A

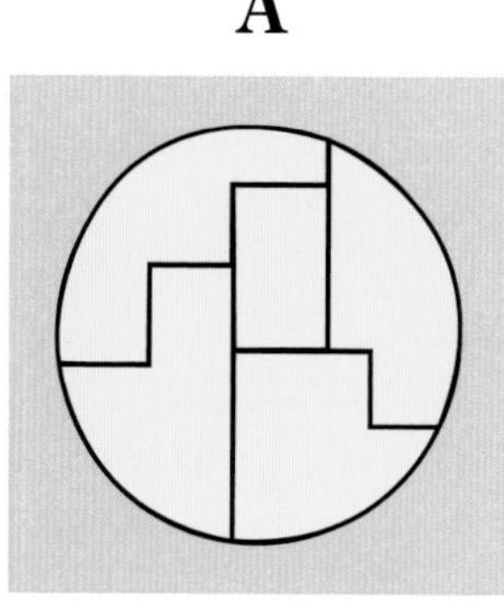

B

C

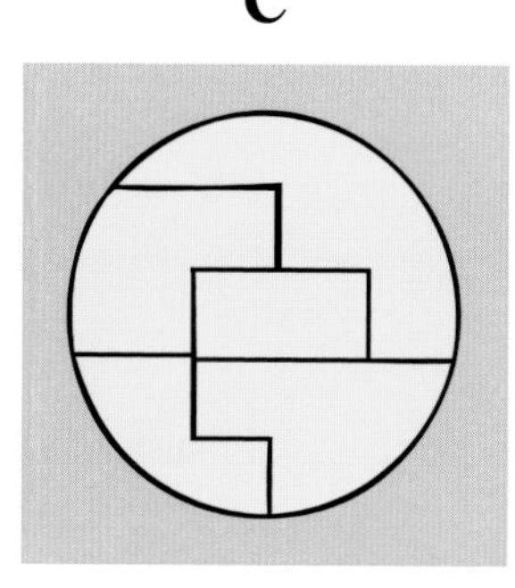

D

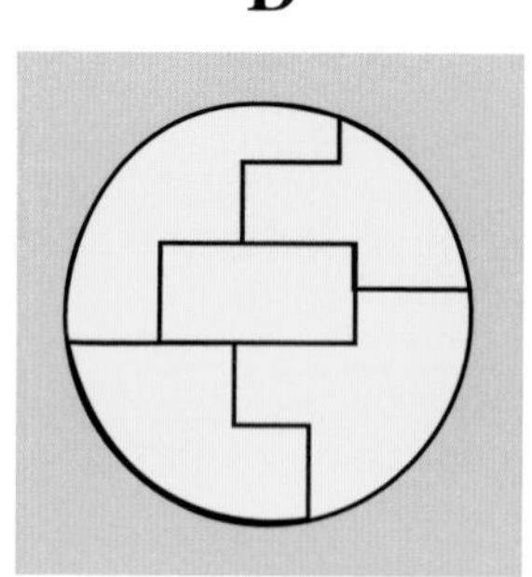

9.

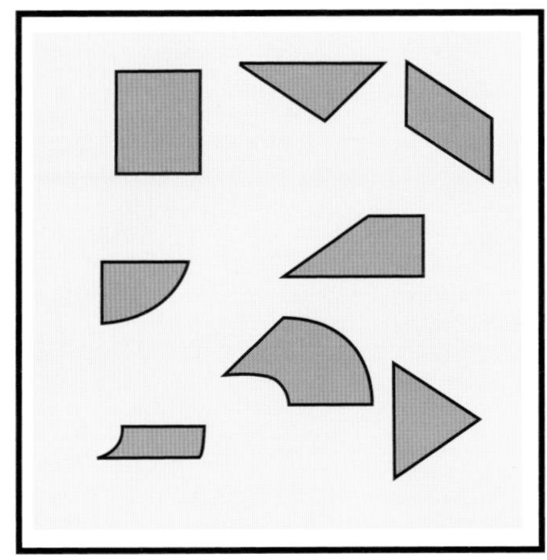

A

B

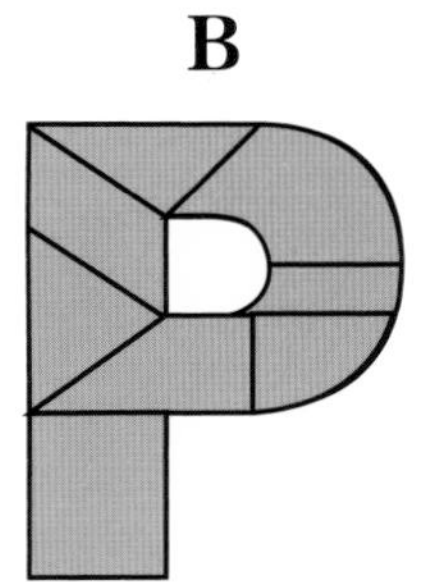

C

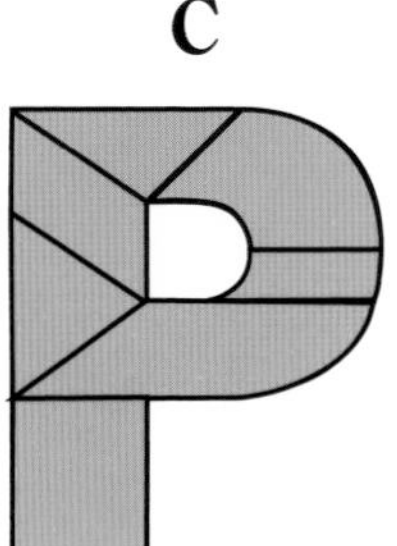

D

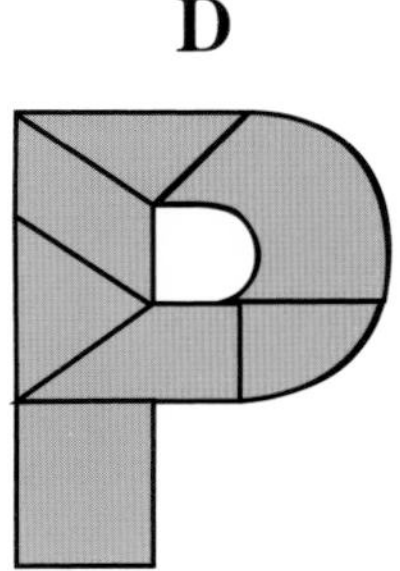

10.

A

C

B

D

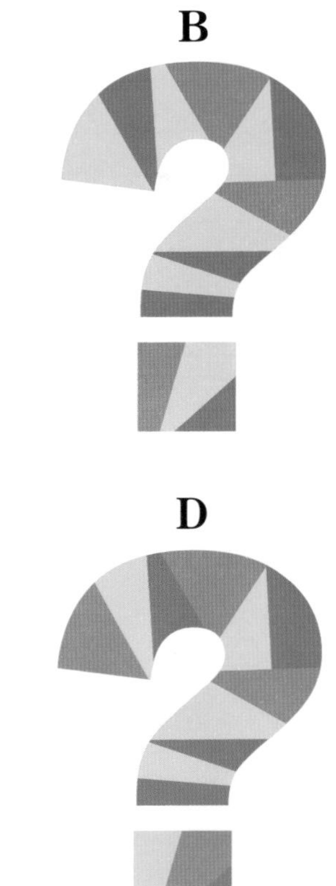

11.

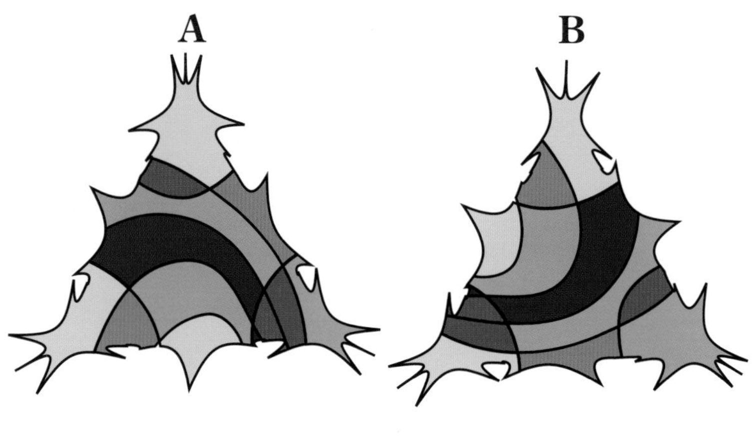

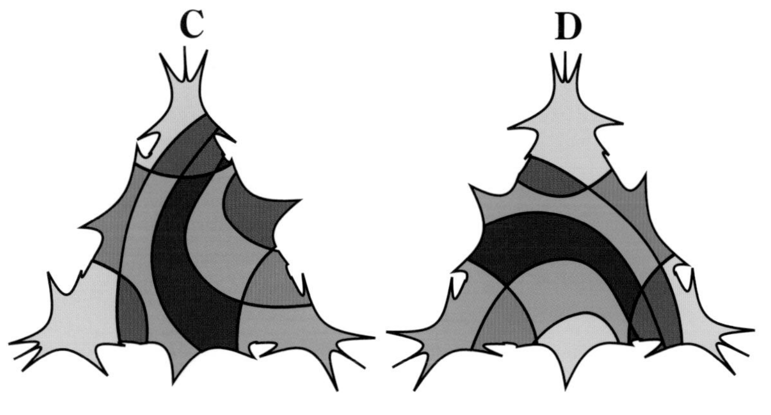

12.

A

B

D

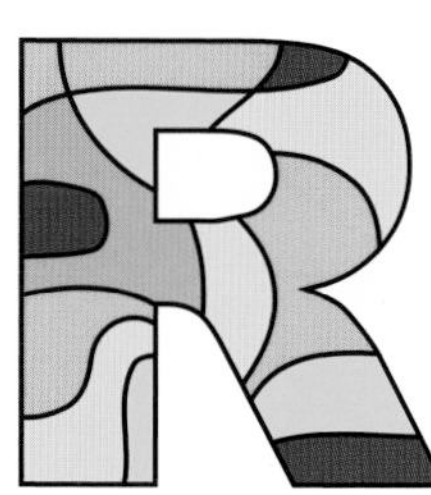

13.

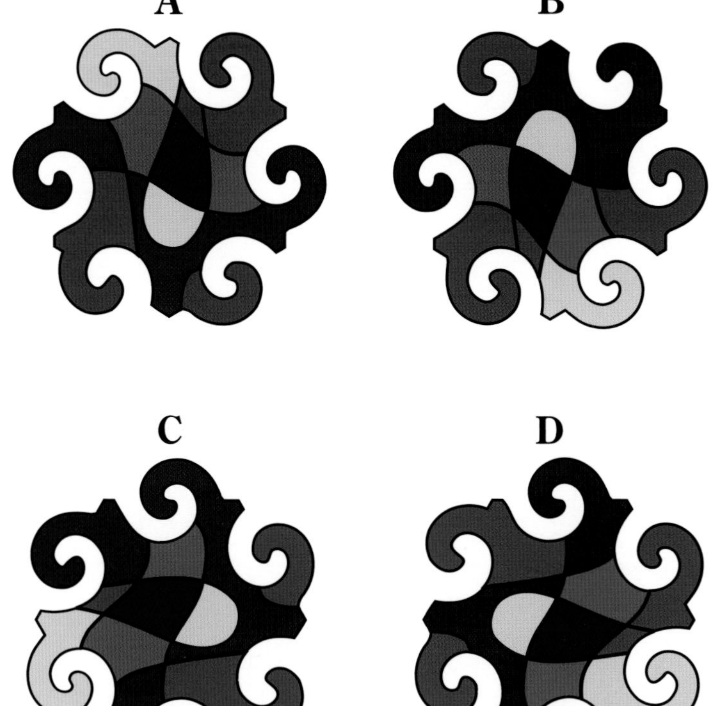

14.

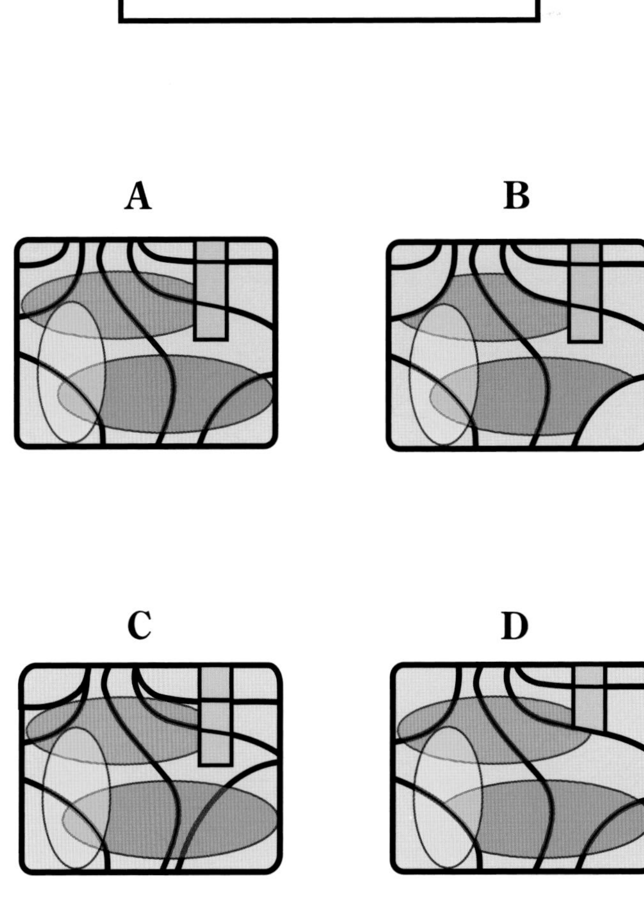

15.

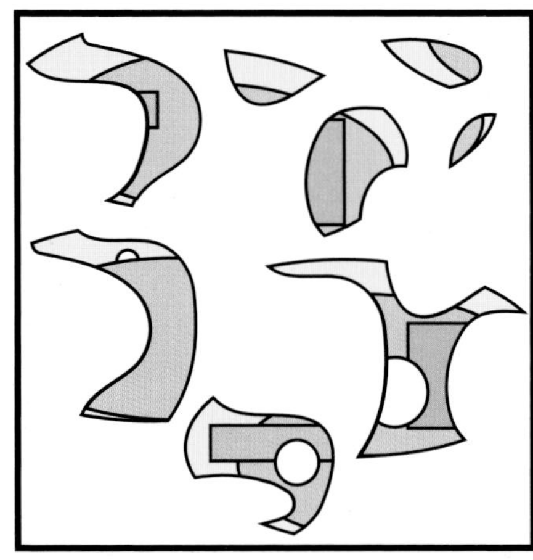

A

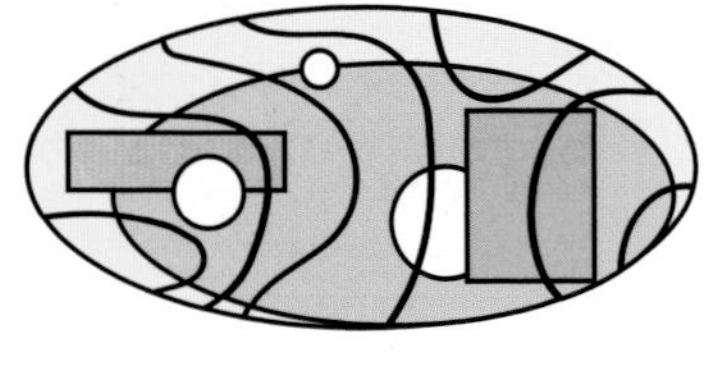

B

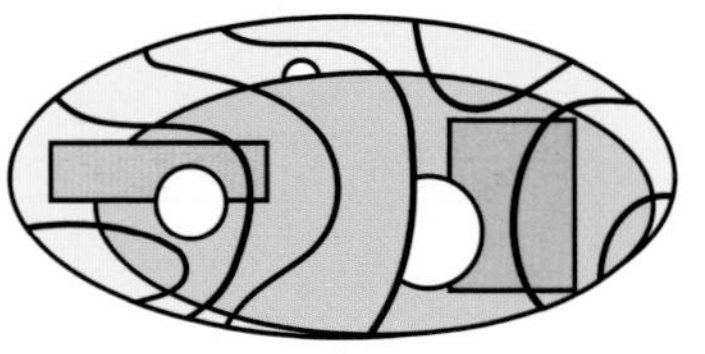

C

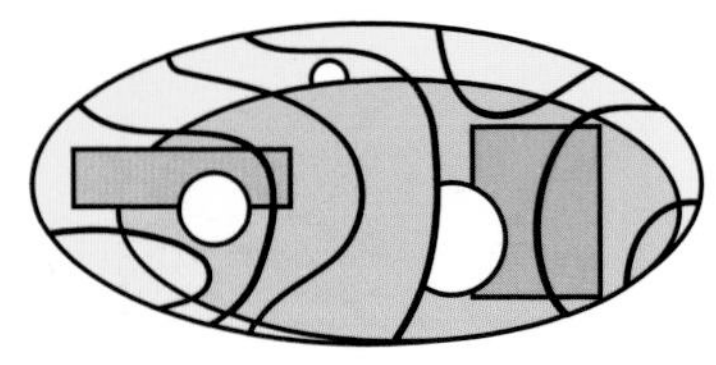

D

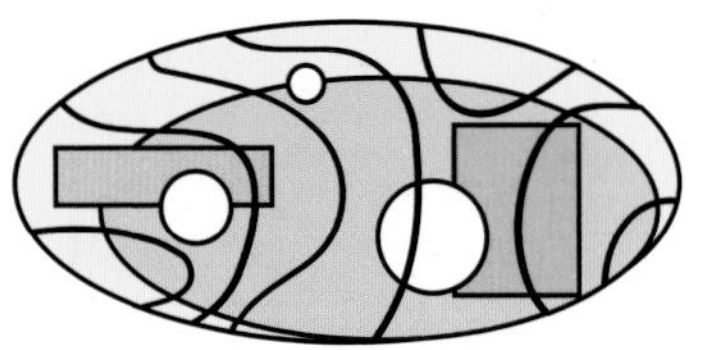

16.

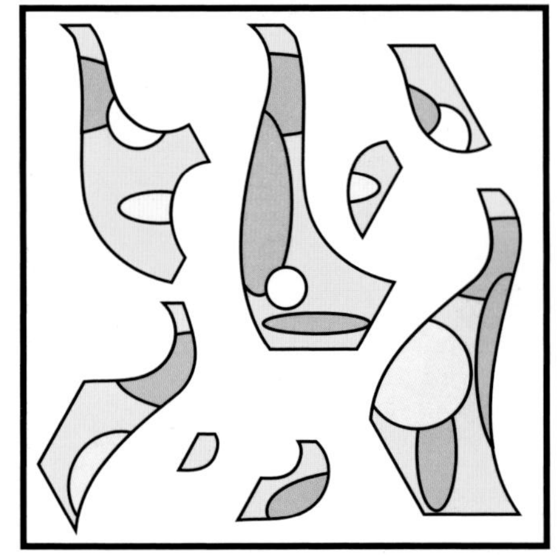

A

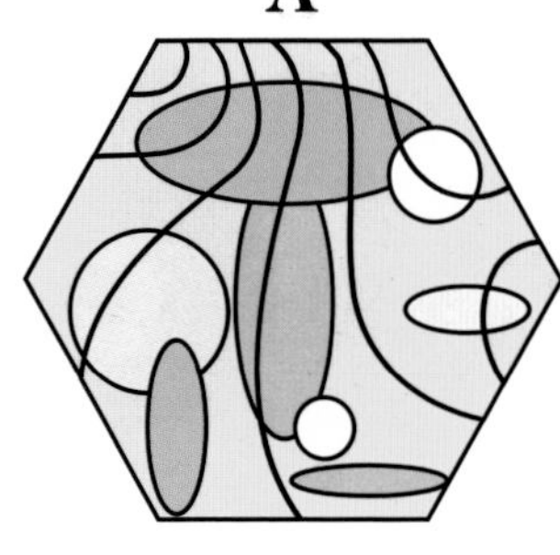

B

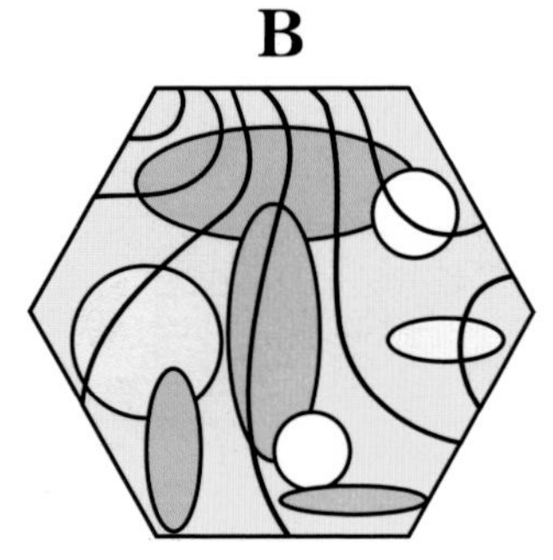

C

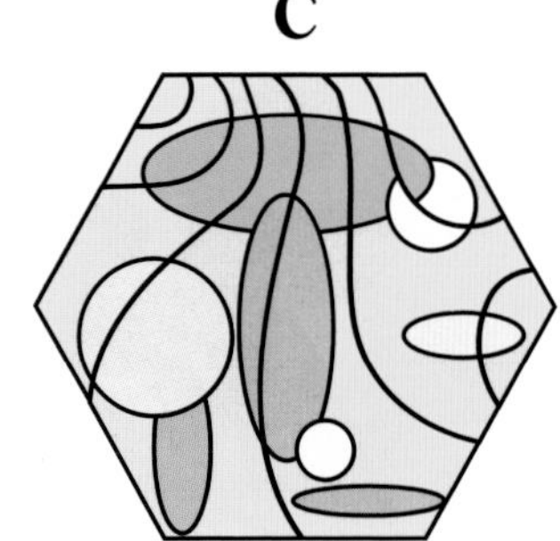

D

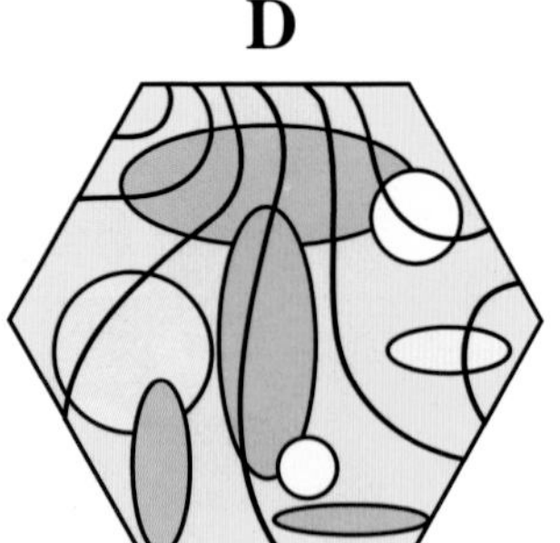

17.

A

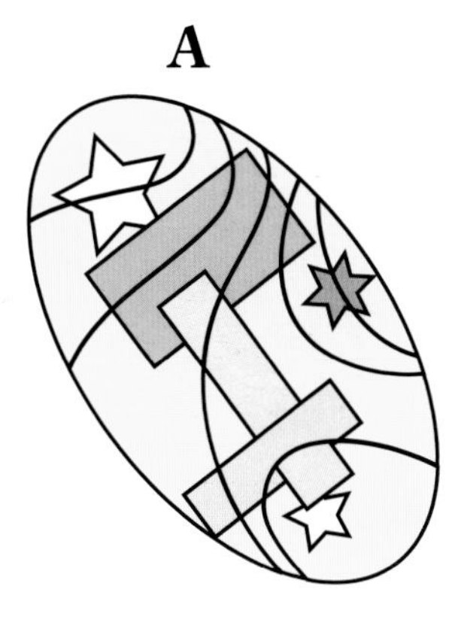

B

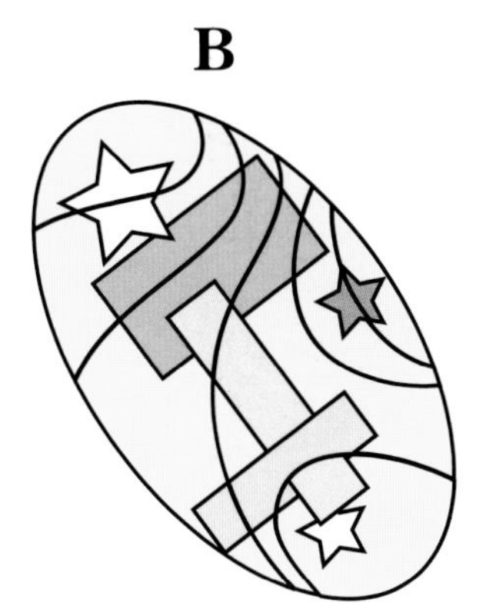

C

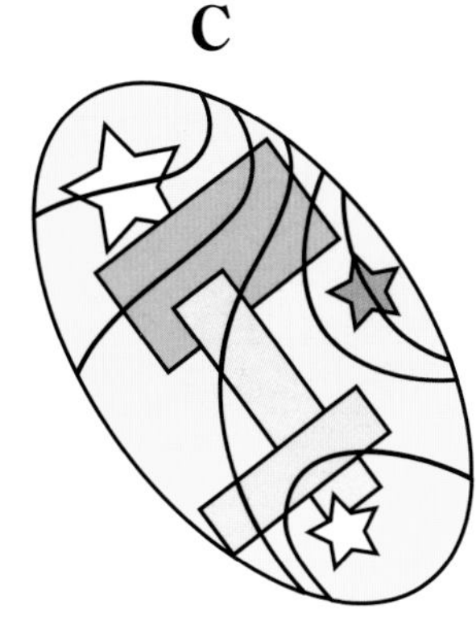

D

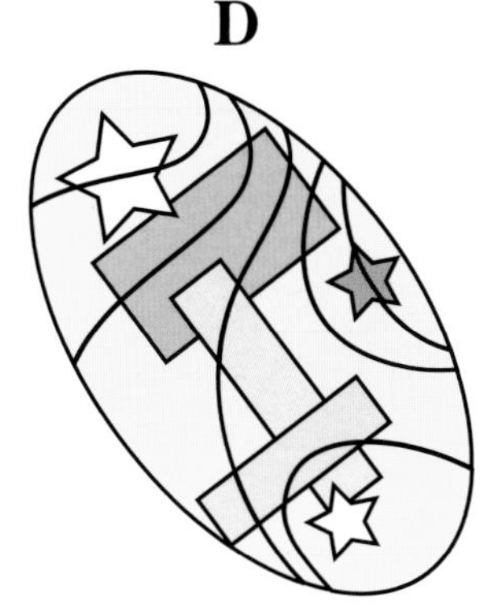

18.

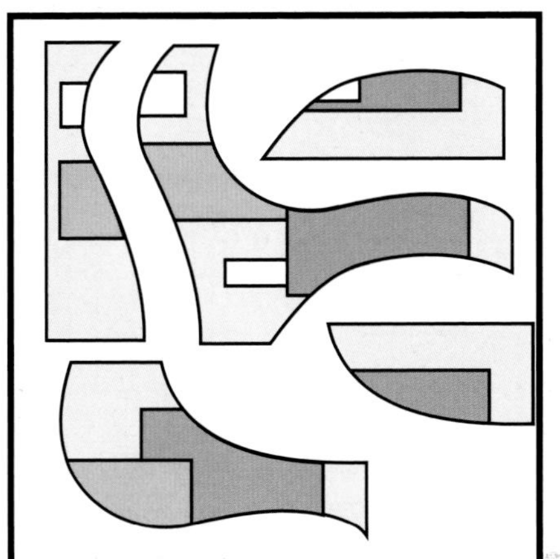

A

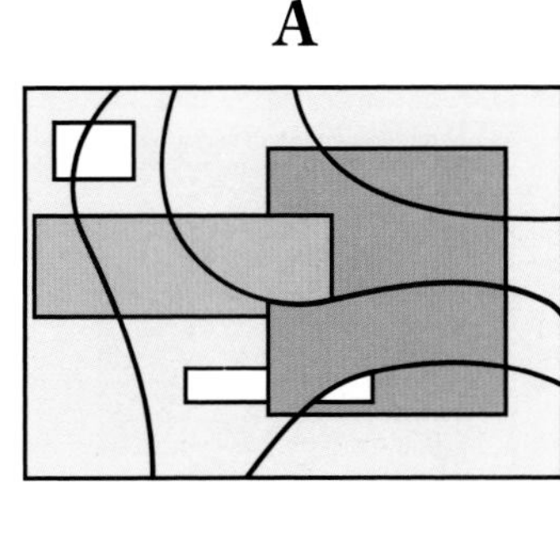

B

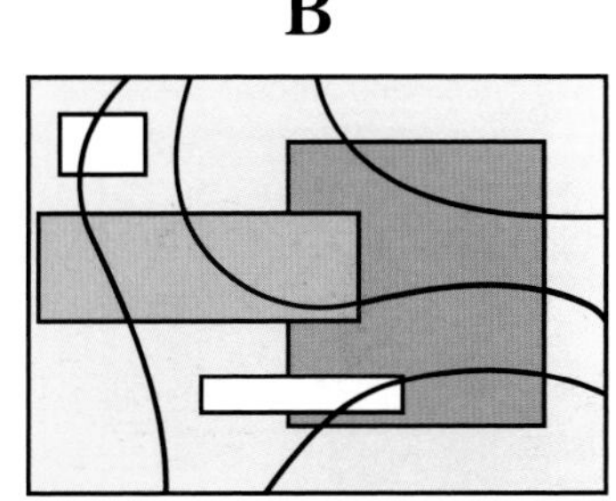

C

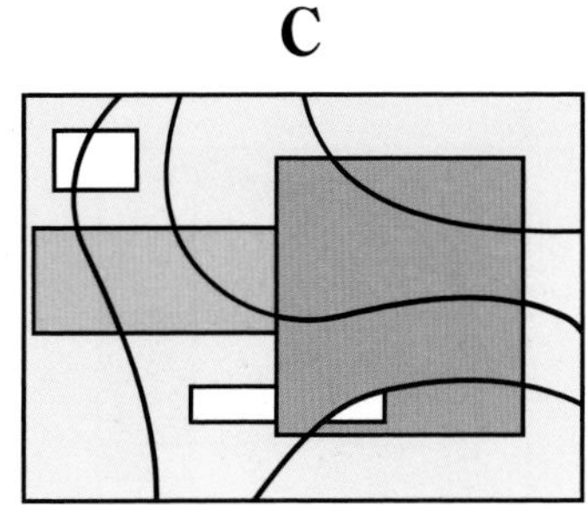

D

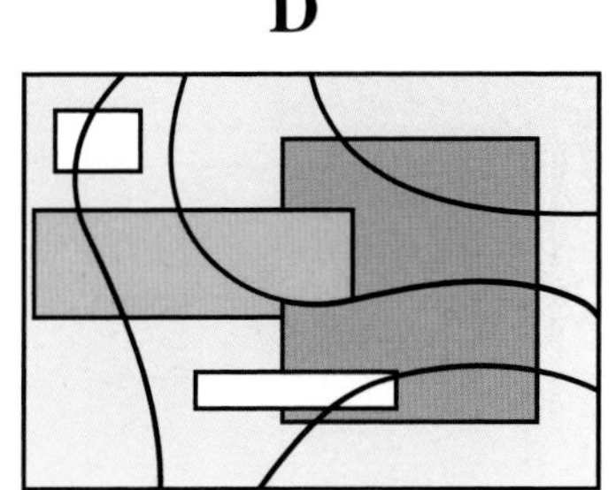

19.

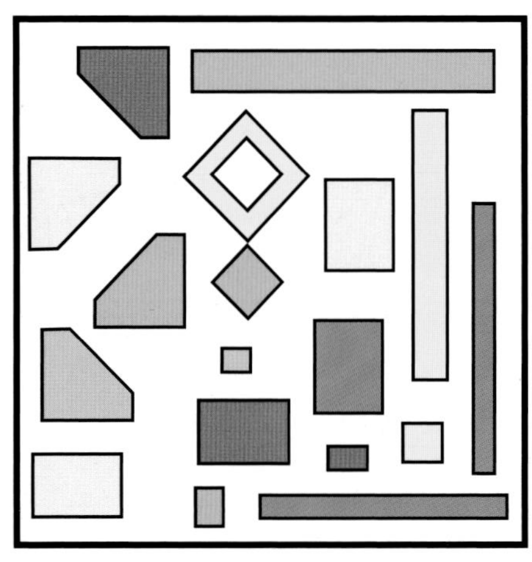

A

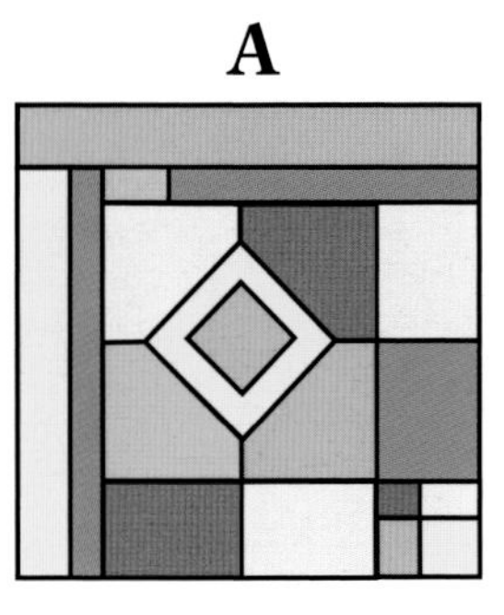

B

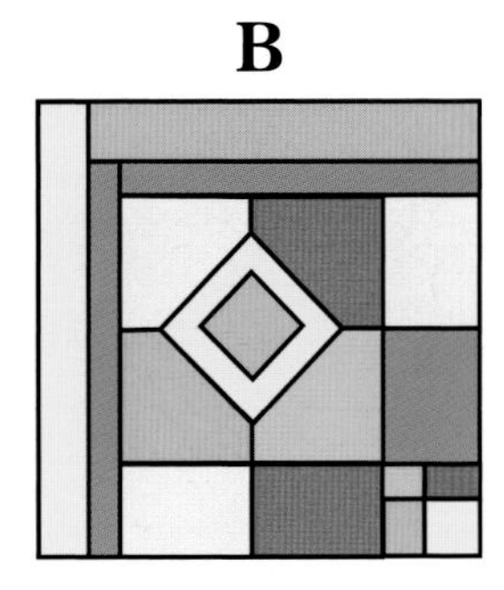

C

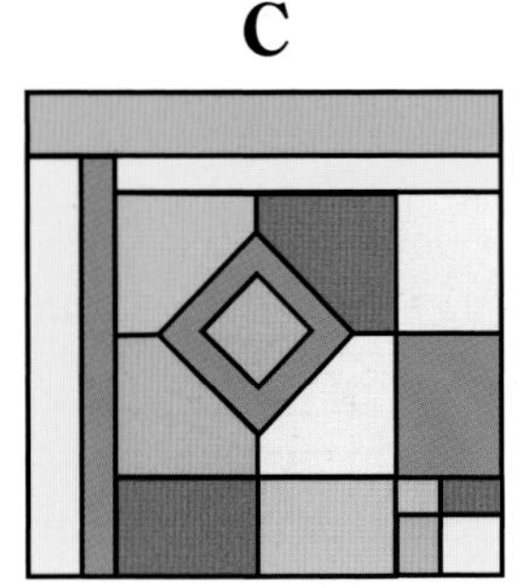

D

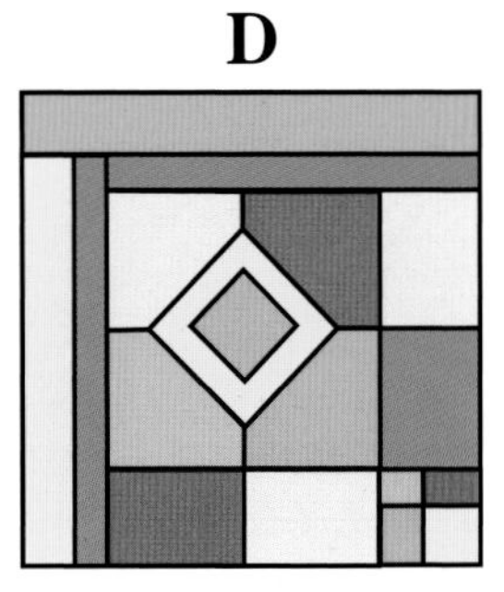

20.

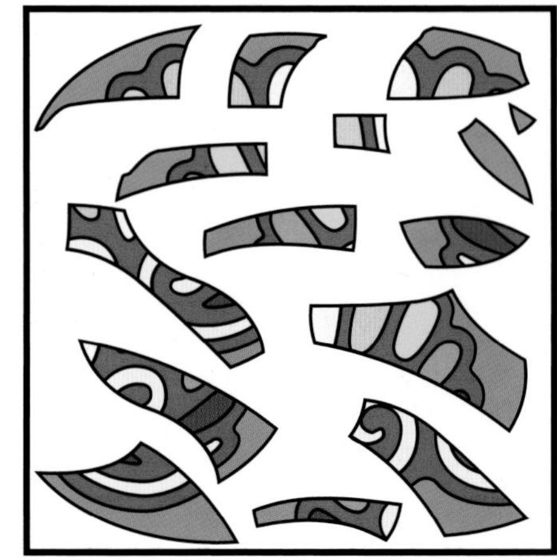

A

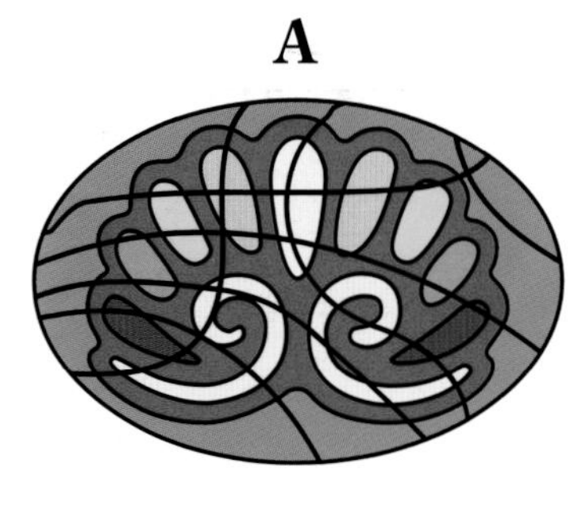

B

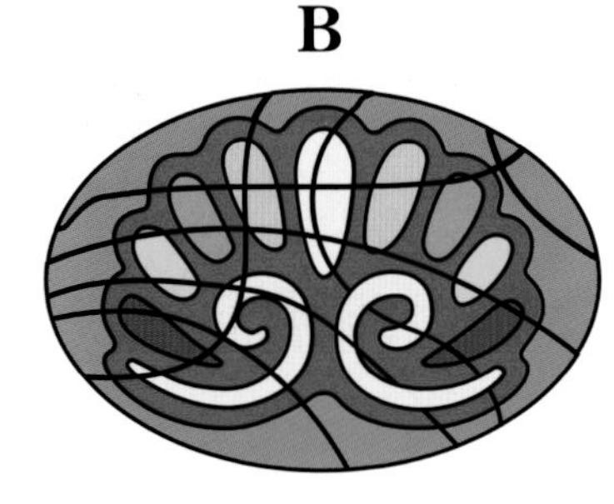

C

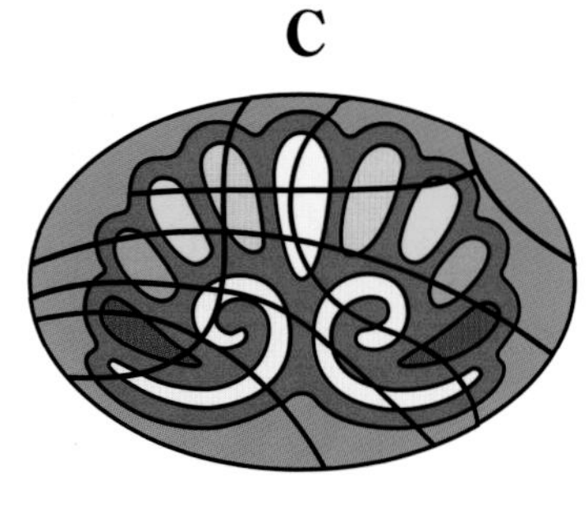

D

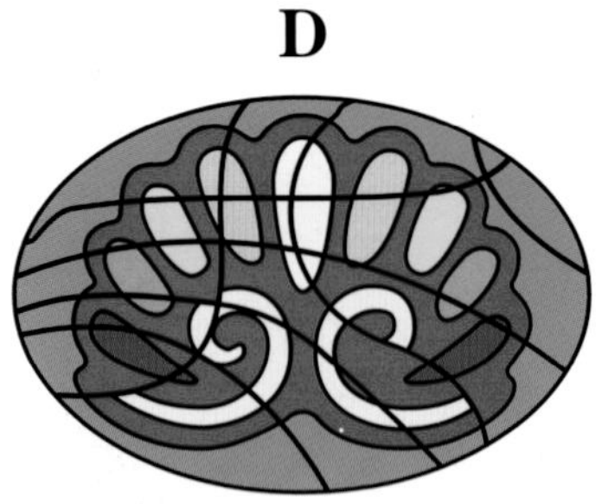

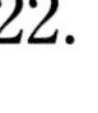

21.

A

B

C

D

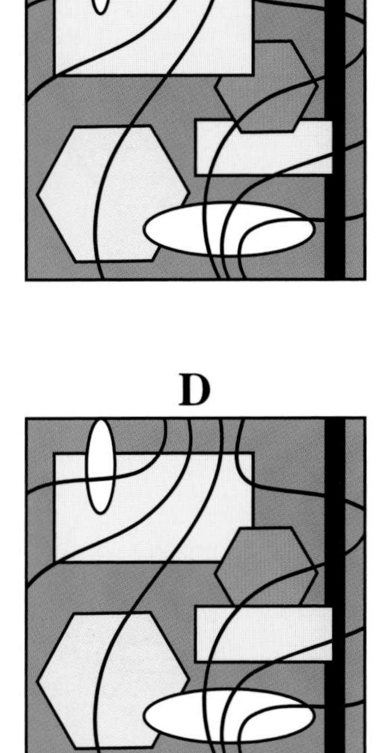

22.

A

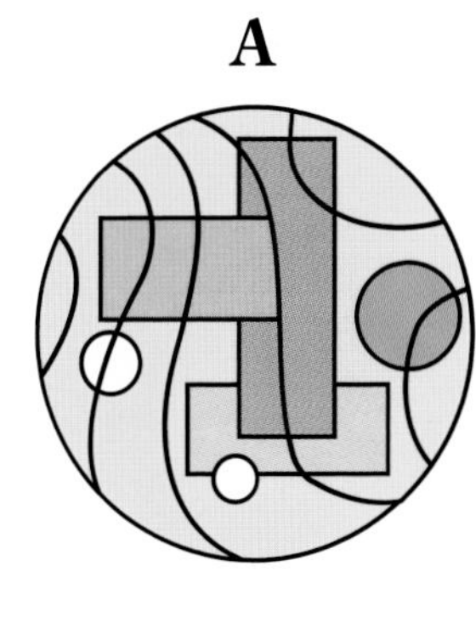

B

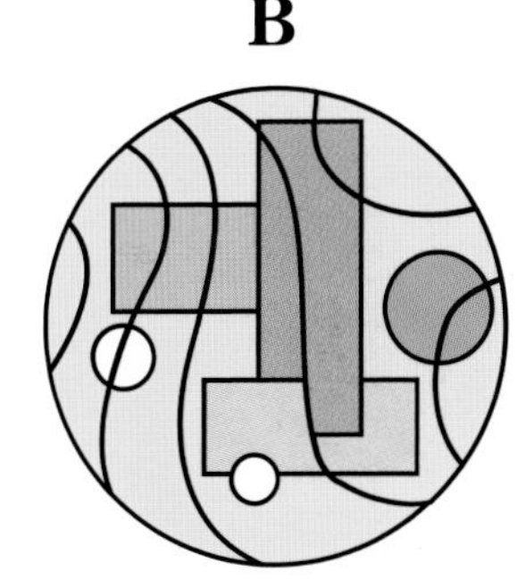

C

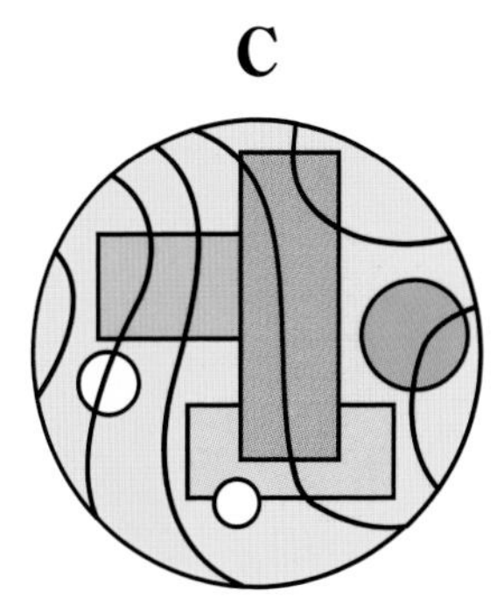

D

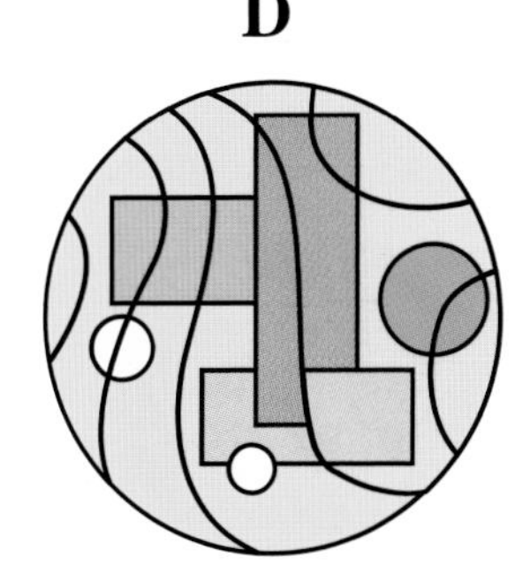

23.

A

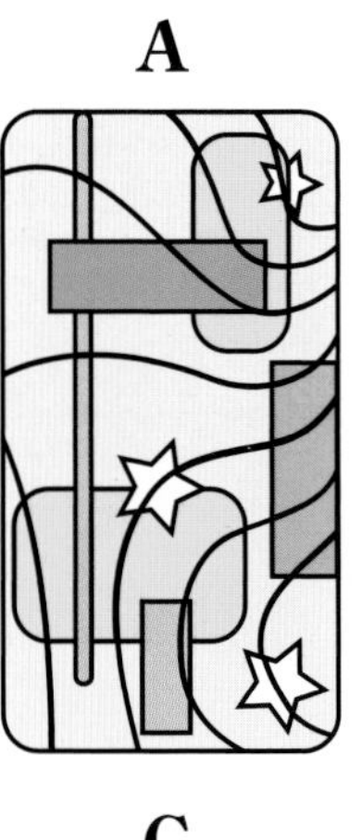

B

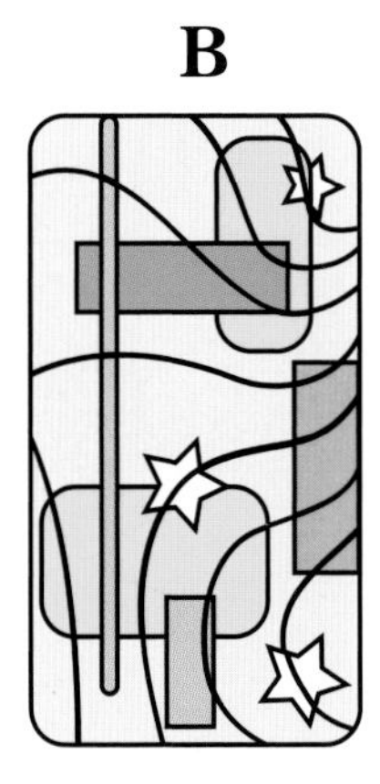

C

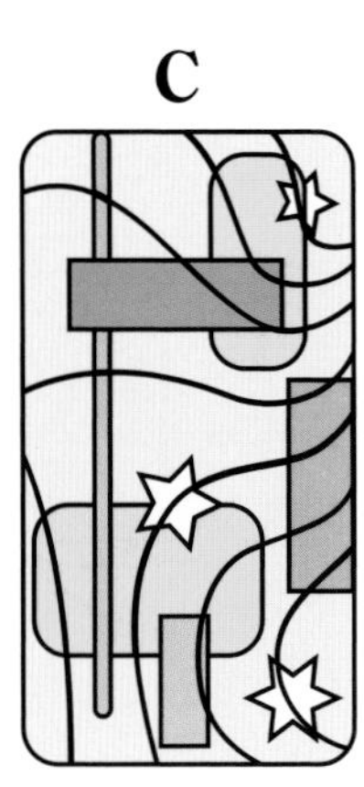

D

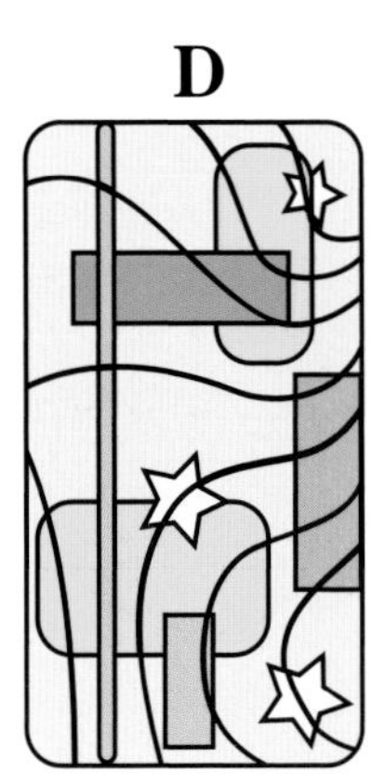

24.

A

B

C

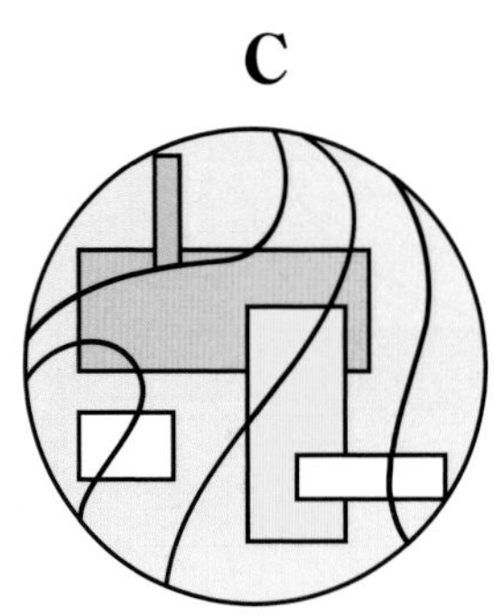

D

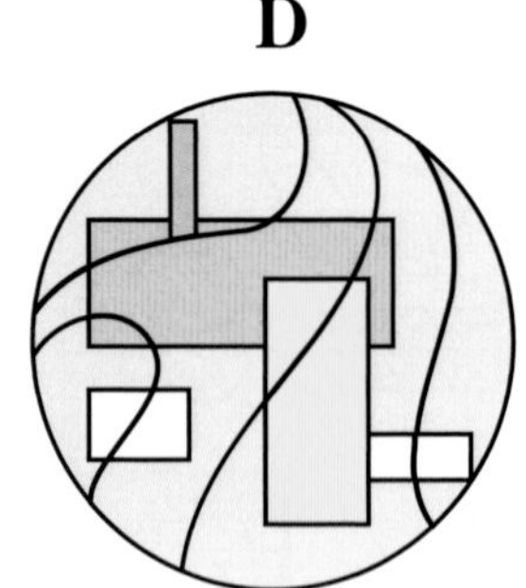

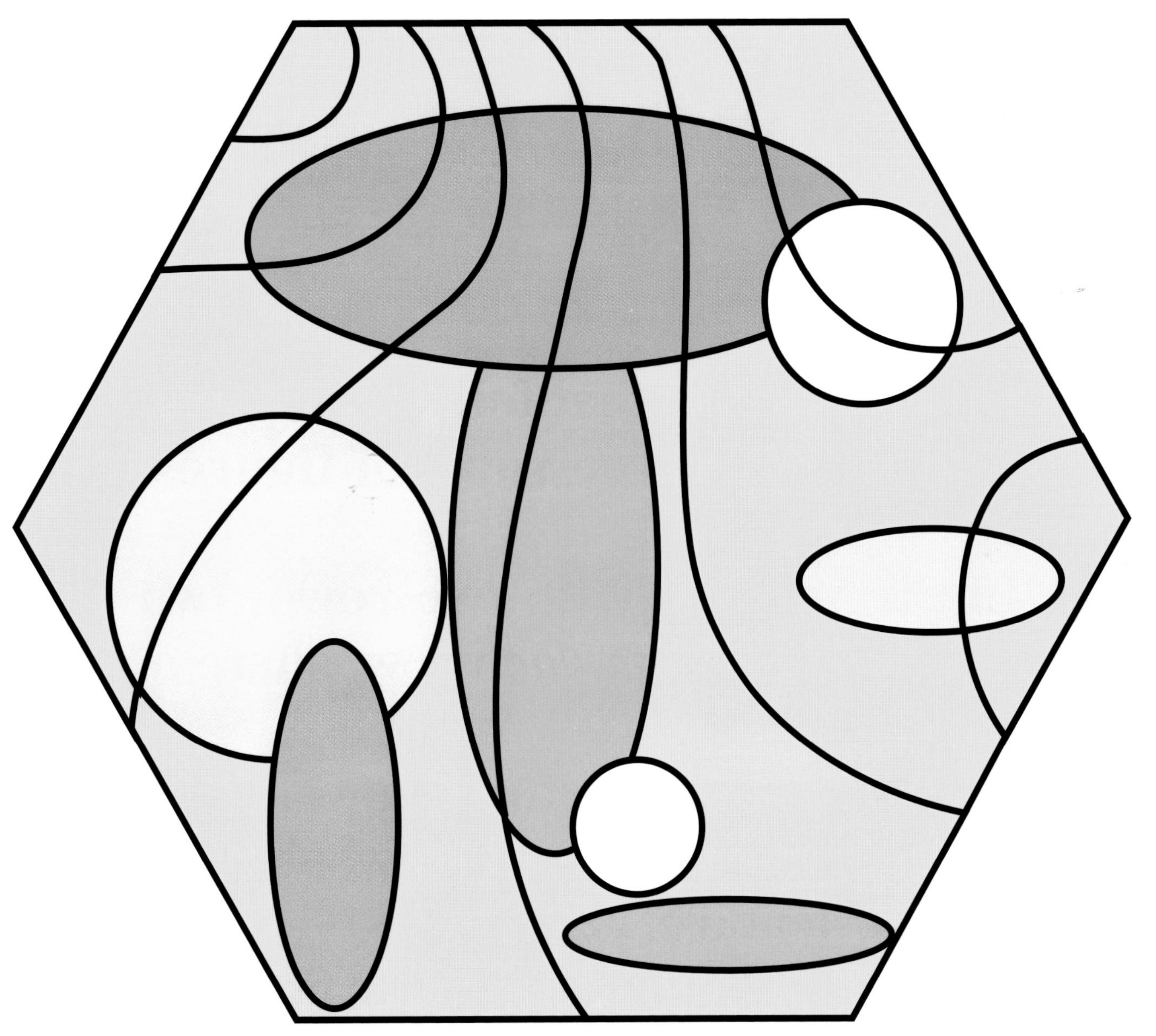

SIMILARITY

- In the puzzles that follow, you will find two or three rows of figures given.
- In the puzzles with two rows, two figures, one from each row, share a similar feature.
- In the puzzles with three rows, three figures, one from each row, share a similar feature.
- Try and identify the similar figures.

1.

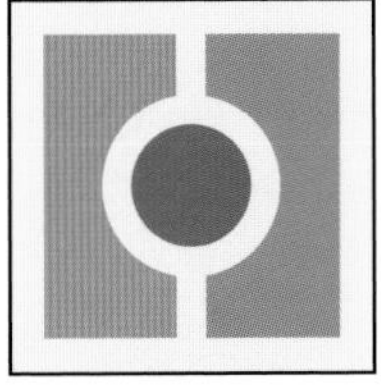
1

2

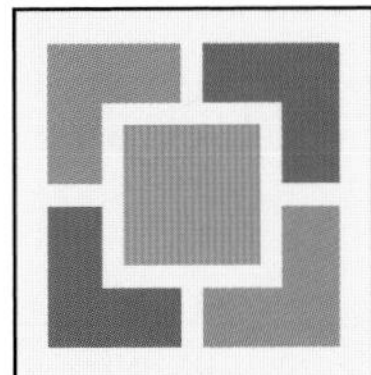
3

4

5

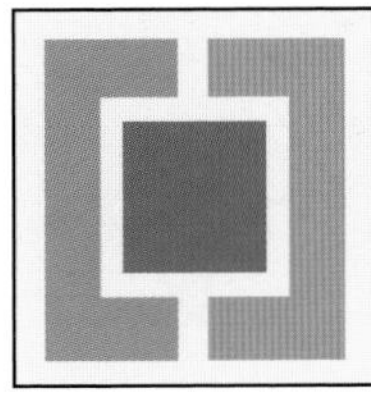
6

3 & 4	2 & 4	2 & 6	1 & 5	3 & 6	1 & 4
A	B	C	D	E	F

2.

1

2

3

4

5

6

1 & 6	1 & 5	3 & 6	3 & 5	2 & 5	2 & 6
A	B	C	D	E	F

3.

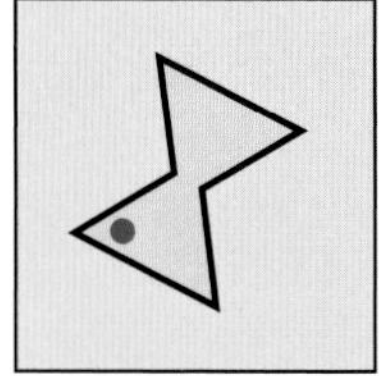
1

2

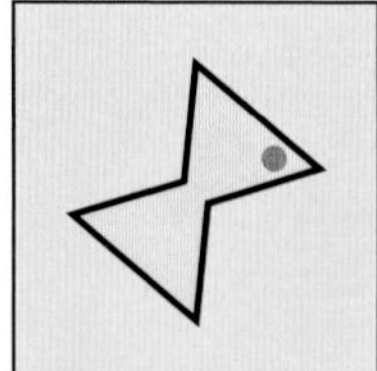
3

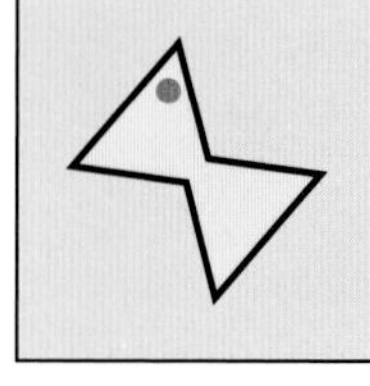
4

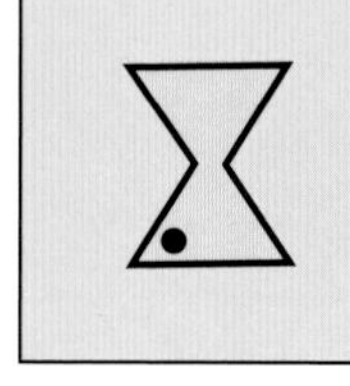
5

6

1 & 4	3 & 6	2 & 6	3 & 4	2 & 5	1 & 6
A	B	C	D	E	F

4.

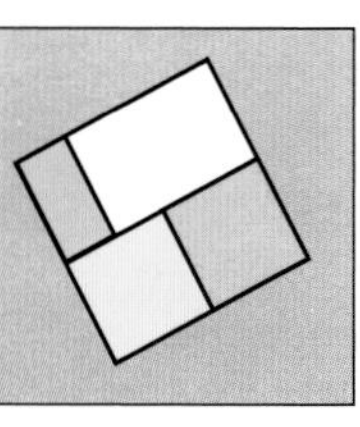
1

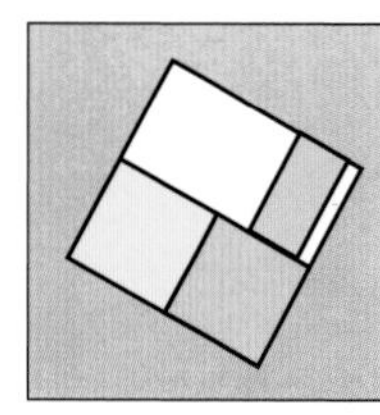
2

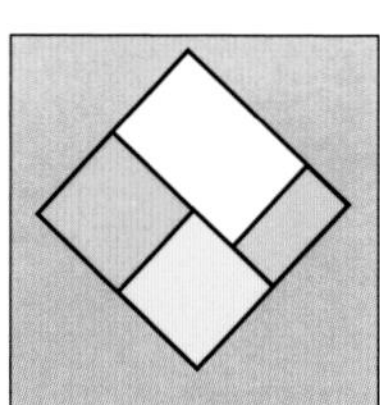
3

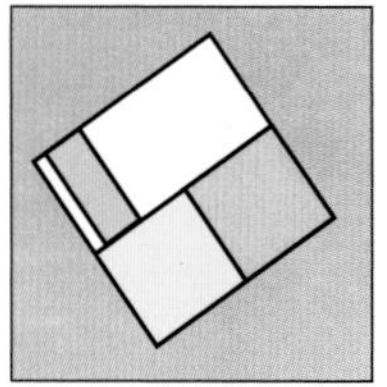
4

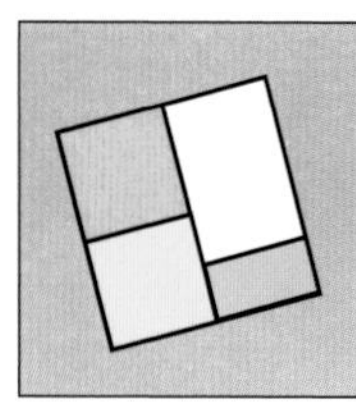
5

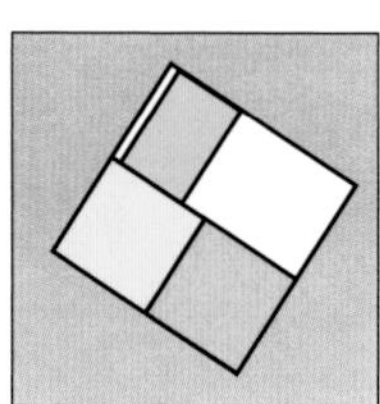
6

2 & 4	3 & 4	1 & 6	1 & 5	3 & 5	2 & 6
A	B	C	D	E	F

5.

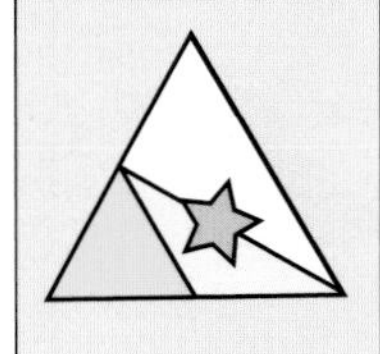
1

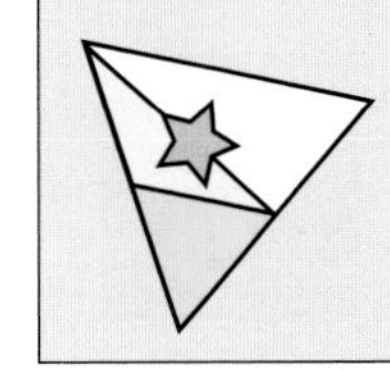
2

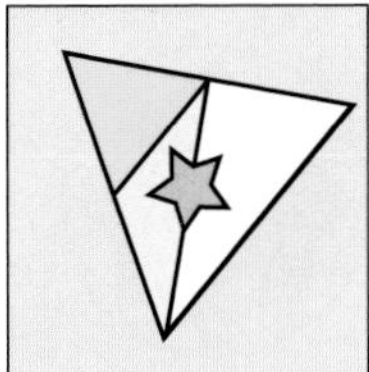
3

4

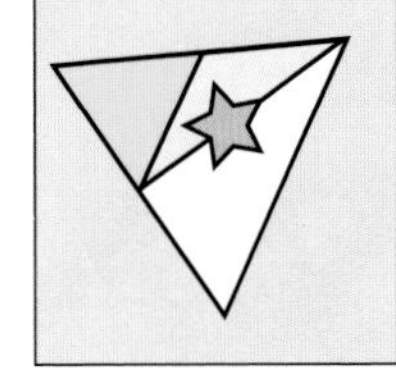
5

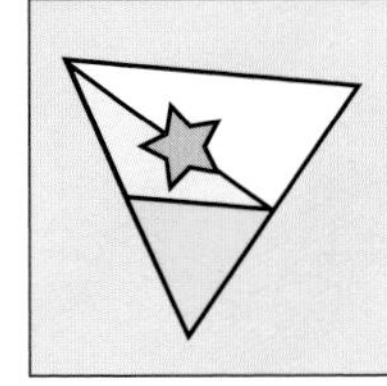
6

2 & 4	2 & 5	3 & 6	3 & 5	1 & 4	1 & 6
A	B	C	D	E	F

6.

1

2

3

4

5

6

3 & 4	1 & 4	1 & 5	3 & 5	2 & 4	2 & 6
A	B	C	D	E	F

7.

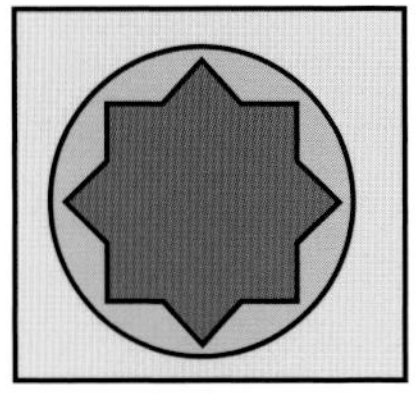
1

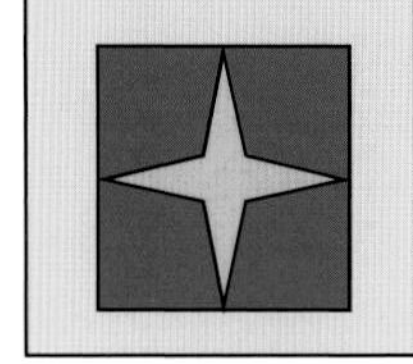
2

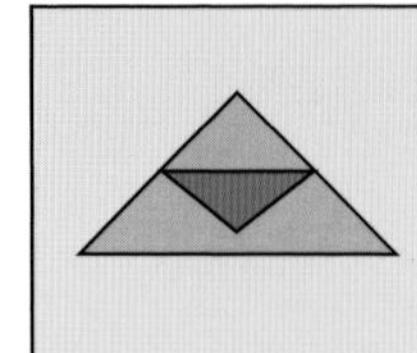
3

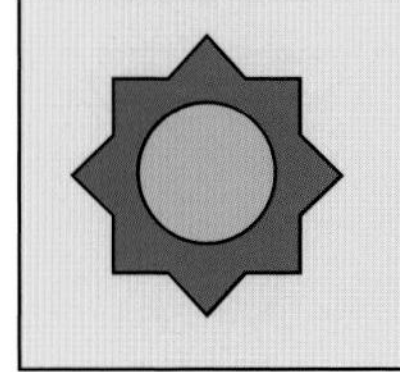
4

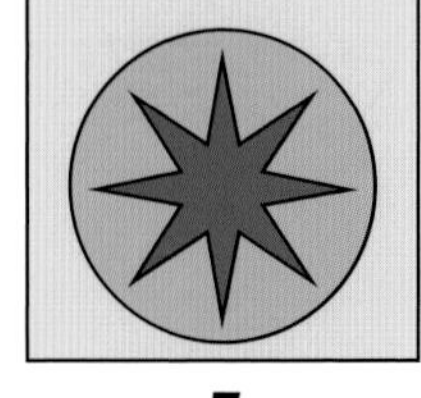
5

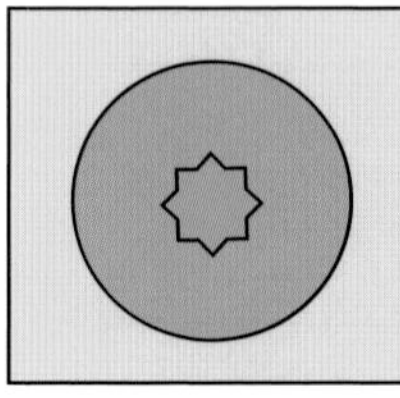
6

2 & 4	1 & 6	2 & 5	2 & 6	3 & 4	1 & 4
A	B	C	D	E	F

8.

1

2

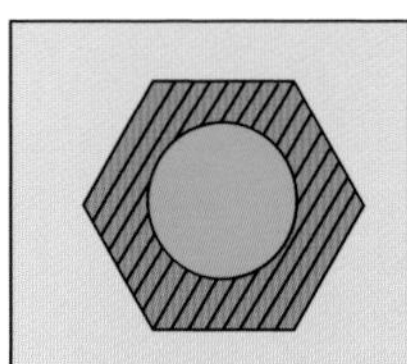
3

4

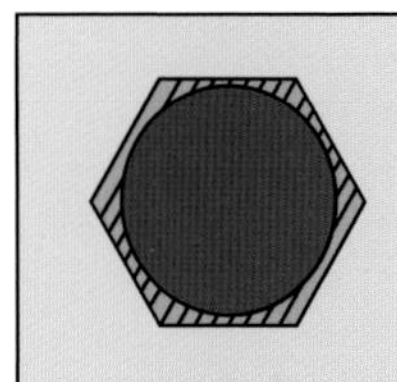
5

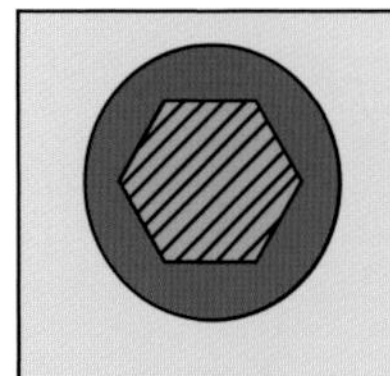
6

2 & 4	1 & 6	2 & 5	3 & 5	3 & 4	3 & 6
A	B	C	D	E	F

9.

	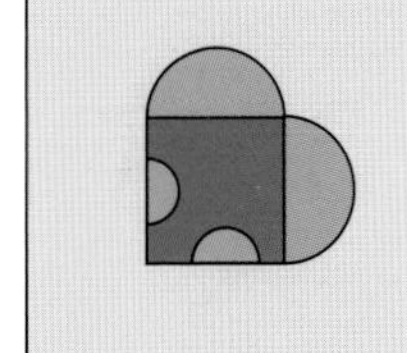	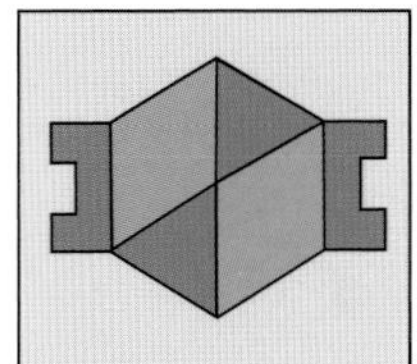
1	**2**	**3**
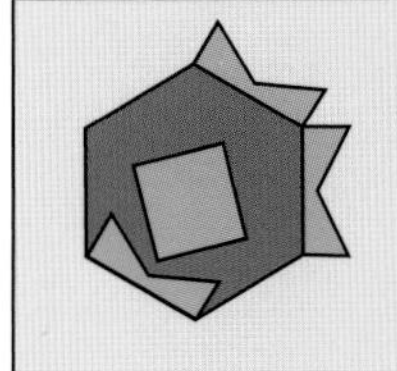	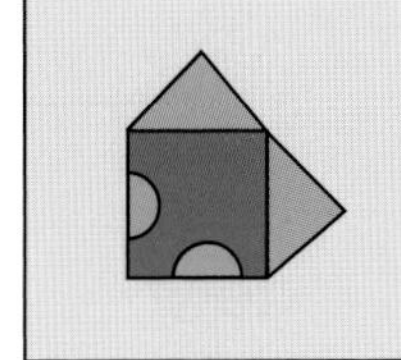	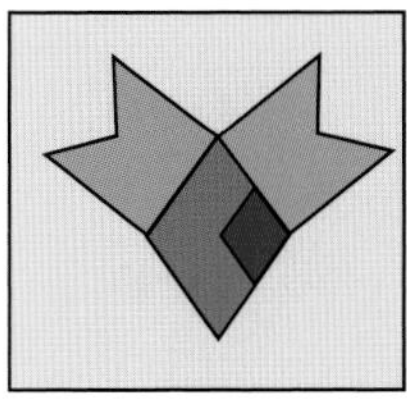
4	**5**	**6**

1 & 6	3 & 4	1 & 5	2 & 5	2 & 4	2 & 6
A	**B**	**C**	**D**	**E**	**F**

10.

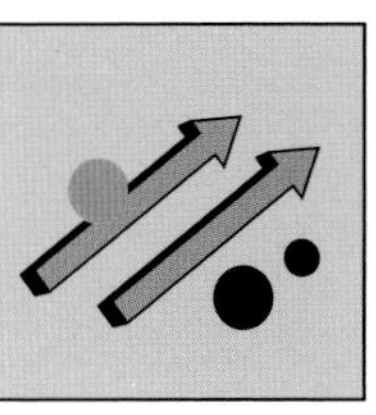	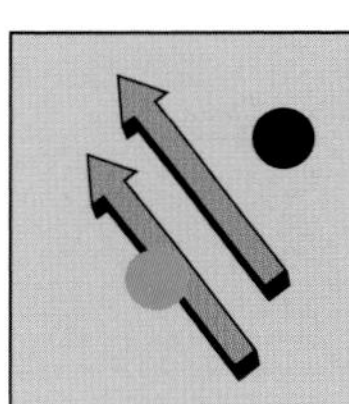	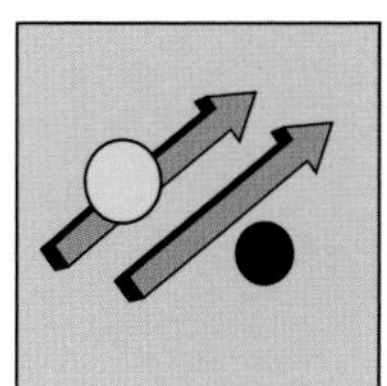
1	**2**	**3**
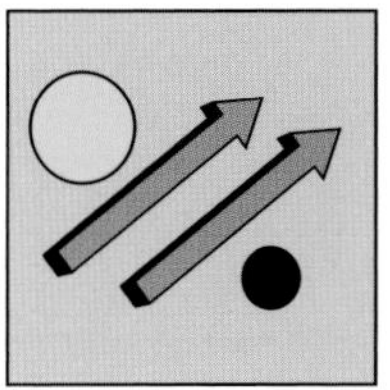	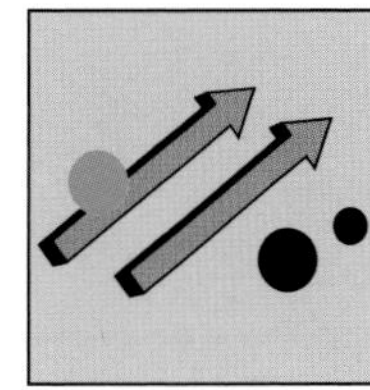	
4	**5**	**6**

1 & 6	3 & 4	2 & 5	1 & 4	3 & 6	2 & 6
A	**B**	**C**	**D**	**E**	**F**

11.

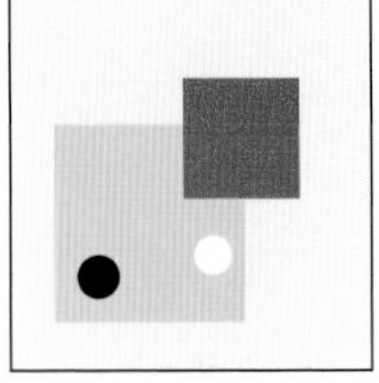

1

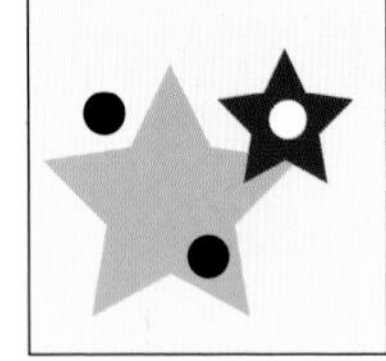

2

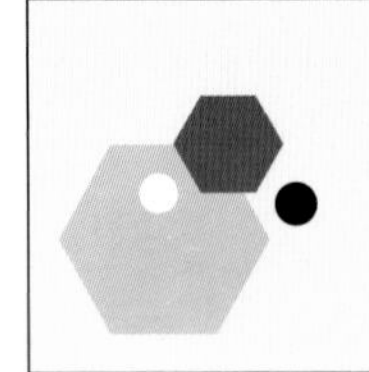

3

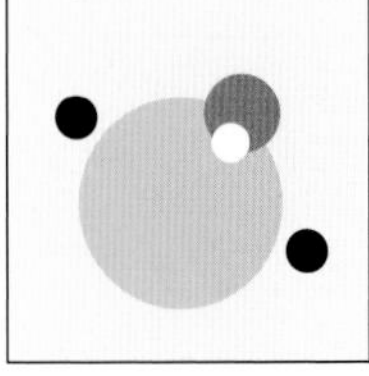

4

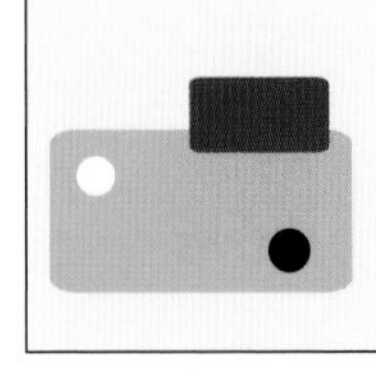

5

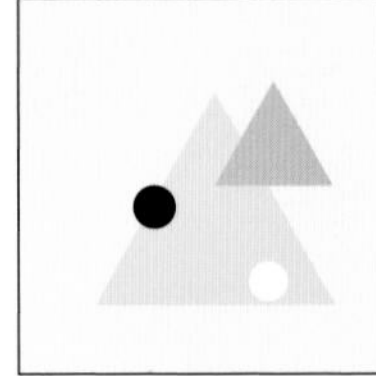

6

2 & 4	3 & 6	2 & 5	3 & 5	1 & 5	1 & 6
A	**B**	**C**	**D**	**E**	**F**

12.

1

2

3

4

5

6

1 & 6	3 & 6	2 & 5	3 & 5	1 & 5	2 & 6
A	**B**	**C**	**D**	**E**	**F**

13.

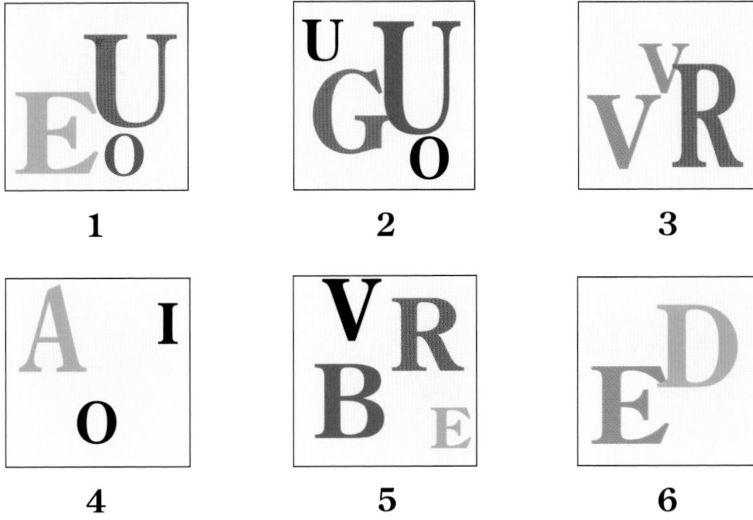

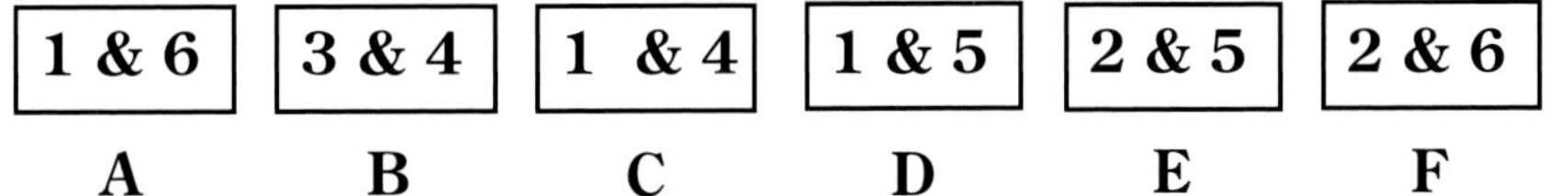

14.

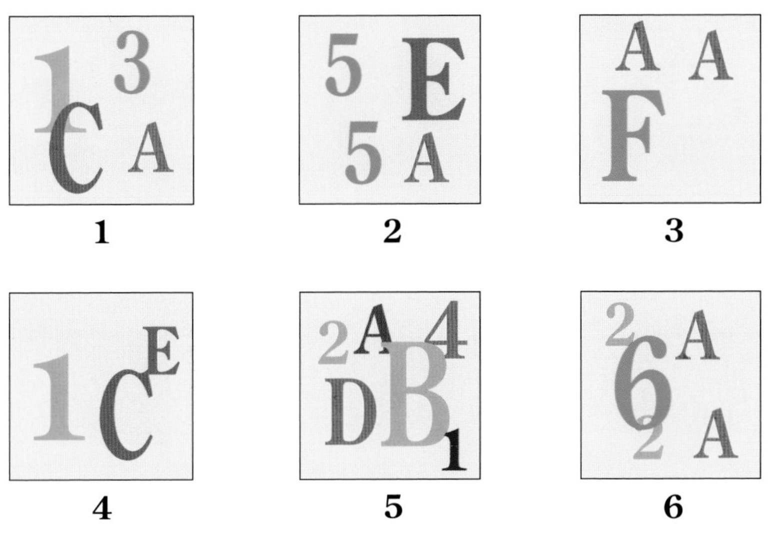

1 & 6	3 & 4	3 & 5	2 & 4	1 & 5	2 & 6
A	B	C	D	E	F

15.

1

2

3

4

5

6

1 & 6	1 & 4	3 & 4	2 & 6	1 & 5	3 & 5
A	B	C	D	E	F

16.

1

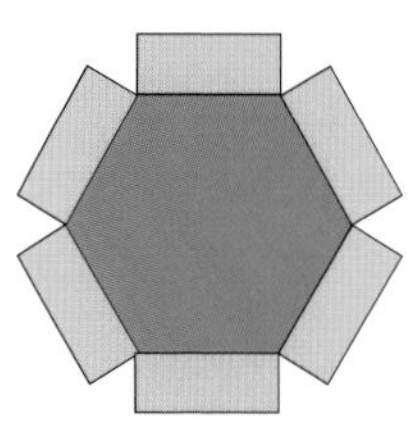
2

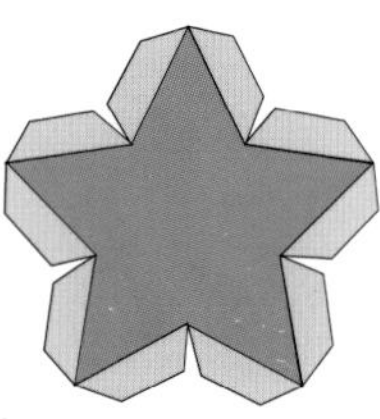
3

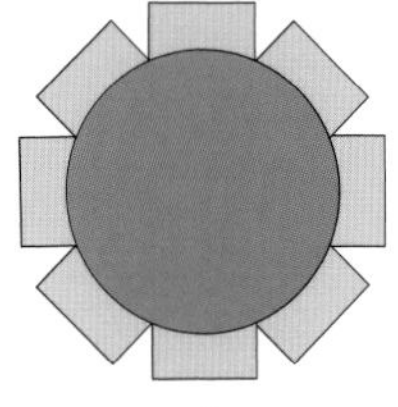
4

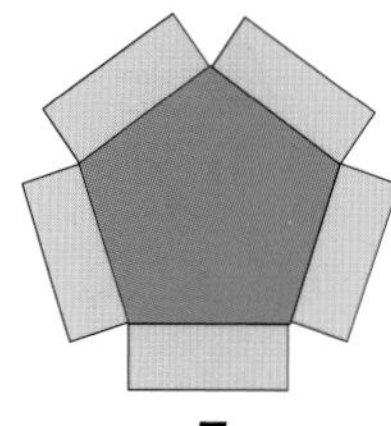
5

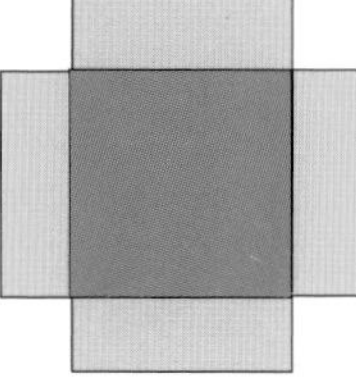
6

2 & 4	3 & 4	1 & 6	3 & 6	3 & 5	1 & 5
A	B	C	D	E	F

17.

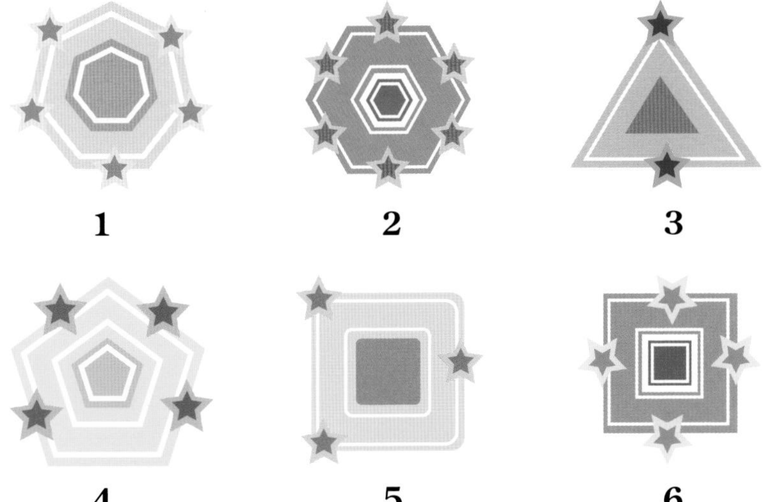

2 & 4	2 & 5	1 & 5	3 & 5	2 & 6	3 & 4
A	B	C	D	E	F

18.

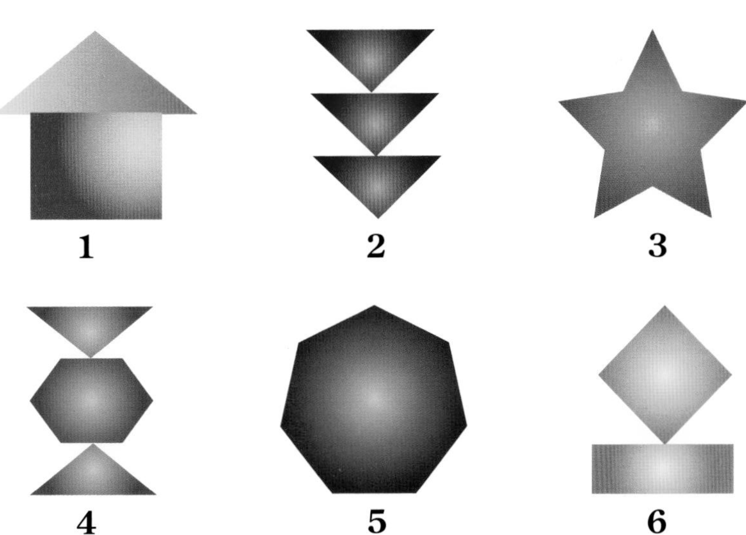

3 & 5	1 & 6	2 & 6	1 & 5	3 & 4	3 & 6
A	B	C	D	E	F

19.

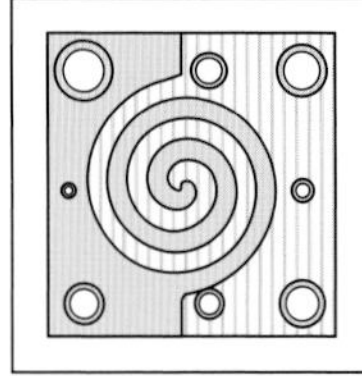
1

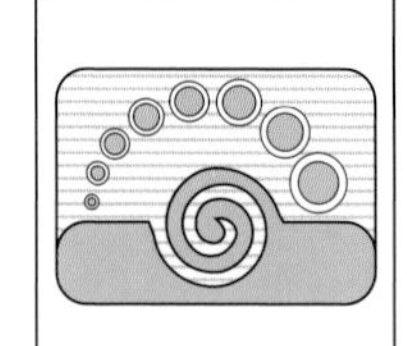
2

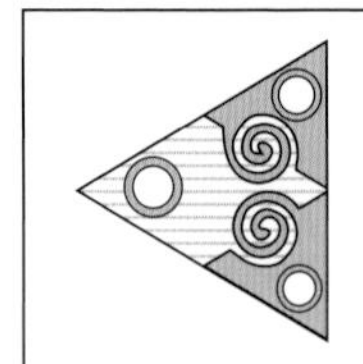
3

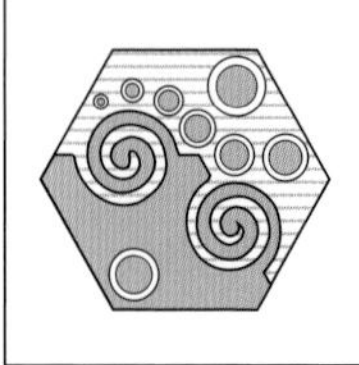
4

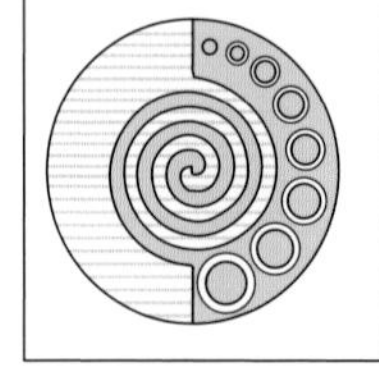
5

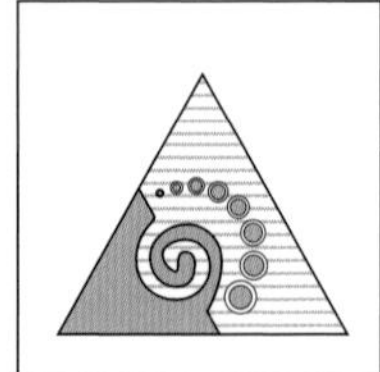
6

2 & 4	2 & 6	1 & 5	3 & 5	2 & 5	3 & 4
A	B	C	D	E	F

20.

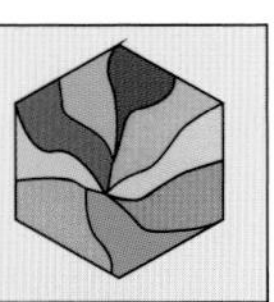
1

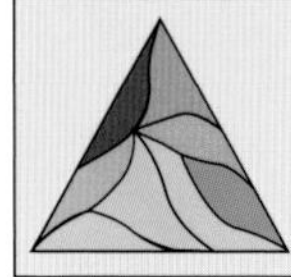
2

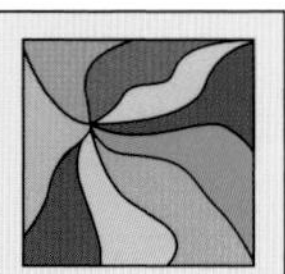
3

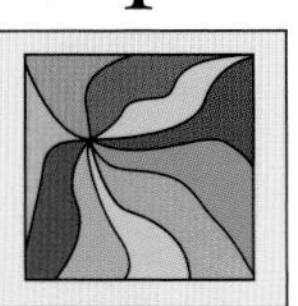
4

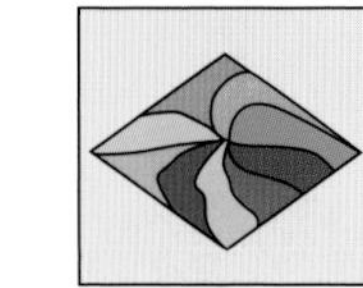
5

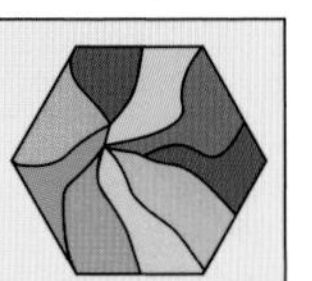
6

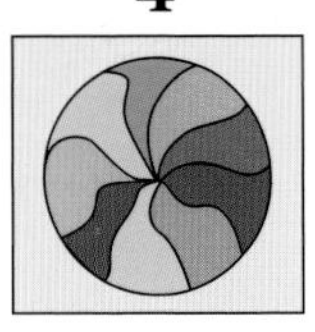
7

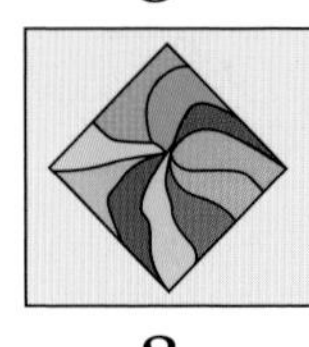
8

9

3, 5 & 7	1, 5 & 9	1, 6 & 7	2, 5 & 7	3, 4 & 8	2, 5 & 9
A	B	C	D	E	F

21.

1

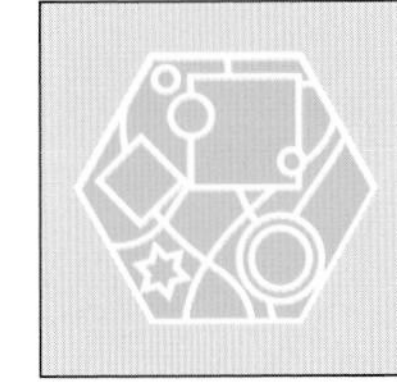

2

3

4

5

6

2 & 5	1 & 4	3 & 5	1 & 5	3 & 4	3 & 6
A	B	C	D	E	F

22.

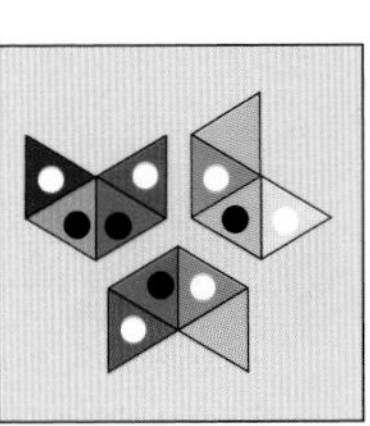

1

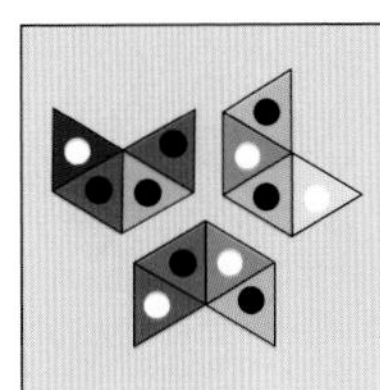

2

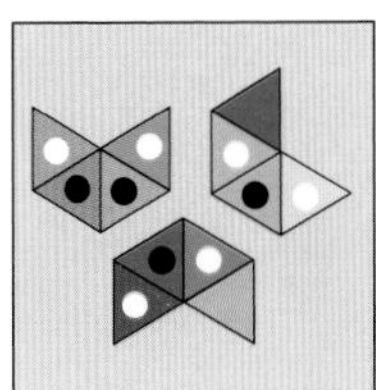

3

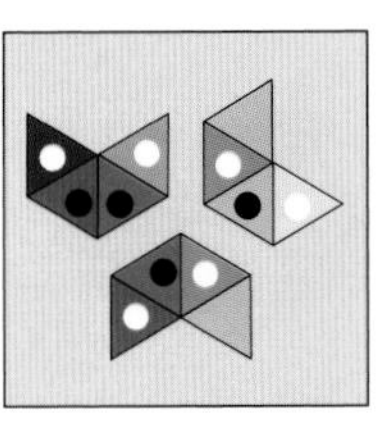

4

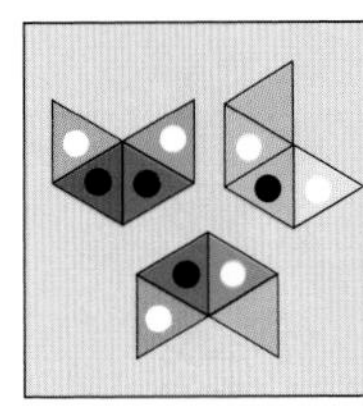

5

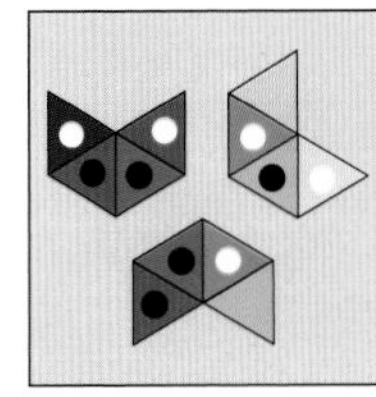

6

1 & 6	1 & 5	2 & 4	1 & 4	3 & 5	3 & 6
A	B	C	D	E	F

23.

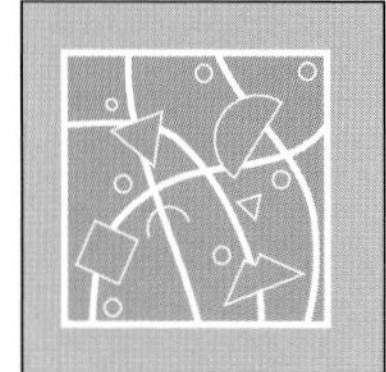
1

2

3

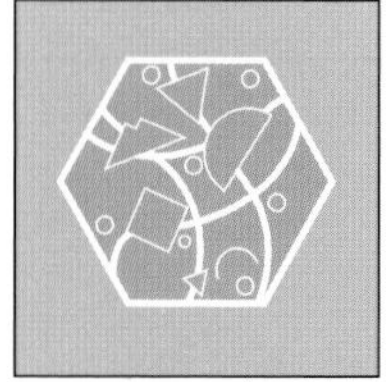
4

5

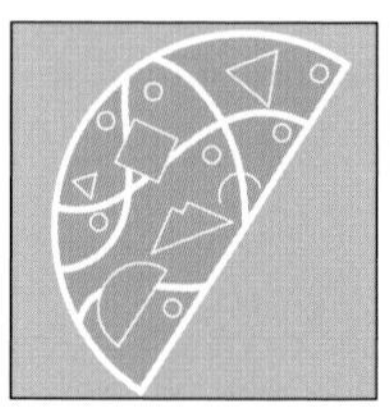
6

2 & 5	2 & 6	3 & 5	1 & 5	1 & 4	3 & 6
A	B	C	D	E	F

24.

1

2

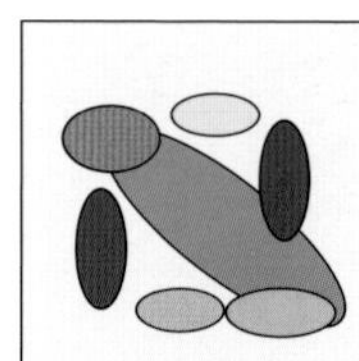
3

4

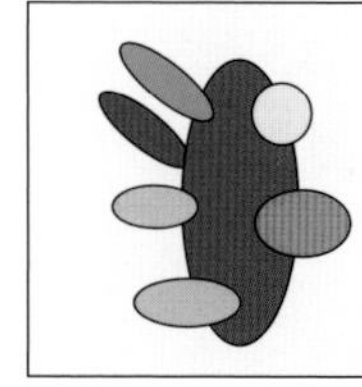
5

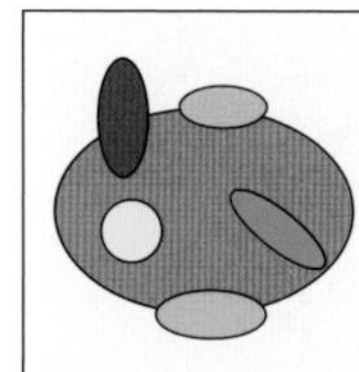
6

2 & 5	3 & 6	1 & 4	1 & 5	2 & 4	3 & 5
A	B	C	D	E	F

25.

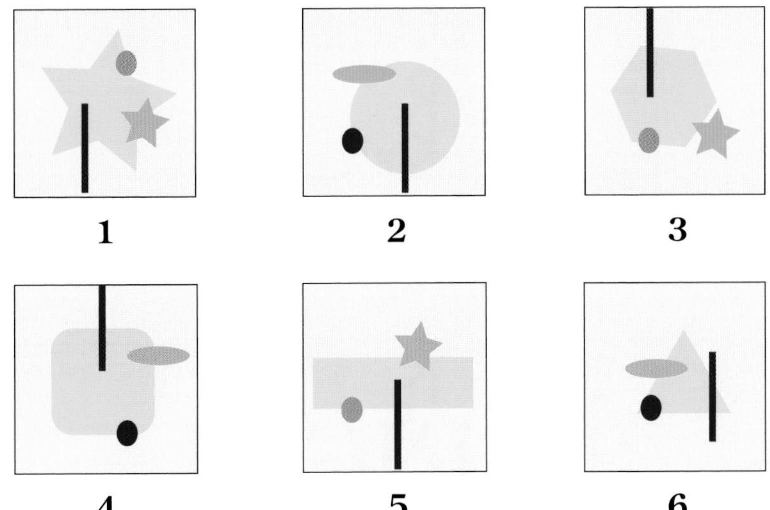

2 & 5	1 & 6	1 & 4	2 & 4	3 & 4	3 & 5
A	B	C	D	E	F

26.

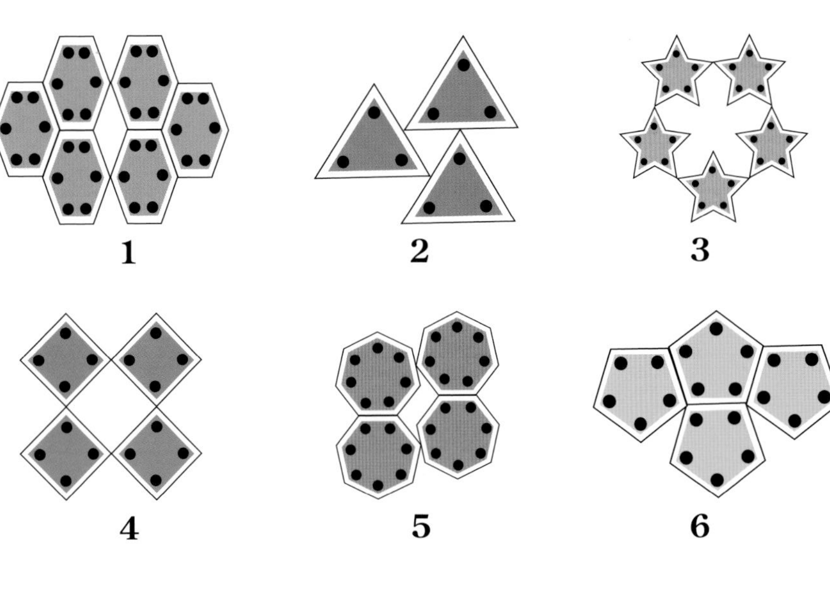

2 & 5	3 & 6	1 & 4	1 & 5	2 & 4	3 & 4
A	B	C	D	E	F

BRICKS

- **In each of the puzzles that follow, the cut-shapes are to be fitted in the given grid. These cut-shapes can be rotated in any angle, however no cut-shape can be repeated, changed or reversed.**
- **Find the correct answer from the options given.**

1.

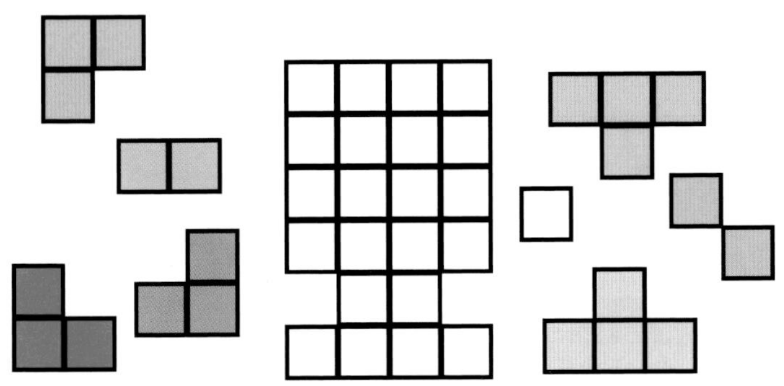

A

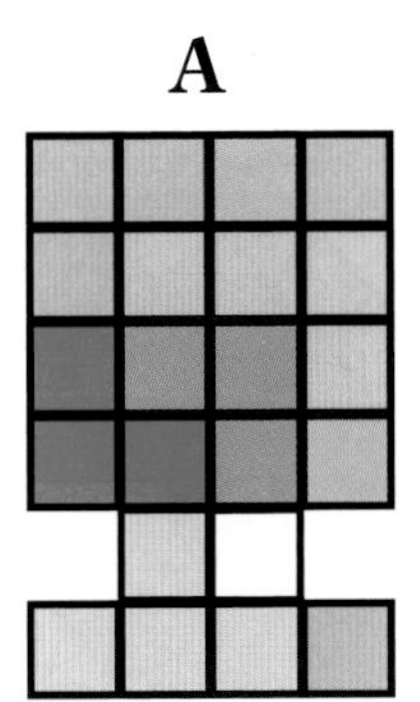

B

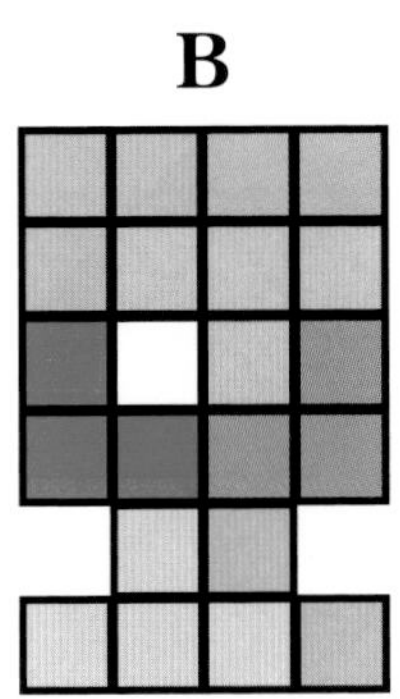

C

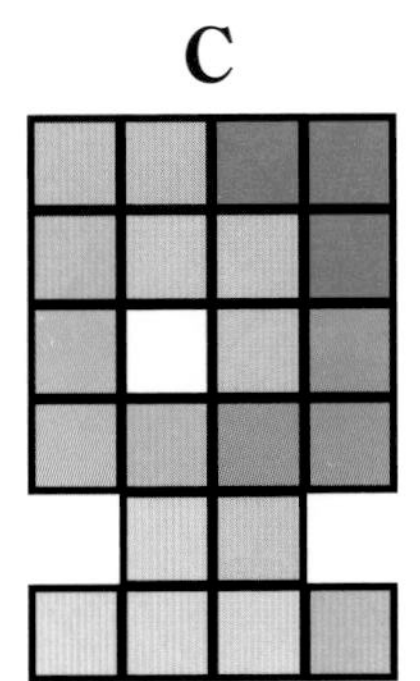

D

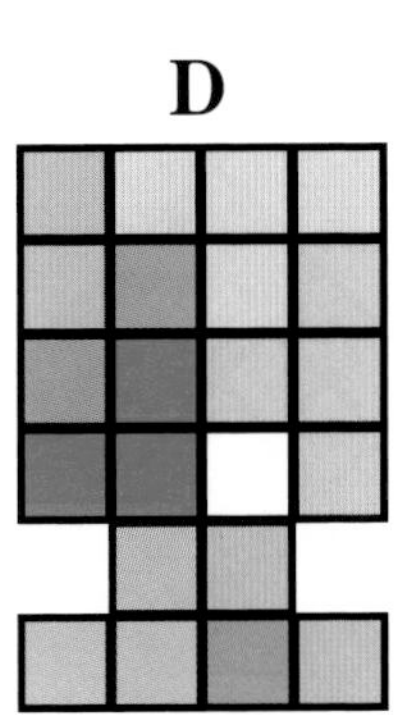

2.

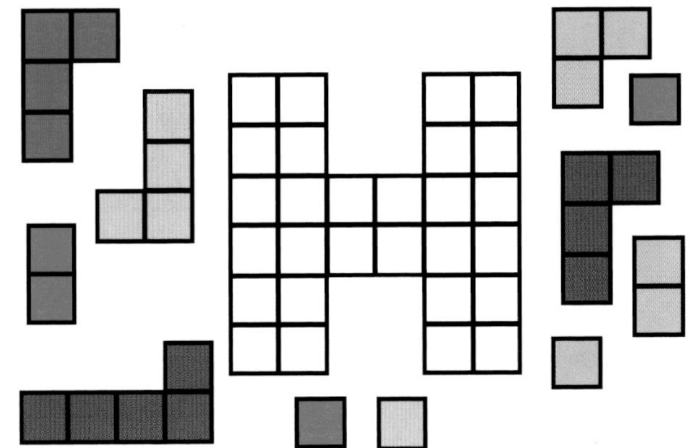

A

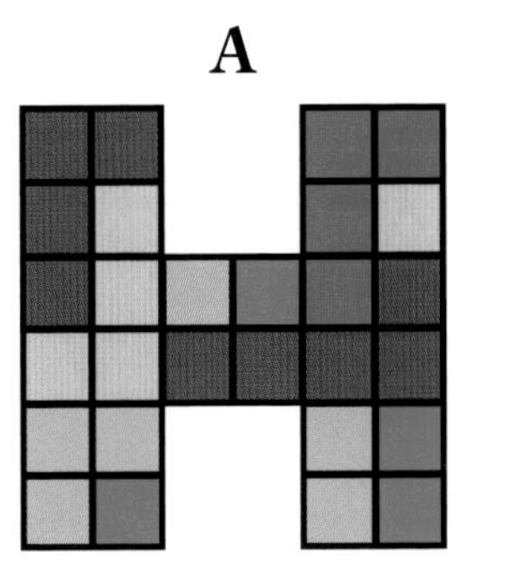

B

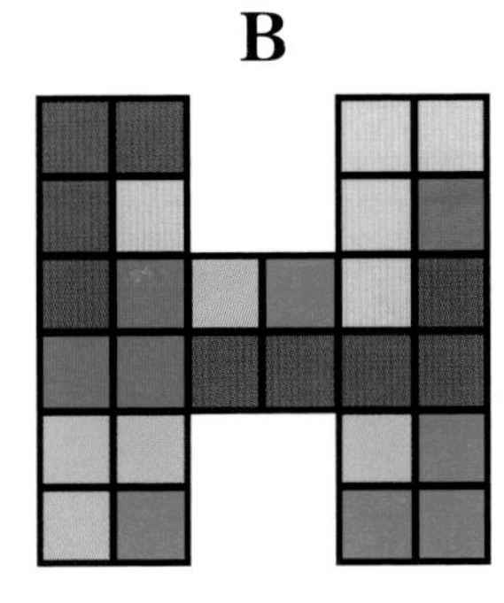

C

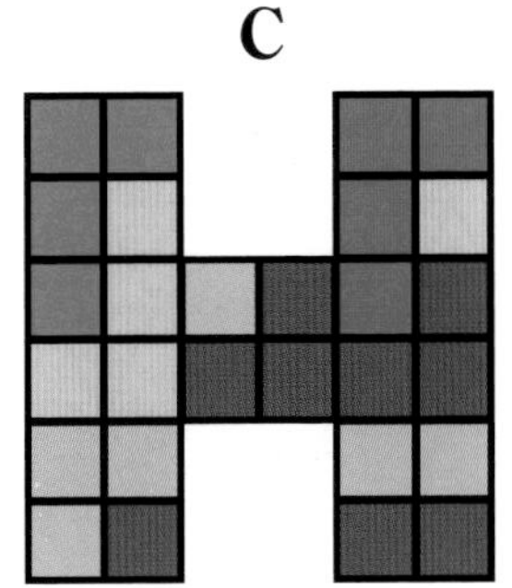

D

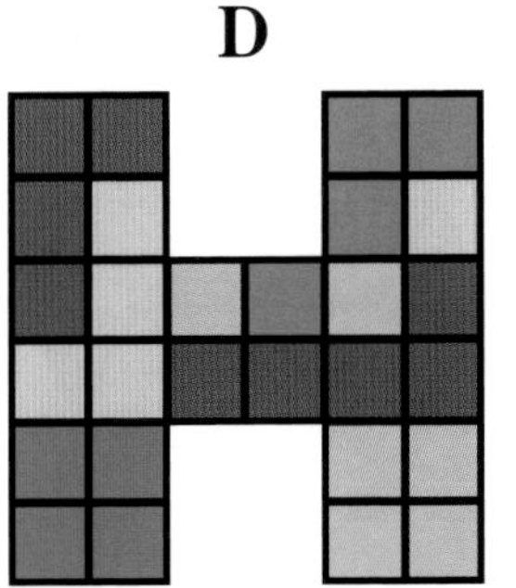

3.

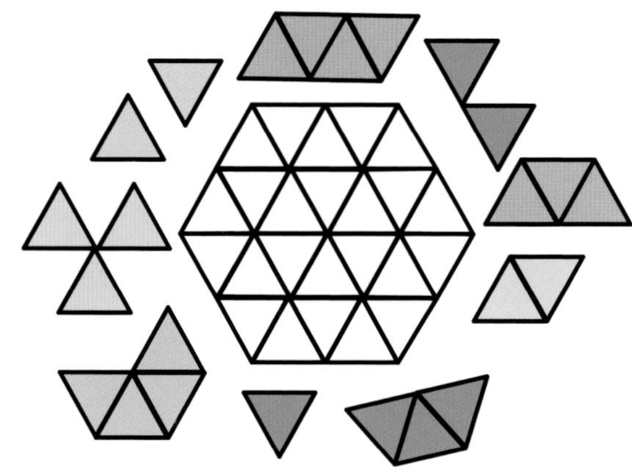

A

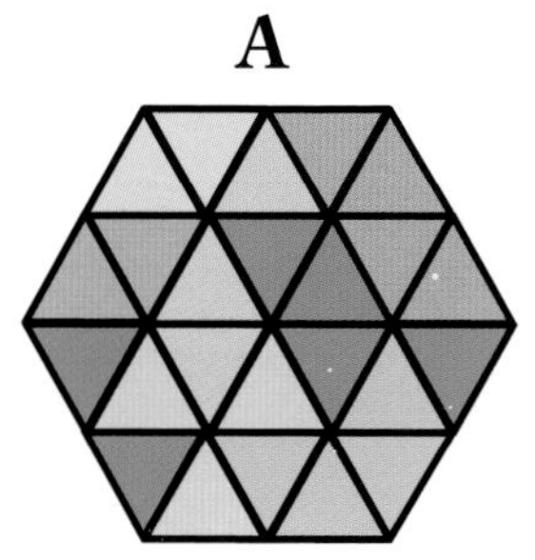

B

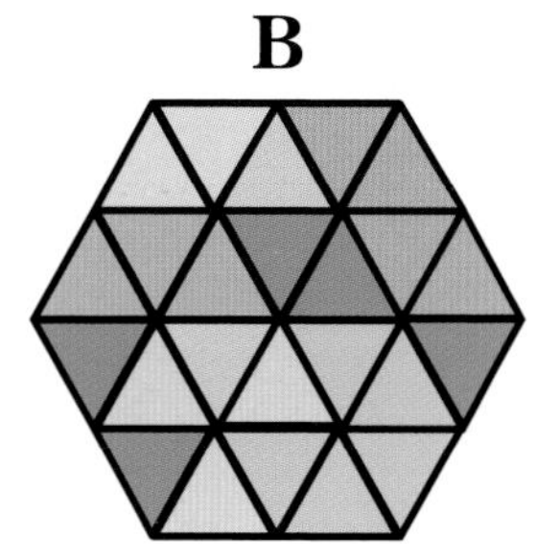

C

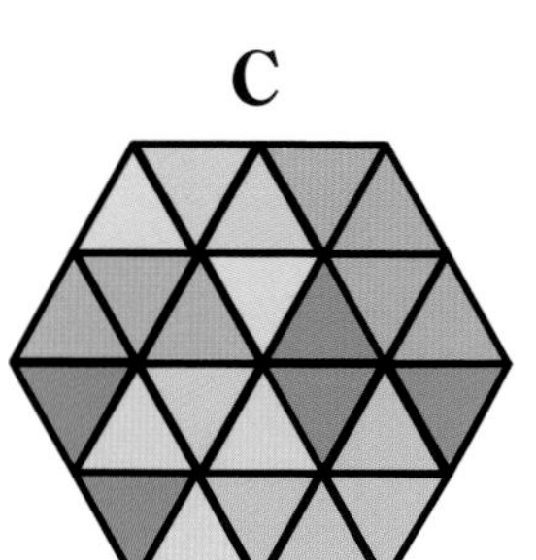

D

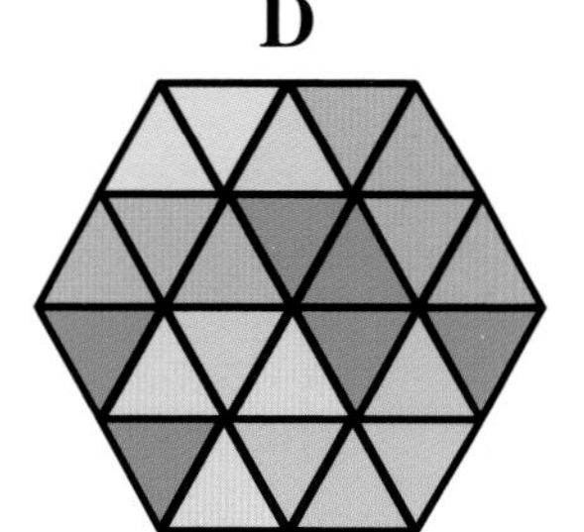

4.

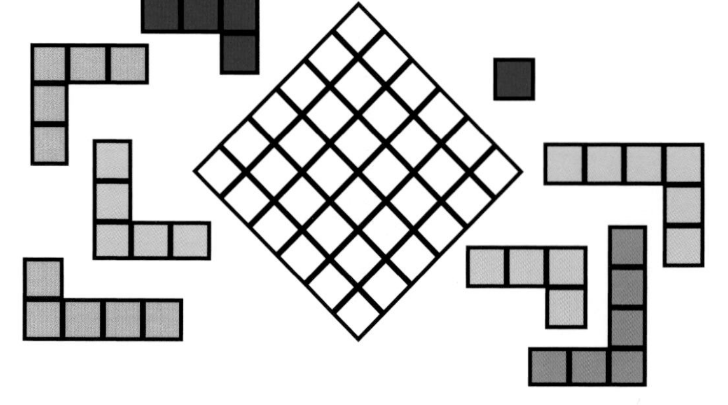

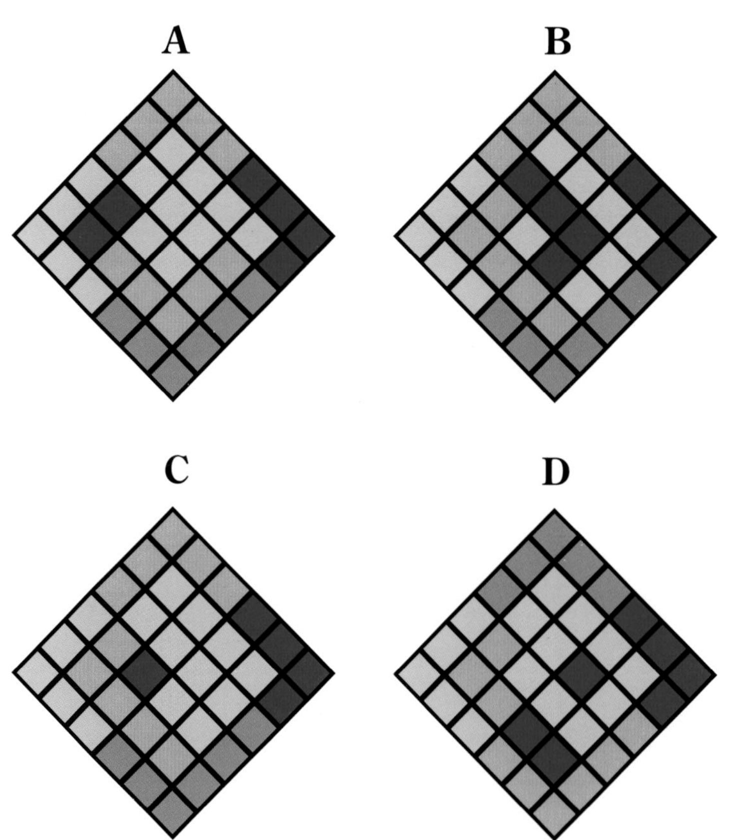

5.

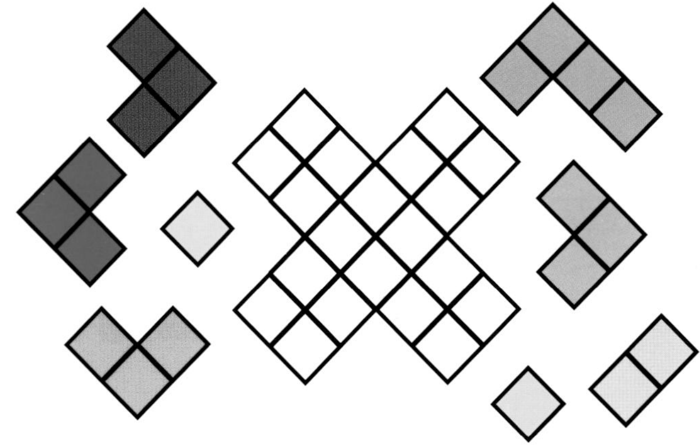

A

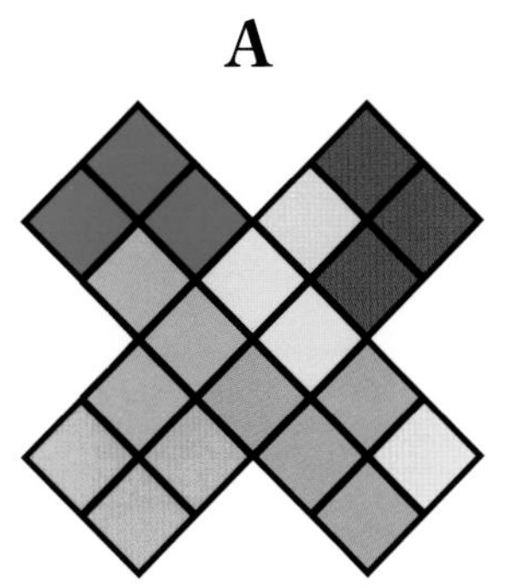

B

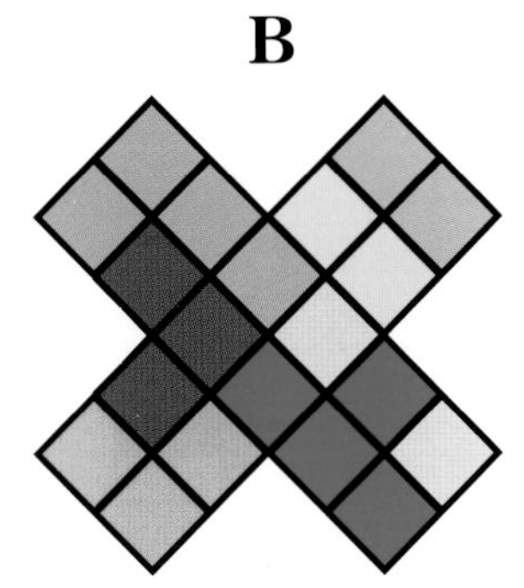

C

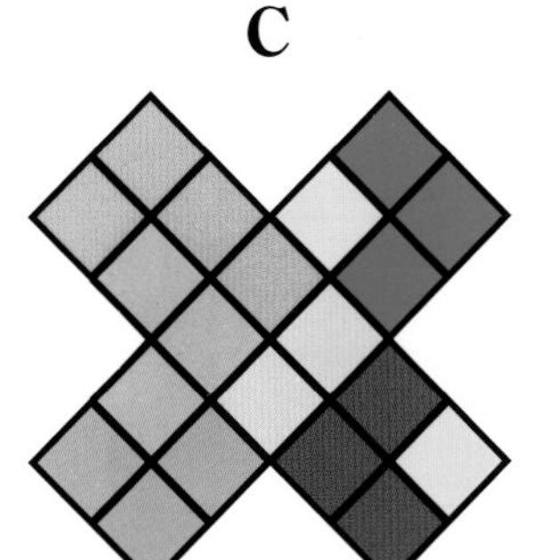

D

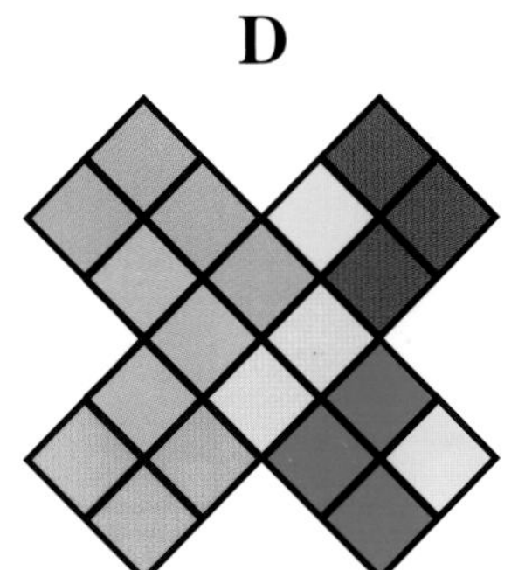

6.

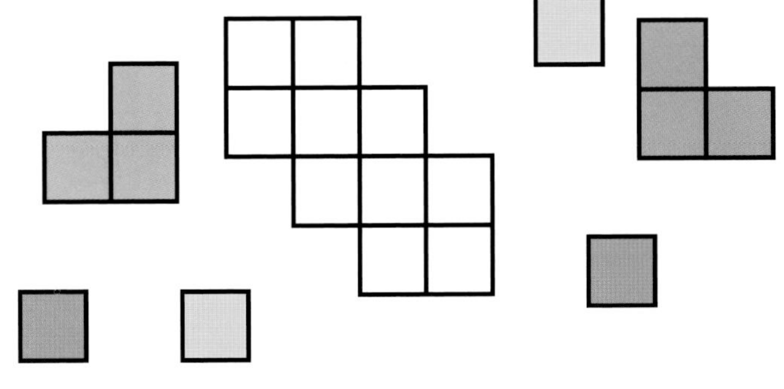

A B

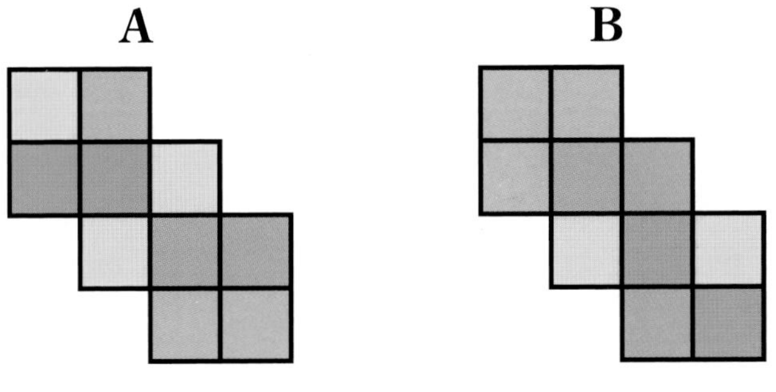

C

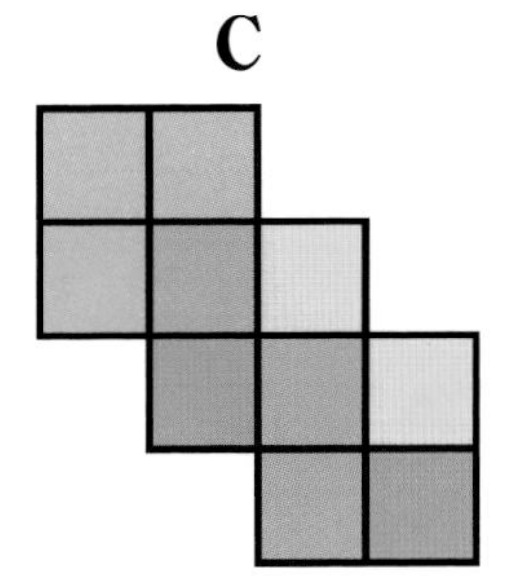

D

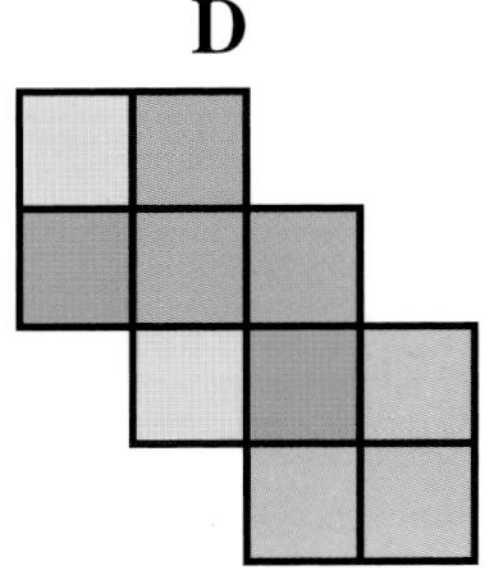

7.

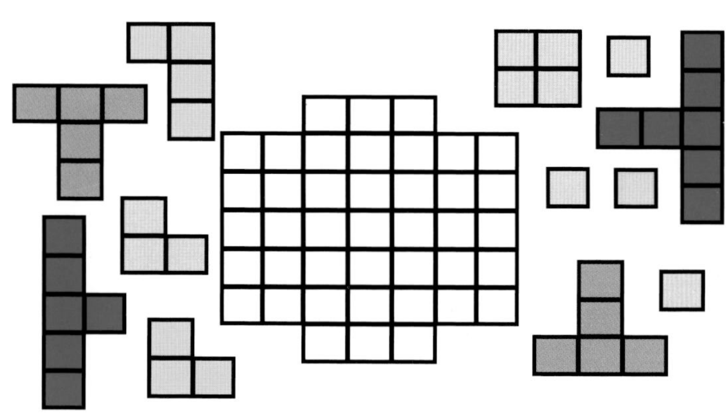

A

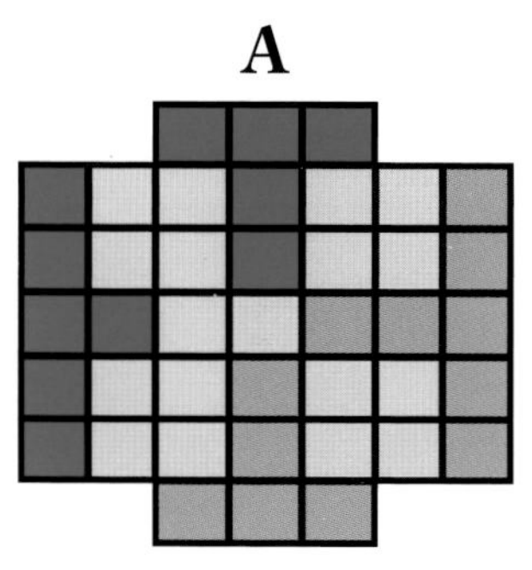

B

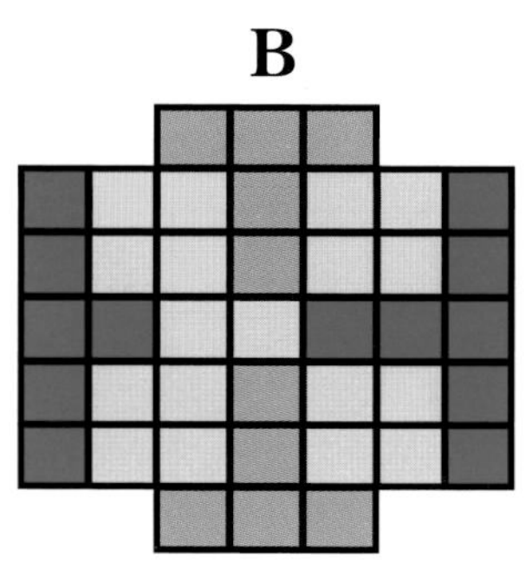

C

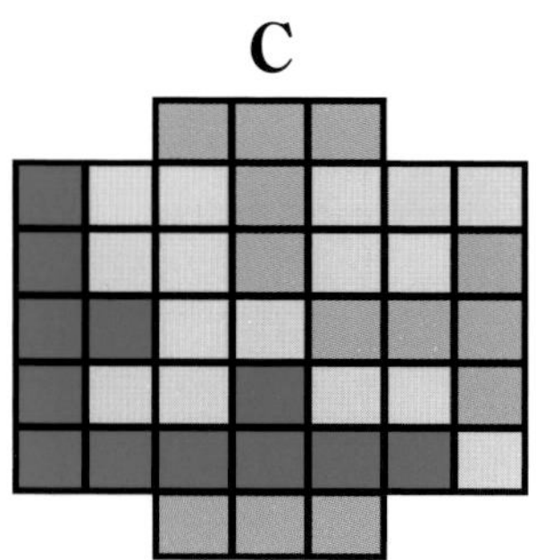

D

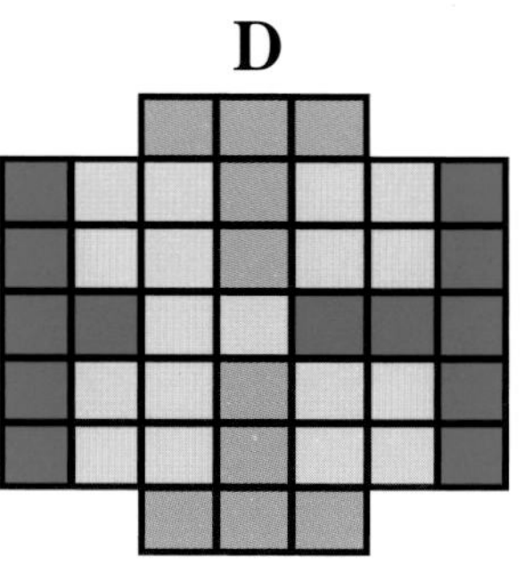

8.

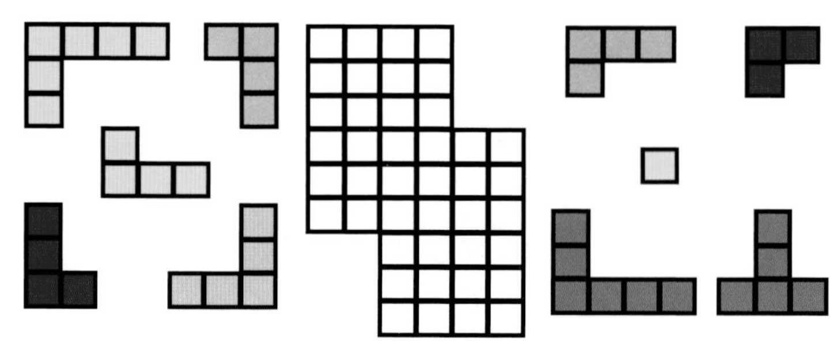

A

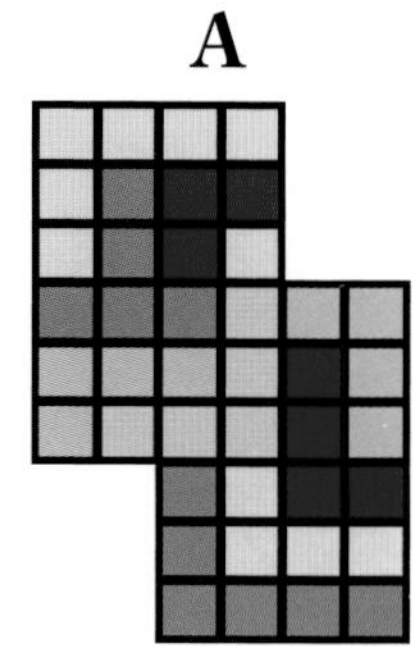

B

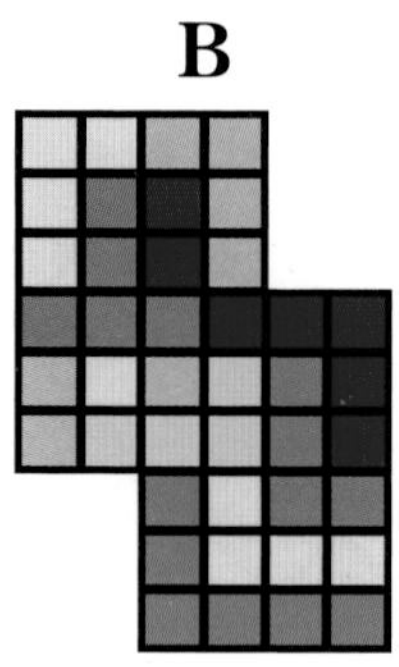

C

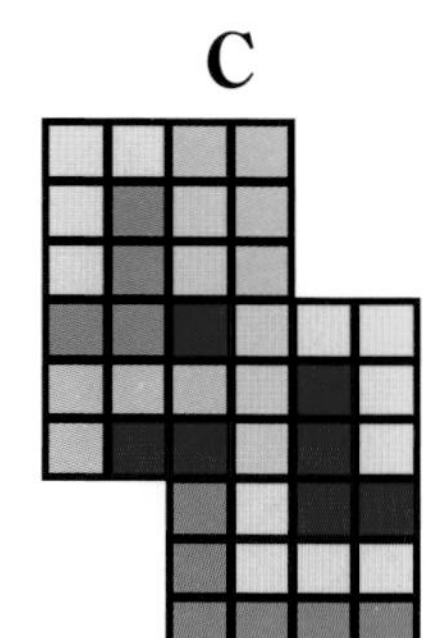

D

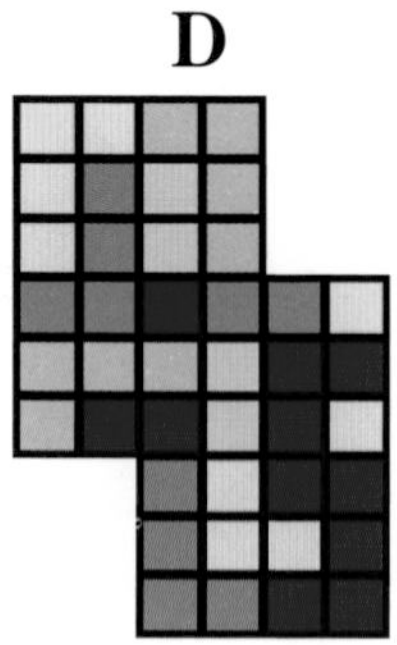

9.

A

B

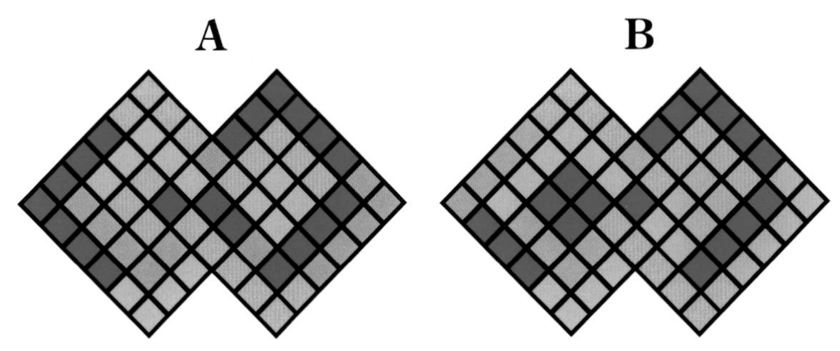

C

D

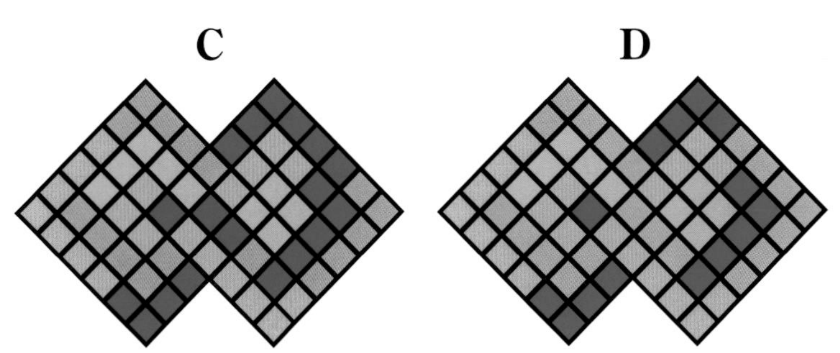

10.

A

B

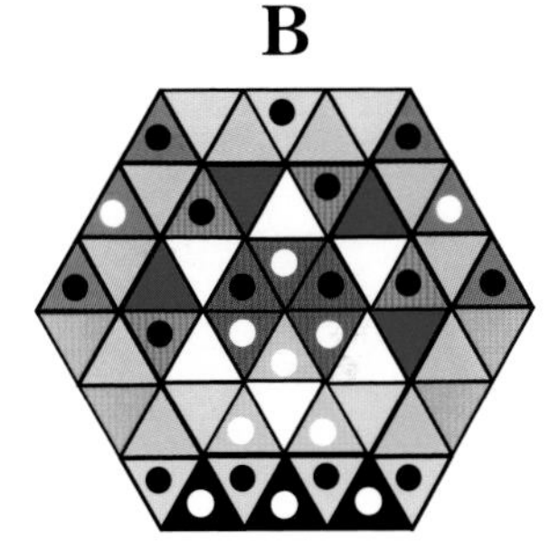

C

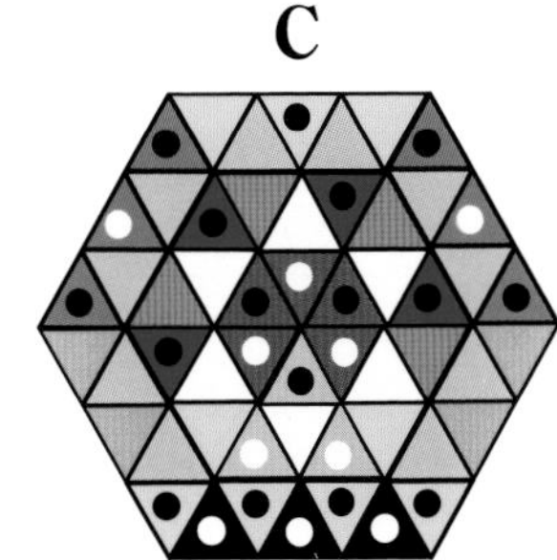

D

11.

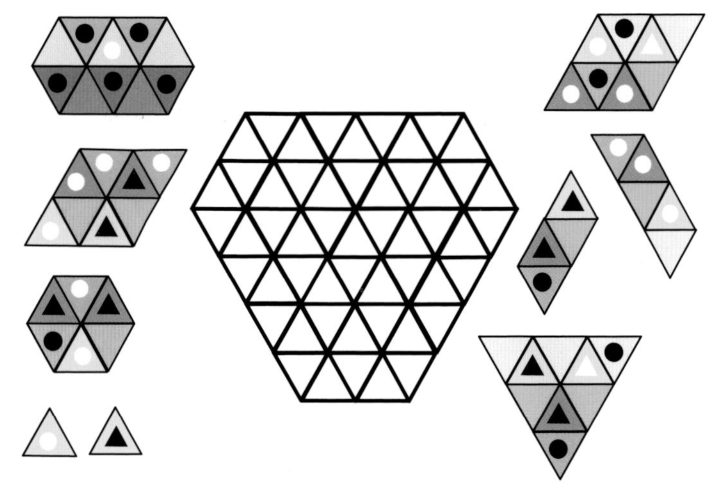

A

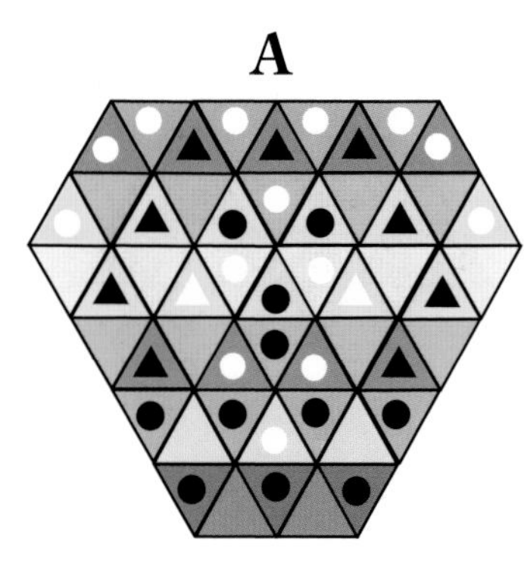

B

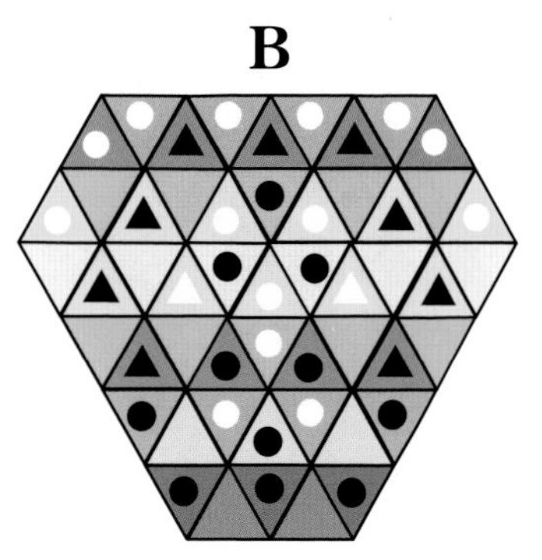

C

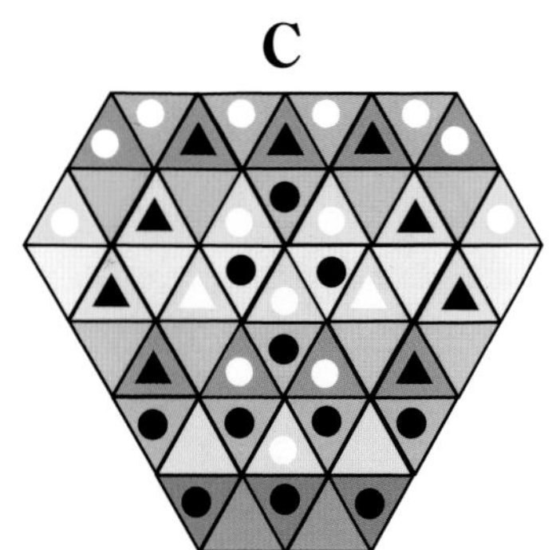

D

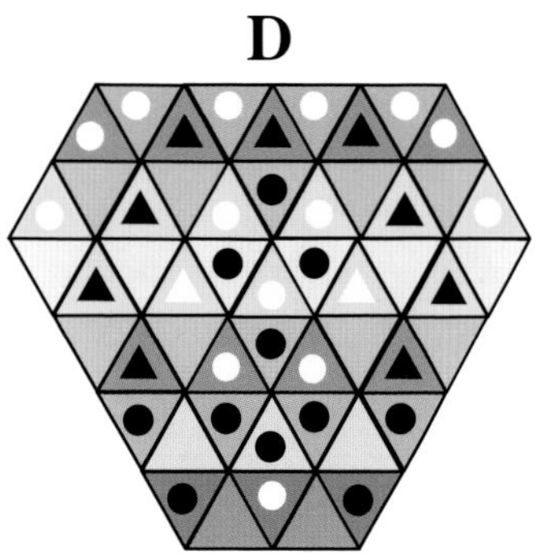

12.

A

B

C

D

13.

A **B**

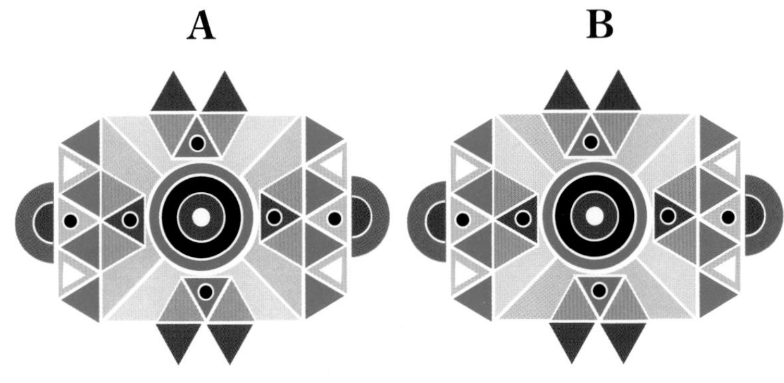

C **D**

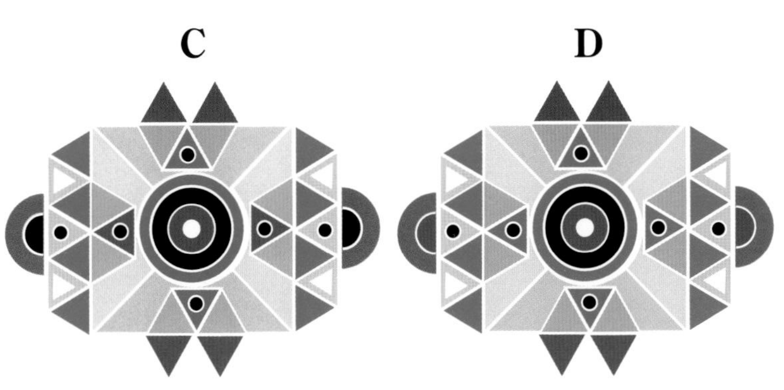

14.

A

B

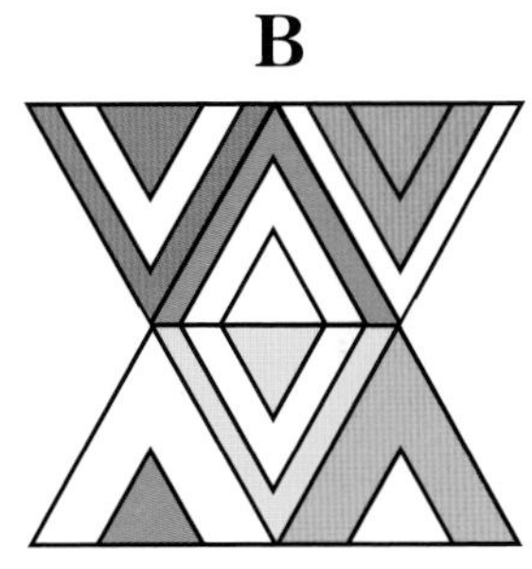

C

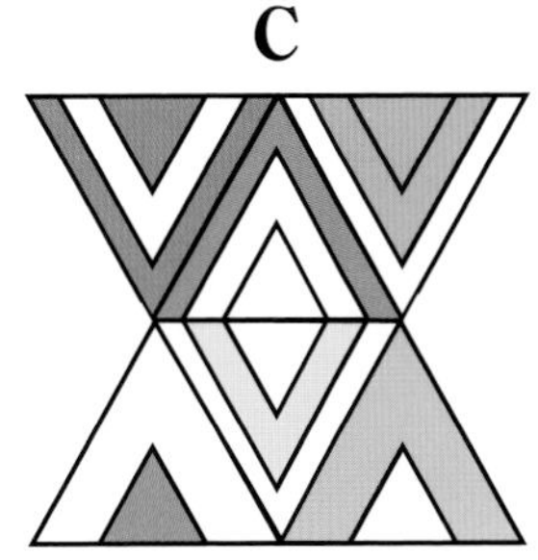

D

15.

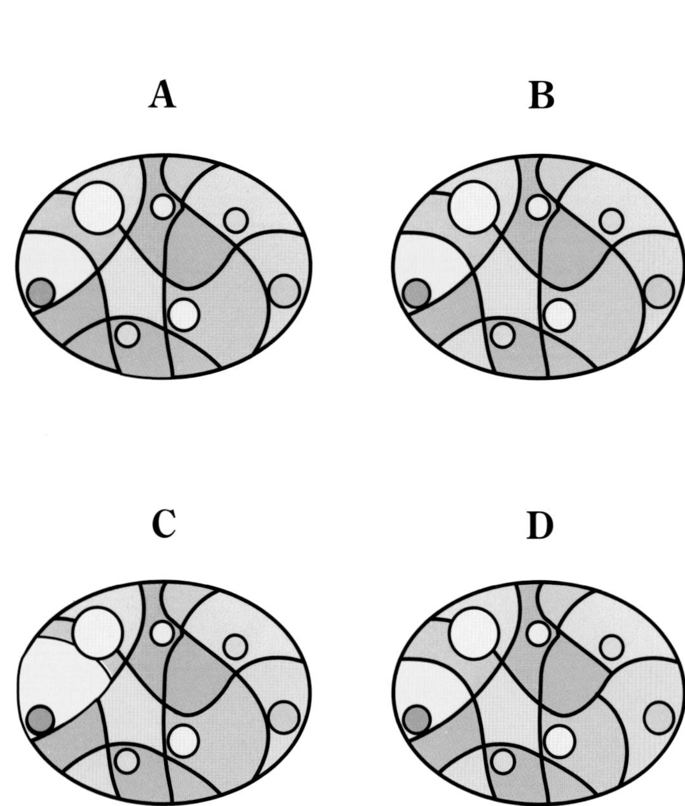

16.

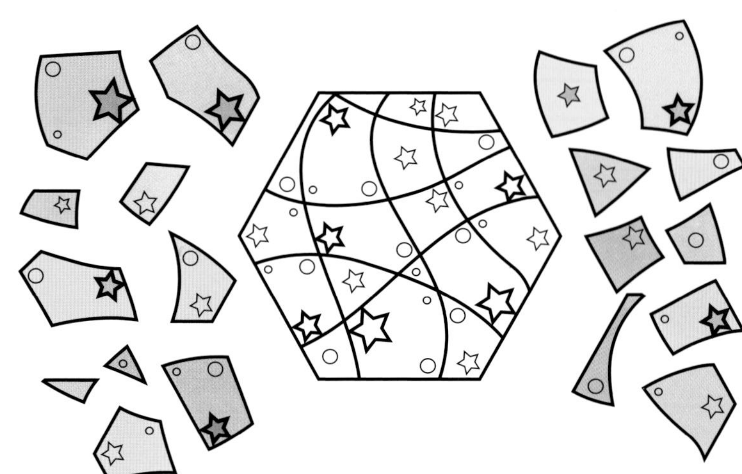

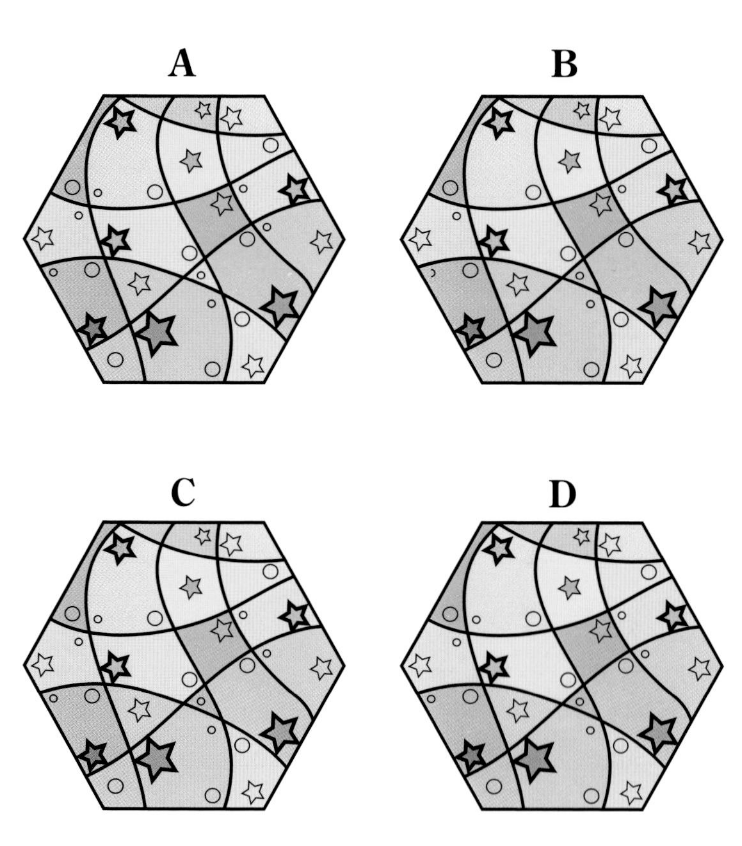

17.

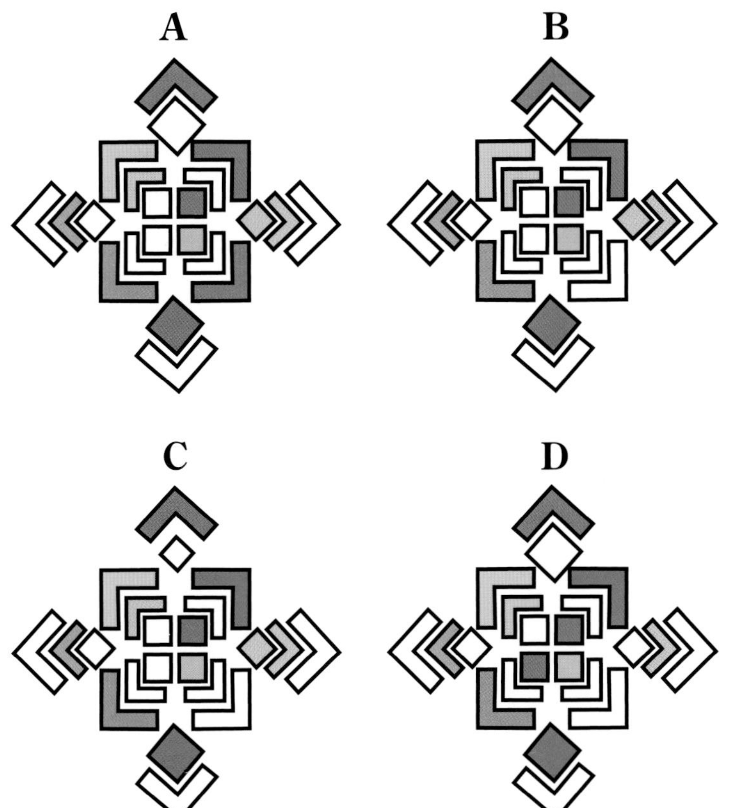

18.

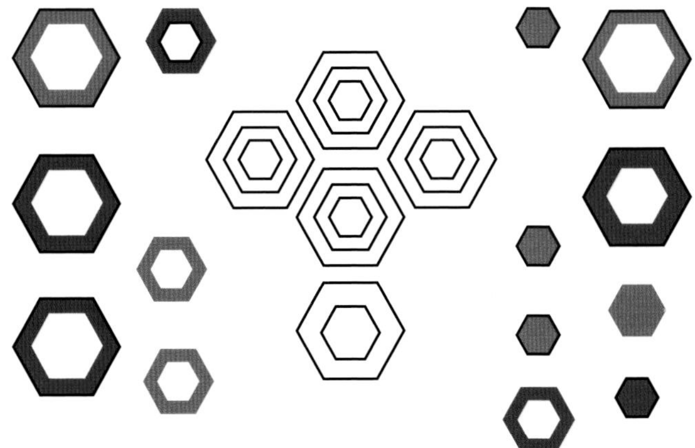

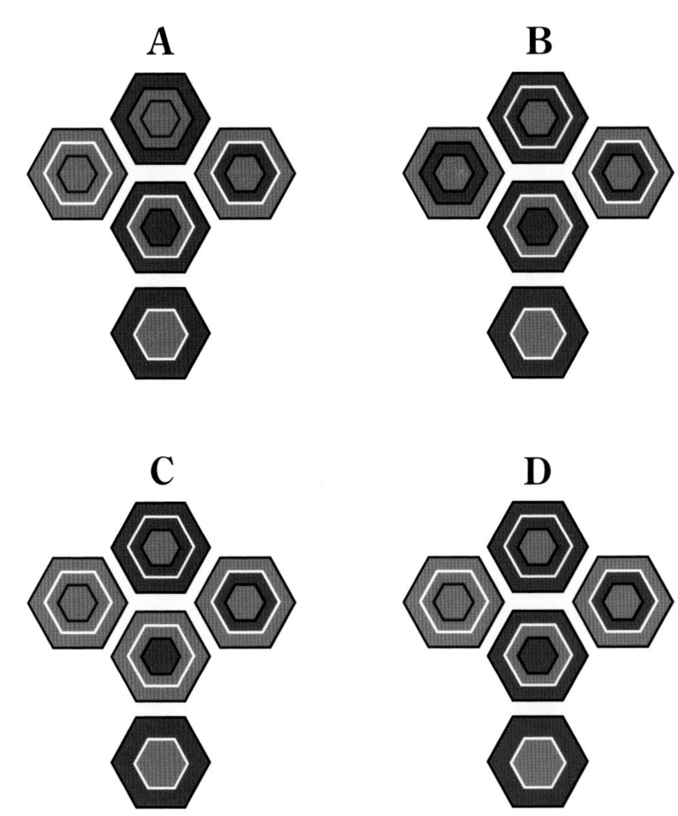

19.

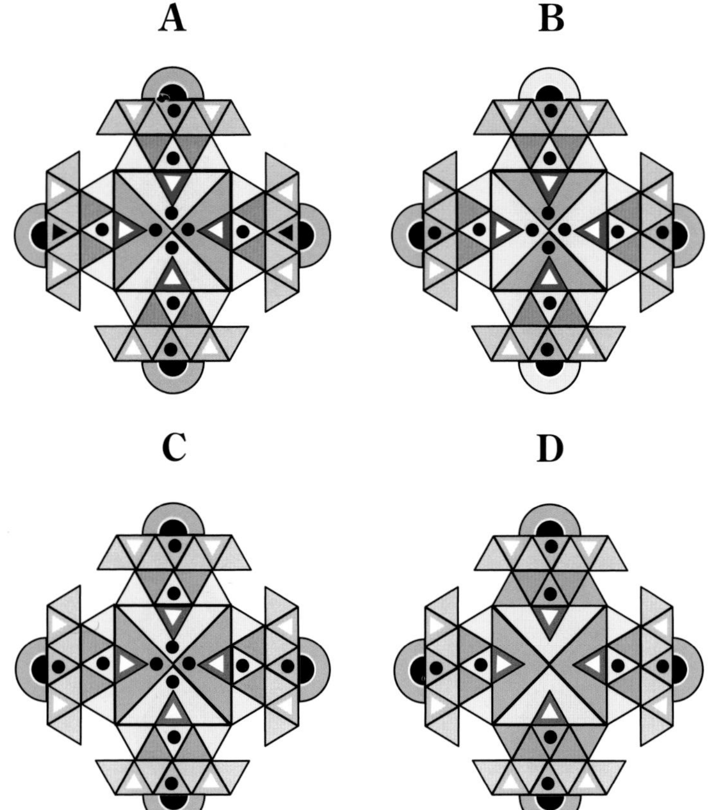

20.

21.

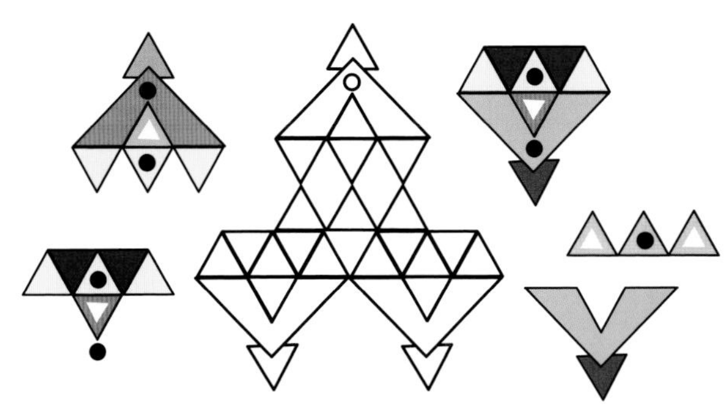

A

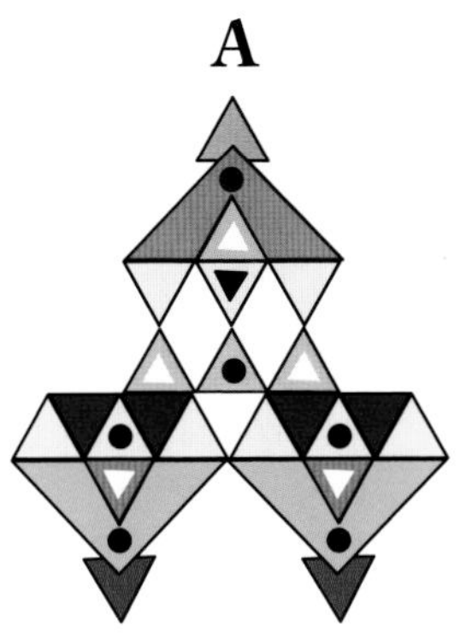

B

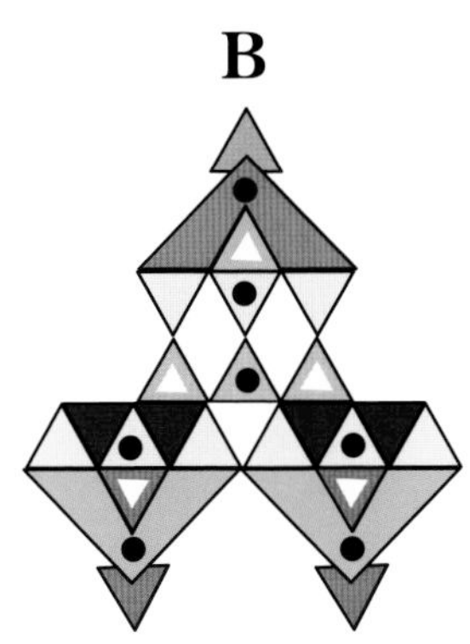

C **D**

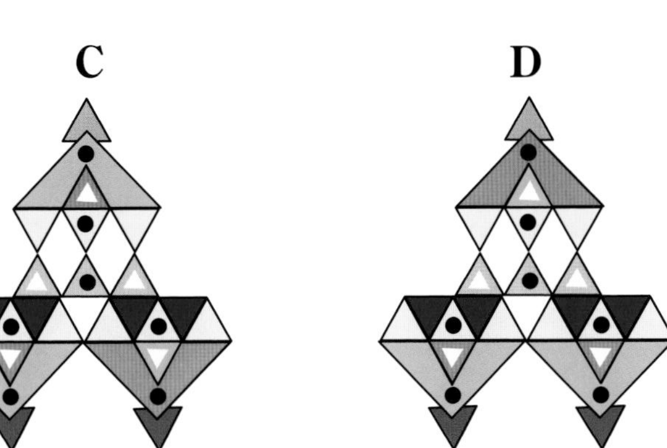

22.

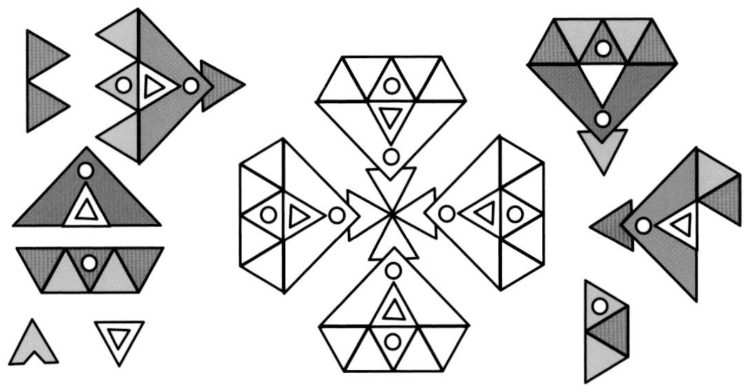

A

B

C **D**

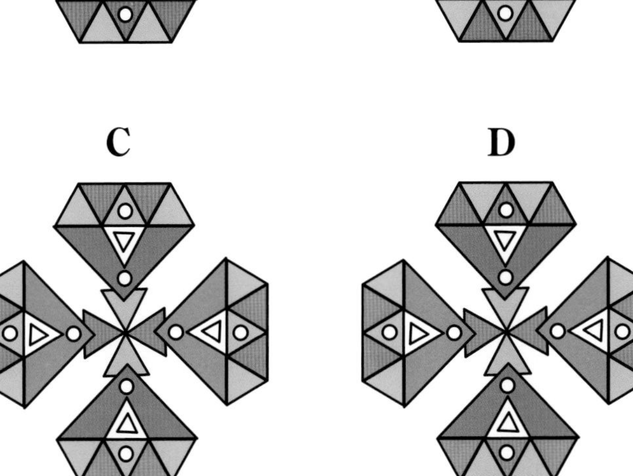

23.

A

B

C

D

24.

A

B

C

D

COLOR PERCEPTION

- In this category you would have to reason with colors. The problem figure is a complete figure with four answer options. Only one answer option is an identical 'part' of the 'whole' problem figure. You have to find this option.

1.

A B C D

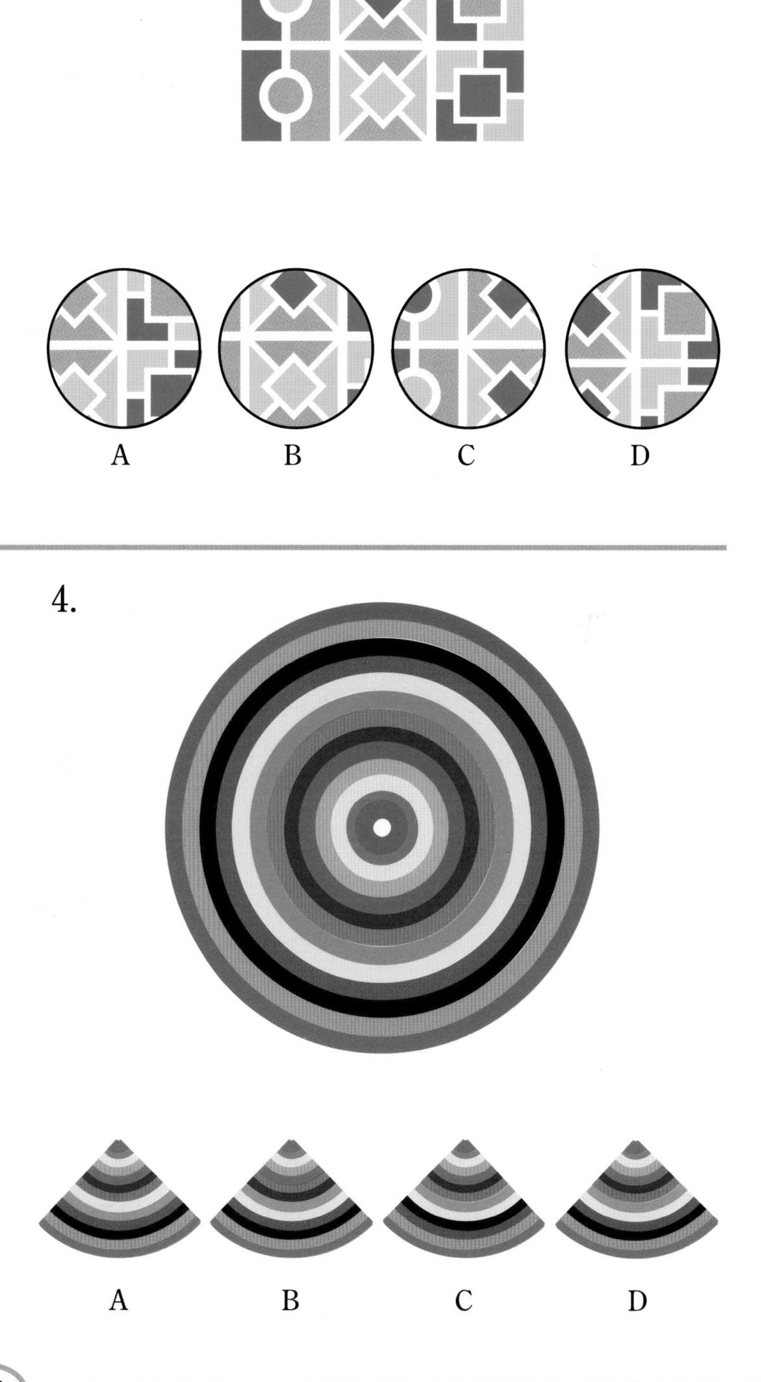

3.

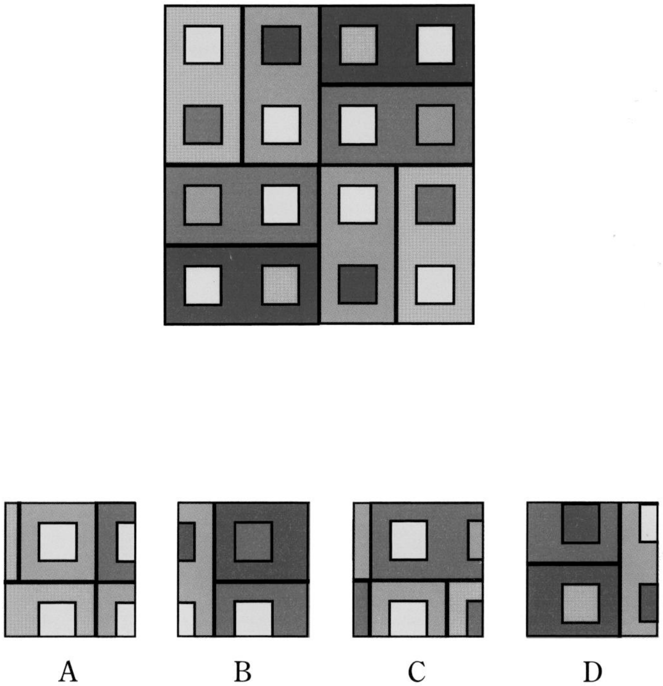

A B C D

5.

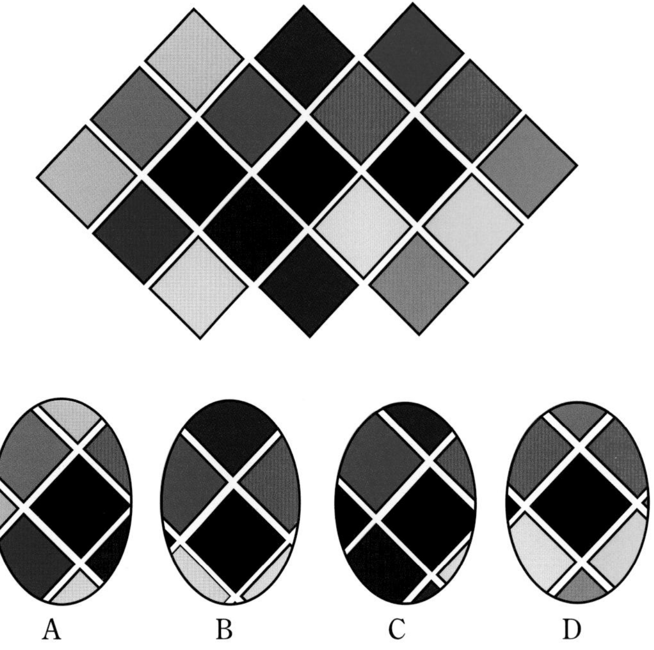

A B C D

6.

A B C D

7.

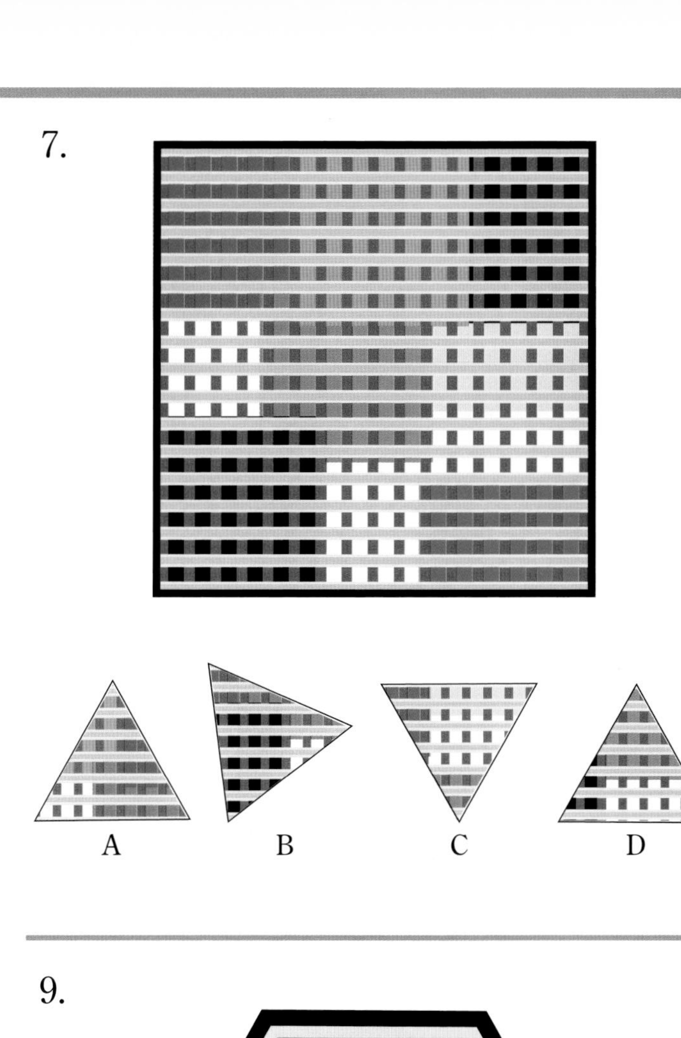

8.

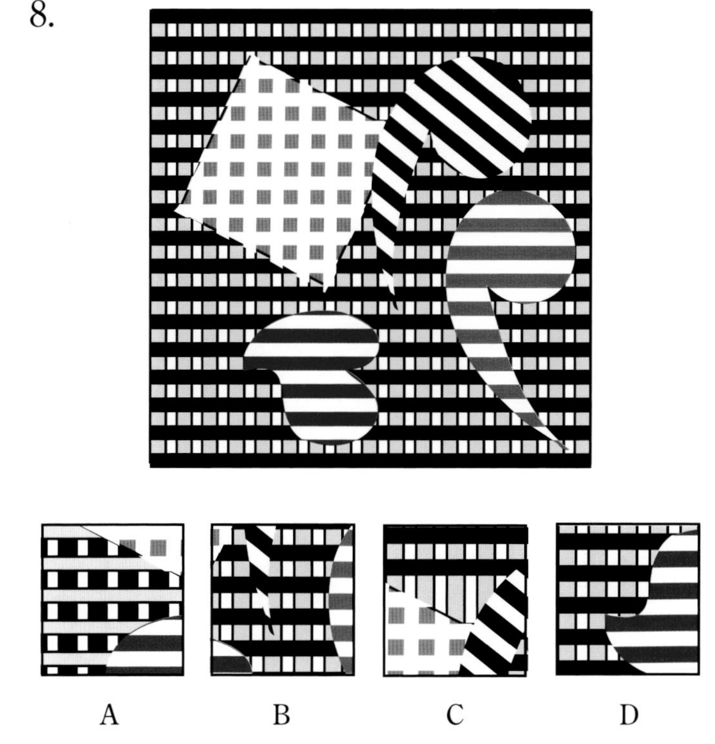

9.

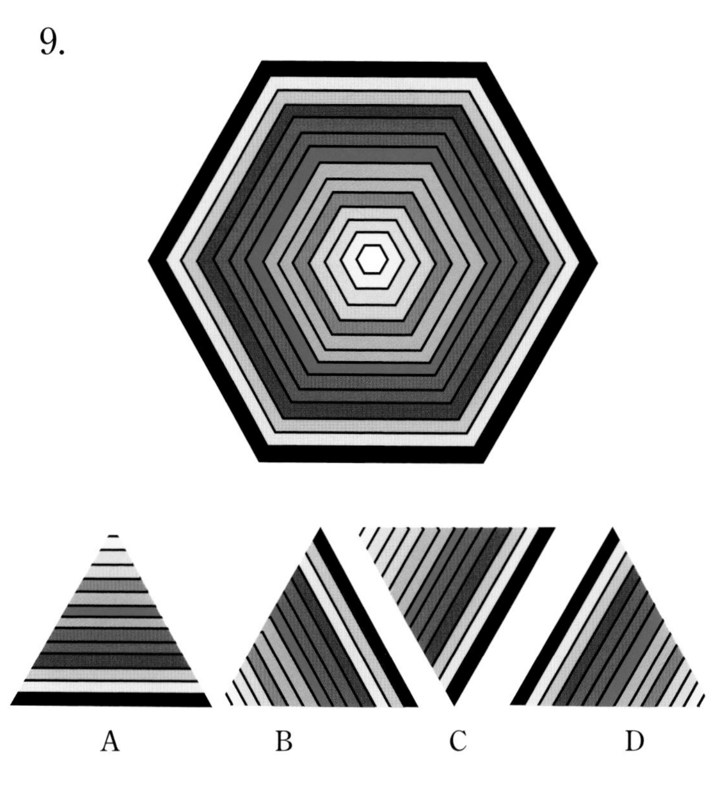

10.

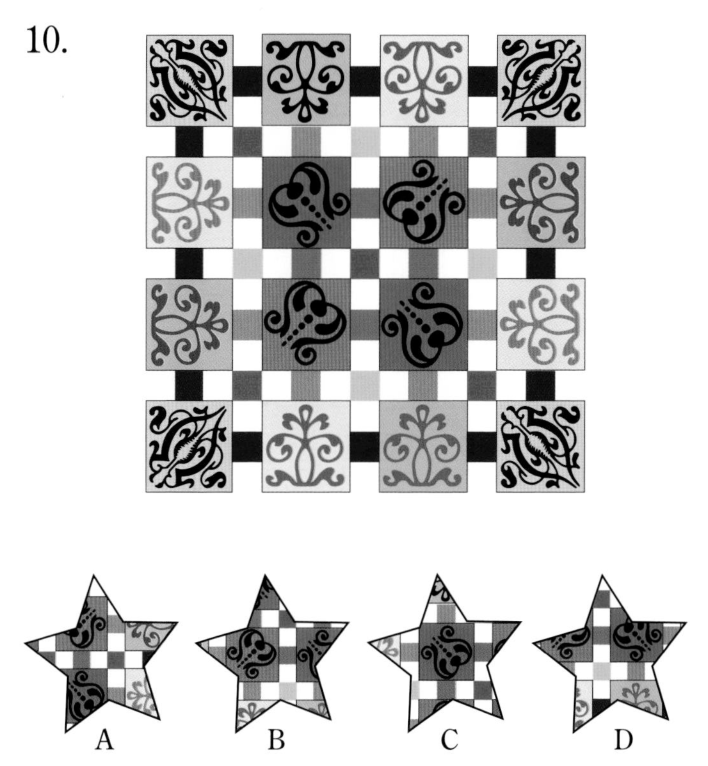

11.

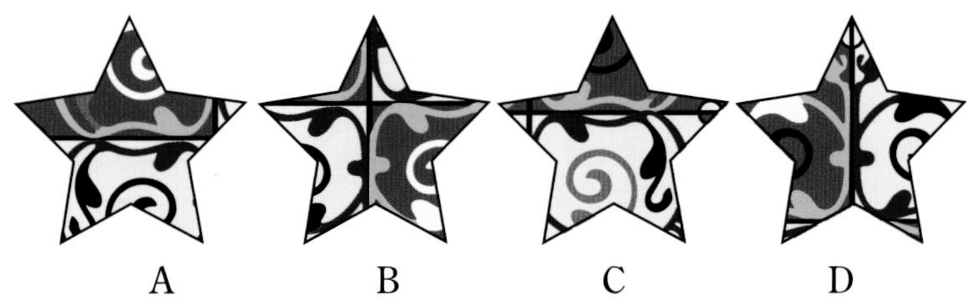

A B C D

12.

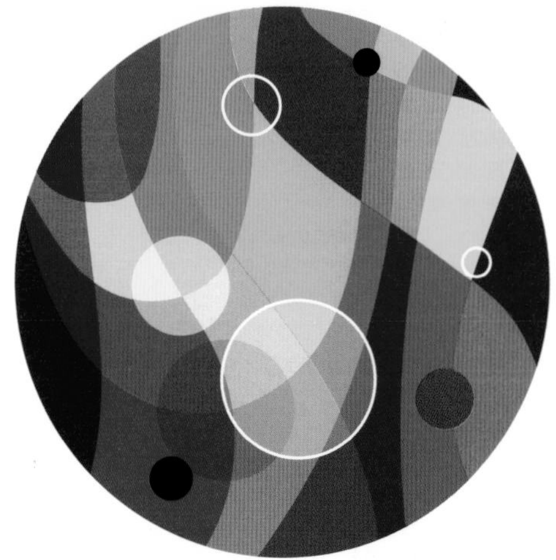

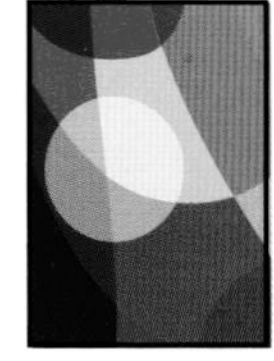
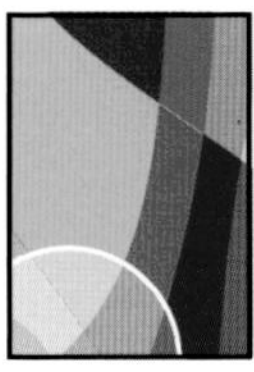
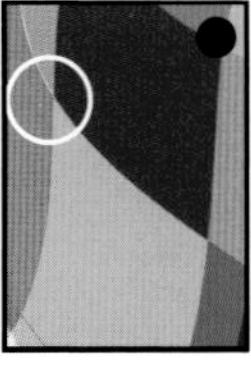
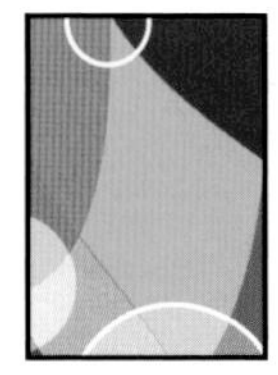

A B C D

13.

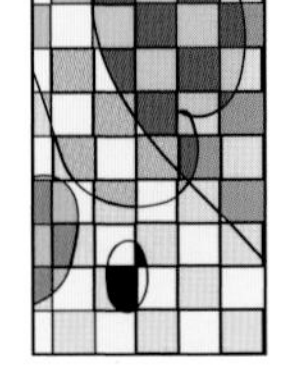
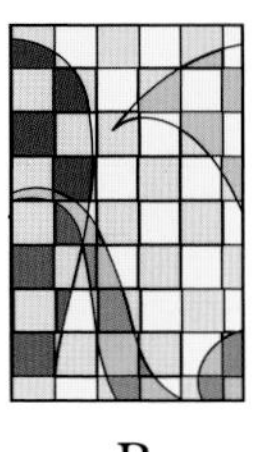
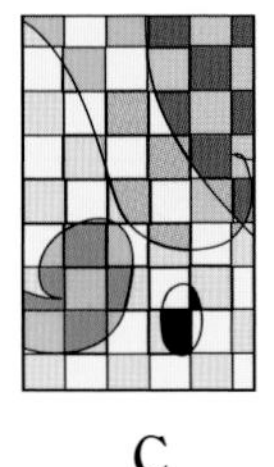
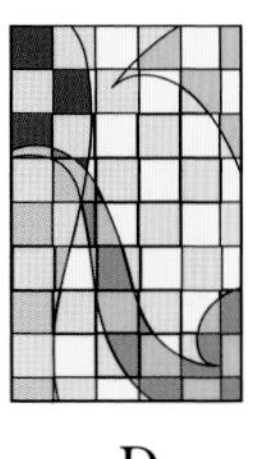

A B C D

14.

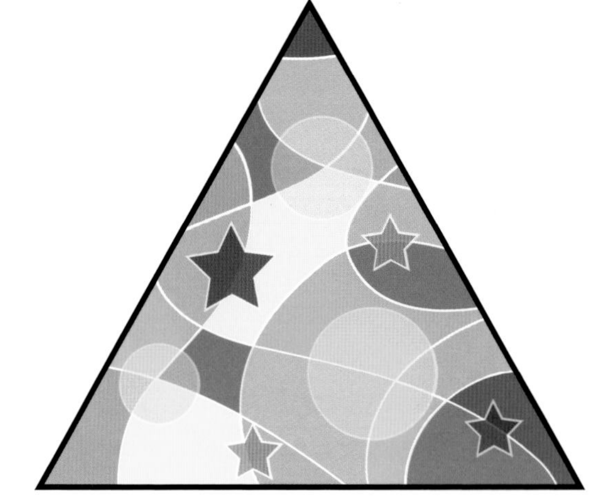

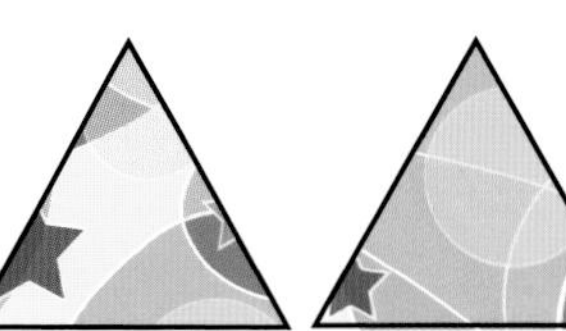
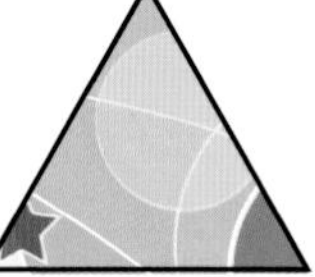

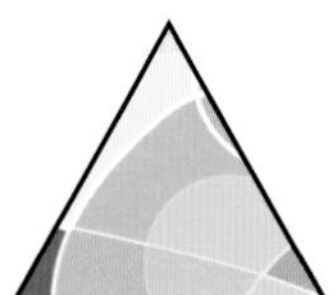

A B C D

15.

A

B

C

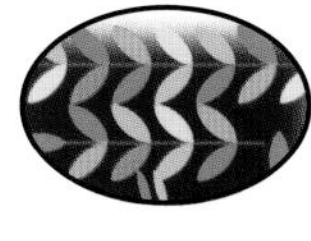
D

16.

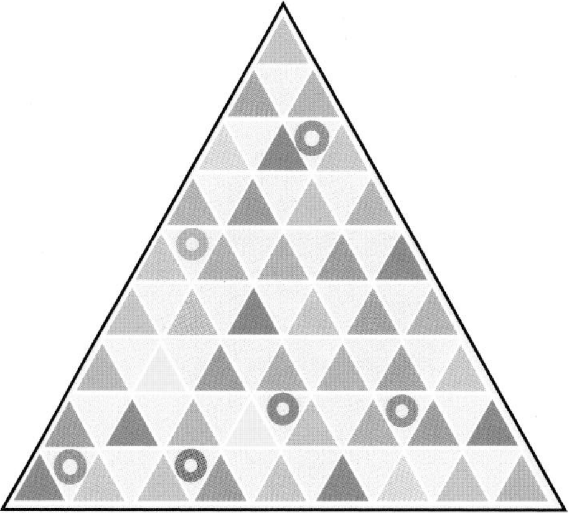

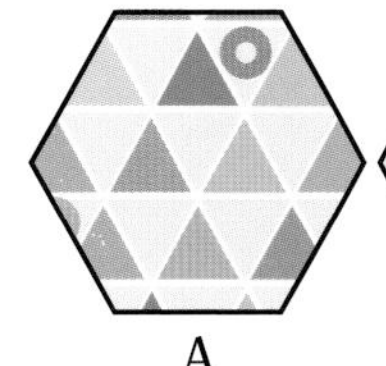
A

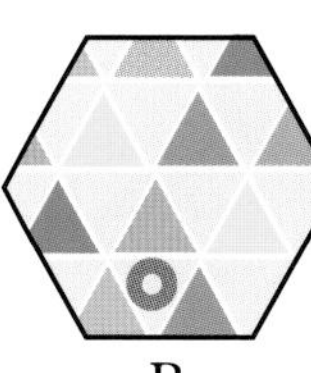
B

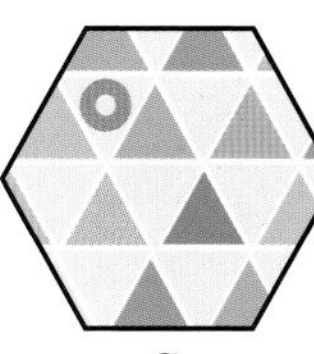
C

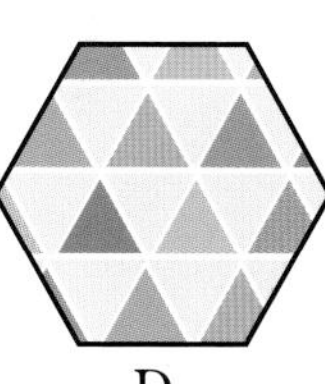
D

17.

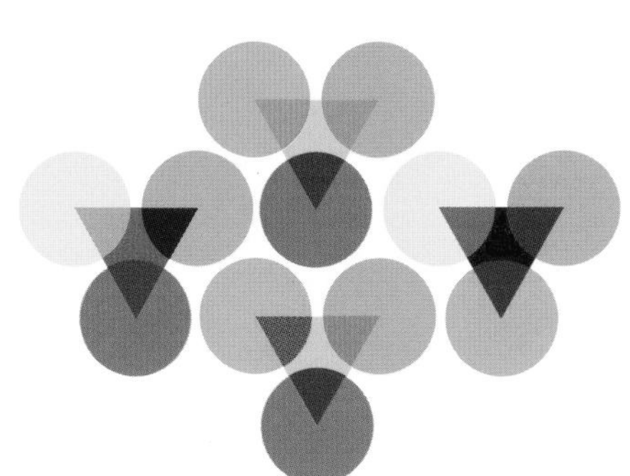

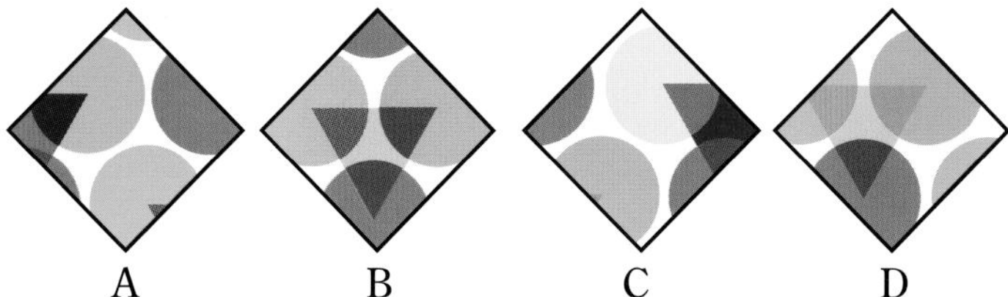

A B C D

18.

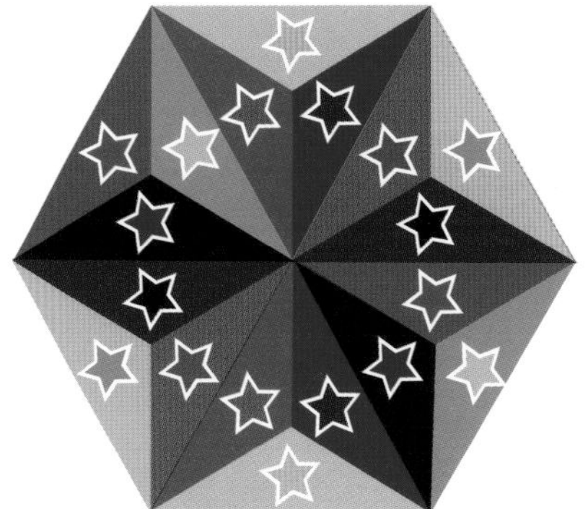

A

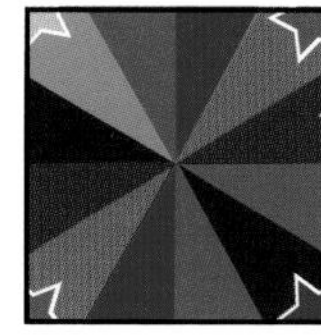
B

C

D

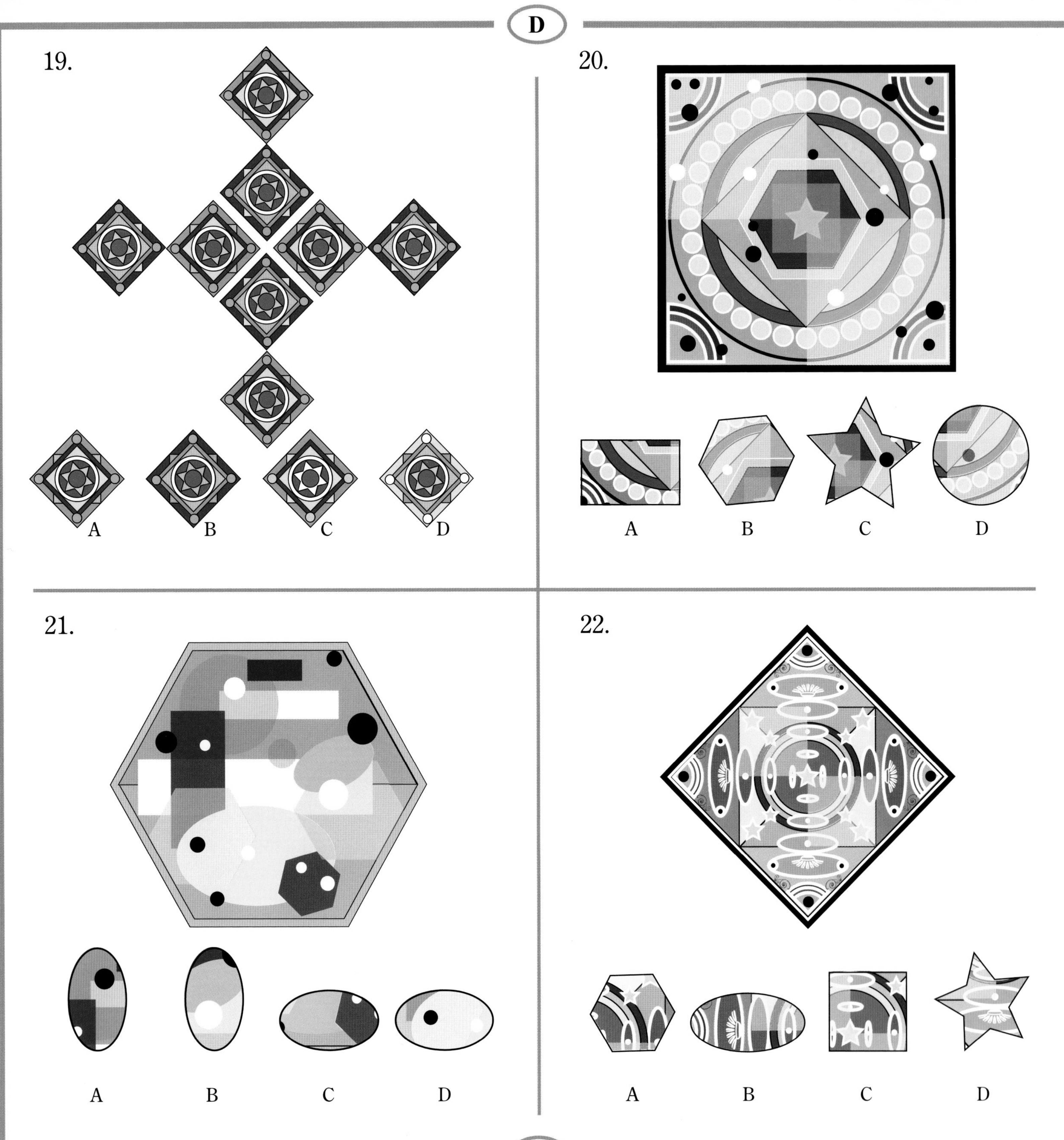
19.
A
B
C
D
20.
A
B
C
D
21.
A
B
C
D
22.
A
B
C
D

23.

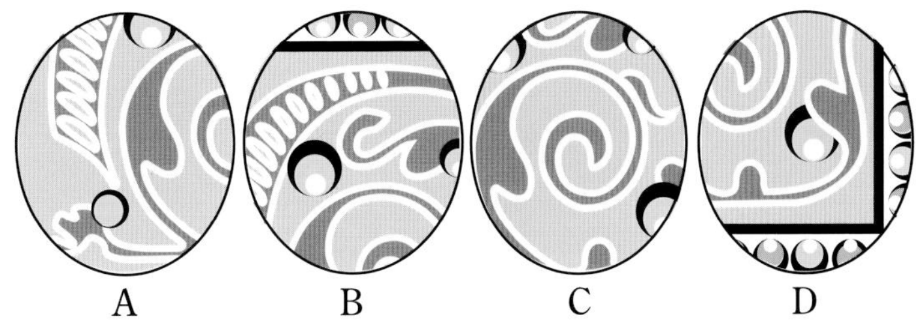

24.

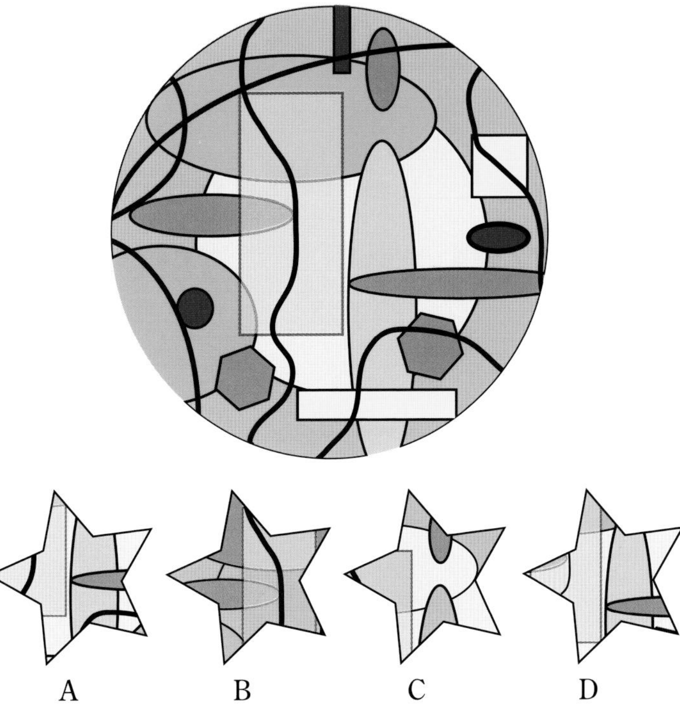

MATRIX

- **One piece from each of the matrices is missing.**
- **To complete each matrix, choose the most appropriate option from the choices given.**

1.

A

B

C

D

2.

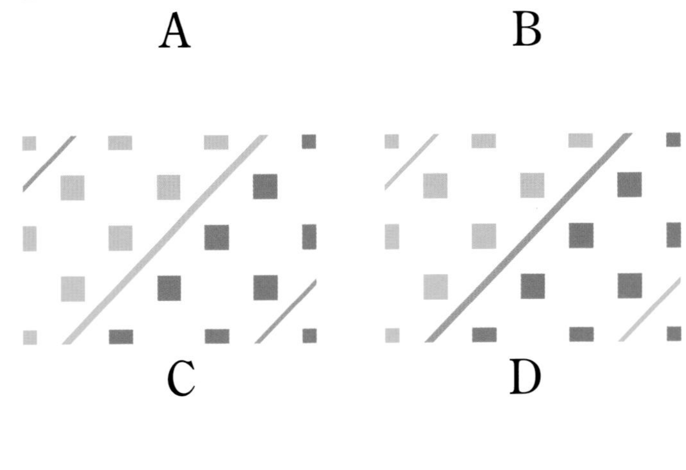

3.

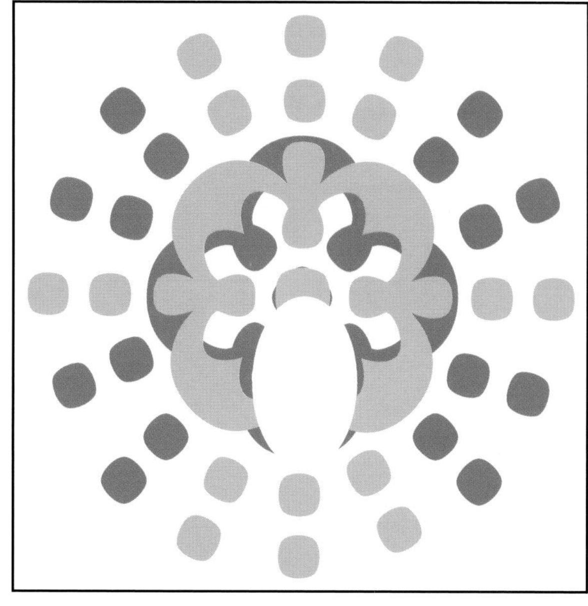

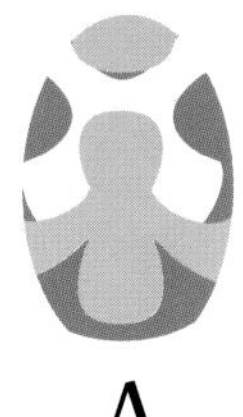

A

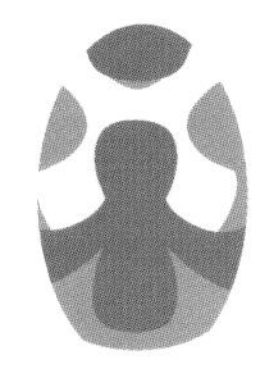

B

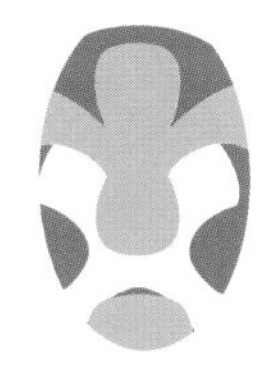

C

D

4.

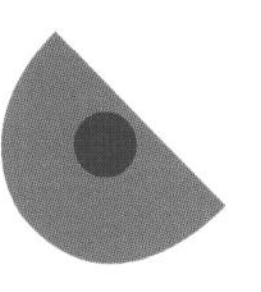

A

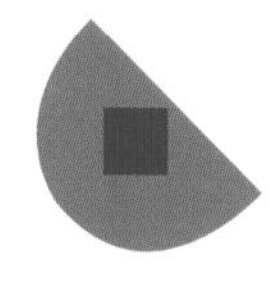

B

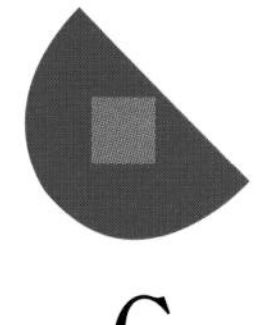

C

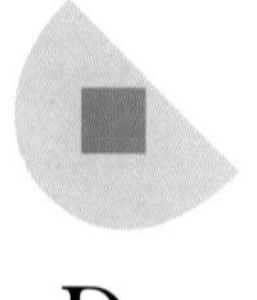

D

5.

A

B

C

D

6.

A

B

C

D

7.

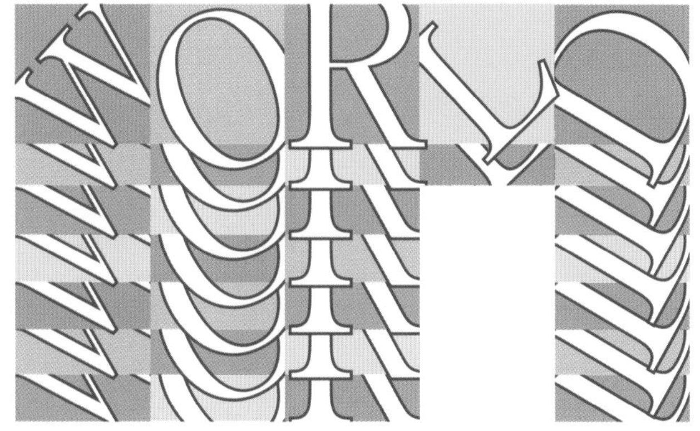

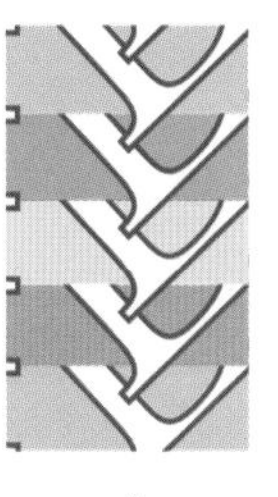

A

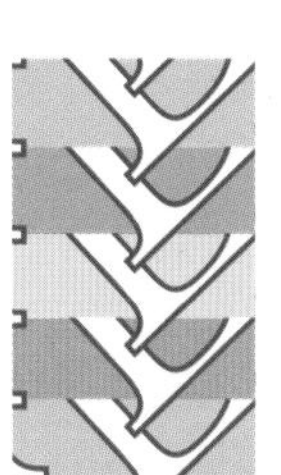

B

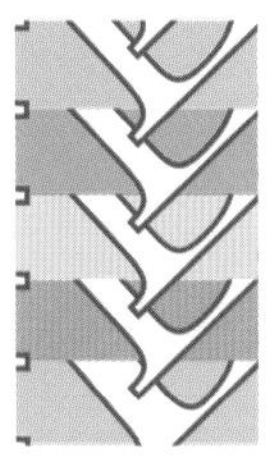

C

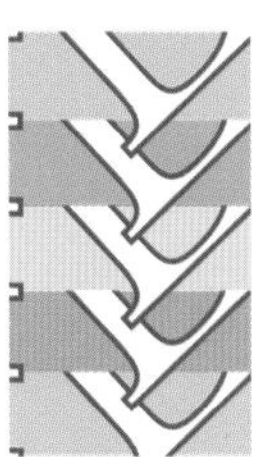

D

8.

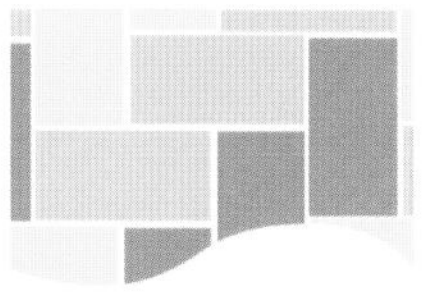

A

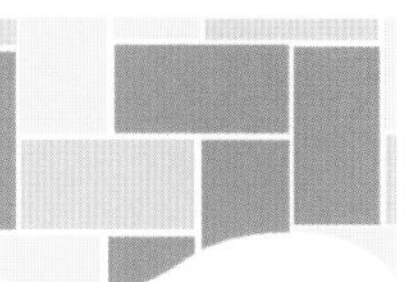

B

C

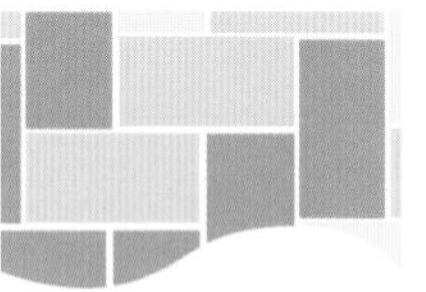

D

9.

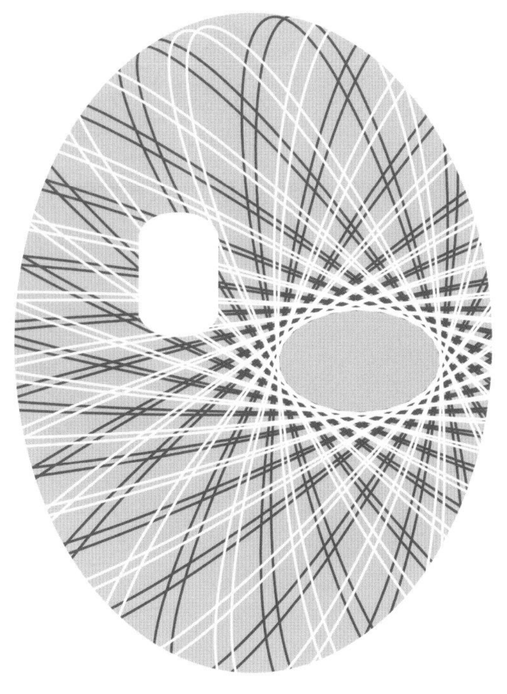

A

B

C

D

10.

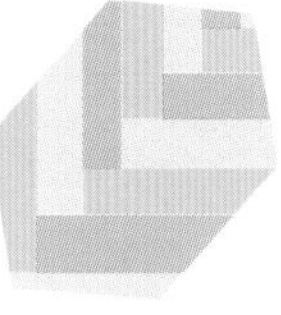

A

B

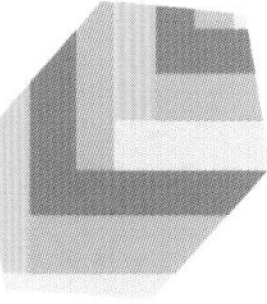

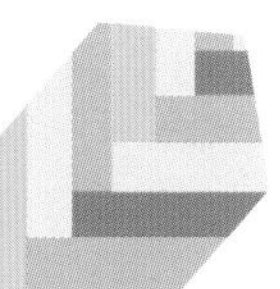

C

D

11.

A

B

C

D

12.

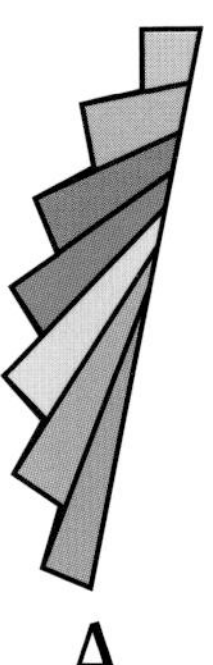

A

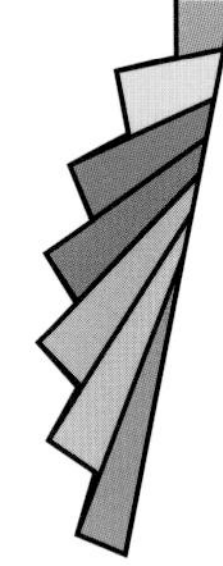

B

C

D

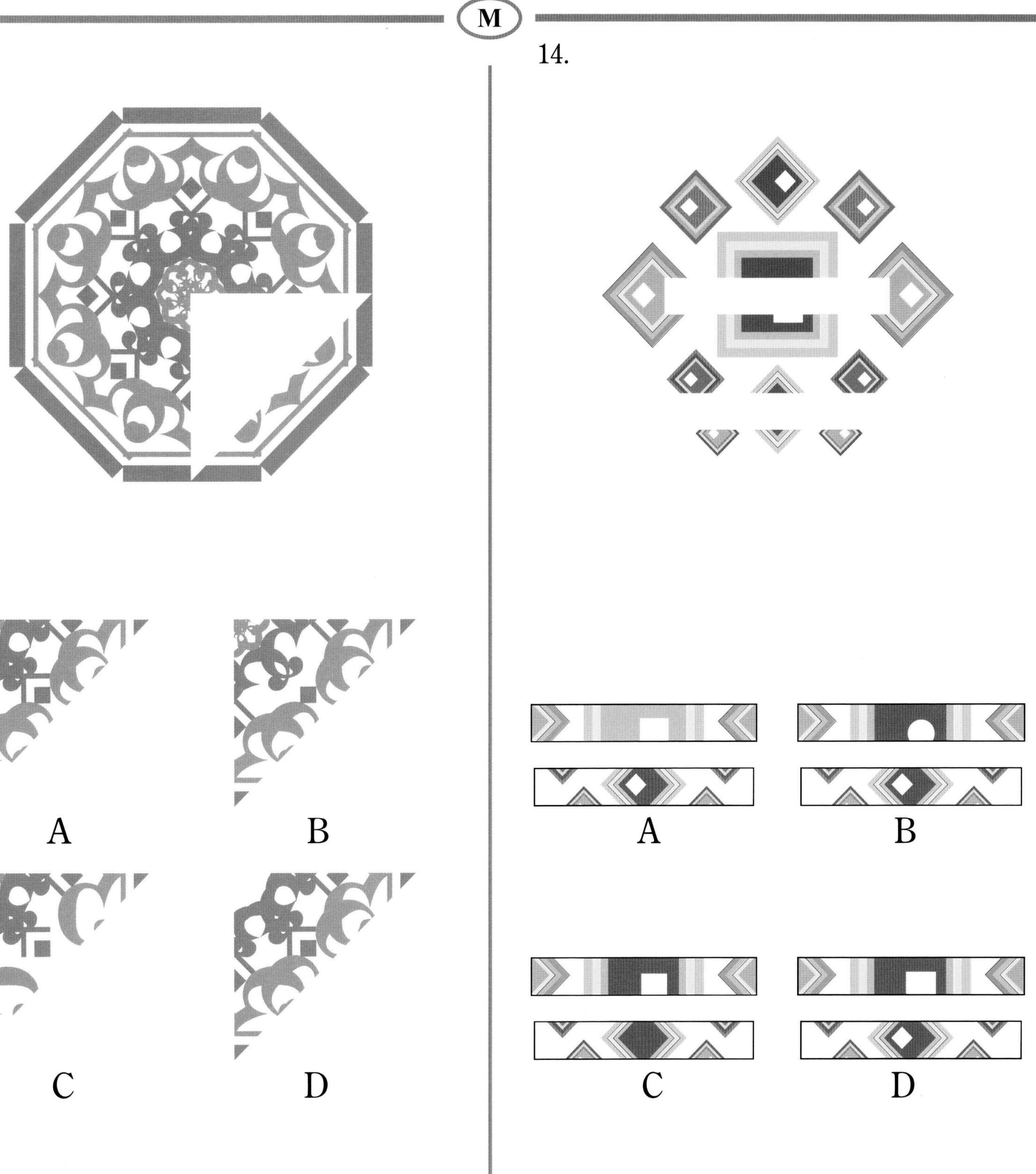
13.
A
B
C
D
14.
A
B
C
D

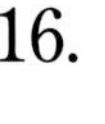

15.

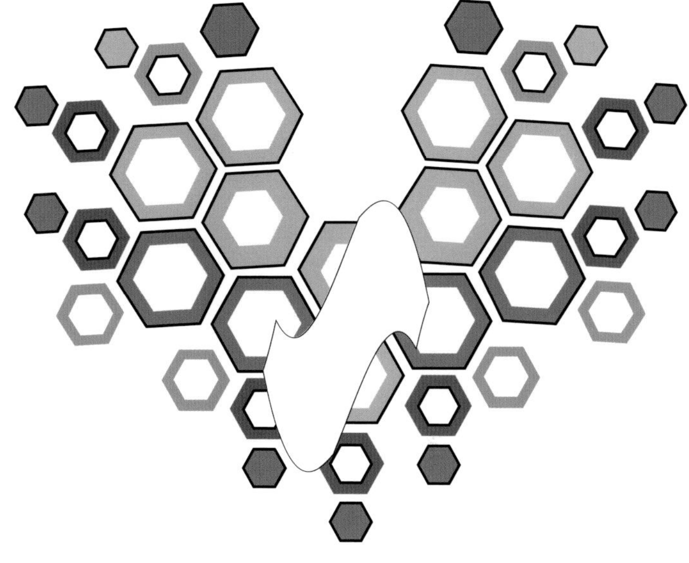

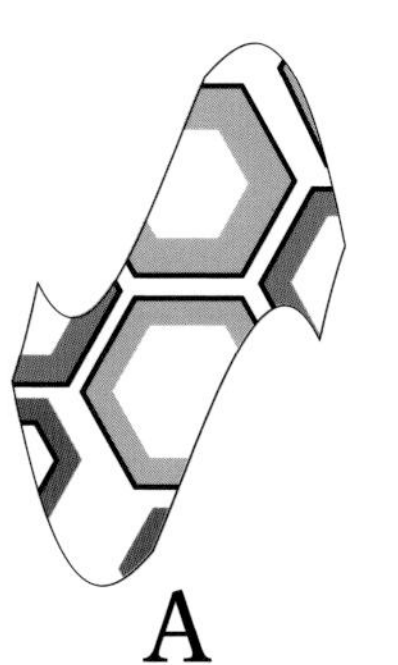

A

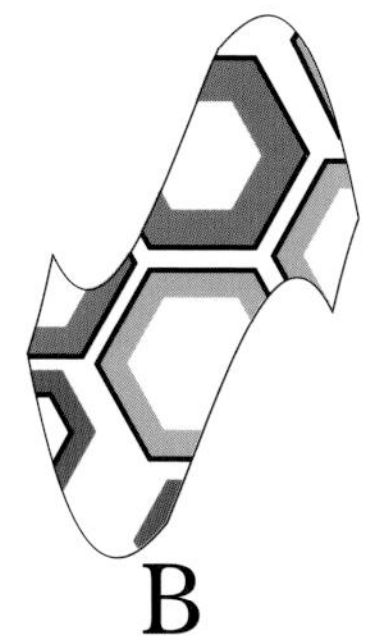

B

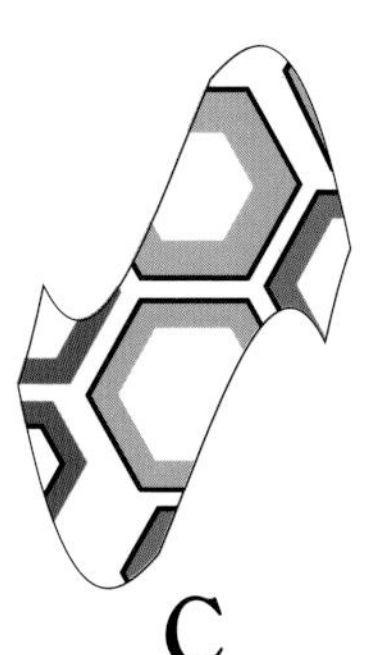

C

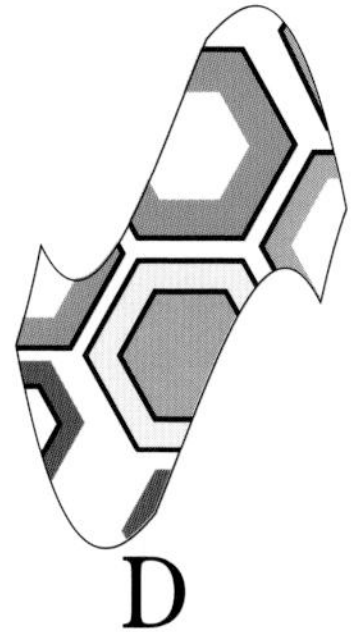

D

16.

A

B

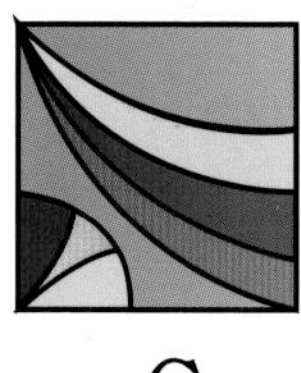

C

D

17.

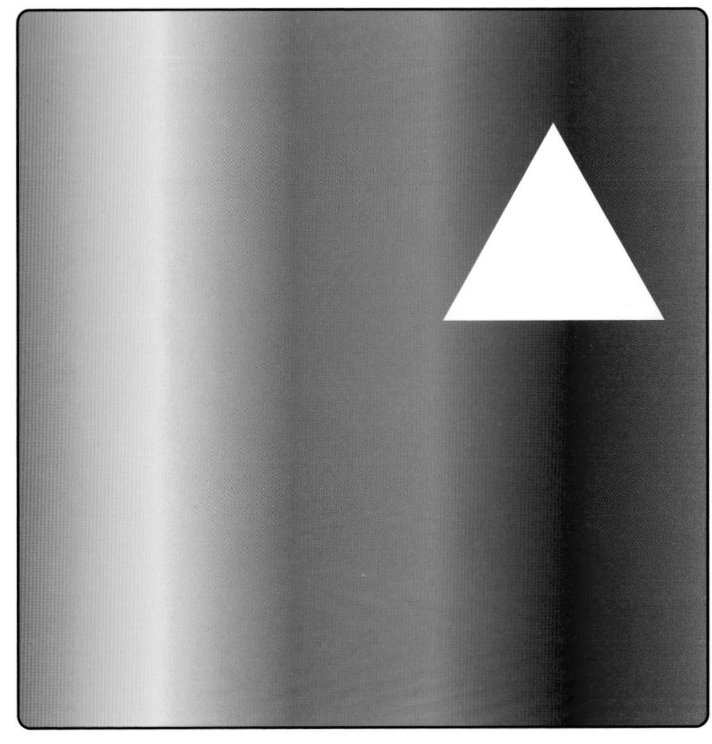

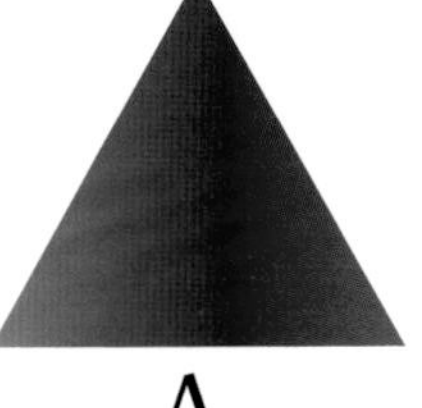

A

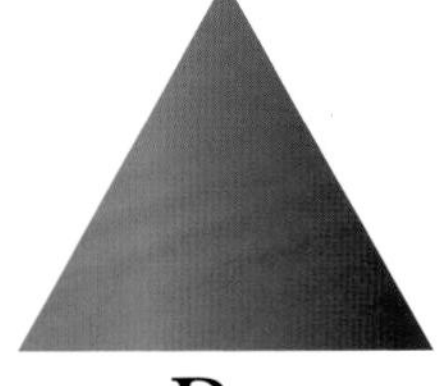

B

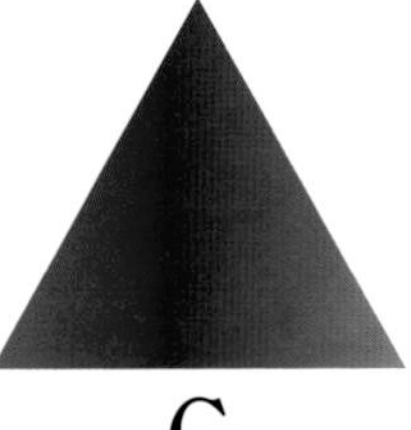

C

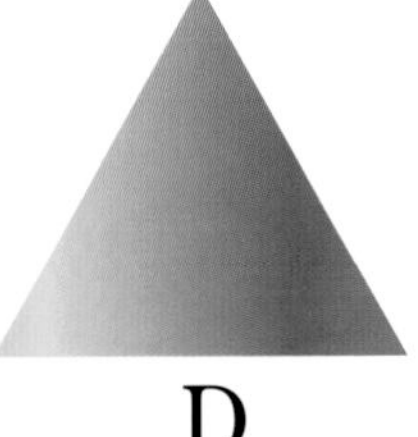

D

18.

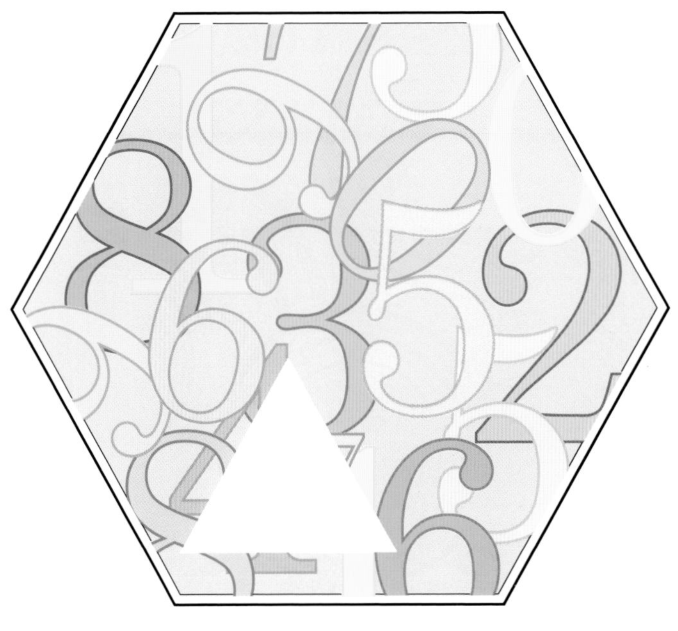

A

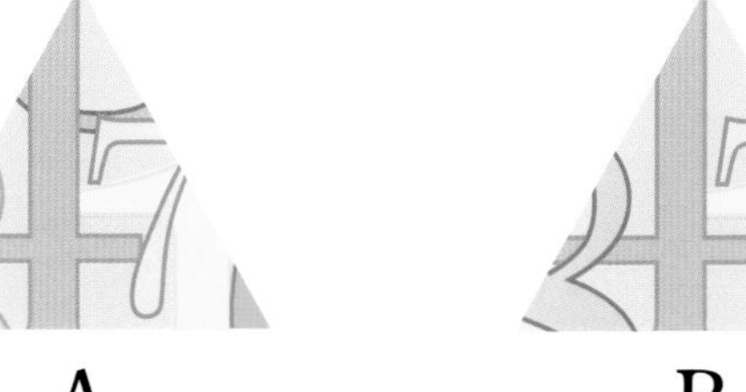

B

C

D

19.

A

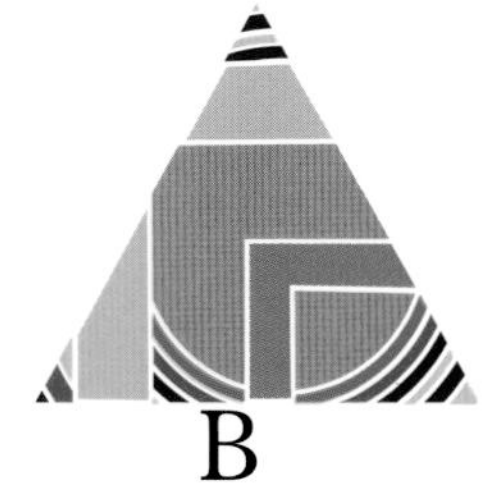

B

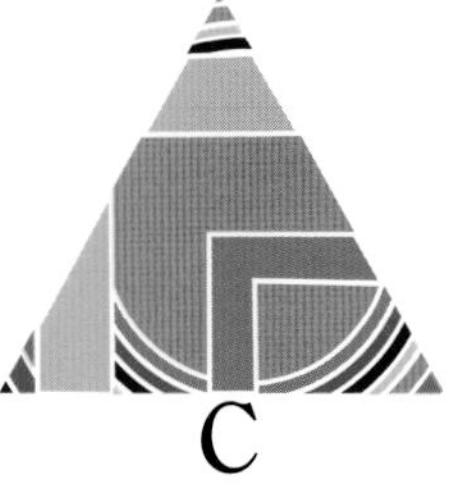

C

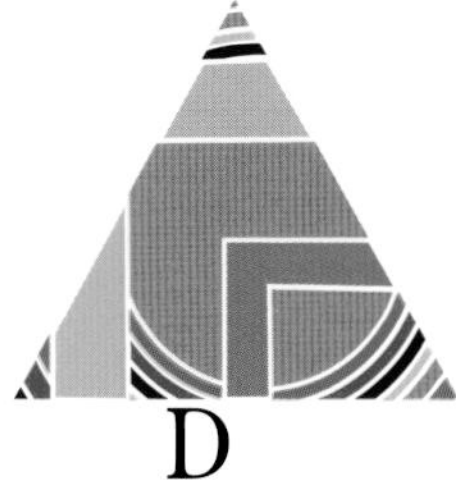

D

20.

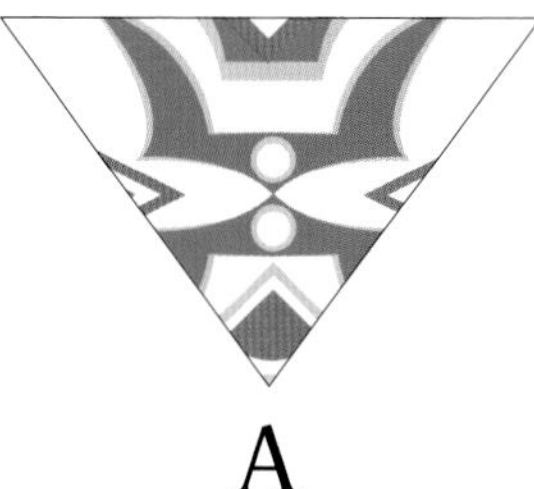

A

B

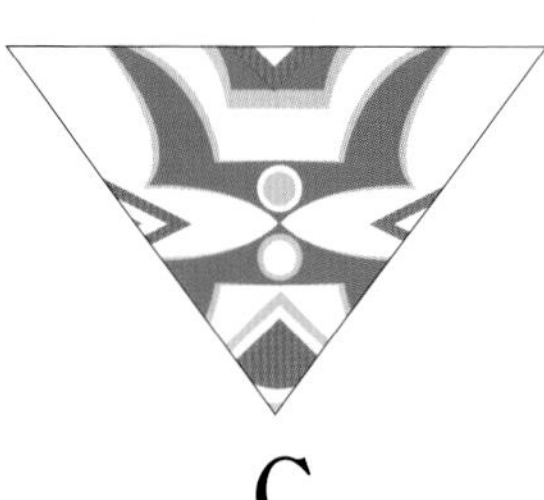

C

D

21.

A

B

C

D

22.

A B

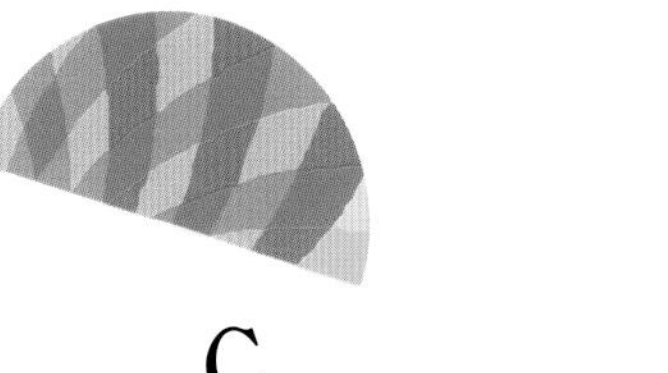

C

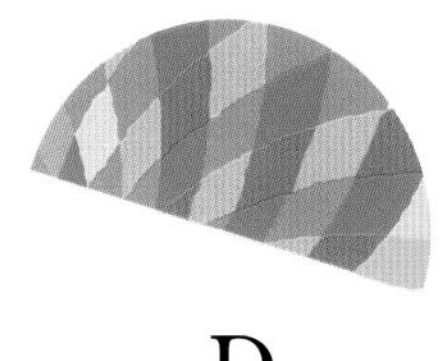

D

23.

A

B

C

D

24.

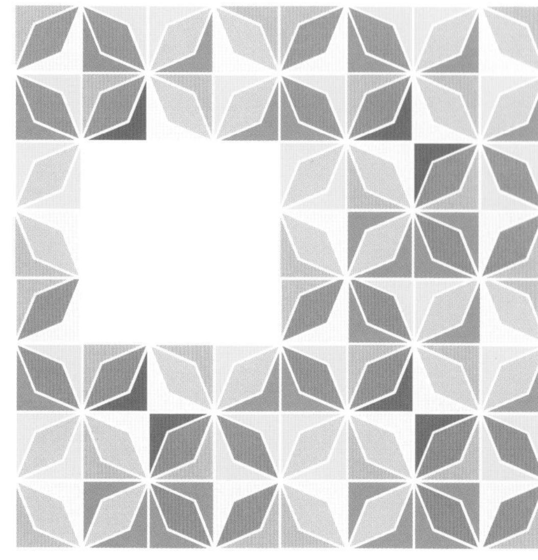

A

B

C

D

WORD POWER

- **Each puzzle in this section has specific instructions.**
- **Read each question carefully before you solve the puzzle.**
- **Try solving puzzles in the easy and medium category in two minutes, and puzzles in the difficult category in one minute.**

1.
Unscramble the letters to get a 9 letter word. Make as many 4 - 9 letter words from the letters given below. Remember each word can use a letter only once.

I E T
E G A
N R M

2.
Unscramble the letters to get a 9 letter word. Make as many 4 - 9 letter words from the letters given below. Remember each word can use a letter only once.

P
A M
R A T
E R
E

3.
How many words of 4 or more letters can you make from the letters shown? Each word can use a letter only once and must contain the central letter. There should be one 10 letter word.

E S C S F L U S C
L

4.
How many words of 3 or more letters can you make from the letters shown? Each word can use a letter only once and must contain the central letter. There should be one 7 letter word.

5.
How many words of 4 or more letters can you make from the letters shown? Each word can use a letter only once and must contain the central letter. There should be one 9 letter word.

B R A A S T C O
D

6.
How many words of 3 or more letters can you make from the letters shown? Each word can use a letter only once and must contain the central letter. There should be one 11 letter word.

7.
How many words of 4 or more letters can you make from the letters shown? Each word can use a letter only once and must contain the central letter. There should be one 9 letter word.

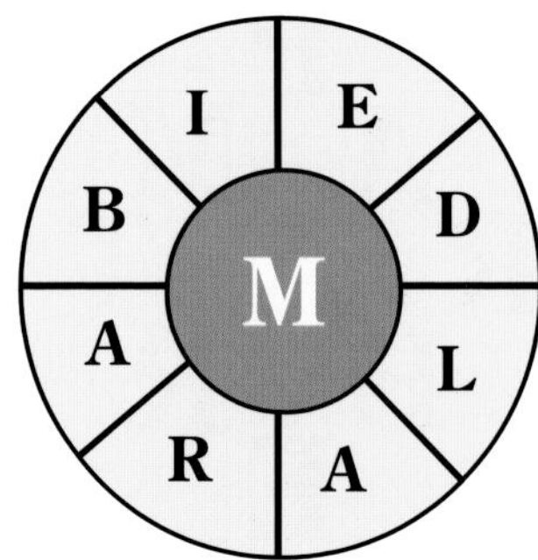

8.
How many words of 4 or more letters can you make from the letters shown? Each word can use a letter only once and must contain the central letter. There should be one 9 letter word.

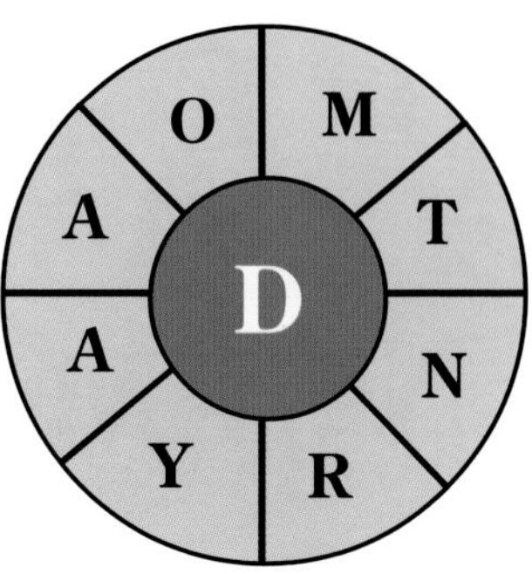

9.
How many words of 3 or more letters can you make from the letters shown? Each word can use a letter only once and must contain the central letter. There should be one 7 letter word.

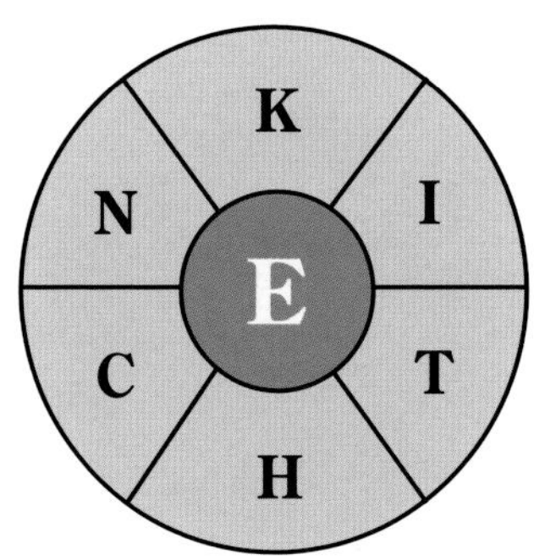

10.
How many words of 4 or more letters can you make from the letters shown? Each word can use a letter only once and must contain the central letter. There should be one 8 letter word.

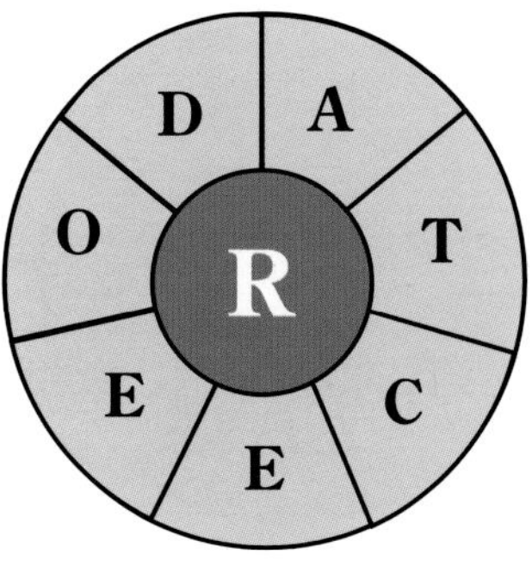

11.
How many words of 4 or more letters can you make from the letters shown? Each word can use a letter only once and must contain the central letter. There should be one 9 letter word.

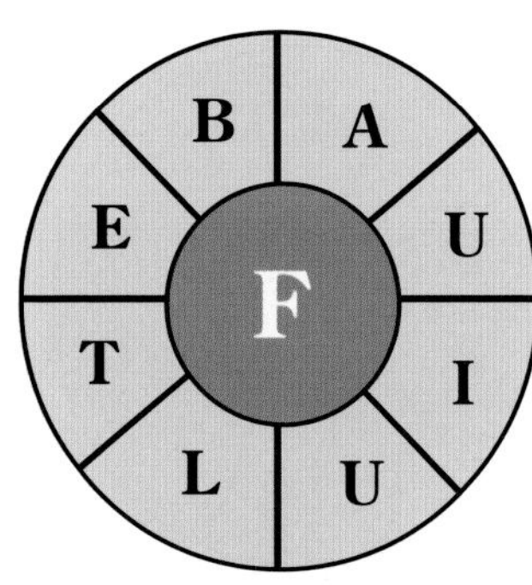

12.
How many words of 4 or more letters can you make from the letters shown? Each word can use a letter only once and must contain the central letter. There should be one 13 letter word.

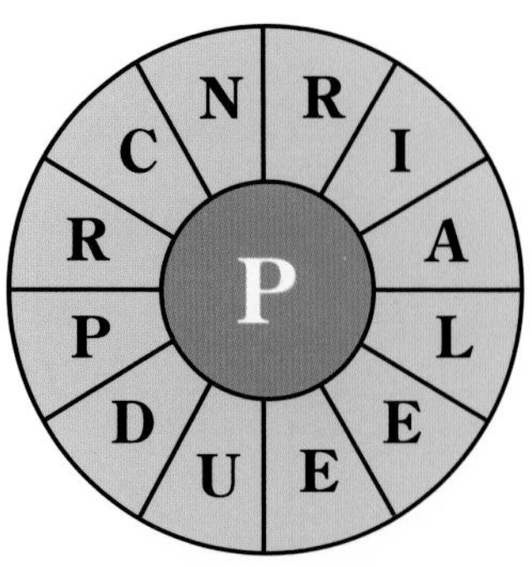

13\. How many words of 3 or more letters can you make from the letters shown? Each word can use a letter only once and must contain the central letter. There should be one 9 letter word.

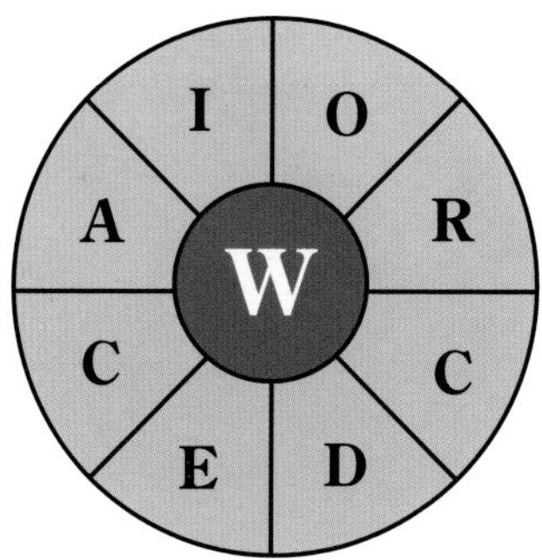

14\. How many words of 3 or more letters can you make from the letters shown? Each word can use a letter only once and must contain the central letter. There should be one 7 letter word.

15\. How many words of 3 or more letters can you make from the letters shown? Each word can use a letter only once and must contain the central letter. There should be one 9 letter word.

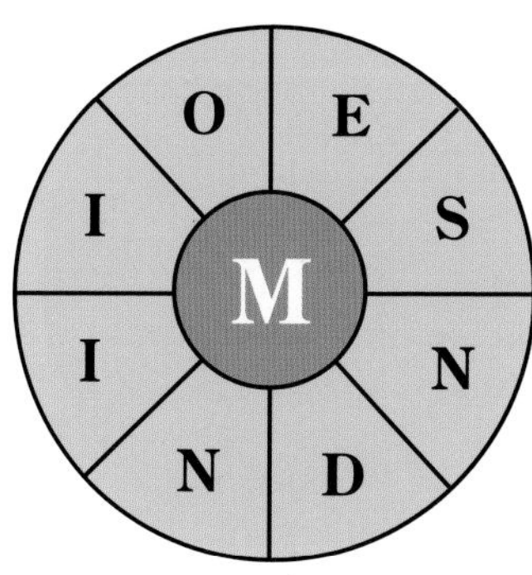

16\. How many words of 4 or more letters can you make from the letters shown? Each word can use a letter only once and must contain the central letter. There should be one 12 letter word.

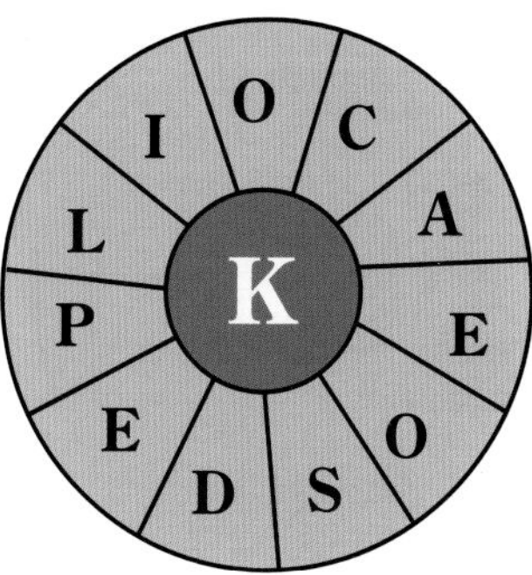

17\. How many words of 3 or more letters can you make from the letters shown? Each word can use a letter only once and must contain the central letter. There should be one 8 letter word.

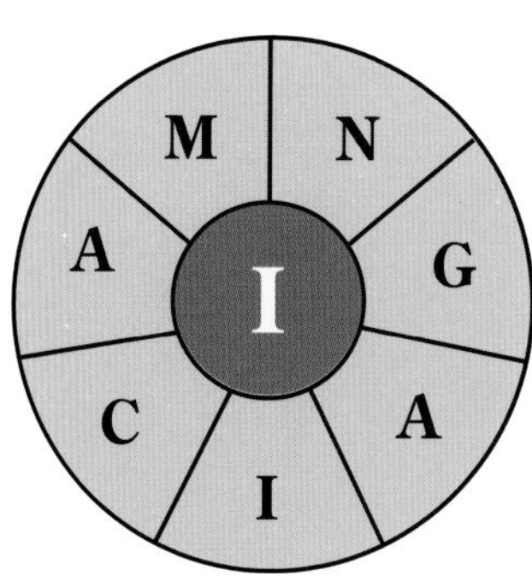

18\. How many words of 4 or more letters can you make from the letters shown? Each word can use a letter only once and must contain the central letter. There should be one 8 letter word.

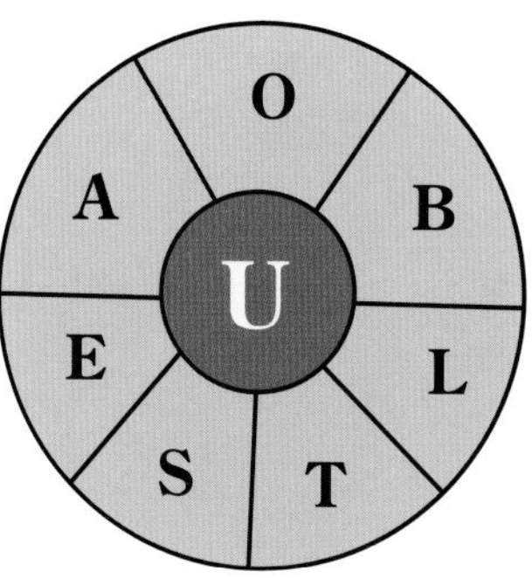

19.

How many words of 4 or more letters can you make from the letters shown? Each word can use a letter only once and must contain the central letter. There should be one 10 letter word.

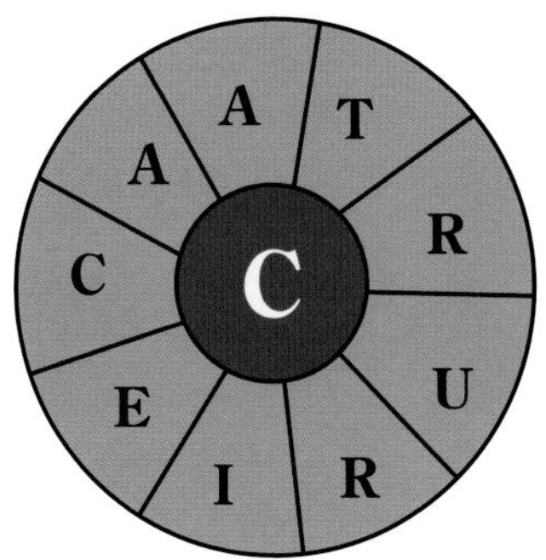

20.

How many words of 3 or more letters can you make from the letters shown? Each word can use a letter only once and must contain the central letter. There should be one 9 letter word.

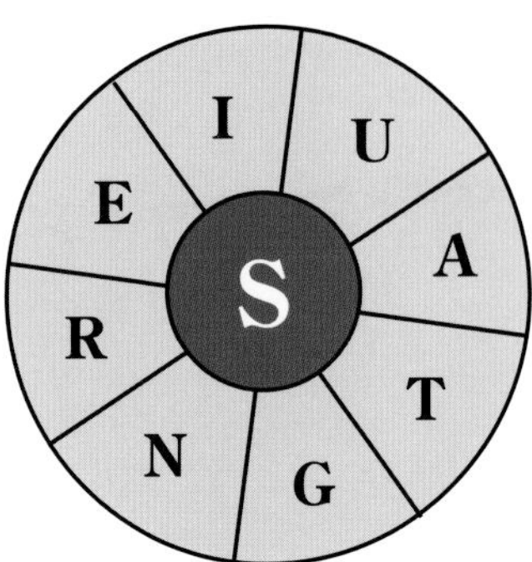

21.

How many words of 4 or more letters can you make from the letters shown? Each word can use a letter only once and must contain the central letter. There should be one 13 letter word.

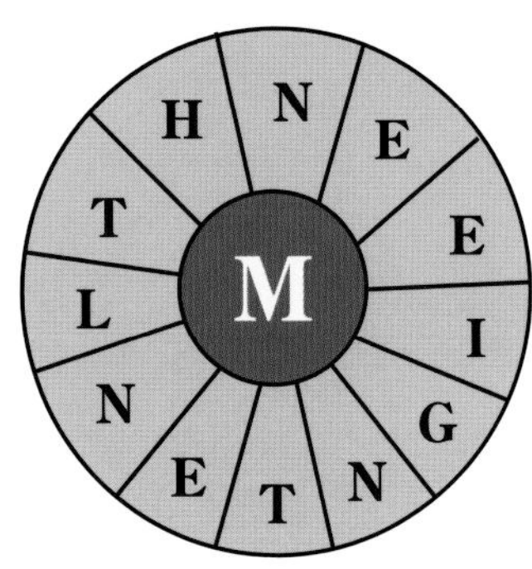

22.

How many words of 4 or more letters can you make from the letters shown? Each word can use a letter only once and must contain the central letter. There should be one 10 letter word.

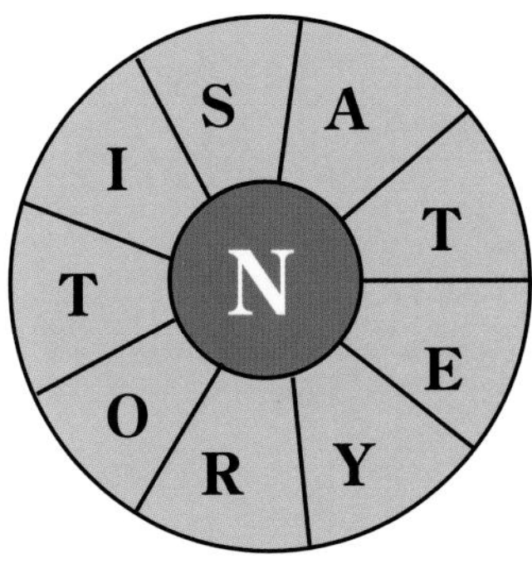

23.

Unscramble the letters to get a 10 letter word. Make as many 3 - 10 letter words from the letters given below. Remember each word can use a letter only once.

24.

Unscramble the letters to get a 11 letter word. Make as many 4 - 11 letter words from the letters given below. Remember each word can use a letter only once.

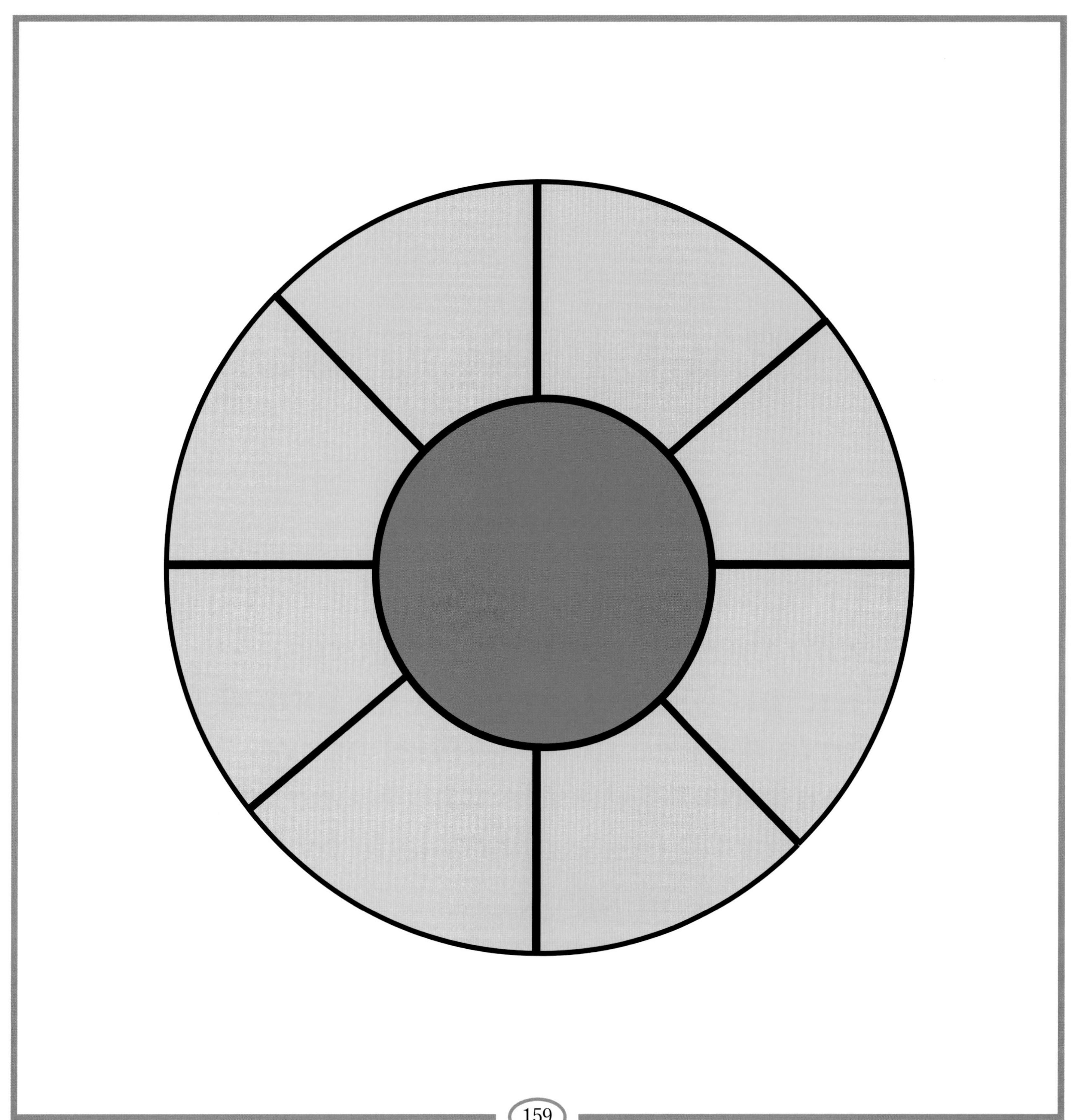

SPACE PERCEPTION

- **In this category, you will be dealing with three dimensional figures.**
- **The problem figure can be folded to form a three dimensional figure.**
- **You have to decide which one of the answer figures can be made by folding the problem figure.**
- **There is only one right answer.**

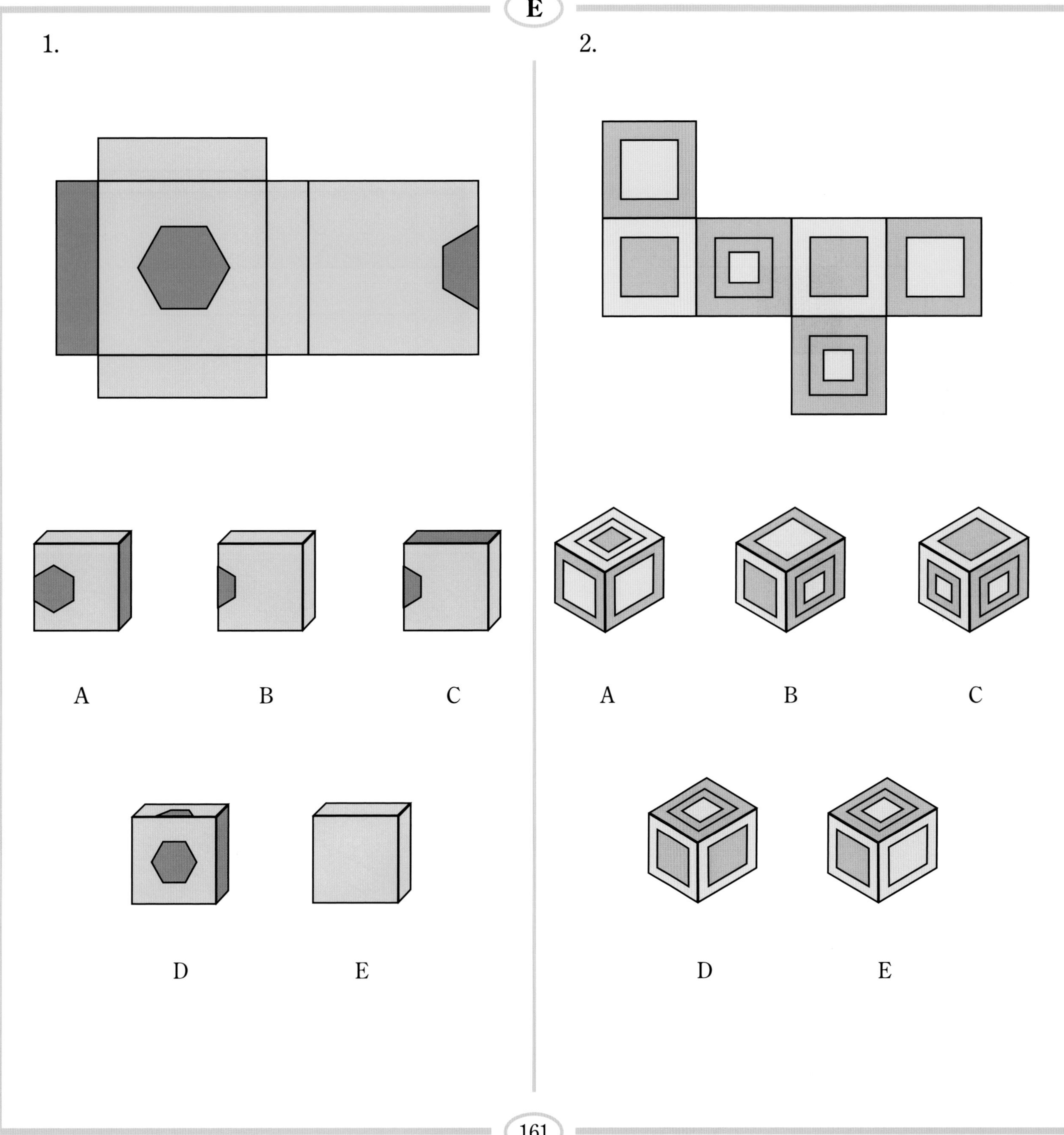
1.
A
B
C
D
E
2.
A
B
C
D
E

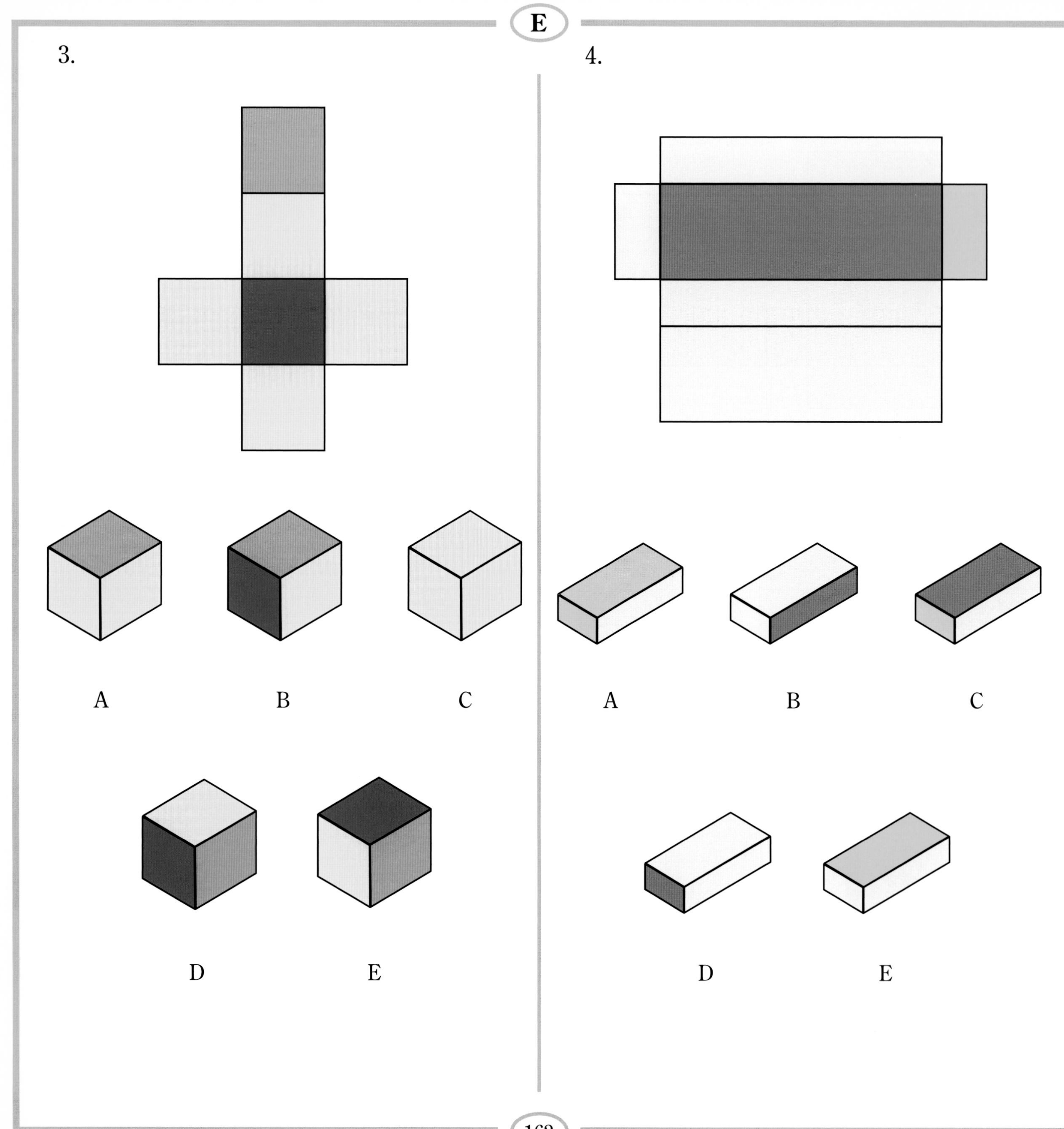
3.
A
B
C
D
E
4.
A
B
C
D
E

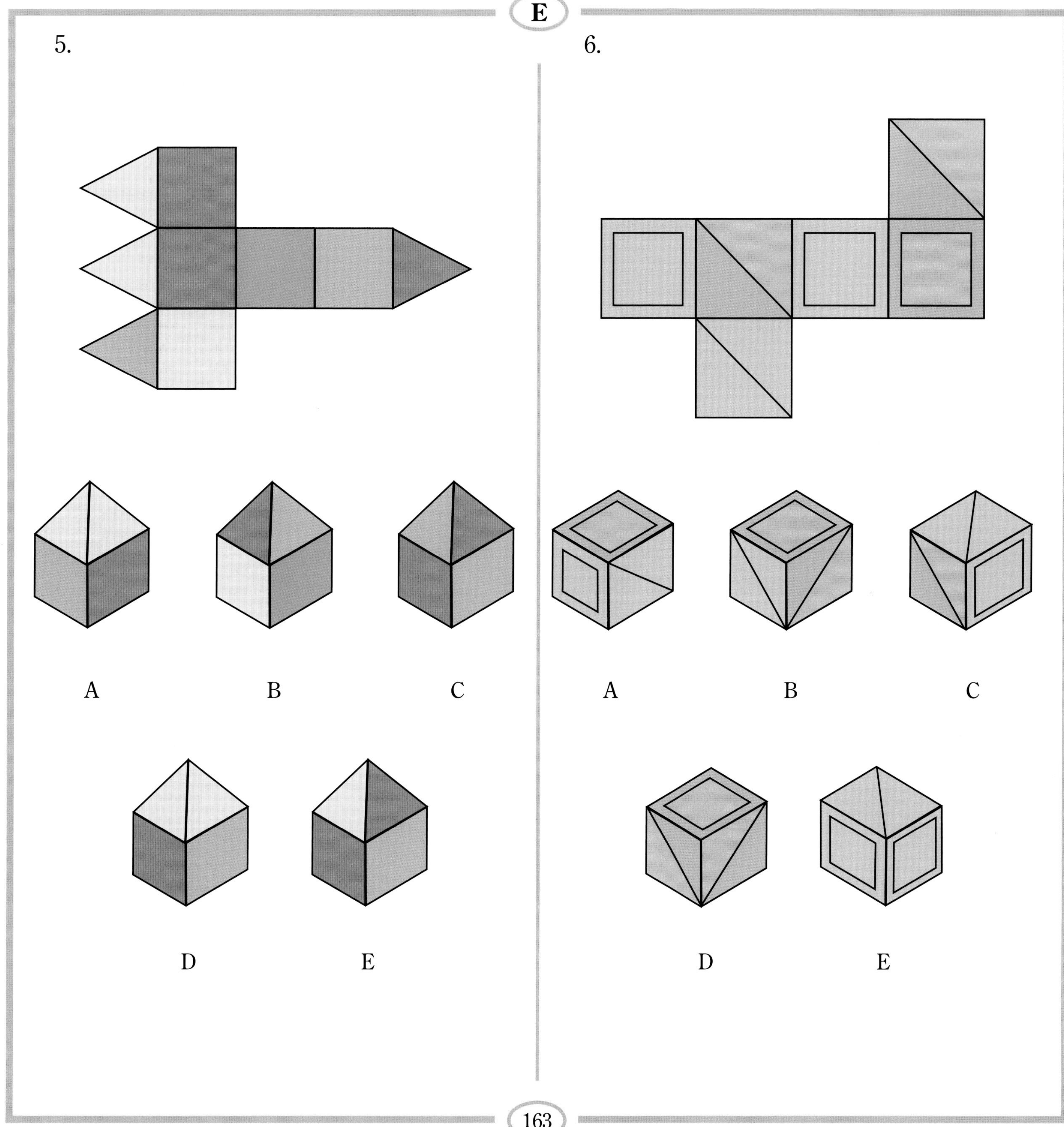
5.
6.
A
B
C
D
E
A
B
C
D
E

7.

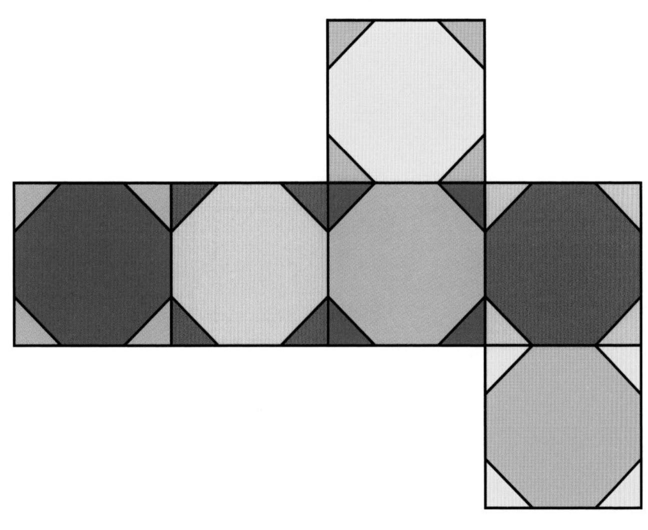

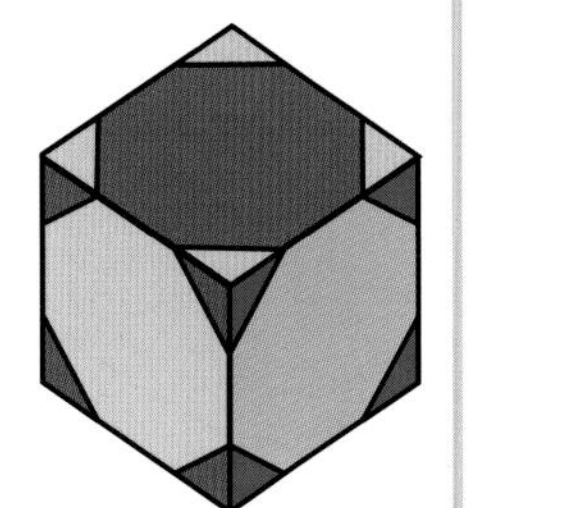

A B C

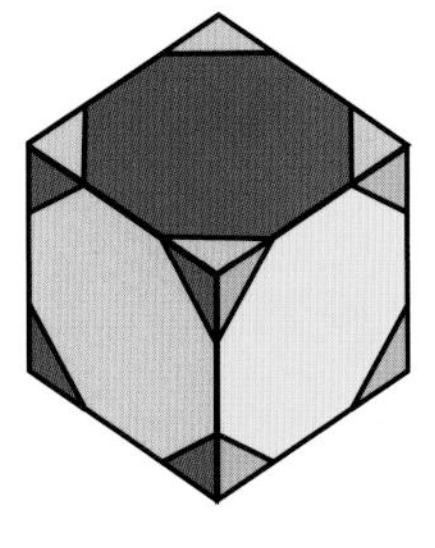

D E

8.

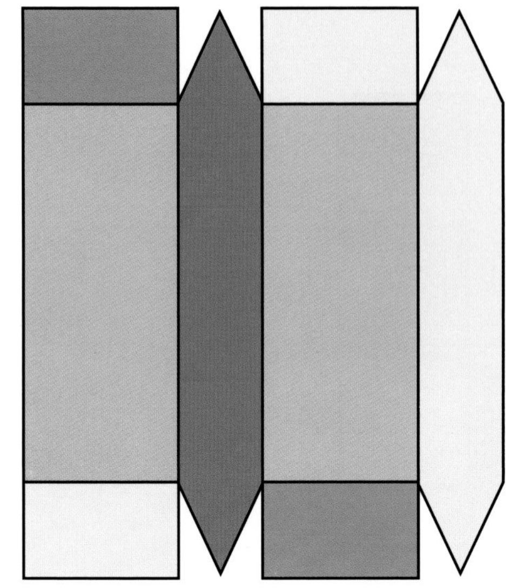

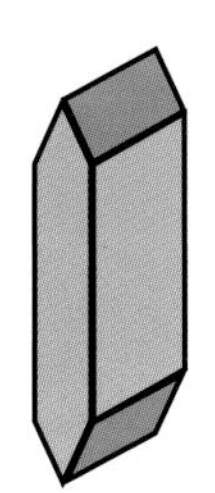

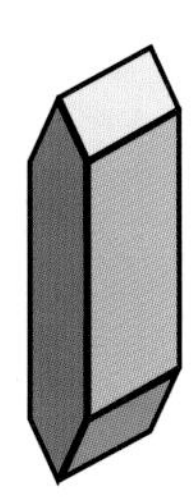

A B C

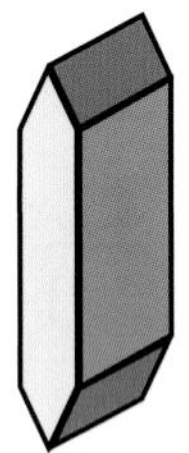

D E

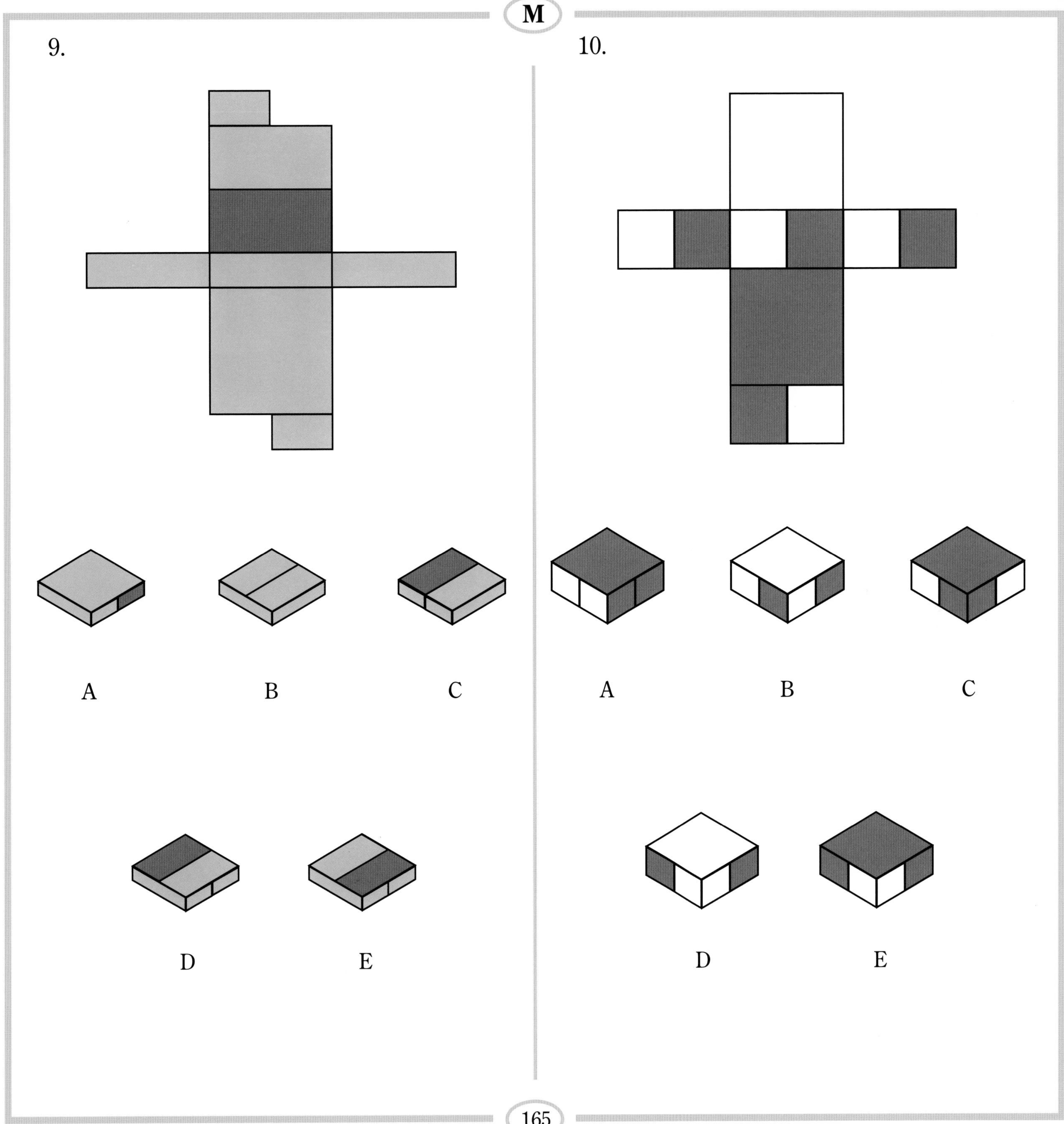
9.
A
B
C
D
E
10.
A
B
C
D
E

11.

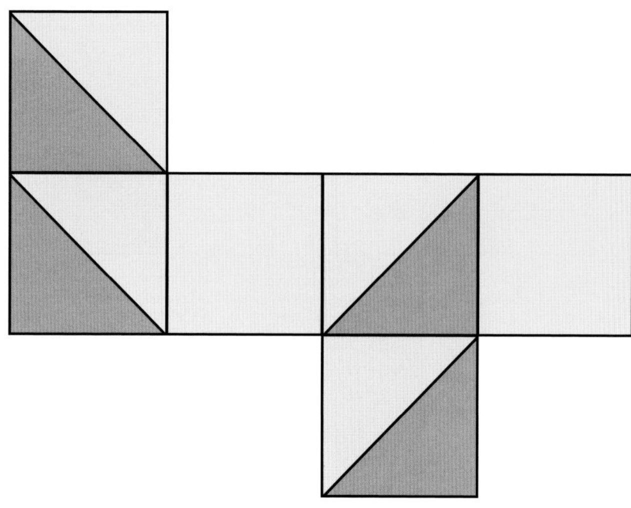

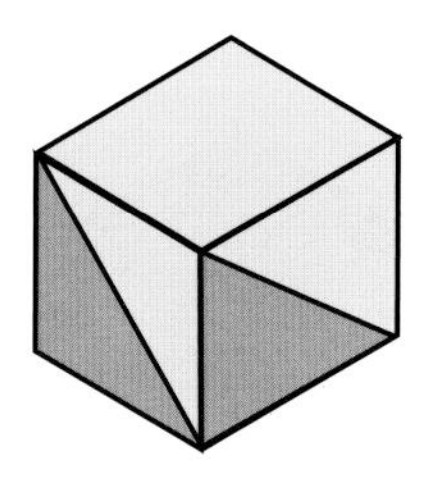

A

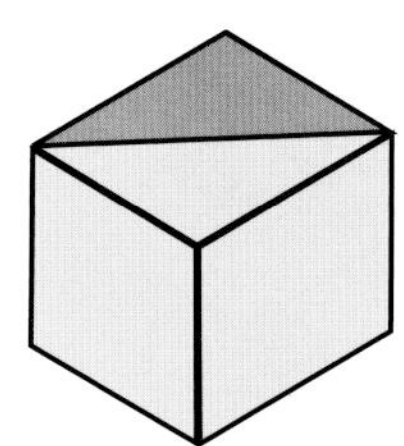

B

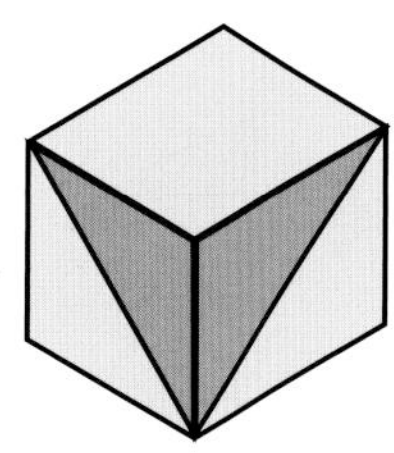

C

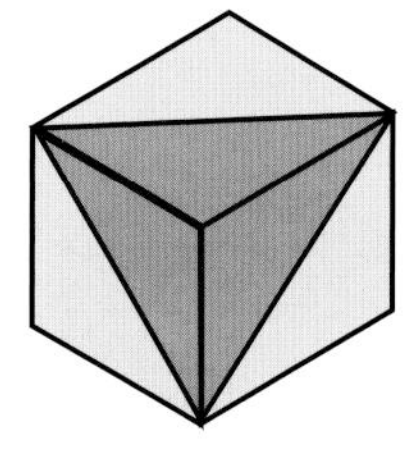

D

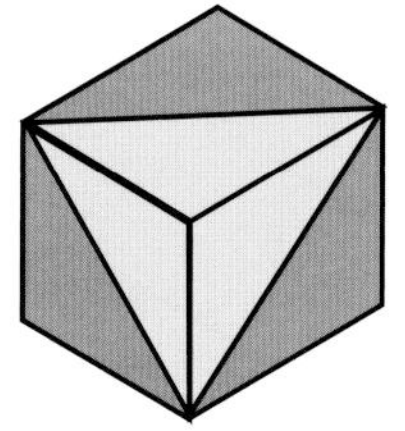

E

12.

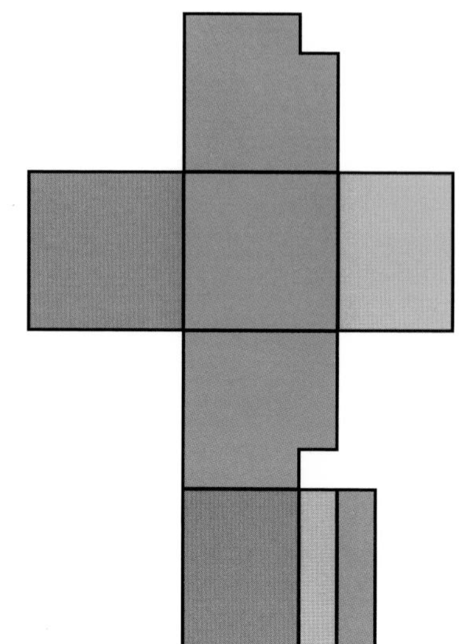

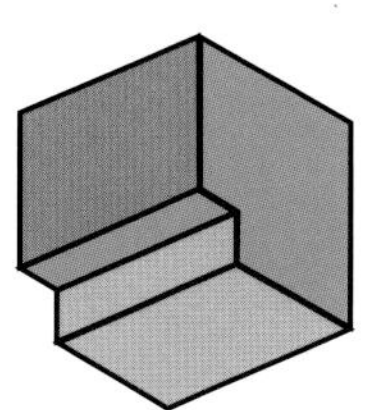

A

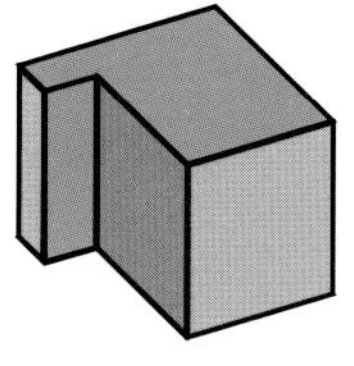

B

C

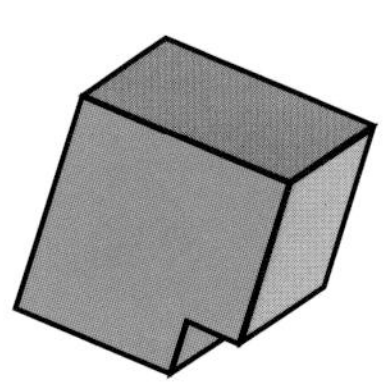

D

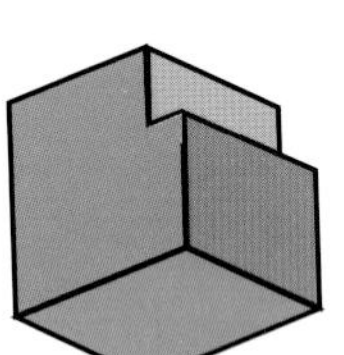

E

13.

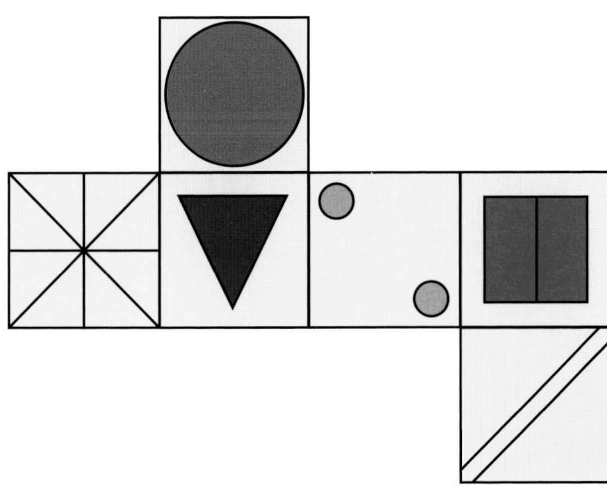

A

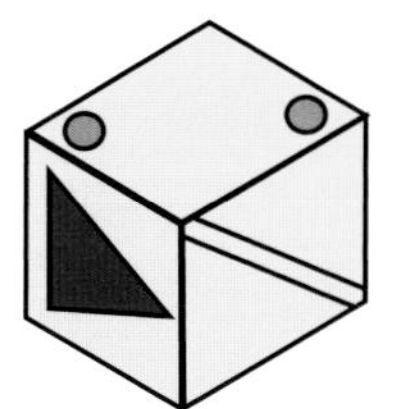

B

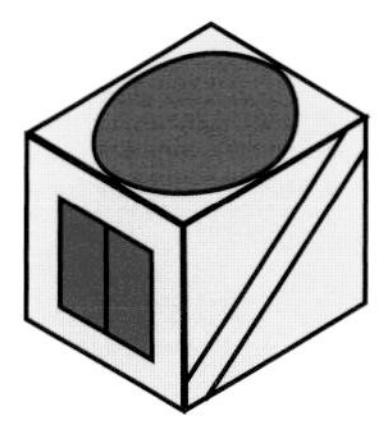

C

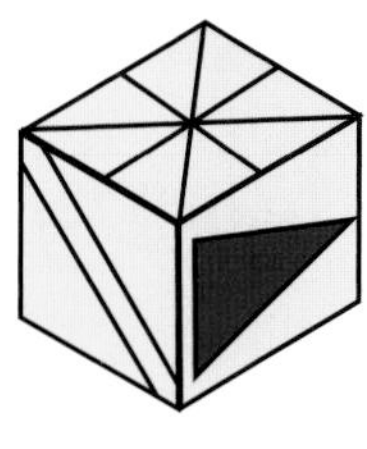

D

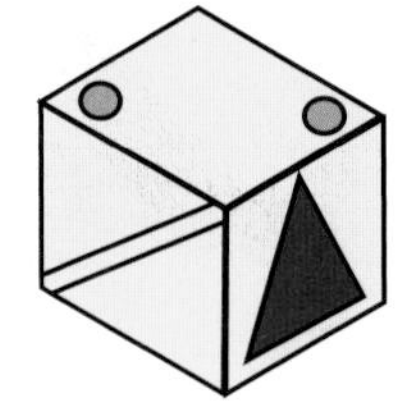

E

14.

A

B

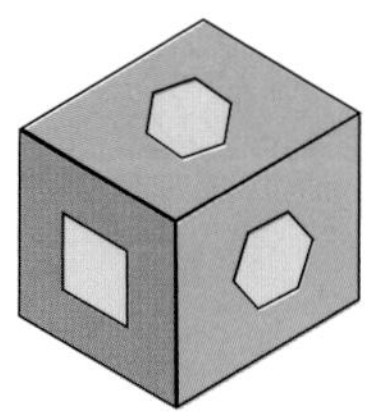

C

D

E

15.

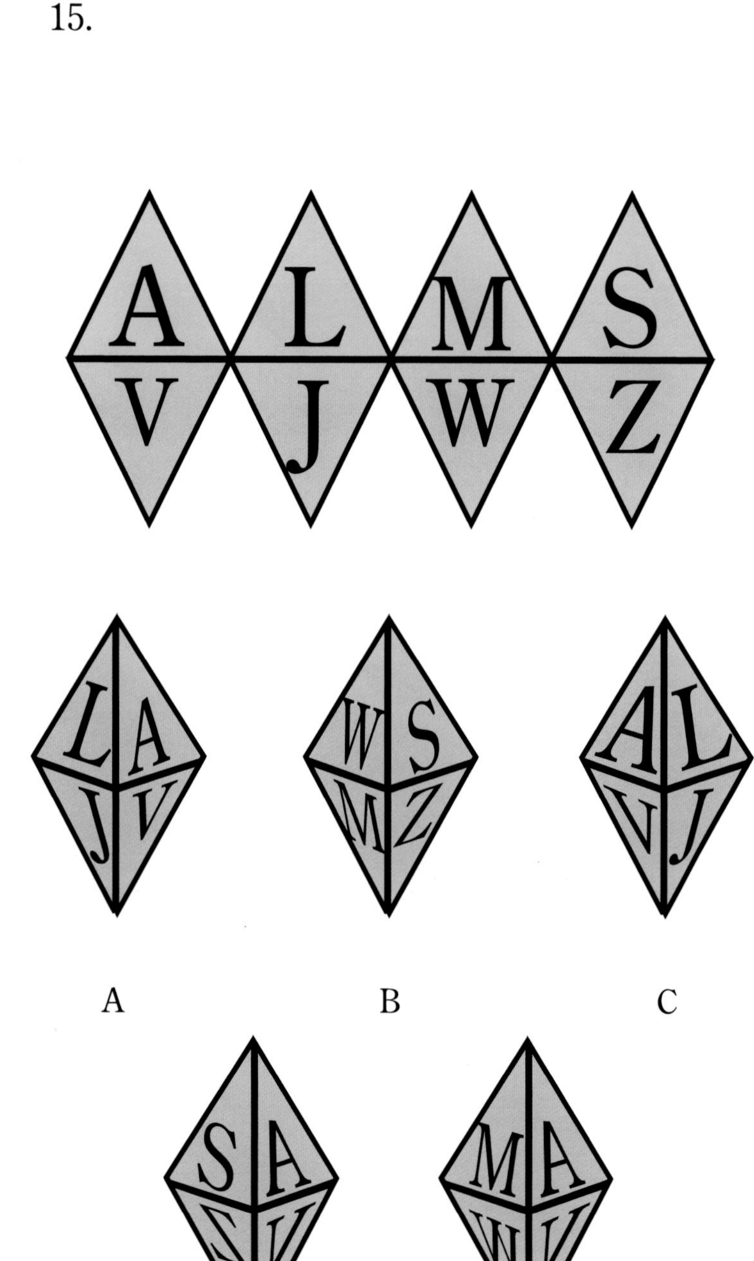

16.

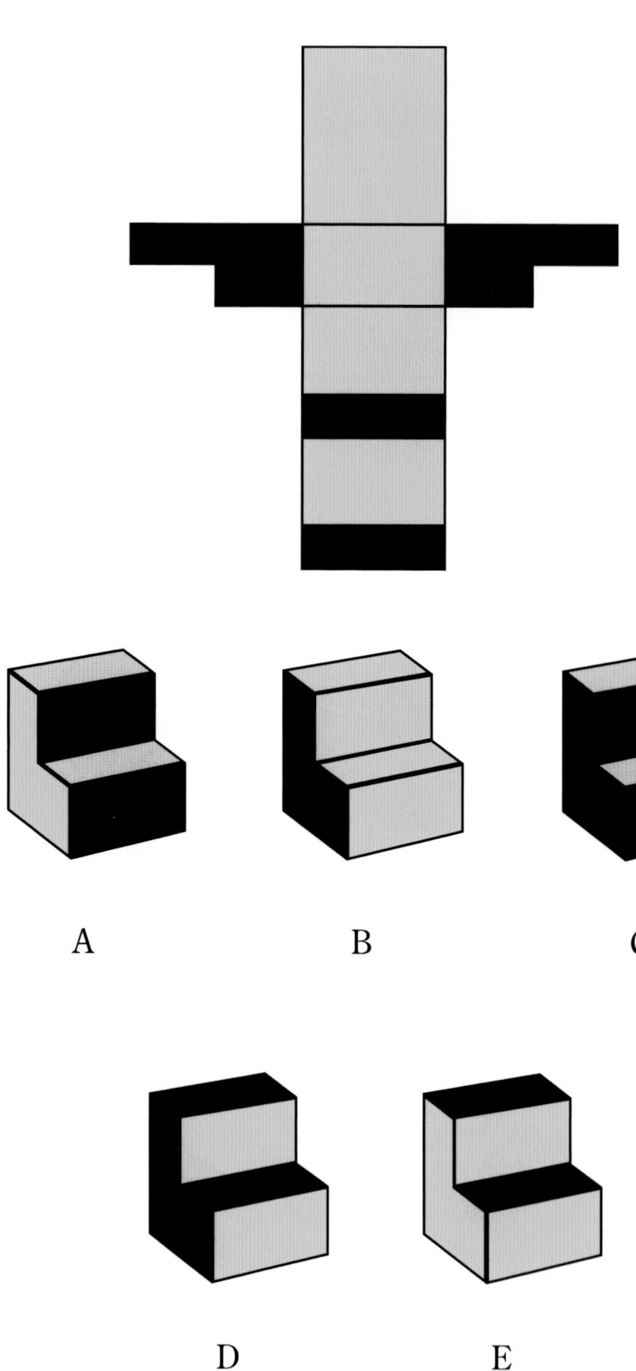

17.

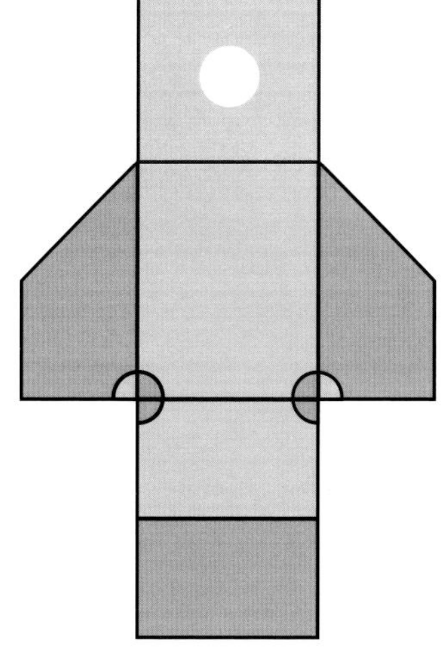

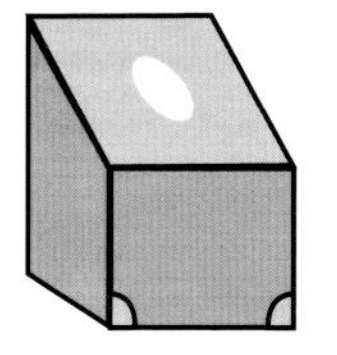

A

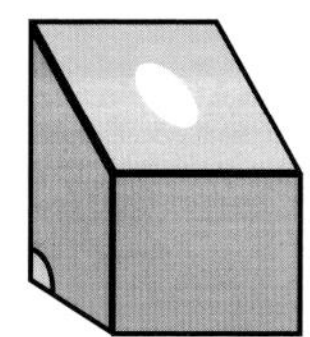

B

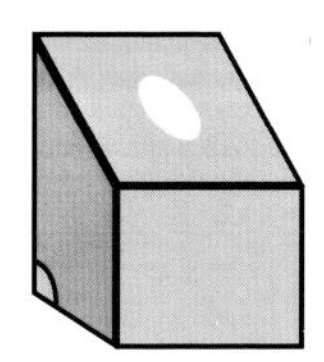

C

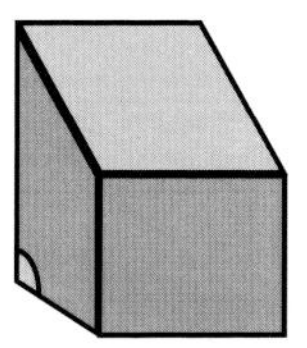

D

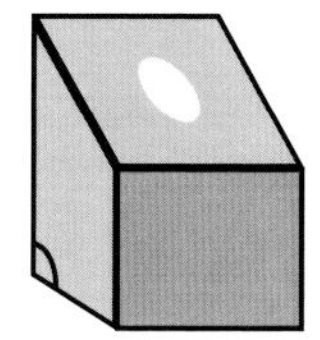

E

18.

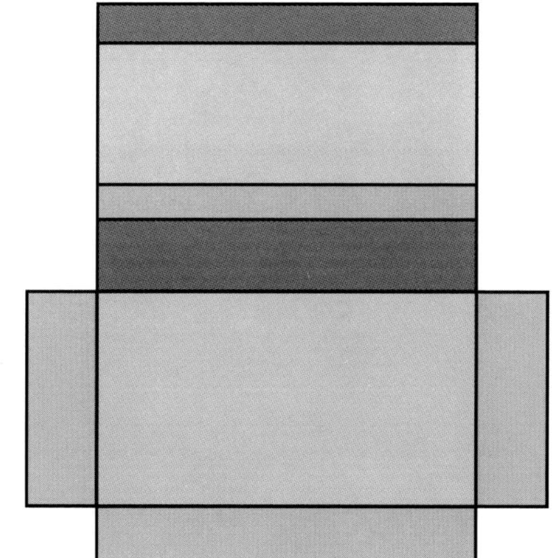

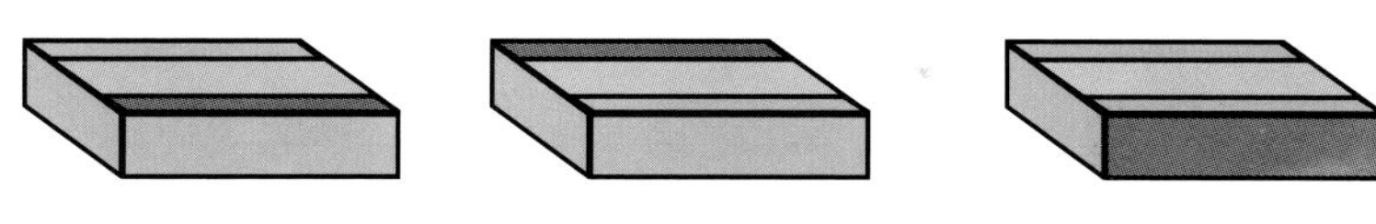

A B C

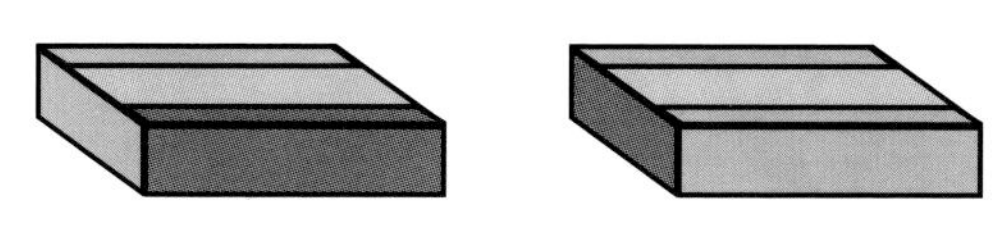

D E

19.

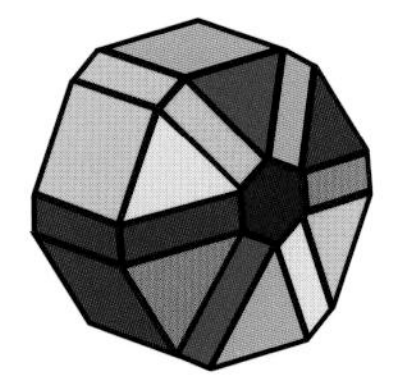

A

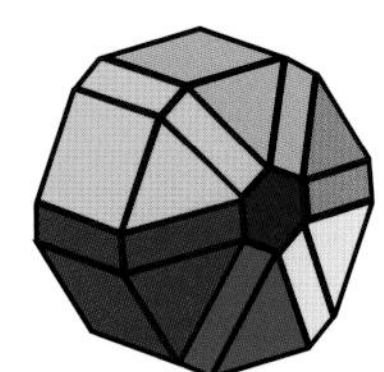

B

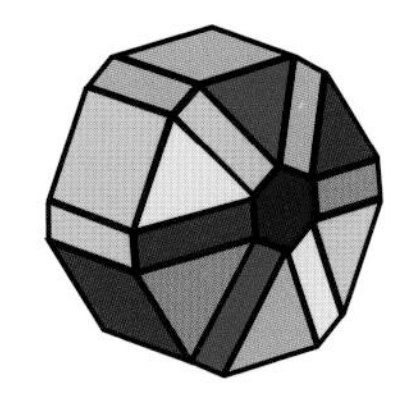

C

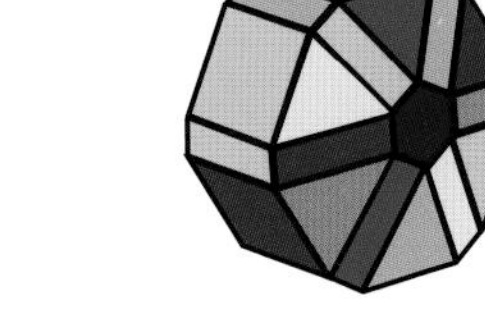

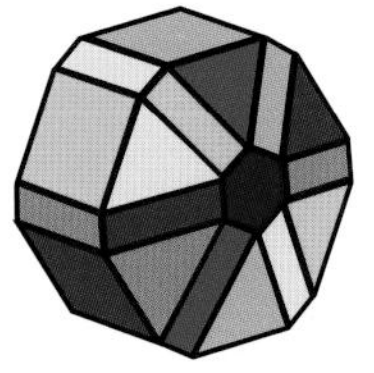

D

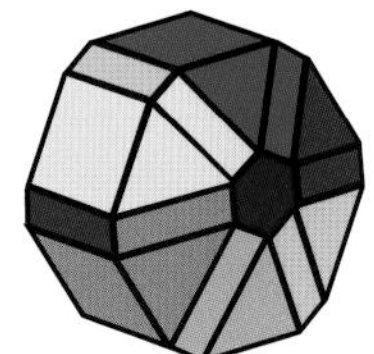

E

20.

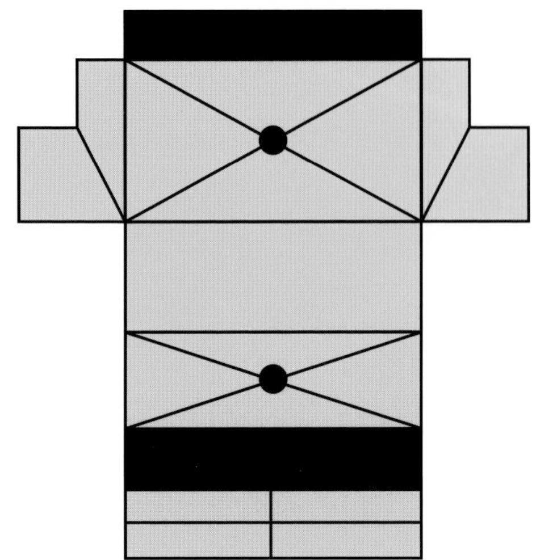

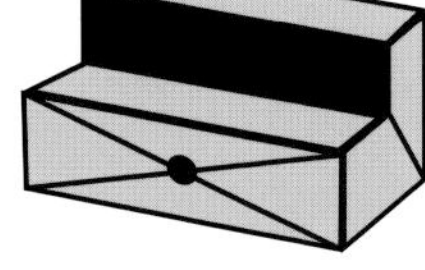

A

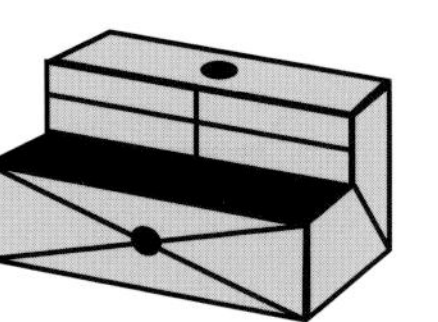

B

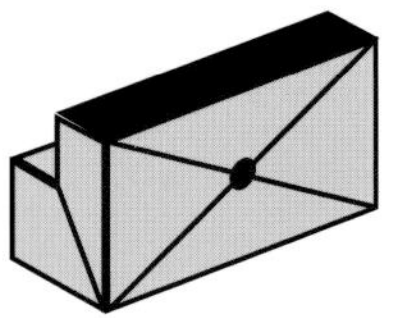

C

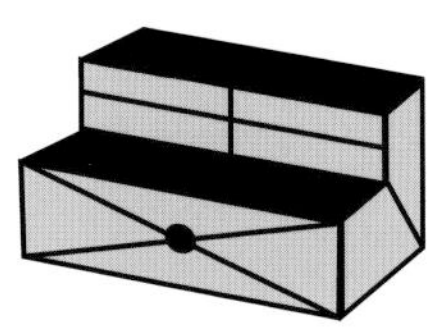

D

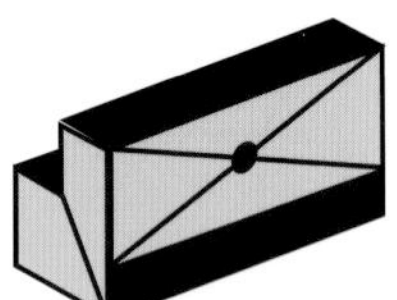

E

21.

A

B

C

D

E

22.

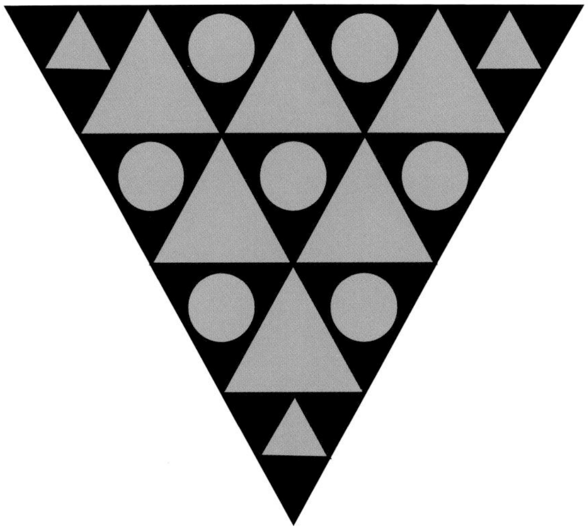

A

B

C

D

E

23.

A

B

C

D

E

24.

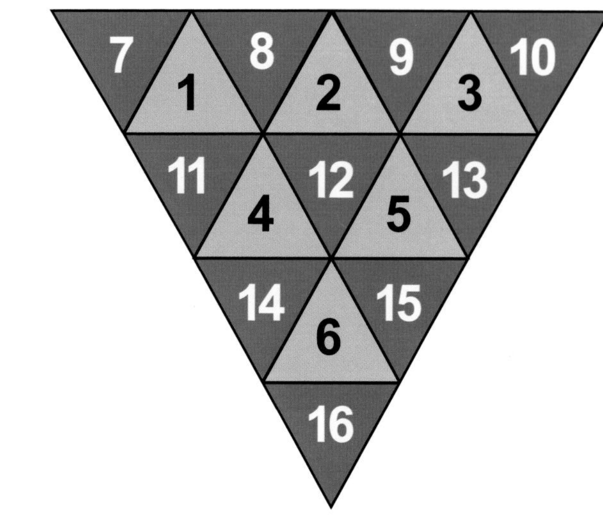

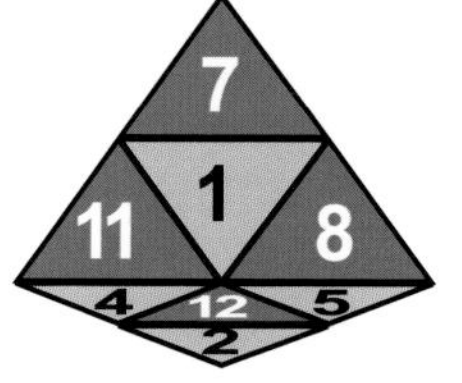

A

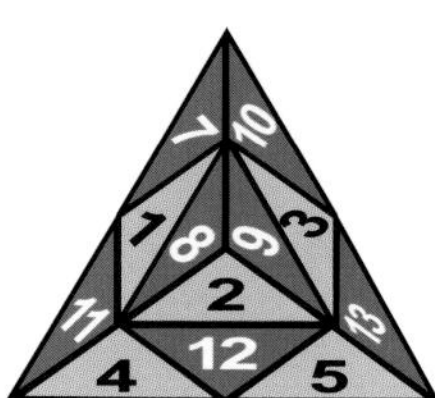

B

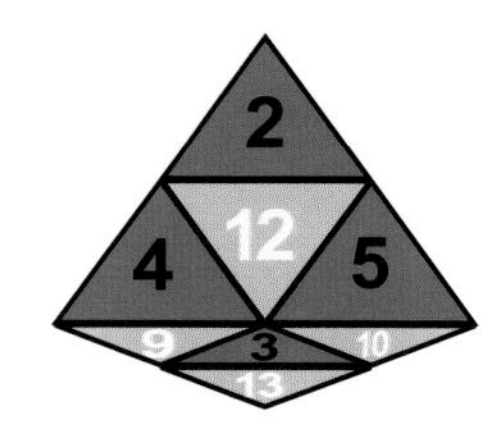

C

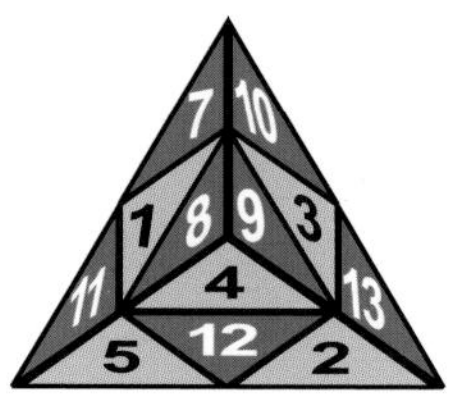

D

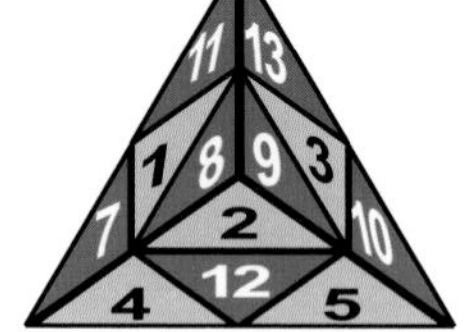

E

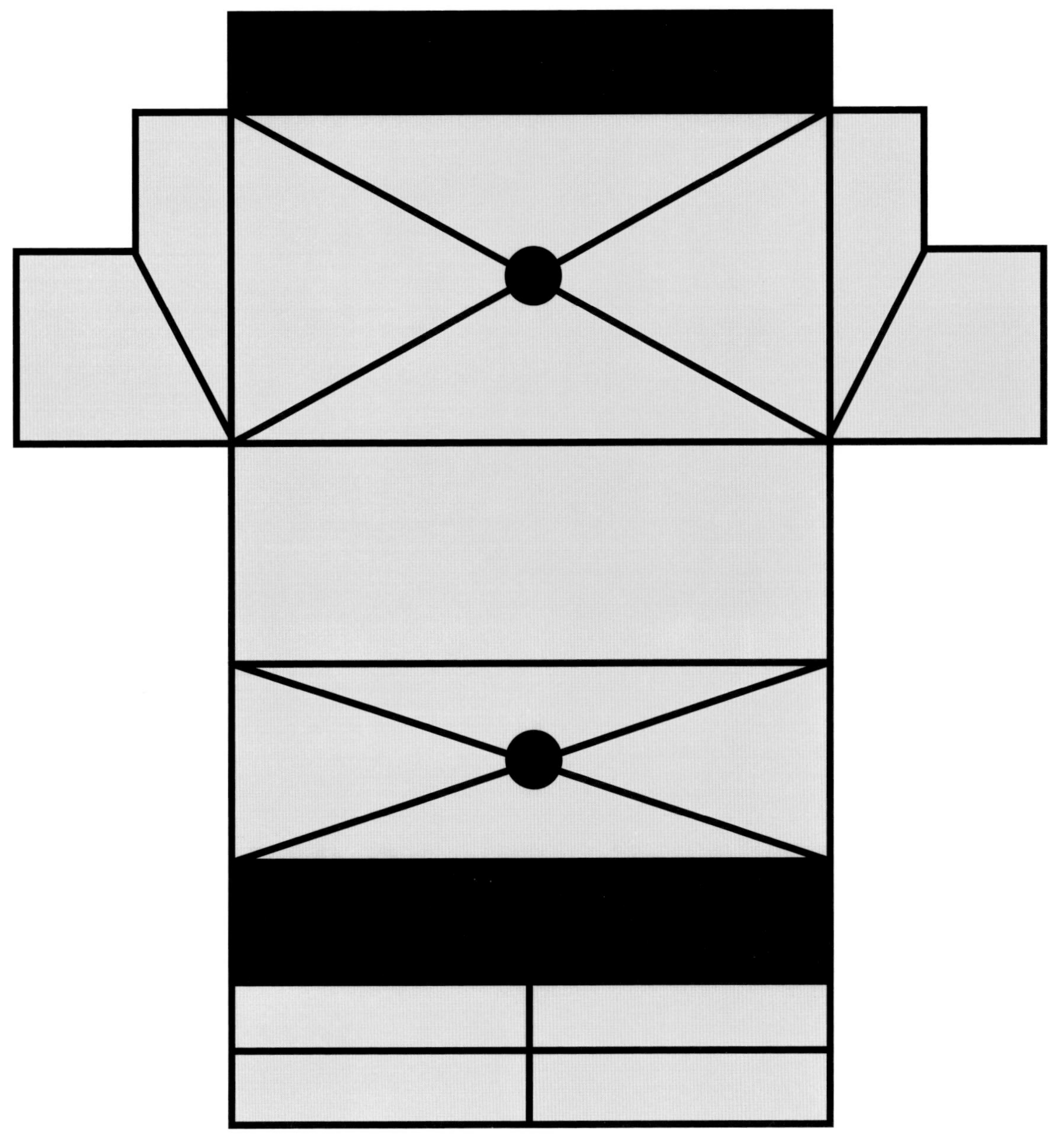

CLUSTER

- **In the series of puzzles that are to follow, instructions would differ from puzzle to puzzle.**
- **Read each question carefully before you solve the puzzle.**

1.

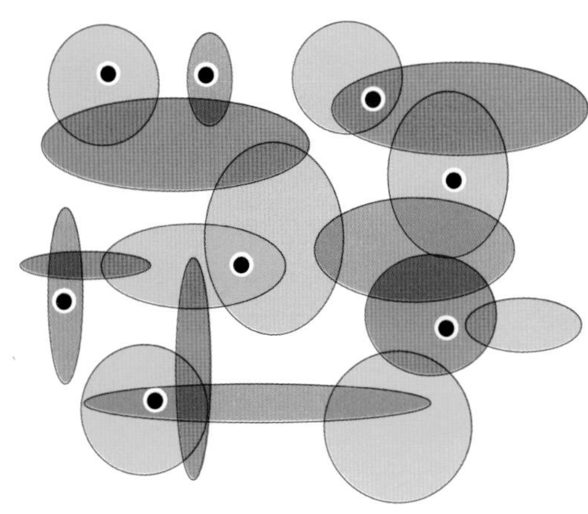

- **Find the number of pink ellipses containing black dots.**

3	4	5	2
A	B	C	D

2.

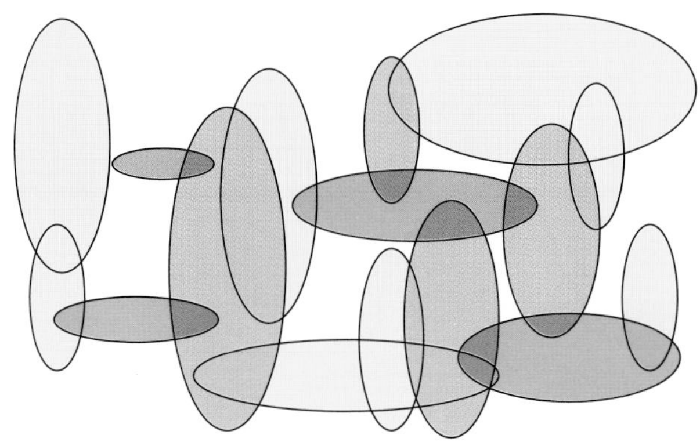

- **How many yellow ellipses intersect pink ellipses?**

2	3	4	5
A	B	C	D

3.

- **Find the number of stars having six points.**

3	4	6	7
A	B	C	D

4.

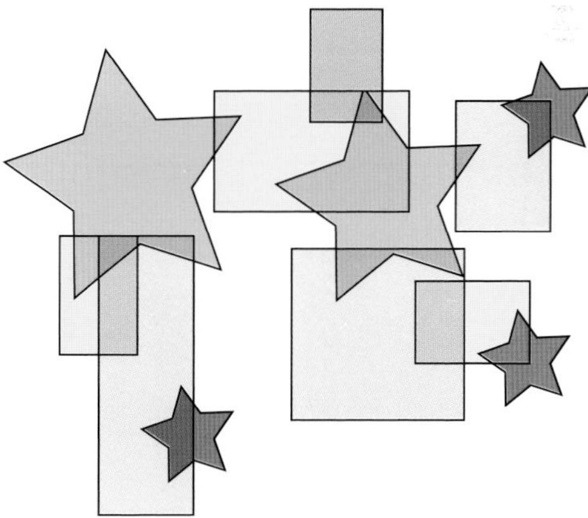

- **Find the number of rectangles intersecting pink stars.**

8	5	6	9
A	B	C	D

5.

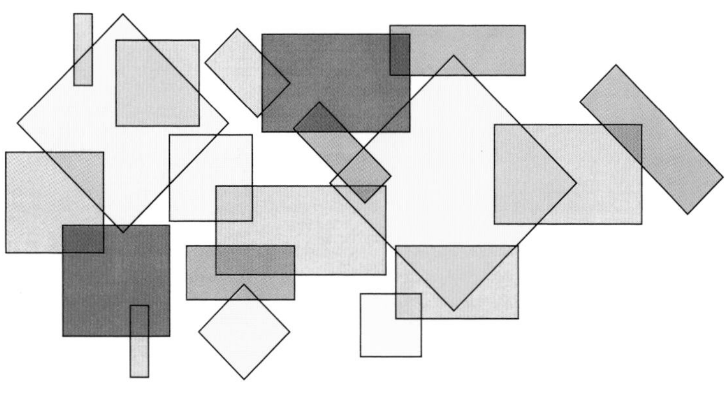

- **Find the number of yellow squares intersecting pink rectangles.**

6	2	7	4
A	B	C	D

6.

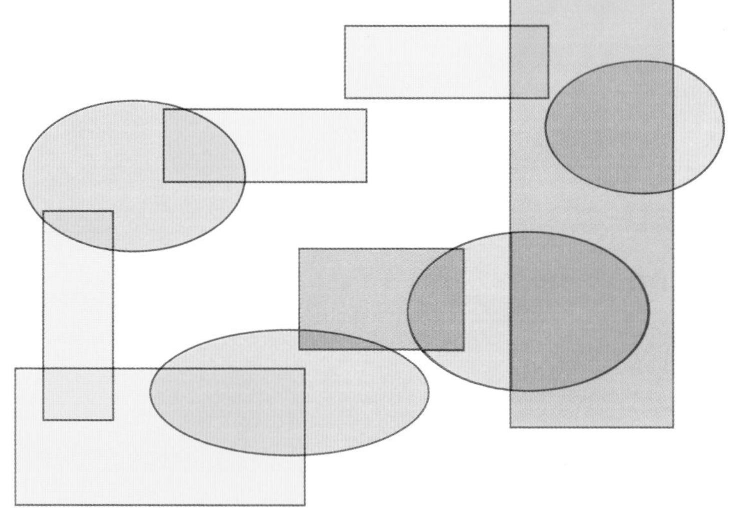

- **Find the number of rectangles which do not intersect ellipses.**

1	3	4	6
A	B	C	D

7.

• **Find the total number of triangles intersecting pink circles.**

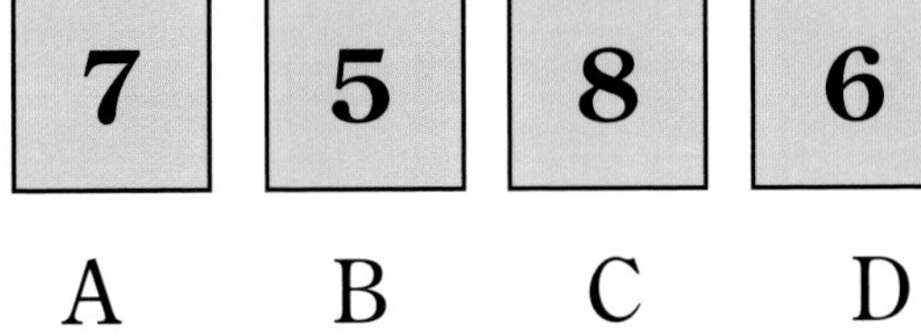

A B C D

8.

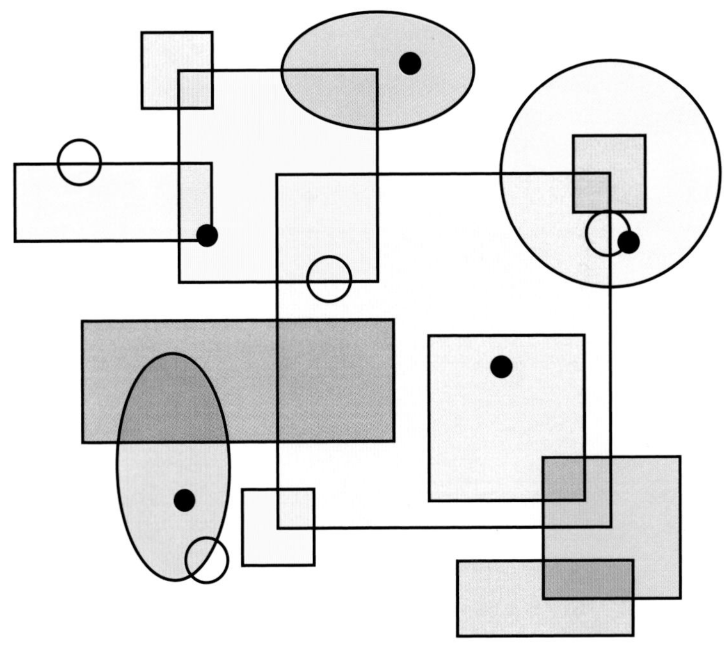

• **Find the total number of squares.**

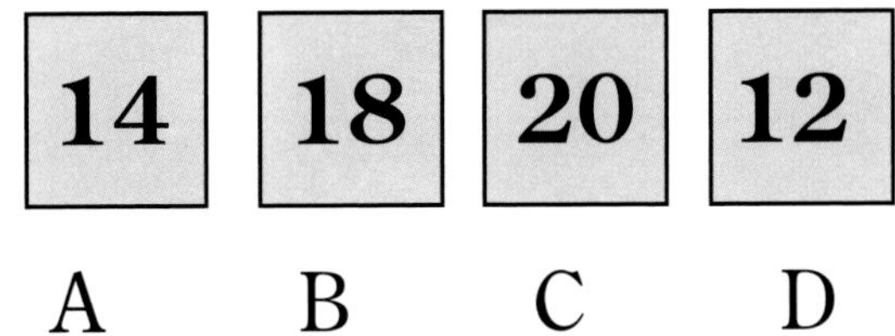

A B C D

9.

• **How many rectangles add up to 7?**

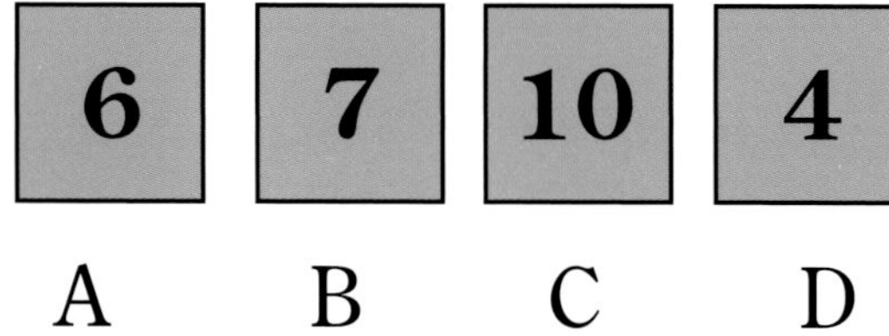

A B C D

10.

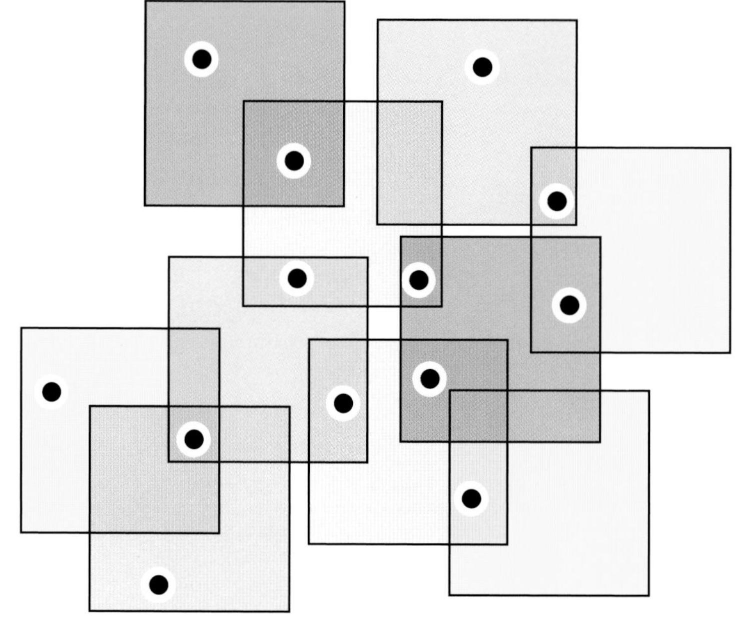

• **How many rectangles contain black dots?**

9 **7** **10** **4**

A B C D

11.

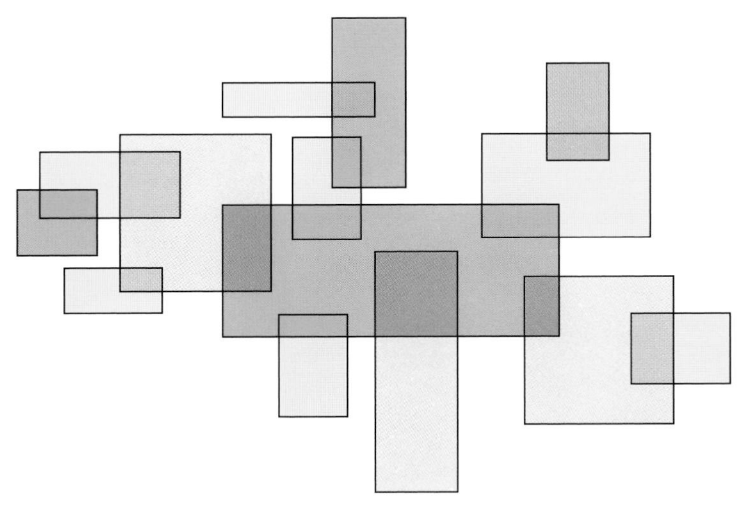

• **How many yellow rectangles intersect pink rectangles?**

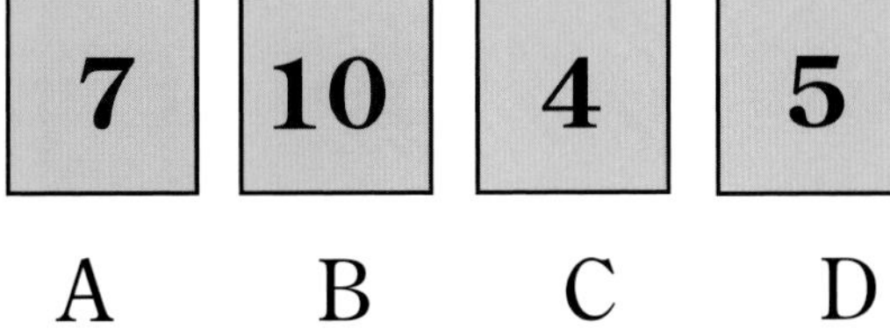

A B C D

12.

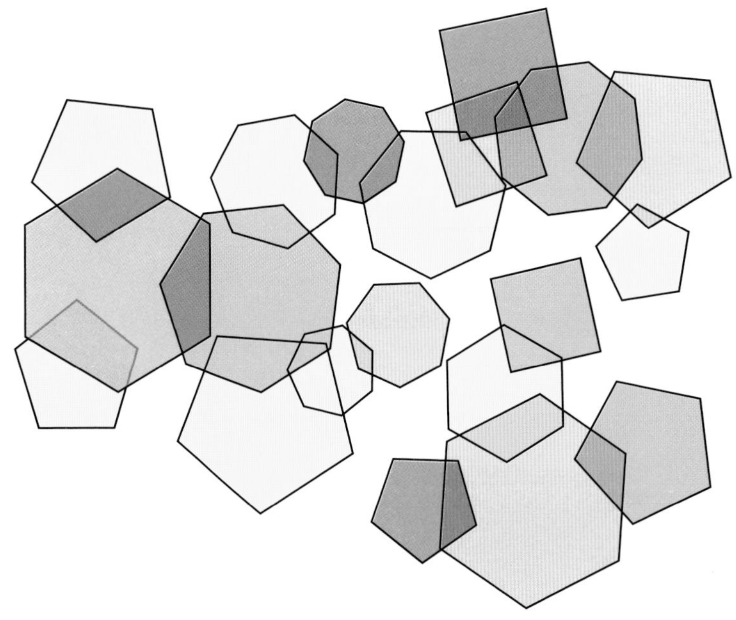

• **Find the number of yellow polygons having 5 sides.**

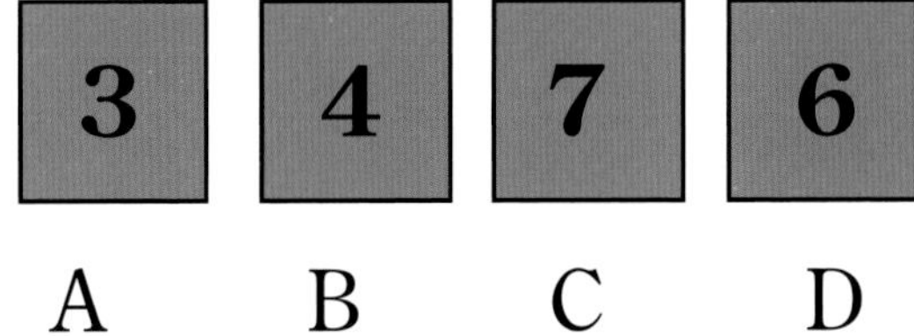

A B C D

13.

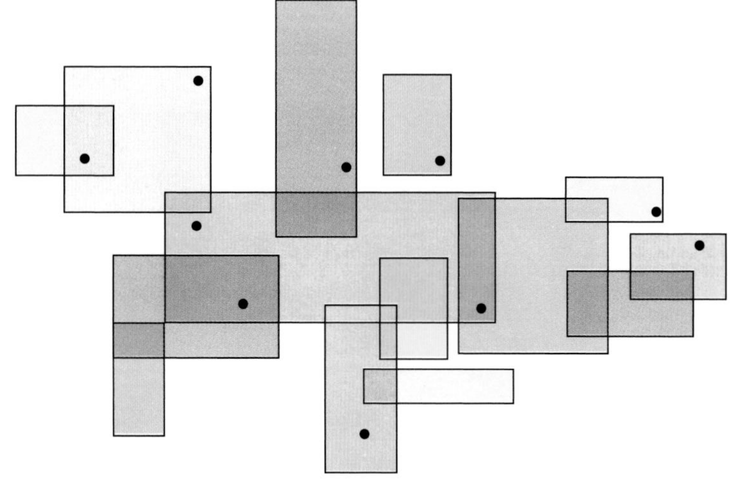

- **Find the number of rectangles which do not contain black dots.**

A	B	C	D
19	**25**	**21**	**18**

14.

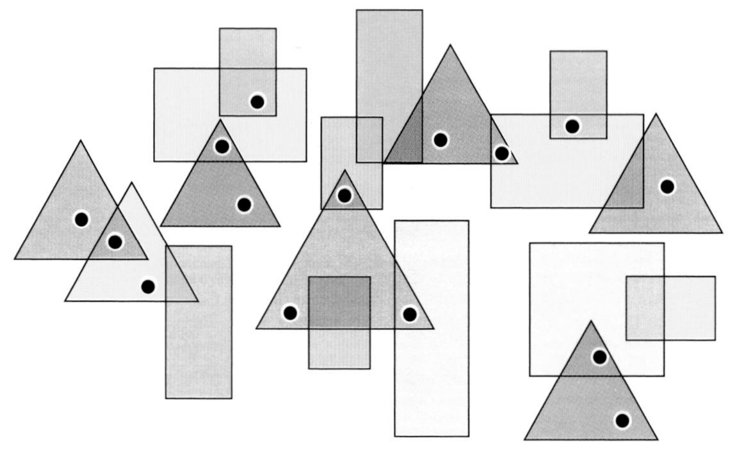

- **Find the number of triangles containing black dots.**

A	B	C	D
13	**06**	**10**	**11**

15.

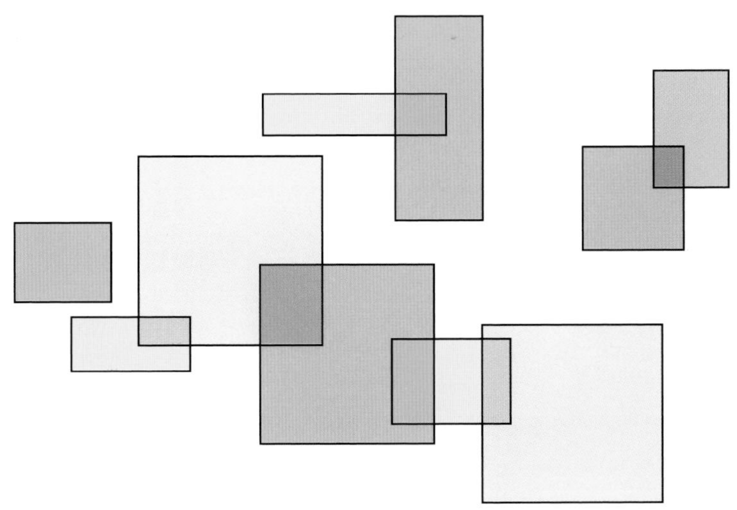

• **How many yellow rectangles intersect squares?**

1	2	3	4
A	B	C	D

16.

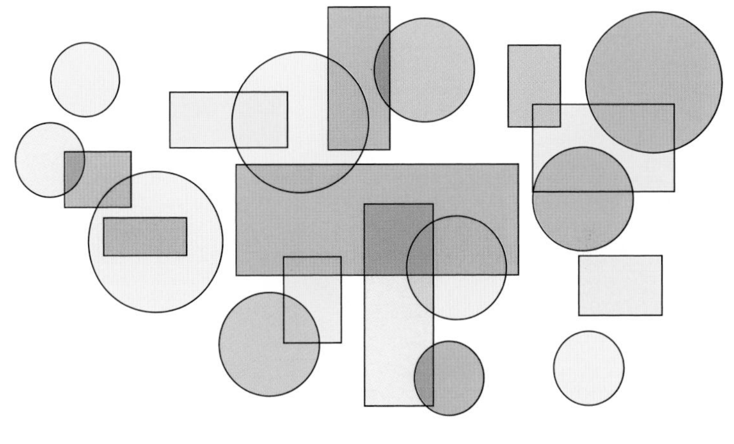

• **Find the number of yellow circles intersecting pink rectangles.**

5	4	10	3
A	B	C	D

17.

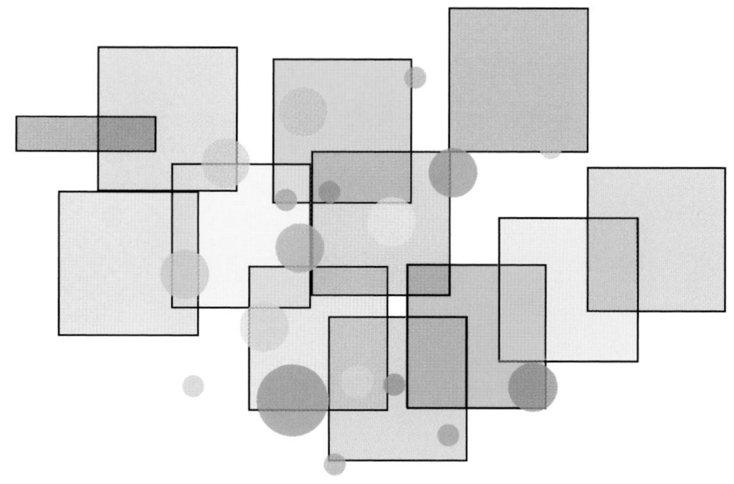

• **Find the total number of rectangles.**

15	18	21	13
A	B	C	D

18.

• **How many times do the green circles intersect pink rectangles?**

4	5	6	7
A	B	C	D

19.

- **How many six pointed stars contain digit 1.**

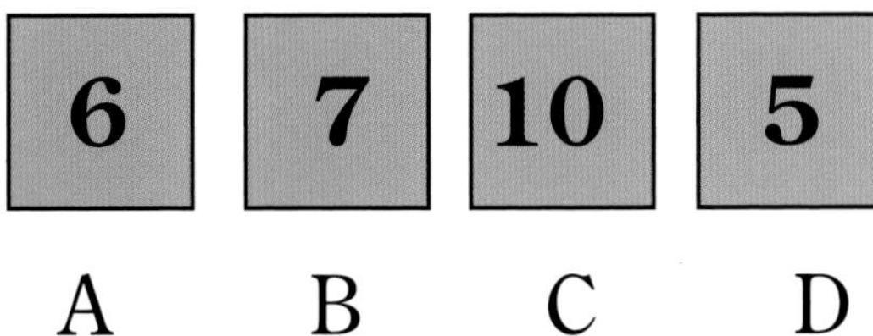

A B C D

20.

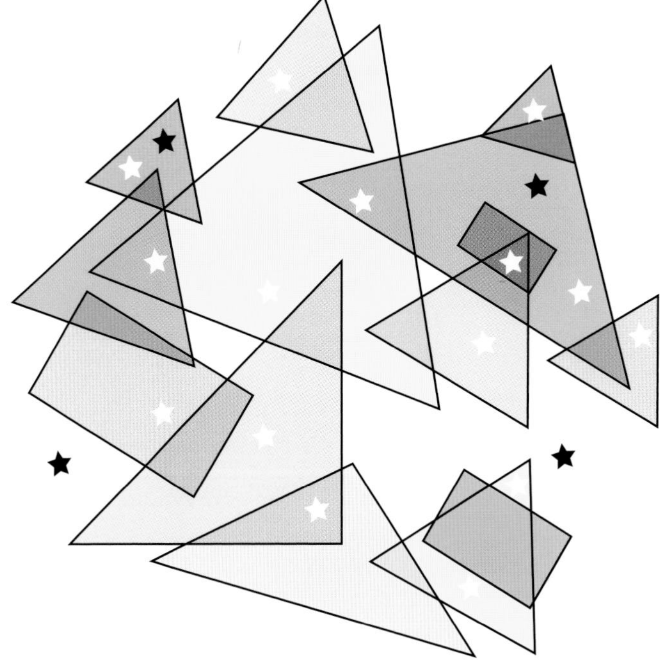

- **Count the total number of equilateral triangles.**

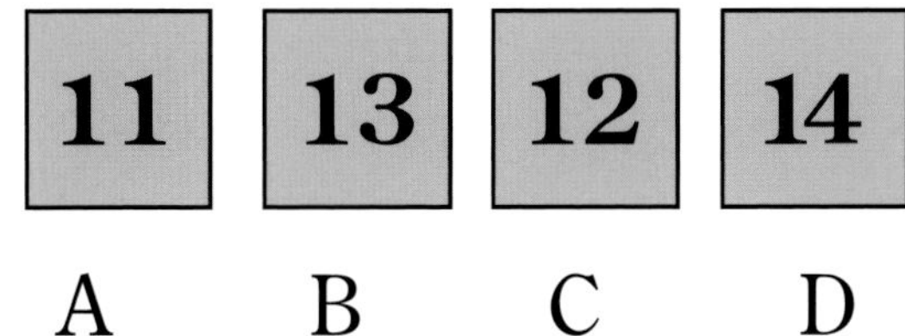

A B C D

21.

• **Find the total number of ellipses.**

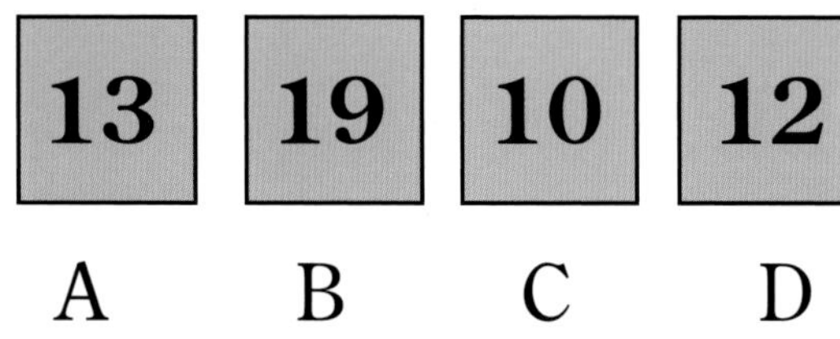

A B C D

22.

• **Count the total number of hexagons.**

38	37	36	34
A	B	C	D

23.

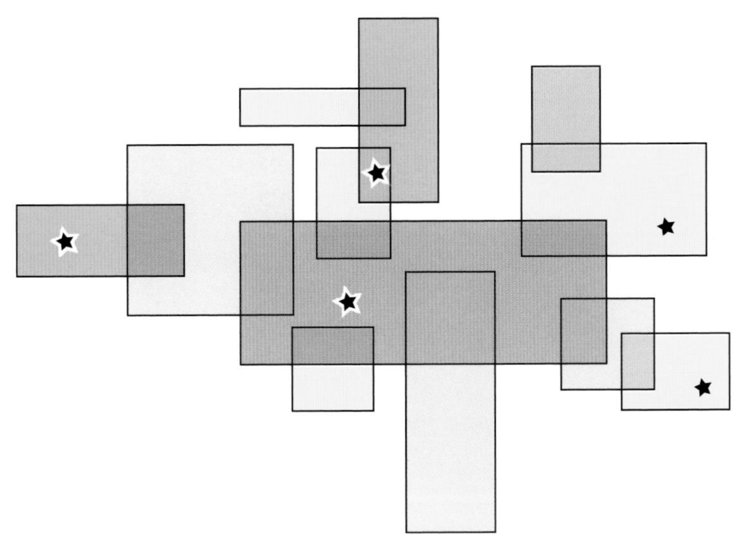

- **Find the number of rectangles having stars.**

5	8	13	17
A	B	C	D

24.

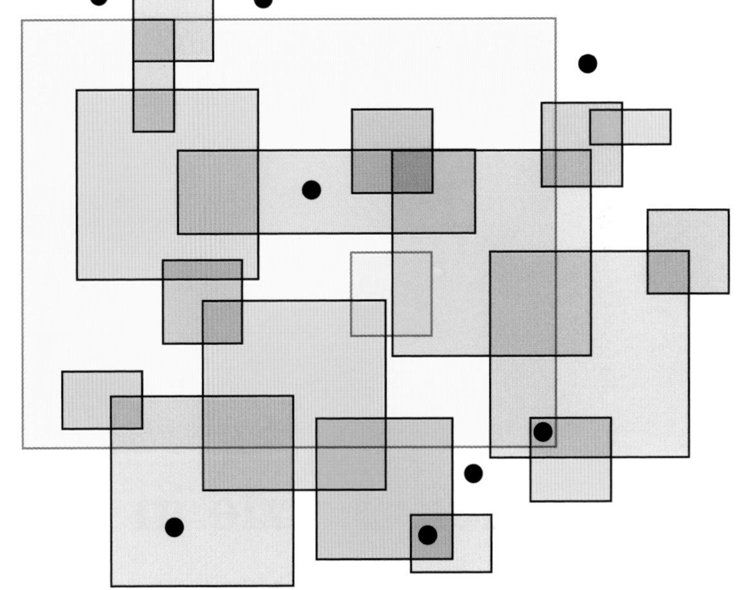

- **Count the squares which do not have black dots in it.**

18	22	17	25
A	B	C	D

WORD FIND

- **Each puzzle in this section has specific instructions.**
- **Read each question carefully before you solve the puzzle.**
- **Try solving puzzles in the easy and medium category in two minutes, and puzzles in the difficult category in one minute.**

1\. 5 words related to hospital are hidden in the puzzle given below. Try to locate them.

S	T	E	L	B	A	T
Y	E	S	E	D	S	M
R	D	E	A	E	N	N
J	E	E	D	L	E	U
K	N	A	E	D	R	R
U	S	Y	B	E	U	S
R	T	A	C	E	E	E
S	Y	R	I	N	G	E

2\. The names of 7 continents are hidden in the puzzle given below. Try to locate them.

A	U	S	T	N	A	T	B	B	A	T
U	E	S	A	O	B	S	D	D	I	S
C	H	I	N	R	H	T	I	R	N	O
E	S	R	N	T	E	R	E	E	D	U
A	L	A	N	H	L	M	A	E	L	T
N	E	U	M	A	A	D	F	D	I	H
E	B	S	R	M	E	U	R	N	A	A
N	Y	T	G	E	R	G	I	E	I	M
A	E	I	L	R	A	I	C	L	M	E
F	P	P	A	I	B	S	A	D	R	R
R	O	D	G	C	T	R	E	A	A	I
Y	R	U	N	A	T	E	D	E	T	C
A	U	S	T	S	A	M	E	E	N	A
N	E	E	U	G	L	A	N	D	A	R
E	B	A	N	T	A	R	T	I	C	A
S	D	N	A	F	R	I	H	T	E	N

3\. The names of 7 types of fish are hidden in the puzzle given below. Try to locate them.

C	H	O	C	Y	D	I	P	E	N
C	B	H	T	T	B	L	E	Z	T
K	E	A	A	R	E	T	S	Y	O
X	L	D	Q	W	H	A	L	E	T
V	A	O	C	T	O	P	U	S	J
Z	O	L	B	E	S	R	E	R	O
E	R	P	Q	S	J	L	W	E	V
H	J	H	O	D	T	D	A	O	R
G	C	I	N	T	N	E	Q	E	I
O	Y	N	O	E	Q	R	R	R	W
F	R	O	N	U	G	Q	R	O	O
A	M	K	R	S	H	A	R	K	U
E	I	P	D	F	V	P	U	W	Y
S	T	A	R	F	I	S	H	G	T

4\. The names of 10 computer devices are hidden in the puzzle given below. Try to locate them.

O	P	H	F	X	V	D	S	K	T	U	N	K	F	S	Q
H	Q	V	T	M	N	Q	B	L	I	G	X	N	C	I	L
F	L	O	P	P	Y	X	Q	E	C	O	A	Z	R	C	W
Q	Z	D	I	O	S	N	S	H	W	X	G	C	W	M	G
W	E	T	I	R	S	Y	H	A	R	D	D	I	S	K	B
X	I	C	W	T	A	S	E	F	R	R	A	X	L	N	M
W	A	S	E	R	V	O	O	A	S	A	C	U	E	S	D
E	J	E	N	O	K	I	O	M	O	B	A	R	O	I	A
V	R	L	U	T	G	B	C	E	V	A	T	I	C	A	J
H	J	D	Q	X	Y	U	T	O	M	O	N	I	T	O	R
M	C	N	R	E	R	S	K	E	O	X	Q	R	T	L	D
C	U	R	K	S	G	S	A	S	U	B	A	N	H	L	R
J	E	O	S	U	H	N	S	O	S	M	N	P	E	R	N
R	M	U	R	C	A	M	C	D	E	T	B	I	B	K	T
O	I	P	D	F	V	J	A	W	F	X	W	H	H	J	G
P	L	C	O	M	P	A	C	T	D	I	S	C	K	C	B

5.

The names of 15 birds are hidden in the puzzle given below. Try to locate them.

C	M	S	W	O	O	D	P	E	C	K	E	R	B
C	W	L	W	L	I	A	M	G	M	T	E	S	E
R	R	I	I	E	I	P	A	R	O	R	W	R	R
C	K	A	R	L	A	A	B	S	C	O	H	T	I
S	I	N	N	R	E	R	Y	P	K	S	I	W	A
T	W	M	R	E	E	A	D	A	I	L	I	N	R
O	J	A	I	E	C	K	I	R	N	K	D	U	C
P	S	C	N	S	R	E	B	R	G	S	L	O	U
L	F	L	A	M	R	E	E	O	B	L	V	S	R
A	U	A	R	U	A	T	N	W	I	E	E	T	N
T	U	R	K	E	Y	R	M	D	R	F	R	R	A
T	A	L	M	I	E	T	U	N	D	R	E	I	O
O	N	D	C	N	U	L	W	A	H	I	H	C	G
G	O	O	S	E	L	N	O	E	E	B	A	H	N
N	R	L	U	S	A	C	L	A	I	O	W	F	U
I	R	L	B	I	R	D	S	R	M	R	K	N	M
M	A	C	A	W	A	R	C	N	E	U	T	O	E
A	P	I	M	P	R	T	O	R	A	L	A	C	L
L	B	U	D	P	A	M	L	N	I	B	O	R	F
F	E	N	S	E	T	U	T	H	O	M	S	R	A

6.

The names of 10 countries are hidden in the puzzle given below. Try to locate them.

A	T	E	L	B	A	T	B	B	A	T
U	E	S	E	D	B	S	D	D	Y	I
C	H	I	N	A	T	Y	N	N	T	N
E	R	R	N	E	E	R	A	E	E	D
R	L	A	N	D	L	M	E	E	L	I
N	E	N	M	D	R	D	F	D	A	A
E	B	D	Y	E	T	E	R	L	T	E
N	Y	R	G	E	R	G	A	E	O	A
A	L	E	L	I	A	I	N	B	A	M
J	A	P	A	N	B	S	C	D	B	E
S	T	D	G	D	T	Y	E	A	T	R
E	I	U	N	I	T	E	D	E	E	A
R	L	N	I	E	L	E	E	E	L	E
N	E	E	N	G	L	A	N	D	A	D
E	B	D	Y	L	T	E	L	L	T	E
S	D	N	A	L	R	E	H	T	E	N

7.

The names of 12 professionals are hidden in the puzzle given below. Try to locate them.

Y	A	S	T	R	O	N	O	M	E	R	I	B	T	P
U	P	E	S	A	O	D	A	N	S	E	U	S	E	E
U	P	H	O	L	S	T	E	R	E	R	O	G	O	D
P	H	P	U	B	L	I	S	H	E	R	R	E	U	I
A	A	H	C	O	U	N	T	A	N	C	Y	L	C	A
H	N	Y	U	G	A	R	C	H	I	V	I	S	T	T
E	G	S	S	N	R	E	B	M	U	L	P	A	S	R
J	N	I	T	I	C	R	G	H	E	I	A	I	T	I
A	A	C	I	S	H	A	I	A	L	M	I	M	I	C
G	M	I	D	I	I	I	N	E	D	R	H	R	D	I
R	H	S	T	A	T	I	S	T	I	C	I	A	N	A
Y	H	T	U	R	E	T	E	L	E	T	Y	T	P	N
G	A	U	S	E	C	A	M	O	E	N	S	N	Y	S
N	S	E	N	A	T	O	R	G	D	A	P	A	R	N
E	V	B	A	D	T	A	R	Y	I	C	A	C	A	A
C	O	M	M	U	N	I	T	Y	W	A	R	D	E	N

8.

The names of 8 most influential people are hidden in the puzzle given below. Try to locate them.

C	F	M	S	E	R	O	L	I	V	C	R	W	S	J
H	W	P	S	L	G	L	O	R	G	H	B	I	I	O
R	I	R	D	I	E	I	P	N	A	U	R	L	R	H
I	L	I	U	Z	S	V	R	O	U	R	E	L	W	A
S	L	N	N	U	R	E	A	Y	T	C	S	I	I	N
T	I	T	S	A	I	L	U	N	A	B	L	A	N	N
O	I	E	D	I	E	C	W	I	M	I	L	M	S	E
P	J	S	U	R	W	R	I	U	B	L	S	S	T	S
H	R	S	N	I	A	O	H	E	U	L	L	H	O	G
E	O	D	E	S	S	A	F	N	D	C	I	A	N	U
R	O	I	D	A	M	W	R	L	D	L	E	K	C	T
C	S	A	C	M	I	E	E	A	H	I	W	E	H	E
O	H	N	E	C	N	L	Y	P	A	N	E	S	U	N
L	A	D	O	N	G	L	N	C	E	T	I	P	R	B
U	K	N	B	E	T	A	C	I	N	O	S	E	C	E
M	E	N	I	W	R	A	D	S	E	L	R	A	H	R
B	H	O	R	A	S	S	A	R	N	S	N	T	H	G
U	S	I	R	I	S	A	A	C	N	E	W	T	O	N
S	I	E	L	O	I	S	P	R	U	S	L	E	L	I
L	A	B	R	N	H	A	M	L	Q	N	C	O	L	N
A	L	B	E	R	T	E	I	N	S	T	E	I	N	N

9.

The names of 8 mountain ranges are hidden in the puzzle given below. Try to locate them.

K	P	H	O	T	Q	D	A	A	Z	U	N	K	F	S
E	E	R	L	A	X	W	L	I	V	B	X	C	G	I
P	M	N	Y	B	A	L	P	S	C	D	D	C	B	E
A	V	D	M	I	C	K	I	S	O	U	G	C	B	E
C	Z	S	P	X	Z	Y	L	K	H	D	U	L	X	E
X	Z	U	I	Z	D	B	L	U	E	R	I	D	G	E
S	A	R	C	B	S	R	E	E	S	C	S	C	S	Y
S	I	U	M	Z	B	I	S	M	O	W	T	R	N	I
A	Y	A	U	L	N	E	C	E	N	X	K	T	S	R
Y	T	T	N	U	H	S	S	N	I	P	Q	Y	E	K
A	S	S	S	R	J	S	A	S	D	E	R	N	D	L
L	U	E	O	E	K	O	U	N	S	C	H	A	R	Z
A	B	T	H	W	K	I	R	I	D	X	R	D	V	F
M	B	N	W	G	L	K	Q	E	G	E	U	R	L	K
I	N	O	Q	F	N	Y	B	L	O	R	S	T	O	M
H	X	M	G	S	O	J	N	Y	G	R	R	Y	B	C

10.

The names of 8 great British people are hidden in the puzzle given below. Try to locate them.

F	M	S	E	R	O	L	I	V	C	R	W	S	S
W	P	S	L	G	L	O	R	G	H	B	I	I	H
I	R	D	I	E	I	P	N	B	U	R	L	R	I
L	I	U	Z	O	V	R	O	L	R	E	L	W	B
L	N	N	G	R	E	A	Y	N	C	S	I	I	E
I	C	S	S	G	R	H	D	H	B	L	A	N	N
I	E	D	I	E	C	W	I	T	I	L	M	S	J
A	S	U	R	W	R	I	N	E	L	S	S	T	A
R	S	N	I	A	O	N	E	B	L	L	H	O	M
O	D	E	S	S	M	F	N	A	C	I	A	N	I
O	I	D	A	H	W	R	L	Z	L	E	K	C	N
S	A	C	A	I	E	E	A	I	I	W	E	H	F
H	N	E	C	N	L	Y	P	L	N	E	S	U	R
A	A	O	N	G	L	N	C	E	T	I	P	R	A
K	N	B	E	T	A	C	I	N	O	S	E	C	N
E	N	I	W	R	A	D	S	E	L	R	A	H	C
T	N	N	T	N	N	U	O	E	L	L	R	I	L
I	E	L	O	I	S	P	R	U	S	L	E	L	I
A	B	R	N	H	A	M	L	Q	N	C	O	L	N
S	H	O	R	A	T	I	O	N	E	L	S	O	N

11.

The names of 10 best films of Alfred Hitchcock are hidden in the puzzle given below. Try to locate them.

A	S	G	T	B	U	O	D	F	O	W	O	D	A	H	S	X
E	M	P	N	O	C	I	R	P	A	C	R	E	D	N	U	R
S	R	F	S	L	A	R	T	U	U	E	Y	P	Z	N	E	I
G	I	E	F	Y	O	W	S	R	J	H	F	G	F	B	F	V
F	U	P	A	E	C	M	O	I	C	F	B	U	E	B	U	G
B	A	A	S	R	F	H	O	W	M	K	L	C	R	M	T	L
L	F	M	H	Y	W	R	O	P	E	H	C	X	N	G	D	E
B	A	H	I	U	L	I	E	C	E	A	L	E	Q	M	T	A
P	R	A	O	L	S	B	N	O	T	O	R	I	U	S	B	T
K	G	J	T	N	Y	T	L	D	M	I	M	W	D	S	O	D
H	F	U	L	T	E	P	E	K	O	S	D	E	B	P	B	V
A	F	G	H	A	N	T	L	A	M	W	O	W	A	S	U	D
A	S	G	F	G	O	W	S	O	J	H	F	Z	F	E	F	X
L	A	R	T	U	U	E	Y	P	T	N	R	C	Z	N	H	F
F	R	E	S	A	C	E	N	I	D	A	R	A	P	E	H	T

12.

The names of 10 most popular plays by William Shakespeare are hidden in the puzzle given below. Try to locate them.

R	O	M	E	O	A	N	D	J	U	L	I	E	T	Y	F	K
S	D	F	H	L	A	R	T	U	U	E	Y	P	Z	N	R	I
G	I	X	C	O	R	I	O	L	A	N	U	S	Z	A	G	N
U	R	P	P	E	K	M	O	I	C	F	B	U	X	B	U	G
B	A	H	A	M	L	E	T	U	M	K	L	M	M	M	T	L
L	F	H	H	Y	S	P	H	S	L	H	Z	X	N	G	D	E
B	A	H	F	U	L	T	E	C	E	K	L	E	Q	M	T	A
P	R	A	O	W	S	B	L	A	H	P	D	F	B	V	B	R
K	G	J	T	N	L	T	L	E	M	I	M	W	D	S	U	D
M	A	C	B	E	T	H	O	S	H	S	D	E	B	V	B	V
F	A	G	H	A	N	T	D	A	M	A	O	W	T	S	U	D
A	S	G	F	G	O	W	S	R	J	H	F	G	F	E	F	X
T	I	M	O	N	O	F	A	T	H	E	N	S	Z	N	H	F
F	R	S	U	C	I	N	O	R	D	N	A	S	U	T	I	T

13.

The names of 9 Roman emperors are hidden in the puzzle given below. Try to locate them.

P	R	A	O	W	S	B	V	F	D	A	H	R	I	A	N	I
S	C	J	M	A	R	C	U	S	A	U	R	E	L	I	U	S
G	D	A	G	K	H	Q	D	T	I	B	E	R	I	U	S	X
J	S	I	L	R	O	J	O	D	F	I	F	G	I	Y	F	X
B	A	H	O	I	L	T	W	N	A	I	S	A	P	S	E	V
O	K	C	K	C	G	M	O	F	C	F	B	U	X	B	U	G
K	G	S	T	N	L	U	D	S	M	I	O	N	D	S	U	D
L	F	H	U	Y	S	E	L	F	L	H	A	X	N	G	N	M
B	N	H	F	I	L	T	T	A	K	I	L	E	Q	E	T	D
A	U	A	N	C	D	B	N	I	R	S	D	F	R	V	B	V
F	R	F	J	W	S	U	V	D	A	S	D	O	B	V	B	V
S	G	J	T	A	A	T	A	L	U	N	Y	P	Z	N	J	F
A	S	G	F	G	R	H	S	L	J	H	F	G	F	Y	F	X
S	H	U	W	K	V	T	D	S	C	A	O	W	D	S	U	D

14.

The names of 8 ancient war weapons are hidden in the puzzle given below. Try to locate them.

P	R	A	O	W	S	B	V	F	H	S	D	F	B	V	B	V
C	G	J	A	V	E	L	I	N	M	A	O	W	D	S	U	D
L	F	H	H	S	S	W	G	F	S	N	Z	X	N	G	D	M
J	S	A	R	R	O	W	S	G	F	H	F	G	F	Y	F	X
B	A	H	F	U	L	T	W	S	M	K	L	E	Q	M	T	D
A	C	E	G	I	K	M	O	F	C	F	W	O	X	B	U	G
S	G	J	T	U	L	T	R	L	U	E	Y	P	Z	N	J	F
G	I	X	G	K	H	Q	D	O	V	B	M	C	Z	I	G	X
H	G	J	T	U	R	T	S	L	F	H	H	S	S	W	M	F
F	S	N	Z	A	N	G	A	X	E	E	Y	P	Z	N	J	Z
P	R	F	E	W	S	B	V	F	H	S	D	F	B	V	B	V
B	W	P	F	U	L	T	R	U	M	P	E	T	E	R	U	D
J	S	G	F	G	C	L	U	B	J	H	F	G	F	Y	F	X
Q	B	O	W	T	S	W	G	F	S	N	Z	X	N	G	D	M

15.

The names of the 7 wonders of the modern world are hidden in the puzzle given below. Try to locate them.

A	N	N	T	K	U	R	N	I	K	O	S	G	T
G	N	S	A	D	B	S	D	D	B	S	E	R	H
R	E	D	J	N	T	Y	N	N	T	Y	R	E	E
A	R	U	M	E	E	R	N	E	E	U	E	A	G
N	N	N	A	K	U	R	N	I	H	O	N	T	R
D	N	S	H	D	B	S	D	C	B	S	G	P	E
C	E	D	A	N	T	Y	C	N	T	Y	E	Y	A
A	R	U	L	E	E	I	N	E	E	R	T	R	T
N	L	N	O	E	P	E	E	E	L	E	I	A	W
Y	E	E	G	U	A	D	D	D	A	T	M	M	A
O	A	D	H	L	Z	G	L	L	A	E	I	I	L
N	N	C	R	E	R	G	A	M	O	G	G	D	L
I	A	E	F	B	I	T	P	S	A	T	R	O	O
M	S	O	G	A	P	A	L	A	G	L	A	F	F
H	R	D	D	N	A	Y	G	N	A	I	T	G	C
O	P	U	E	S	I	R	N	N	E	R	I	I	H
R	A	N	R	E	N	E	O	E	L	E	O	Z	I
S	E	E	E	D	A	R	D	D	A	D	N	A	N
E	S	D	R	L	S	E	L	L	T	E	L	T	A
S	A	R	F	O	L	L	A	W	S	T	E	R	G

16.

The names of 6 manned spacecrafts are hidden in the puzzle given below. Try to locate them.

B	P	H	F	X	V	D	S	A	M	U	N	K	F	V
D	E	R	R	T	M	S	B	I	L	E	X	C	O	O
P	A	N	A	F	S	O	C	S	C	B	D	S	B	S
A	P	O	L	L	O	N	S	H	H	U	K	C	W	T
N	E	T	I	C	Y	Y	H	A	E	H	X	X	X	O
A	L	C	A	L	U	E	E	F	O	C	A	X	A	K
S	T	E	G	N	Z	R	A	D	S	G	C	U	L	S
O	C	E	N	O	K	I	A	M	O	E	A	R	K	I
N	C	C	U	K	G	C	C	E	N	M	S	T	S	R
I	F	A	S	A	C	S	S	N	I	I	Q	Y	E	D
S	A	P	C	I	S	H	E	P	E	N	O	N	D	L
N	N	R	A	C	U	O	M	S	S	I	D	C	Y	D
U	F	O	S	U	H	N	S	I	C	X	R	D	V	F
X	M	E	R	C	U	R	Y	E	G	R	U	R	L	K
X	R	O	D	C	V	Y	A	L	O	R	O	T	O	M
C	I	M	S	F	V	J	G	Y	G	R	B	Y	R	C

17.

The names of 8 movies based on a historical event or person are hidden in the puzzle given below. Try to locate them.

G	L	A	D	I	A	T	O	R	T	U	N	K	F	S
D	E	R	R	T	M	S	B	I	L	E	X	C	G	I
P	A	N	P	E	A	R	L	H	A	R	B	O	U	R
A	F	D	Q	X	S	N	S	H	H	U	G	C	W	M
N	E	T	I	C	S	Y	H	A	E	B	X	X	C	E
A	L	C	A	L	R	E	E	F	L	R	A	X	L	N
W	A	T	E	R	L	O	O	E	S	A	C	U	E	S
O	C	E	N	O	K	I	A	M	O	V	A	R	O	I
N	C	C	U	K	G	C	C	E	N	E	S	T	P	R
I	F	A	S	A	C	S	S	N	I	H	Q	Y	A	D
C	U	R	M	S	L	I	O	N	H	E	A	R	T	L
N	N	R	A	C	U	O	M	S	S	A	D	C	R	D
T	F	O	S	U	H	N	S	I	C	R	R	D	A	F
R	M	E	R	C	A	M	E	L	O	T	U	R	L	K
O	I	O	D	C	V	Y	A	L	O	R	O	T	O	M
Y	N	M	S	F	V	J	G	Y	G	R	B	Y	R	C

18.

The names of 8 best selling books that have been made into films are hidden in the puzzle given below. Try to locate them.

J	I	S	B	D	F	G	H	D	E	N	B	A
A	R	G	A	T	N	A	N	A	F	C	J	F
W	G	A	F	R	S	A	V	M	U	N	I	C
S	P	O	R	G	L	A	G	K	L	V	D	G
T	K	G	A	G	R	D	X	B	X	R	I	E
D	R	Z	H	I	V	A	G	O	I	T	L	R
O	F	E	C	G	L	N	I	K	R	B	V	M
P	L	P	E	B	C	S	T	E	A	R	K	A
R	C	N	R	F	C	R	G	I	G	Z	G	N
P	O	R	U	H	D	N	L	A	N	I	Q	Y
D	H	J	F	L	I	H	Y	S	P	A	I	N
S	G	A	R	F	I	E	L	D	N	L	E	C
D	E	R	D	I	Y	L	F	F	F	T	E	O
A	A	L	I	Y	T	D	D	R	I	X	F	N
R	O	S	T	R	E	H	T	A	F	D	O	G
G	B	F	H	Y	I	H	F	Y	F	O	F	O

19.

The names of 10 types of dinosaurs are hidden in the puzzle given below. Try to locate them.

A	L	B	E	R	T	O	S	A	U	R	U	S	H	S	X	M
P	L	E	S	I	O	S	A	U	R	U	S	U	D	S	U	A
S	R	L	S	L	A	R	T	U	U	E	Y	C	Z	R	E	I
G	I	E	O	Y	O	W	S	R	J	H	F	O	F	O	F	A
F	U	P	A	S	C	M	O	I	C	F	B	D	E	T	U	S
B	A	A	S	R	A	H	O	W	M	K	L	O	R	P	T	A
L	F	M	H	Y	W	U	O	P	E	H	C	L	N	A	D	U
B	A	H	I	U	L	I	R	C	E	A	L	P	Q	R	T	R
P	R	A	O	L	S	B	N	U	T	O	R	I	U	I	B	U
K	G	J	T	N	Y	T	L	D	S	I	M	D	D	C	O	S
H	P	R	O	T	O	C	E	R	A	T	O	P	S	O	B	V
K	I	N	E	T	O	S	A	U	R	S	W	O	W	L	S	U
A	S	G	F	G	C	R	A	H	A	E	O	P	T	E	Y	X
H	A	D	R	O	S	A	U	R	U	S	G	J	K	V	H	F

20.

The names of 13 currencies are hidden in the puzzle given below. Try to locate them.

K	G	J	T	N	Y	T	L	D	S	I	M
P	A	U	N	D	E	L	B	U	R	U	S
E	A	H	I	O	L	I	R	C	U	A	L
S	I	W	E	L	O	S	A	U	P	S	W
O	U	A	A	L	C	M	O	I	E	F	B
B	A	N	S	A	A	H	O	W	E	K	L
T	F	M	H	R	A	H	O	M	E	H	C
A	R	F	S	L	I	R	T	U	D	E	Y
E	R	R	L	L	S	A	N	U	I	O	R
L	L	A	E	O	T	O	L	A	N	R	U
H	A	N	R	O	R	A	U	R	A	S	G
G	I	C	O	Y	O	I	S	R	R	H	F
A	S	G	F	G	A	R	N	H	A	E	O
M	A	H	R	I	D	C	E	R	A	T	O

21.

Every answer is a 8 letter word that reads from left to right in the row that corresponds to the clue alphabet.

a	S							
b		P						
c			A					
d				N				
e					G			
f						L		
g							E	
h								D

a : The internal structure of the body composed of bone and cartilage

b : A bowl-shaped vessel used by tobacco chewers

c : A quilted pad worn by fencers to protect the torso and side

d : To separate the chaff from grain

e : To employ smoke or fumes in order to exterminate or disinfect

f : A group or combination of eight associated by common properties or behaviour

g : Tendency to play pranks or cause embarrassment

h : Something useless or cumbersome

22.

The names of 10 billionaires in the world are hidden in the puzzle given below. Try to locate them.

C	M	S	E	R	O	L	I	V	C	S	W	S	B
H	W	I	L	L	I	A	M	G	A	T	E	S	E
R	R	A	I	E	I	P	N	A	J	R	L	R	R
I	K	A	R	L	A	L	B	R	E	C	H	T	N
S	N	N	U	R	E	A	Y	T	H	S	I	I	A
T	C	M	R	I	E	T	D	A	A	L	A	N	R
L	J	I	I	E	C	N	I	M	N	L	A	S	D
A	S	C	R	S	R	I	B	B	N	S	L	T	A
T	S	H	S	A	R	H	E	U	E	L	B	O	R
T	D	A	S	U	A	A	N	D	F	I	E	S	N
I	I	E	A	N	S	R	M	D	G	F	R	U	A
M	A	L	M	I	E	T	U	N	U	W	E	I	U
I	N	D	C	N	U	L	P	A	H	E	E	T	L
M	D	E	N	G	L	N	L	E	E	O	I	U	T
H	N	L	U	S	A	C	I	A	N	S	J	F	W
S	N	L	W	R	A	D	S	E	L	R	S	N	E
K	N	R	I	S	A	A	C	N	E	U	T	O	N
A	Z	I	M	P	R	E	M	J	I	L	A	C	I
L	B	U	D	H	A	M	L	Q	G	C	I	P	N
D	A	V	I	D	T	H	O	M	S	O	N	O	N

23.

The names of 12 inventors are hidden in the puzzle given below. Try to locate them.

W	I	L	B	U	R	W	R	I	G	H	T	G	T
G	B	S	A	D	S	S	D	D	B	O	E	R	S
E	E	D	J	I	T	Y	N	N	T	R	R	E	I
N	N	U	T	E	E	R	N	E	E	V	E	A	R
R	J	O	H	N	D	E	E	R	E	I	N	T	I
I	A	S	E	D	B	E	D	C	B	L	G	P	S
C	M	D	N	N	E	D	I	S	T	L	E	T	A
O	I	U	R	E	N	I	N	L	L	E	T	H	A
F	N	N	Y	E	J	S	E	E	L	W	I	O	C
E	F	E	F	U	A	D	R	O	A	R	E	M	N
R	R	D	O	L	Z	G	L	L	A	I	I	A	E
M	A	C	R	E	R	G	A	M	R	G	G	S	W
I	N	E	D	B	I	T	P	U	A	H	R	E	T
M	K	O	G	A	P	A	C	A	G	T	A	D	O
A	L	B	E	R	T	E	I	N	S	T	E	I	N
O	I	U	E	S	I	R	N	N	E	R	I	S	H
R	N	N	R	R	N	E	O	E	L	E	O	O	I
S	E	E	A	D	A	H	E	N	R	D	N	N	N
E	S	M	R	L	S	E	L	L	T	E	L	T	A
S	A	R	F	L	L	E	B	M	A	H	A	R	G

24.

The names of 8 characters from Da Vinci code are hidden in the puzzle given below. Try to locate them.

O	P	H	F	X	V	D	S	K	T	U	N	K	F	S	R
H	P	V	T	M	N	Q	B	L	I	G	X	N	C	I	O
P	C	U	P	E	A	Y	T	E	M	P	L	A	R	C	B
Q	Z	D	S	X	S	N	S	H	A	X	G	C	W	M	E
W	E	T	I	D	S	Y	U	A	R	Z	Y	X	C	E	R
X	I	C	W	L	E	S	E	F	Y	R	A	X	L	N	T
W	A	S	E	R	V	I	O	E	S	A	C	U	E	S	L
E	J	E	N	O	K	I	A	M	O	V	A	R	O	I	A
V	R	L	U	T	G	C	C	E	V	A	T	I	C	A	N
H	O	L	Y	G	R	A	I	L	I	H	M	Y	A	D	G
M	C	N	R	W	R	S	K	E	H	X	Q	R	T	L	D
C	U	R	M	S	G	S	A	S	D	B	A	N	H	L	O
J	E	O	S	U	H	N	S	A	S	D	R	D	A	F	N
R	M	U	R	C	A	M	C	L	O	T	B	O	B	K	T
O	I	O	D	F	V	J	A	I	O	X	W	Q	H	J	G
P	R	I	O	R	Y	O	F	S	I	O	N	Y	K	C	B

25.

The names of 12 Nobel prize winners for peace are hidden in the puzzle given below. Try to locate them.

W	A	S	E	R	E	T	R	E	H	T	O	M	S
G	B	S	A	D	S	S	D	D	B	O	E	I	H
E	E	D	J	I	W	R	N	N	T	R	R	K	I
N	N	U	T	E	A	I	N	E	E	V	K	H	R
T	E	N	Z	I	N	G	Y	A	T	S	O	A	I
I	L	S	E	D	G	O	D	C	B	L	F	I	N
C	S	D	D	N	A	B	I	S	T	L	I	L	E
O	O	U	A	E	R	E	N	L	L	E	A	G	B
R	N	N	L	E	I	R	E	N	L	L	N	O	A
E	M	E	A	U	M	T	R	E	A	I	N	R	D
T	A	D	I	L	A	A	L	L	A	E	A	B	I
R	N	C	L	E	A	M	A	S	R	W	N	A	W
A	D	E	A	B	T	E	P	U	A	E	R	C	T
C	E	O	M	A	H	N	C	A	G	I	A	H	O
Y	L	B	A	R	A	C	I	N	S	S	E	E	N
M	A	U	E	S	I	H	N	N	E	E	I	V	H
M	N	N	R	R	N	U	O	E	L	L	O	O	I
I	E	M	A	N	D	H	E	N	R	D	N	N	N
J	O	S	E	P	H	R	O	T	B	L	A	T	A
S	A	R	F	E	B	L	L	M	A	H	G	R	A

26.

The names of 10 great Americans are hidden in the puzzle given below. Try to locate them.

F	M	S	E	R	E	T	R	I	T	R	A	M	S
R	A	S	A	G	E	O	R	G	E	B	U	S	H
A	R	D	J	E	W	P	N	B	I	R	R	K	I
N	T	U	T	O	A	R	O	L	S	E	O	H	B
K	I	N	G	R	N	A	Y	N	T	S	N	A	E
L	N	S	E	G	G	H	D	J	B	L	A	I	N
I	L	D	O	E	A	W	I	S	I	L	L	L	J
N	U	U	R	W	R	I	N	L	L	E	D	G	A
R	T	N	L	A	I	N	E	I	L	L	R	O	M
O	H	E	A	S	M	F	N	E	C	I	E	R	I
O	E	D	I	H	A	R	L	N	L	E	A	B	N
S	R	C	L	I	A	E	A	S	I	W	G	A	F
E	K	E	A	N	T	Y	P	U	N	E	A	C	R
V	I	O	M	G	H	N	C	A	T	I	N	H	A
E	N	B	A	T	A	C	I	N	O	S	E	E	N
L	G	U	E	O	I	H	N	N	N	E	I	V	K
T	N	N	R	N	N	U	O	E	L	L	O	O	L
I	E	L	V	I	S	P	R	E	S	L	E	Y	I
A	B	R	A	H	A	M	L	I	N	C	O	L	N
S	A	W	A	S	H	I	N	C	A	T	O	N	G

Reposition

- In the given puzzles the positions of two symbols have been interchanged once.
- Reposition them in their original place So that the puzzle would follow a proper sequence.
- The legend will provide you with the sequence.
- Remember the sequence can start from any point.

1.

● LEGEND ●

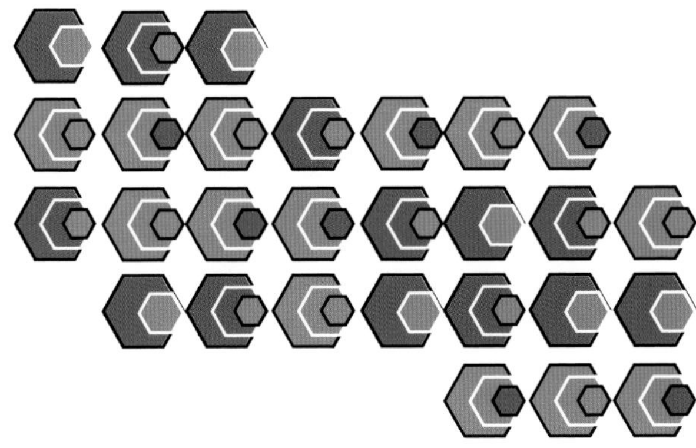

2.

● LEGEND ●

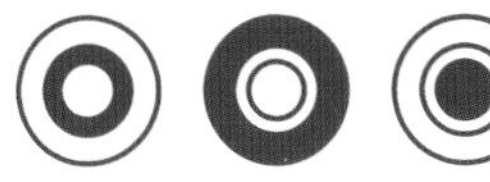

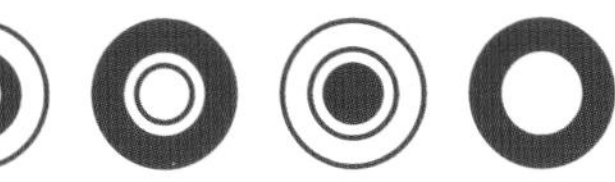

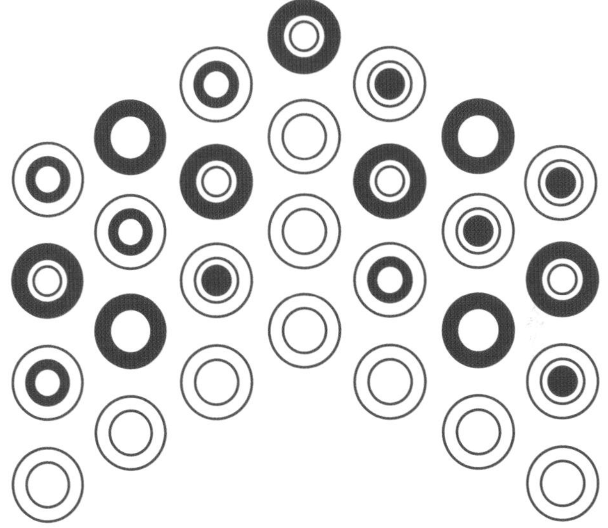

3.

● LEGEND ●

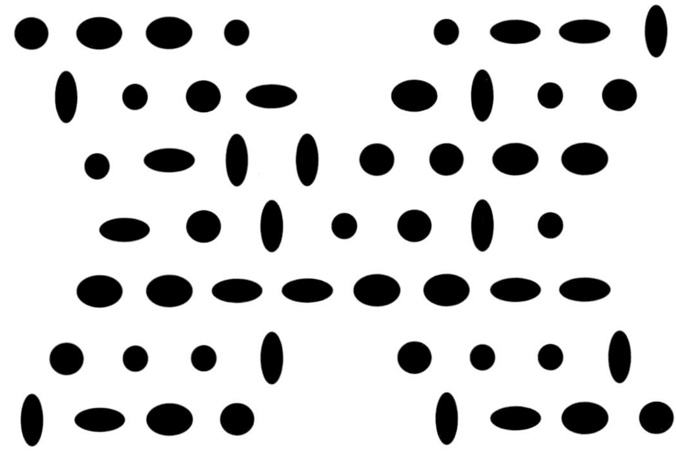

4.

● LEGEND ●

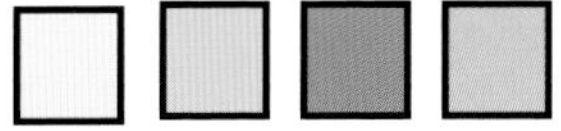

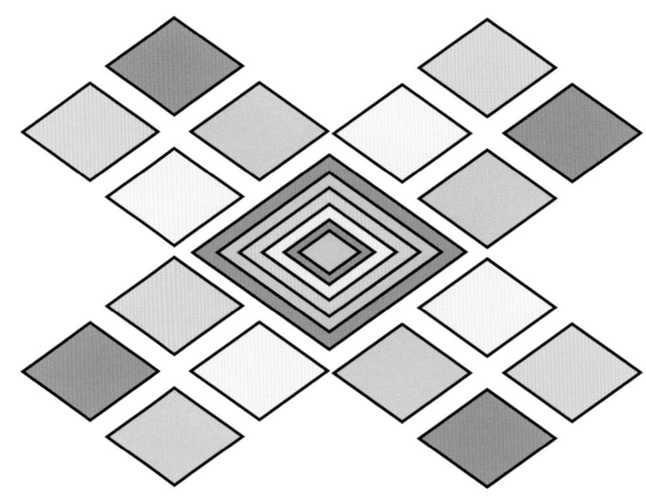

5.

● LEGEND ●

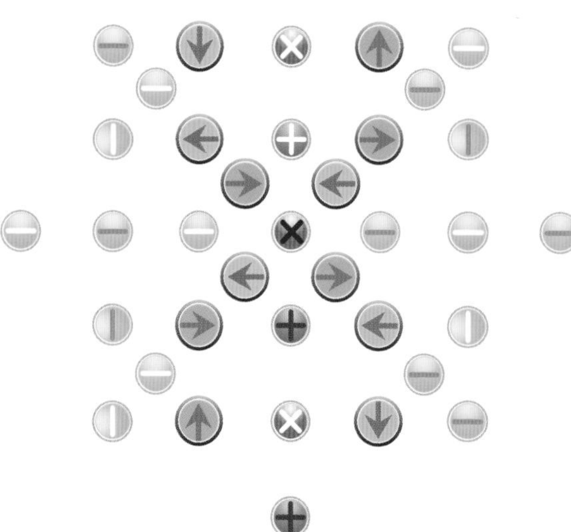

6.

● LEGEND ●

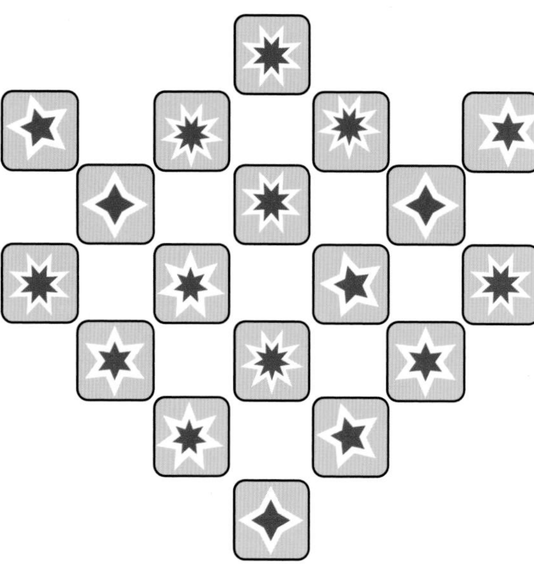

7.

● LEGEND ●

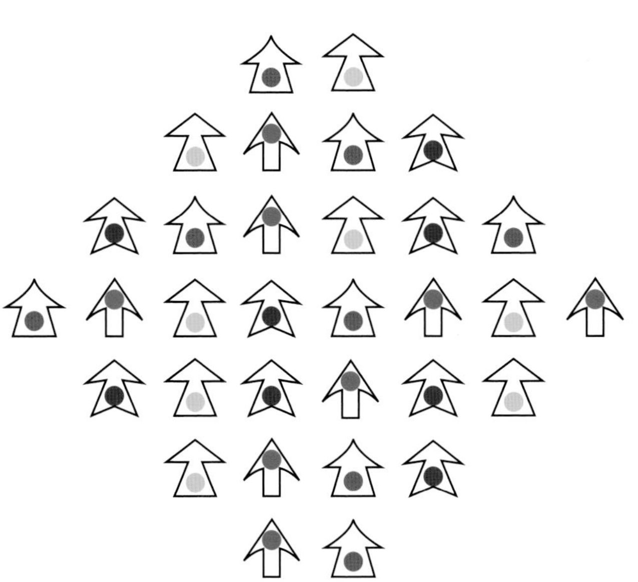

8.

● LEGEND ●

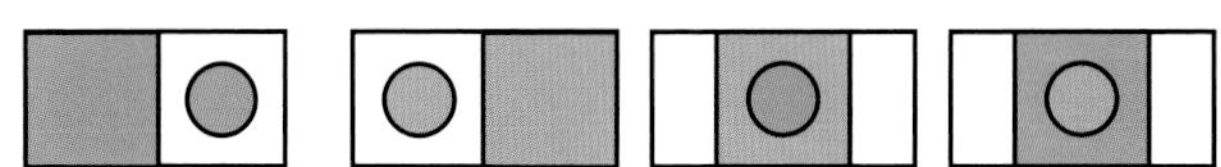

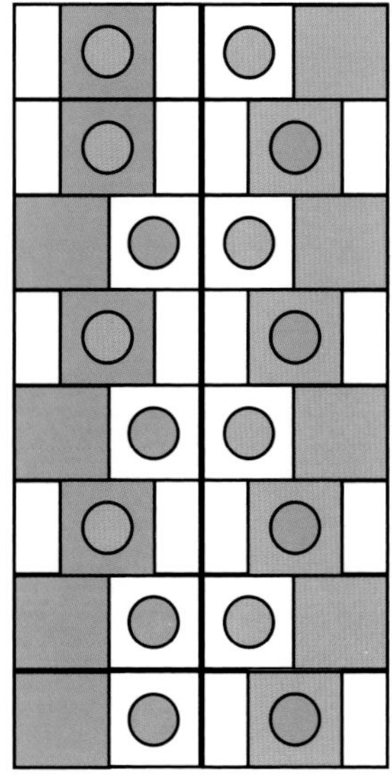

9.

● LEGEND ●

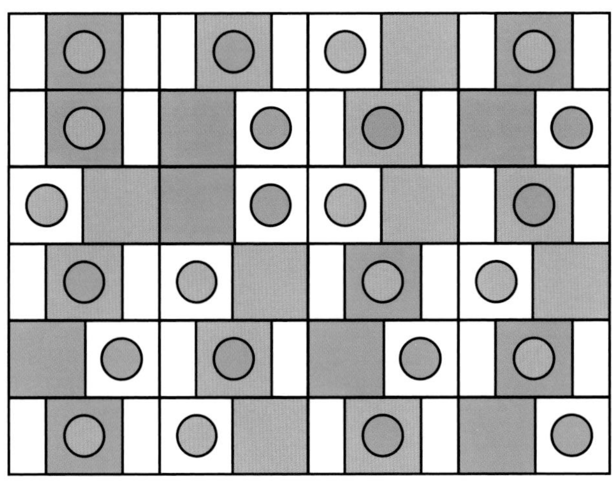

10.

● LEGEND ●

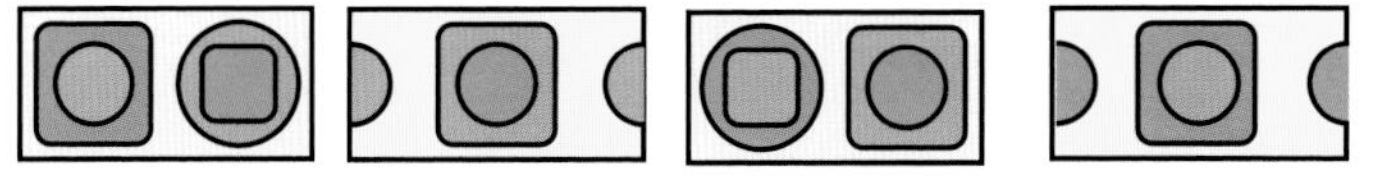

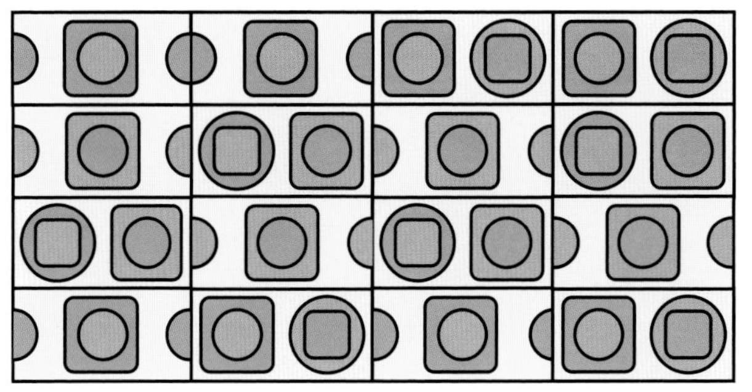

11.

● LEGEND ●

12.

● LEGEND ●

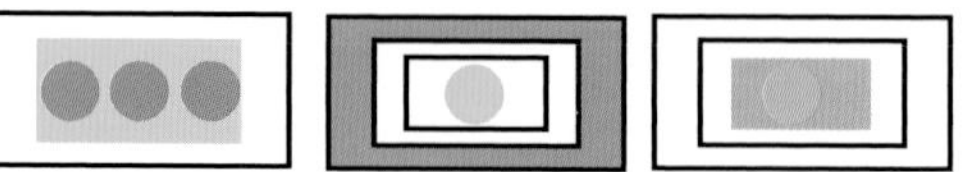

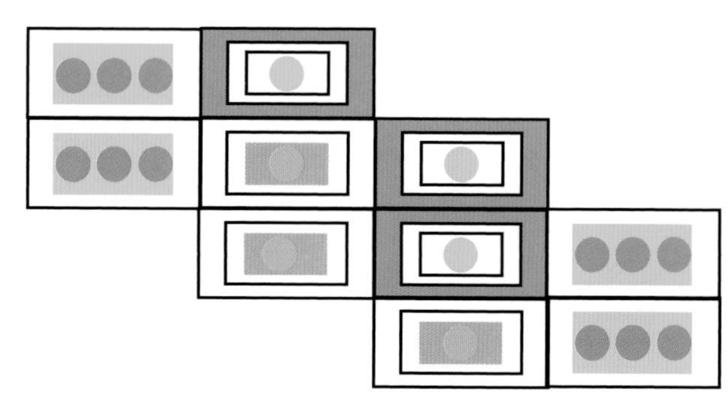

13.

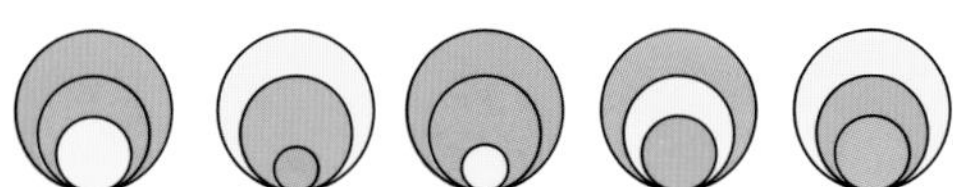

● LEGEND ●

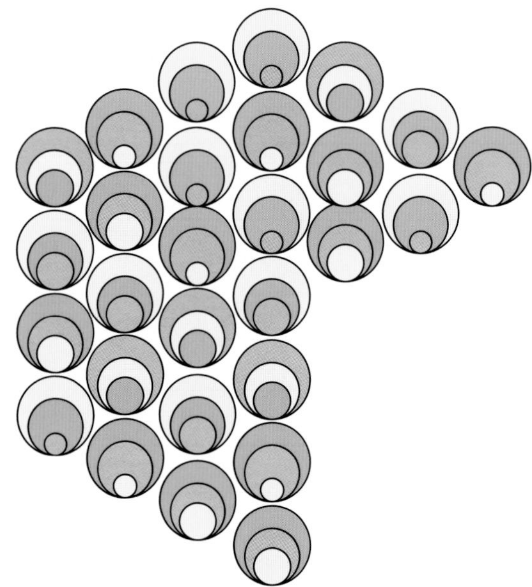

14.

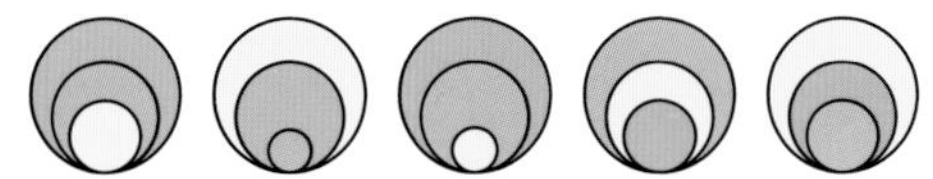

● LEGEND ●

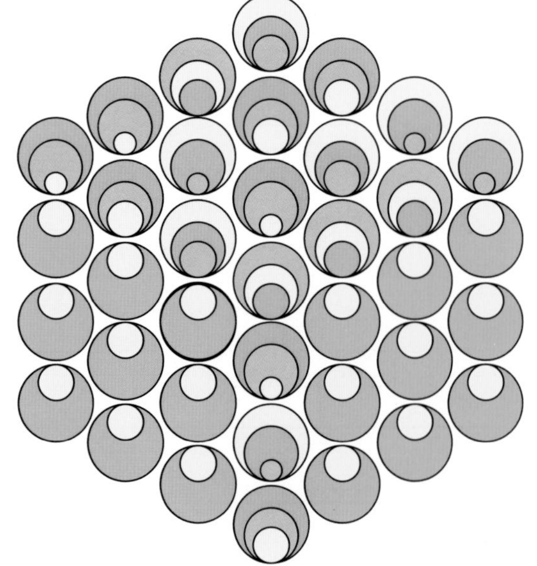

15.

● LEGEND ●

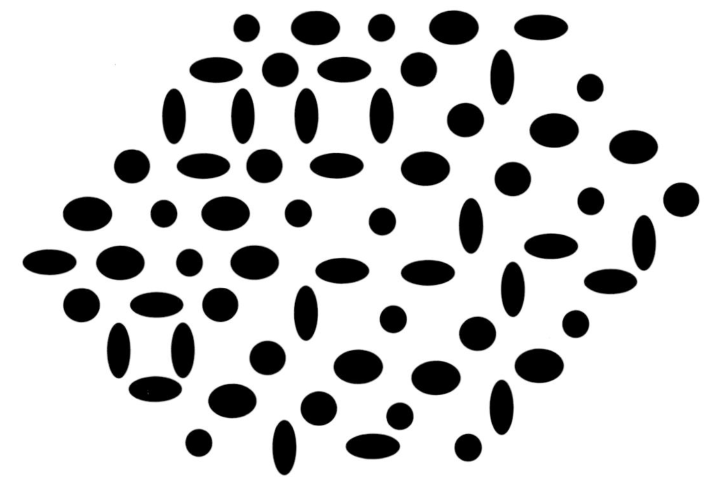

16.

● LEGEND ●

17.

● LEGEND ●

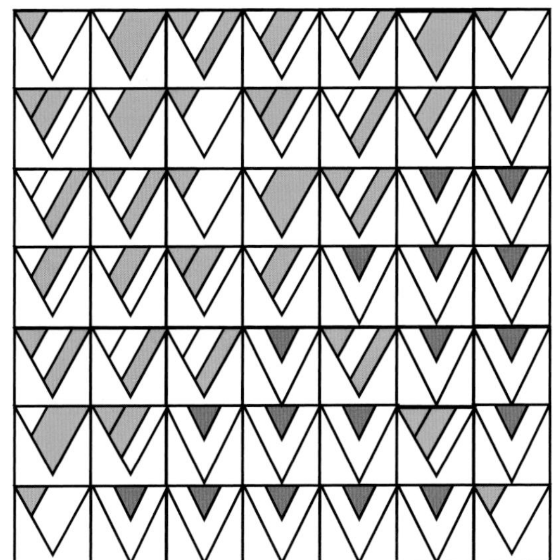

18.

● LEGEND ●

19.

● LEGEND ●

20.

● LEGEND ●

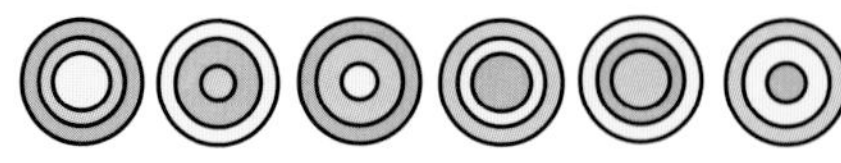

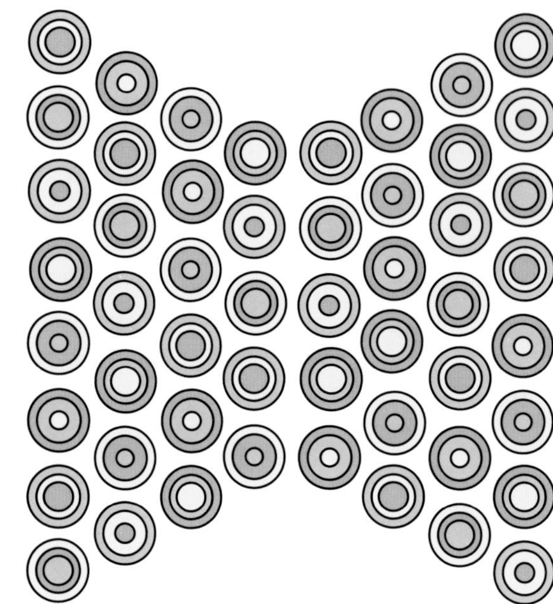

21.

● LEGEND ●

22.

● LEGEND ●

23.

• LEGEND •

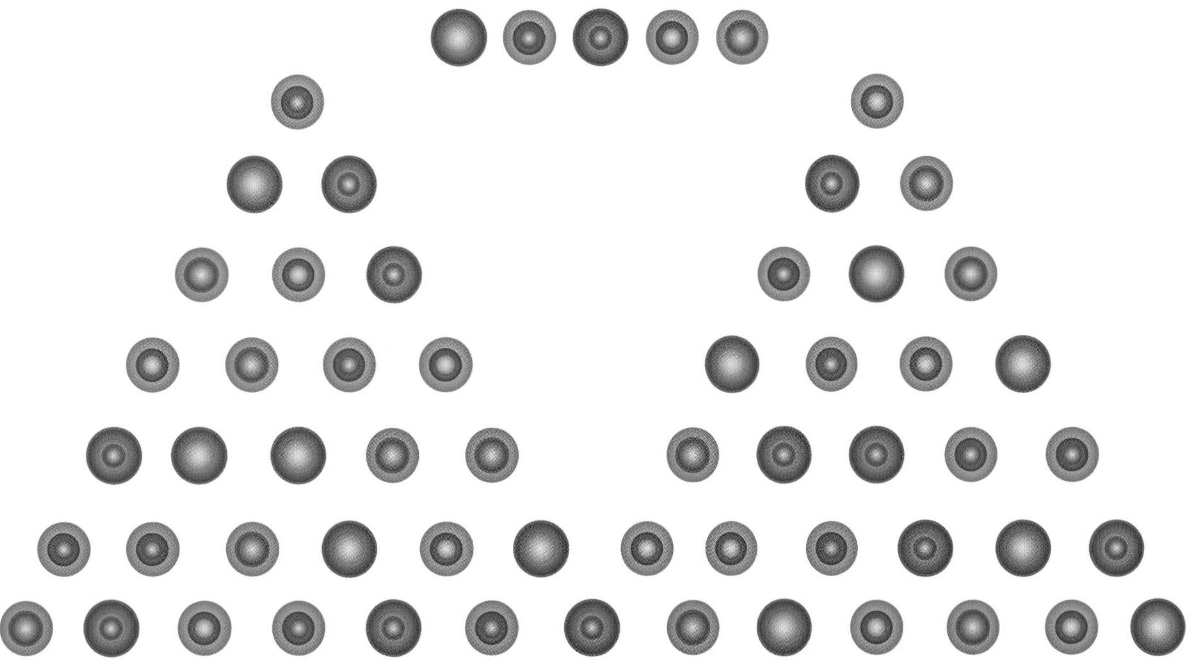

24.

• LEGEND •

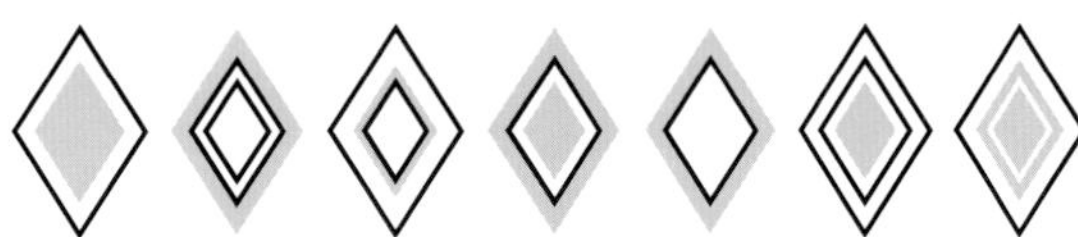

PERFECT CUT

- **In the series of puzzles that follow, instructions would differ from puzzle to puzzle.**
- **Read each question carefully before you solve the puzzle.**

1.

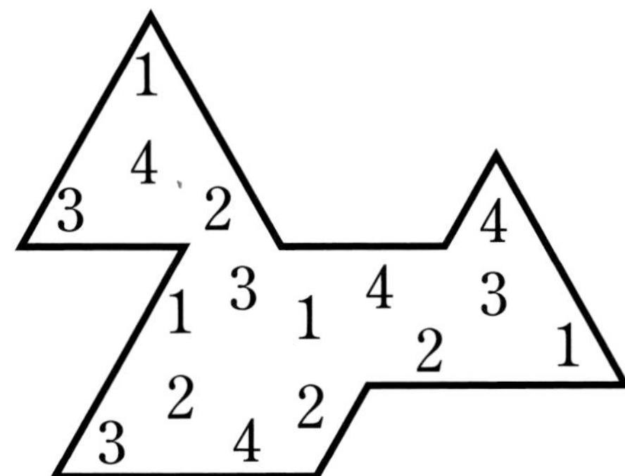

- Divide the diagram into four parts of equal size and shape.
- Each part must contain the numbers 1, 2, 3 and 4.
- The four parts should then be rearranged to form a triangle.

2.

- Divide the diagram into six parts of equal size and shape.
- Each part must contain the symbols ♣, ❖, ◆ and ✥.
- The six parts should then be rearranged to form a star.

3.

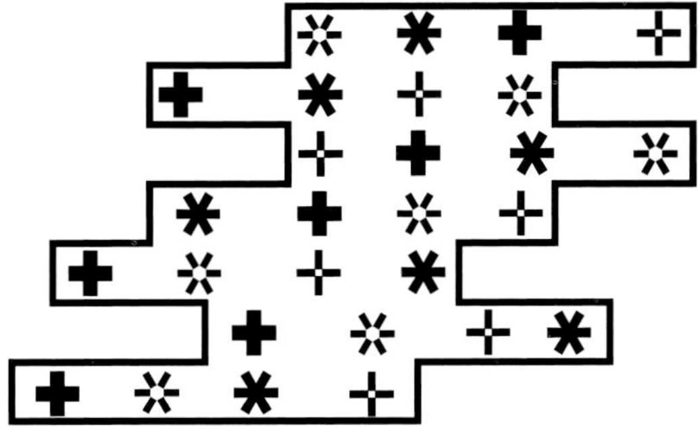

- Divide the diagram into seven parts of equal size and shape.
- Each part must contain the symbols ✛ ,✲ ,✚ and ✱.
- The seven parts should then be rearranged to form a square.

4.

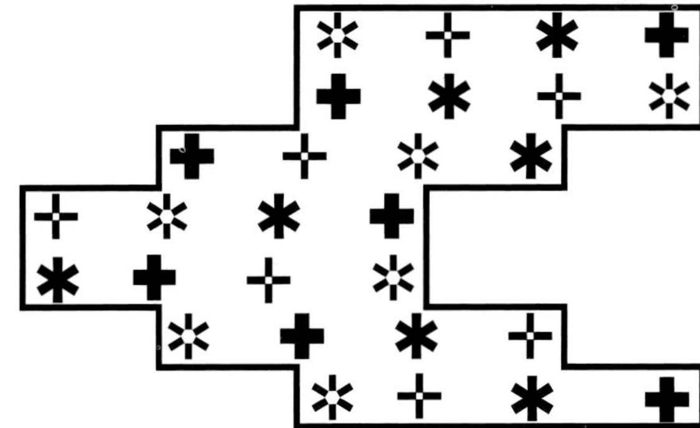

- Divide the diagram into seven parts of equal size and shape.
- Each part must contain the symbols ✛ ,✲ ,✚ and ✱.
- The seven parts should then be rearranged to form a square.

5.

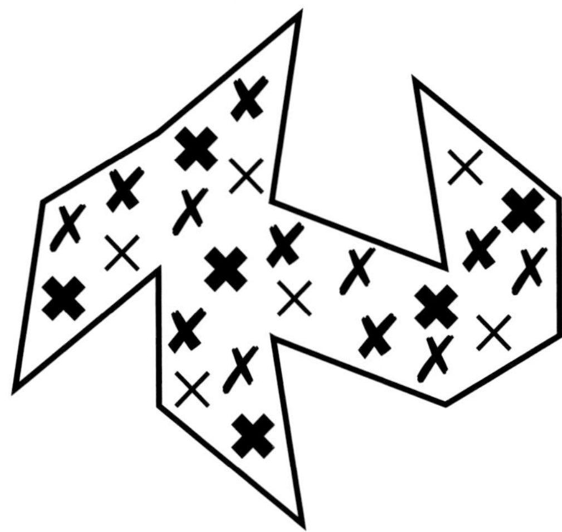

- Divide the diagram into six parts of equal size and shape.
- Each part must contain the symbols ╳, ✗, ✘ and ✖.
- The six parts should then be rearranged to form a star.

6.

- Divide the diagram into six parts of equal size and shape.
- Each part must contain the symbols ✳, ✸, ★ and ✦.
- The six parts should then be rearranged to form a star.

7.

- Divide the diagram into six parts of equal size and shape.
- Each part must contain the symbols ✳, ✸, ★ and ✦.
- The six parts should then be rearranged to form a star.

8.

- Divide the diagram into six parts of equal size and shape.
- Each part must contain the symbols ✳, ✸, ★ and ✦.
- The six parts should then be rearranged to form a star.

9.

- Divide the diagram into six parts of equal size and shape.
- Each part must contain the symbols ✣, ✤, ✢ and ✻.
- The six parts should then be rearranged to form a star.

10.

- Divide the diagram into six parts of equal size and shape.
- Each part must contain the symbols ✣, ✤, ✢ and ✻.
- The six parts should then be rearranged to form a star.

11.

- Divide the diagram into six parts of equal size and shape.
- Each part must contain the symbols ×, ✗, ✘ and ✖.
- The six parts should then be rearranged to form a star.

12.

- Divide the diagram into six parts of equal size and shape.
- Each part must contain the symbols ✳, ✸, ★ and ✦.
- The six parts should then be rearranged to form a star.

13.

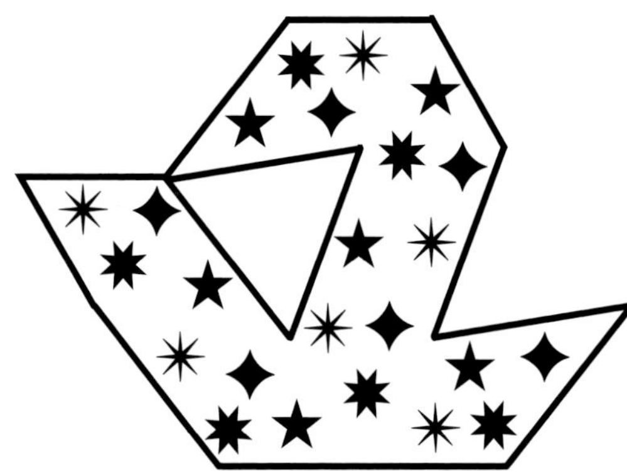

- Divide the diagram into six parts of equal size and shape.
- Each part must contain the symbols ✳, ✸, ★ and ✦.
- The six parts should then be rearranged to form a star.

14.

- Divide the diagram into six parts of equal size and shape.
- Each part must contain the symbols ✳, ✸, ★ and ✦.
- The six parts should then be rearranged to form a star.

15.

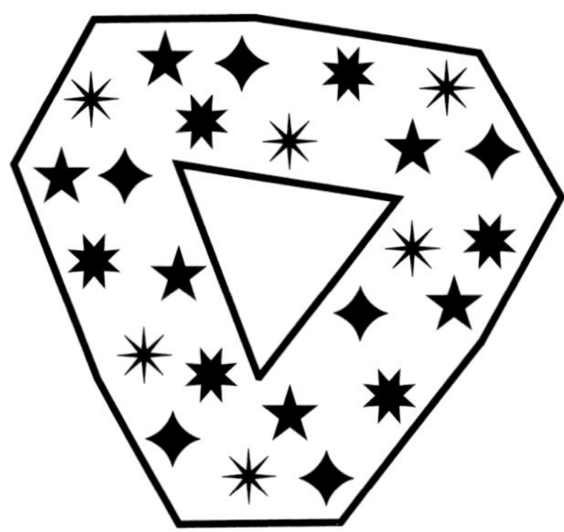

- Divide the diagram into six parts of equal size and shape.
- Each part must contain the symbols ✳, ✸, ★ and ✦.
- The six parts should then be rearranged to form a star.

16.

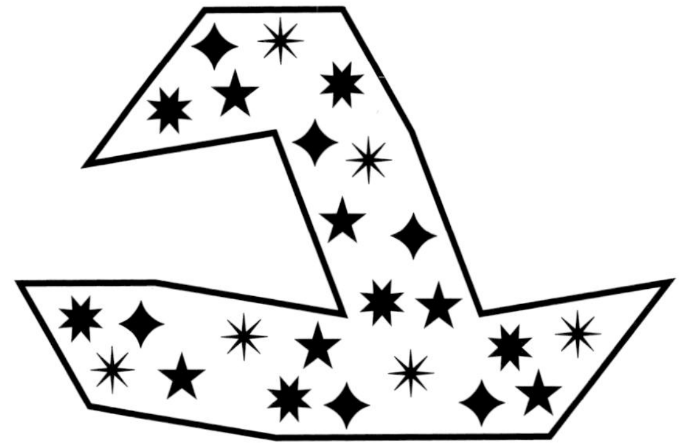

- Divide the diagram into six parts of equal size and shape.
- Each part must contain the symbols ✳, ✸, ★ and ✦.
- The six parts should then be rearranged to form a star.

17.

- Divide the diagram into six parts of equal size and shape.
- Each part must contain the symbols ●, ▲, ■ and ★.
- The six parts should then be rearranged to form a square.

18.

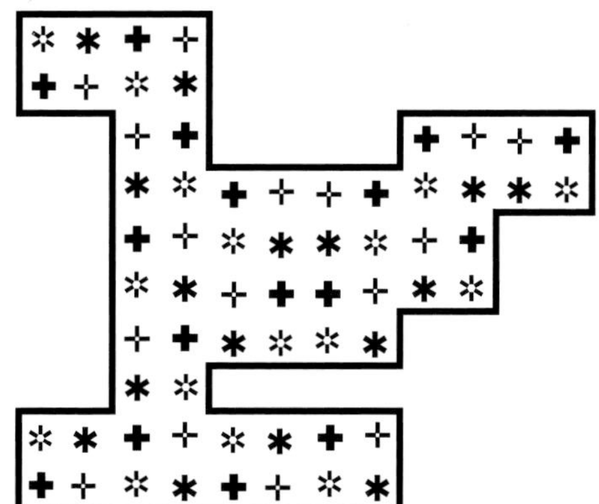

- Divide the diagram into sixteen parts of equal size and shape.
- Each part must contain the symbols ✛, ❊, ✚ and ✱.
- The sixteen parts should then be rearranged to form a square.

19.

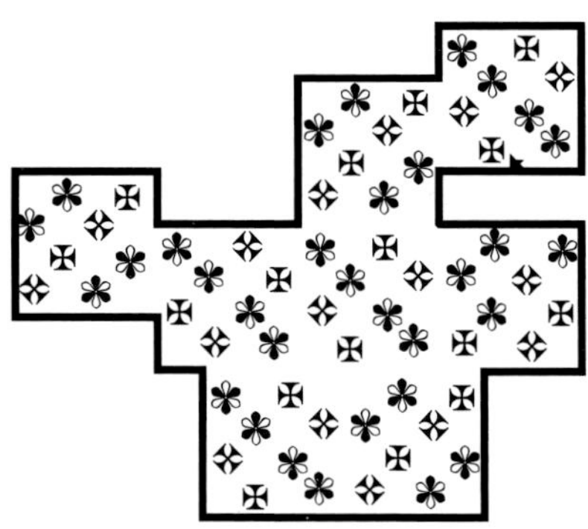

- Divide the diagram into sixteen parts of equal size and shape.
- Each part must contain the symbols ✤, ✠, ✾ and ✧.
- The sixteen parts should then be rearranged to form a rectangle.

20.

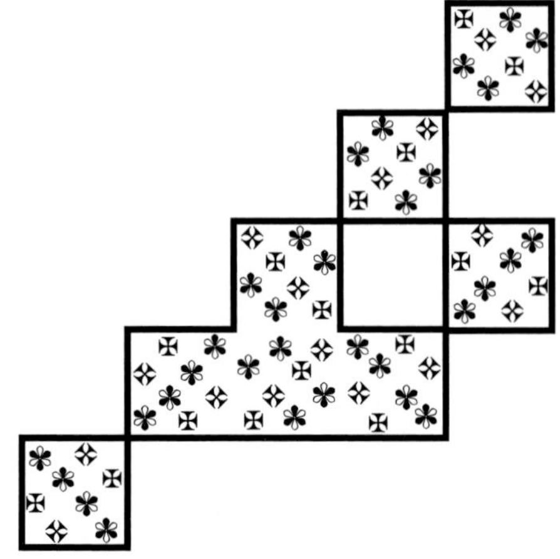

- Divide the diagram into sixteen parts of equal size and shape.
- Each part must contain the symbols ✤, ✠, ✾ and ✧.
- The sixteen parts should then be rearranged to form a rectangle.

21.

- Divide the diagram into sixteen parts of equal size and shape.
- Each part must contain the symbols ✛ , ✲, ✚ and ✱.
- The sixteen parts should then be rearranged to form a square.

22.

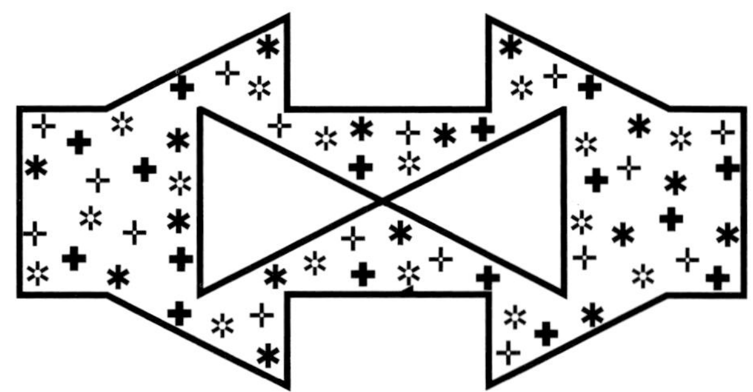

- Divide the diagram into sixteen parts of equal size and shape.
- Each part must contain the symbols ✛ , ✲, ✚ and ✱.
- The sixteen parts should then be rearranged to form a square.

23.

- Divide the diagram into sixteen parts of equal size and shape.
- Each part must contain the symbols ●, ▲, ■ and ★.
- The sixteen parts should then be rearranged to form a square.

24.

- Divide the diagram into sixteen parts of equal size and shape.
- Each part must contain the symbols ●, ▲, ■ and ★.
- The sixteen parts should then be rearranged to form a square.

SUDOKU

- For the puzzles with 4 or 6 boxes, fill each square with a color (from the legend) in such a way that every color appears only once in each horizontal row and vertical column.
- For the puzzles with 9 boxes & color legend given, fill each square with a color (from the legend) in such a way that every color appears only once in each of the nine boxes, as well as once in each horizontal row & vertical column.
- For the puzzles with 9 boxes & symbol legend given, fill each square with a symbol (from the legend) in such a way that every symbol appears only once in each of the nine boxes, as well as once in each horizontal row and vertical column.

1. ●**LEGEND** - 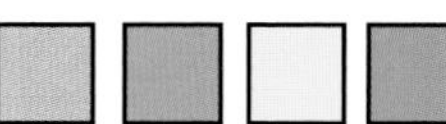

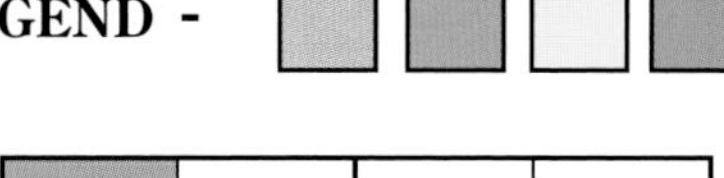

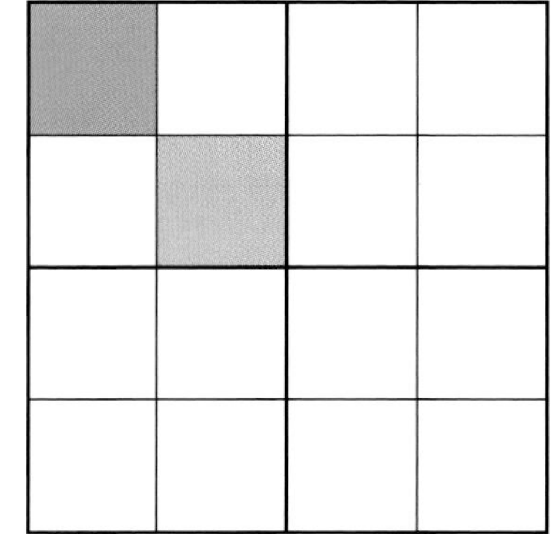

2. ●**LEGEND** - 

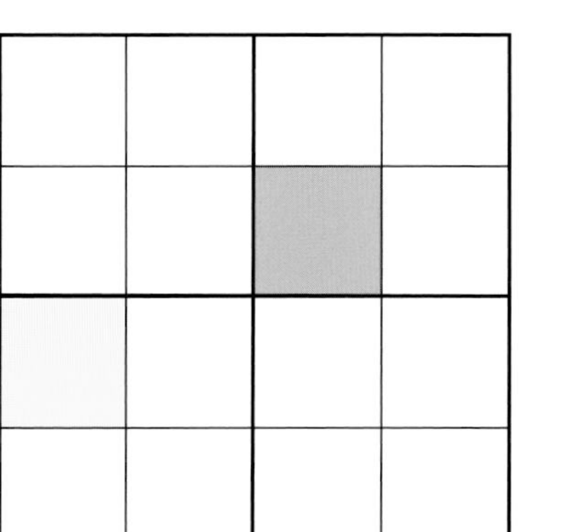

3. ●**LEGEND** - 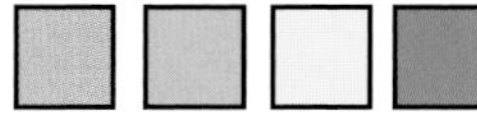

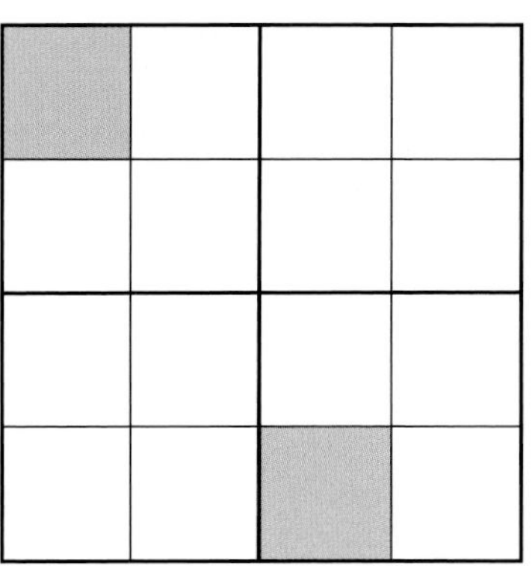

4. ●**LEGEND** - 

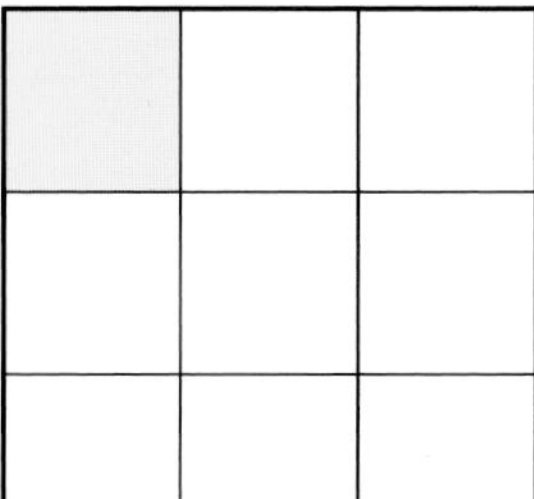

5. ●**LEGEND** - 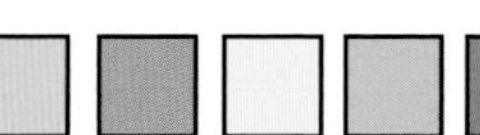

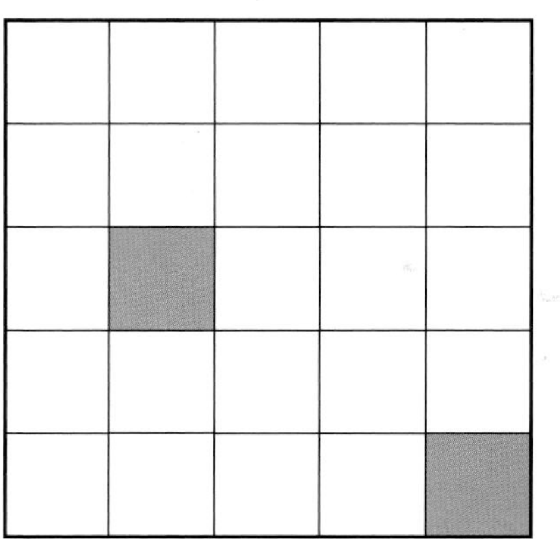

6. ●**LEGEND** -  

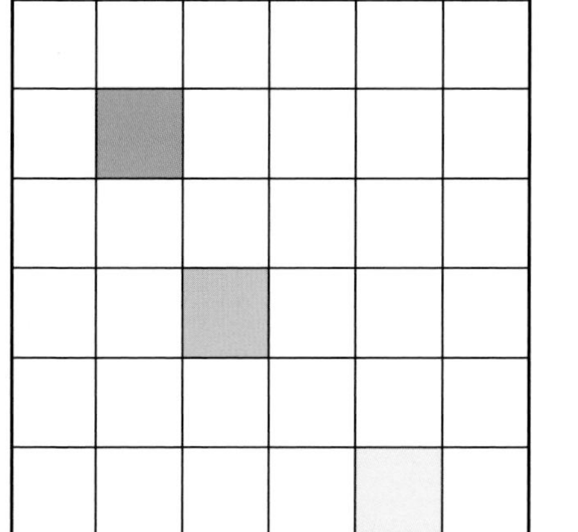

● LEGEND -

7.

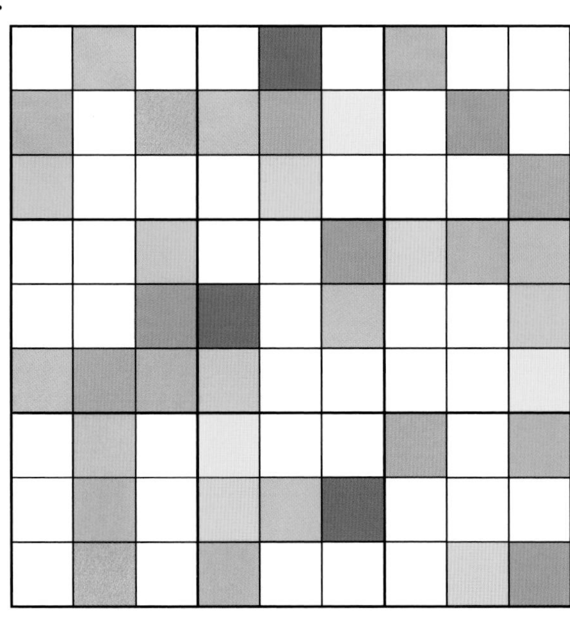

9.

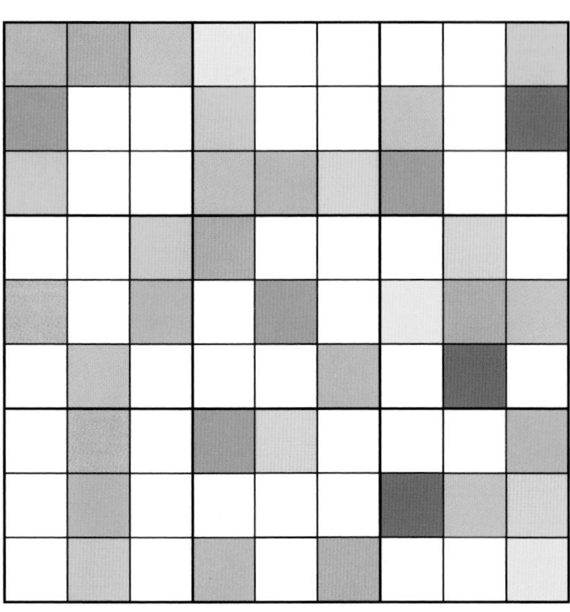

8.

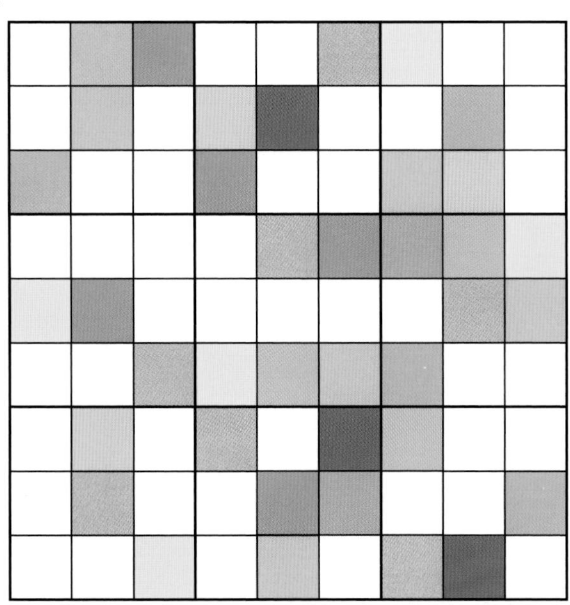

10.

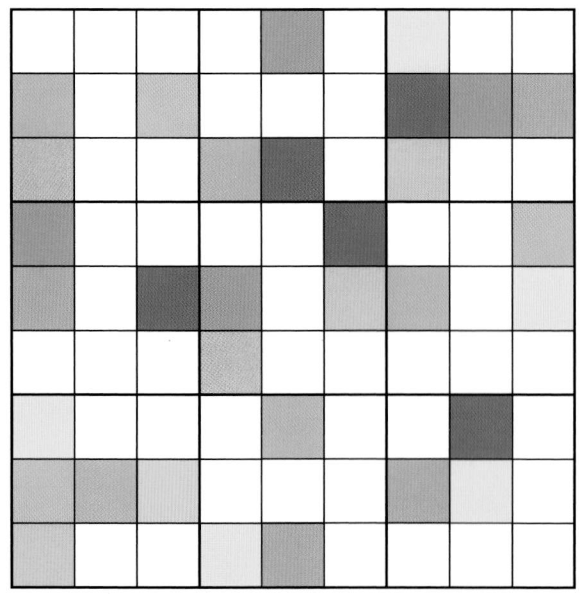

● LEGEND - Δ □ O Ω × ◇ + √ ☆

11.

Δ			◇	O				
Ω	+	☆				O	◇	
◇				+			□	
			√					
O		□	×		Δ	+		◇
×					□			Ω
√			+	□		Δ		
+		Ω				□	×	O
				×		◇		

12.

O		×		√	Ω			
Ω		◇	+		O			×
Δ			☆		×			O
◇			×	+		☆		Δ
□							O	◇
☆		√		◇	Δ			□
√	Δ		□		◇	O		☆
			√			Δ		Ω
				Ω		◇		

13.

			□					O
O	×				Ω	Δ		□
	☆			O		×		Ω
	Ω	+	◇	☆		O	□	
	√	☆	Ω				×	Δ
		O	+		√		Ω	
√					+	☆	Δ	
☆			×	◇	□			
Ω		×		√	Δ			

14.

×				◇			Δ	√
☆		O		Δ			+	
		◇	Ω		√		×	
◇	×	Ω	O					Δ
				Ω		◇		+
	+		Δ		◇			□
Ω	◇		□	×		√		
	☆		◇			Δ	□	
	O				Ω		◇	

● LEGEND - Δ □ O Ω X ◇ + √ ☆

15.

Δ	◇			X		□	O	
√						+	◇	X
+	X			□	◇			
	Δ	◇			X	☆		
☆	O						X	□
			◇	☆		Δ		+
		☆	Δ		√		+	
		Δ	X		□			◇
◇		√	☆			X	□	

16.

X				◇		☆		
				Ω	X	□	+	◇
		□		+		Ω		
		◇	Ω		□	X	☆	O
O	X	√		☆	+			
		☆	O		◇		Δ	+
	☆		X					√
□	◇		+		√		X	
√		X	◇					

17.

	Ω		☆				+	X
X			Ω	◇	Δ			
	O	◇			X	√		Ω
□			◇				√	Δ
	☆			X	Ω			O
O	◇				+	X		
Ω	√	X		+			☆	
◇			O		√	Δ		
		O	X				Ω	√

18.

	√			X		Δ		
Δ		□	√	O	+		☆	
Ω				◇				O
		Ω			☆	◇	Δ	√
		☆	X		√			Ω
√	O	Δ	Ω					+
	Ω		+			O		Δ
	Δ		◇	√	X			
	□		Δ				◇	☆

● LEGEND - △ □ O Ω × ◇ + √ ☆

19.

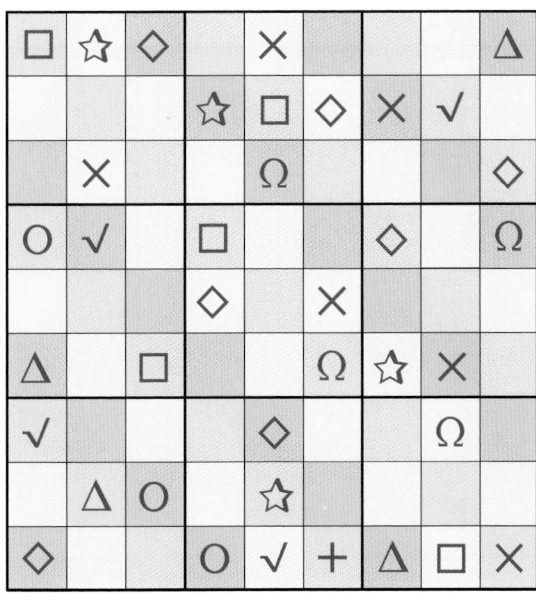

20.

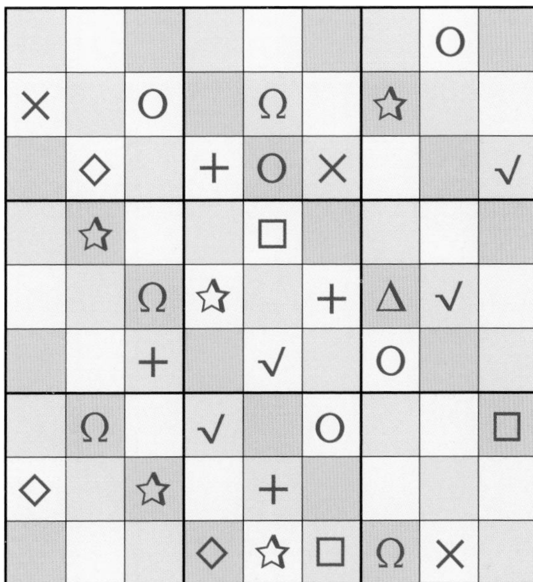

● LEGEND - △ □ O Ω × ◇ + √ ☆

21.

			×			Ω		☆
☆	Ω		+			□		
O	Δ		☆	Ω	◇			
	√	+	□		☆		×	
		O	Ω		+		☆	
	×			√	O	◇		□
+		Ω			×	√	□	
		Δ		+				O
□				Δ			◇	+

23.

☆	◇	Ω	×		+			Δ
	×			Ω				☆
			O		Δ			×
	Ω	◇		□	☆		×	+
□						√		◇
×	Δ		√	◇		☆		
			☆					
			◇	O	×		☆	
Δ	□	☆	Ω			×	◇	O

22.

	√			×		Δ		
Δ		□	√	O	+		☆	
Ω				◇				O
		Ω			☆	◇	Δ	√
		☆	×		√			Ω
√	O	Δ	Ω					+
	Ω		+			O		Δ
	Δ		◇	√	×			
	□		Δ				◇	☆

24.

O		×		√	Ω			
Ω		◇	+		O			×
Δ			☆		×			O
◇			×	+		☆		Δ
□							O	◇
☆		√		◇	Δ			□
√	Δ		□		◇	O		☆
			√			Δ		Ω
				Ω		◇		

● LEGEND - Δ □ O Ω × ◇ + √ ☆

25.

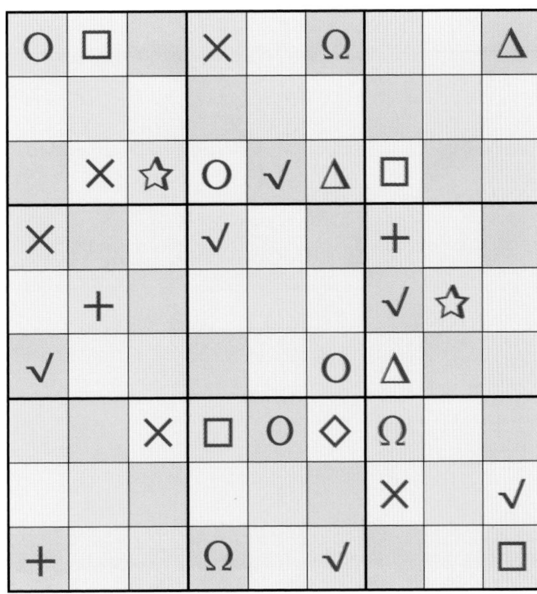

26.

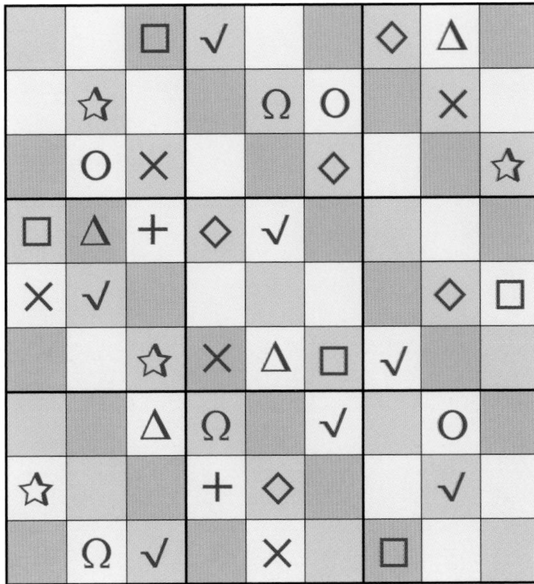

ANSWERS

NUMERICAL

1. A 2. B 3. C 4. C 5. C 6. B 7. D

8. C 9. B 10. D 11. C 12. C 13. B 14. B

15. A 16. A 17. D 18. D 19. B 20. C

21. D. 8+2+4 = 14, 2+5+4 = 11, 5+7+4 = 16, similarly 7+3+4 =11.

22. A. Start from B; jump to alternate segments/ alphabets, work clockwise; skip alphabets in the sequence : B c D ef G hij K lmno P to derive answer.

23. A. 10+7=17, 10+7 +17 = 34, 10+7 +17+34=68;
5+2 = 7, 5+2+7 = 14, 5+2+7+14=28;
4+9 = 13, 4+9+13= 26, 4+9+13+26 = 52;
3+8 = 11, 3+8+11 = 22, 3+8+11+22 = 44.

24. C. 9X5 = 45, 45-4 = 41, 7X5 = 35, 35-7 = 28,
7X6 = 42, 42-3 = 39 and 4X4 = 16, 16-1 = 15.

25. D. 7X3 = 21, 21X2 = 42; 12X8 = 96, 96/2 = 48;
9X4 = 36, 36X2 = 72; 25X6 = 150, 150/2 = 75;
24X2 = 48, 48X2 = 96; 18X9 = 162, 162/2 = 81.

26. C. 2X2 = 4, 4X5 = 20, 20X8 = 160, 160X11 = 1760.
Also 2+3=5; 5+3= 8; 8+3=11; so 11+3=14.
Thus the answer is 14/1760.

OBSERVATION

1. H (Missing Letter - D) 2. V (Missing Letter - O)

3. F (Missing Letter - Y) 4. Y (Missing Letter - P)

5. E (Missing Letter - X) 6. I (Missing Letter - A)

7. C (Missing Letter - X) 8. F (Missing Letter - N)

9. F (Missing Letter - P) 10. L (Missing Letter - A)

11. K (Missing Letter - L) 12. E (Missing Letter - Z)

13. T (Missing Letter - M) 14. P (Missing Letter - R)

15. L (Missing Letter - S) 16. I (Missing Letter - D)

17. Z (Missing Letter - D) 18. R (Missing Letter - W)

19. U (Missing Letter - k) 20. z (Missing Letter - e)

21. K (Missing Letter - W) 22. r (Missing Letter - A)

23. Q (Missing Number - 23) 24. O (Missing Letter - F)

25. a (Missing Letter - b) 26. R (Missing Letter - Q)

ANALOGIES

1. D 2. A 3. C 4. B 5. D 6. B 7. C

8. C 9. A 10. A 11. A 12. C 13. D 14. A

15. B 16. A 17. C 18. D 19. B 20. C

21. B. The shapes reposition from the first figure to the second figure.

22. C. All symbols reposition themselves; lines increase within the shape and outline decreases.

23. C. The second circle has the numerical positions, of the respective alphabets from the first.

24. C. An identical shape is added at the center of the figure.

25. D. 62 is the sum of the numerical values [C=3 + A=1..] of all letters in the word 'Capital'.

26. B. A [1] and B [2] is related to 26 [Z] and 25 [Y]. Similarly 24 [X] and 23 [W] would be related to C [3] and D [4]. The start and end positions of alphabets are related in a particular way.

CATEGORY

1. E 2. C 3. D 4. D 5. D 6. D 7. C

8. E 9. B 10. D 11. E 12. C 13. D 14. A

15. C 16. D 17. D 18. C 19. B 20. D

21. E. Except 'E', all other figures are similar , only rotated.

22. D. Except 'D', all the other figures are similar, only rotated.

23. C. Except 'C', all other figures are the same, only rotated.

24. B. Except in 'B', small shapes impinge on the main shape, so that we are unable to see the corners.

25. E. Except in option 'E', the sum of all the digits, in each sack equals to 14.

26. C. All numbers except 'f and r' are similar to each other. They form by interchanging the digits.

MATCH

1. C 2. D 3. B 4. D 5. D 6. A 7. D

8. C 9. D 10. C 11. D 12. A 13. B 14. D

15. C 16. D 17. B 18. D

19. D. In the other three figures, the colors interchange.

20. B. Only 'B' is identical. In A, the green and blue hexagons change positions; in C, the color of the circle in the center has become white instead of light green and in D, the oval shape in the green colored hexagon is tilted.

21. B. In A, the colors of the oval shapes have interchanged; In C, the green colors in the square have interchanged positions and in D, the colors of the stars have interchanged positions.

22. A. In the other three figures, either the colors or shapes have interchanged.

23. A. In the other three figures, the colors of at least one of the squares has changed.

24. D. In the other three figures, the colors of at least one of the lines has changed.

WATER REFLECTION

• Remember that in all the 'water reflection puzzles' the reflection would always be an inverse image of the problem figure as it is a water reflection i.e. an arrow pointing upwards would have an arrow pointing downwards as its water reflection. Do not confuse it with a mirror image!

1. D 2. B 3. D 4. A 5. D 6. C 7. D

8. B 9. D 10. C 11. D 12. D 13. B 14. C

15. D 16. A 17. D 18. A 19. A 20. D 21. A

22. C 23. B 24. D 25. D 26. D

SEQUENCE

1. D 2. D 3. B 4. B 5. A 6. C 7. A

8. A 9. D 10. B 11. C 12. C 13. B 14. D

15. B 16. B 17. C 18. A 19. A. 20. A.

21. B. The first and fourth problem figure follow the same principle. Hence the second and fifth figure would follow similarly. The symbol below becomes first, second symbol in line remains same, first in line becomes third and fourth remains where it is in the straight line which is formed in the second problem figure. Also the red line below intersects all symbols.

22. B. The upper square has alternately slanting lines, the sequence of hexagons repeats after 3, the black part in the square moves clockwise .

23. D. The curved line moves up and down alternately, the straight line moves towards upper right and bottom left places alternately, the absent line of the hexagon moves clockwise.

24. A. The red circle and blue triangle move clockwise, the green triangle moves alternately in the lower two squares whereas green triangle with the red circle is moving anticlockwise and flipping up and down.

25. C. The number of straight pins decrease by 1 whereas number of curved pins increase by 2. Green triangle moves clockwise. The outside pink portion moves one & then two places ahead alternately, clockwise.

26. B. The number of vertical lines in the inner octagon decrease by 1 and the horizontal lines increase by 1 alternating between up and down. The pink semicircle moves two places and then one place clockwise. The green semicircle moves one place and then two places anticlockwise.

SERIES

1. B 2. D 3. D 4. C 5. B 6. C 7. C

8. B 9. B 10. D 11. A 12. A 13. D 14. D

15. D 16. C 17. A 18. B 19. C 20. D

21. C. The outer shape goes inside and the inside shape comes out. The colors in that positions remain as it is.

22. D. In each row there is one triangle, one circle and one diamond. The color of left half of the shape in first block goes to the left half part of the shape in third block. The color of right half of the shape in second block goes to the right half part of the shape in third block. In each block there are either 2 stars or one star either in right or in left. Also the black ring in each row is either at the center or up or down.

23. C. In each row there are three different shapes with three different colors and each shape and color appears only once in each row. The black figure at the left hand side center is same in any 2 of the 3 blocks and has one side more in the third one. In each row, black ring is placed either towards right, left or center following no particular sequence.

24. C. In this the center part of the figure in first block gets repeated in third block and the upper and bottom part of the second figure gets repeated in the third block. Also the position of the first and third figure remains the same. Both the outer shapes in the first and second blocks appear in the third block.

25. A. The black line rotates in a clockwise direction. The second figure in each row has one side more than the first figure and the third figure in that row has one side more than the second figure. In each row there is only one figure which has double outline. The circles in the first and second block appear in the third block at the same position only their color is the same as the color of the circle in the first block.

26. D. The outer shape of first figure and the center part of the second figure appear in the third figure. Also the corner circles in both the first and second block appear in the third figure in the same position.

PATTERN

1. B 2. D 3. D 4. B 5. D 6. D 7. C

8. A 9. B 10. A 11. D 12. C 13. C 14. A

15. B 16. C 17. A 18. A.

19. D. Answer figures A, B and C cannot be the answers as either the shapes or the colors or both the shapes and colors are changing.

20. A. Answer figures B, C and D cannot be the answers as either the shapes or the colors or both the shapes and colors are changing.

21. C. Answer figures A, B and D cannot be the answers as the shapes are changing.

22. D. Answer figures A, B and C cannot be the answers as the shapes are changing.

23. C. Answer figures A, B and D cannot be the answers as the shapes are changing.

24. B. Answer figures A, C and D cannot be the answers as the shapes are changing.

SIMILARITY

1. B 2. F 3. C 4. E 5. B 6. C 7. B

8. D 9. A 10. A 11. E 12. A 13. C 14. E

15. A 16. C 17. E 18. D 19. B 20. A

21. F. Both the figures contain same number of identical shapes and same number of curved lines.

22. E. Both figures contain 12 triangles of the same colors and same number of black and white dots.

23. B. Both figures are divided by the curved lines to form small parts; all of them contain a single circle.

24. C. Both the figures contain same number of identical smaller shapes [6].

25. D. Both figures contain identical smaller shapes and the line passes through the center of the bigger shape.

26. F. Both the figures contain dots at the corners of each of the shapes & the shapes join at corners.

BRICKS

1. B 2. A 3. D 4. C 5. D 6. D 7. B

8. A 9. D 10. A 11. C 12. A 13. B 14. C

15. B 16. C 17. B 18. D

19. C. In option A, there are 2 black triangles instead of black circles; in option B, colors of 2 semicircles is yellow instead of green, and colors of 4 center triangles get interchanged, in option D, 4 center black dots are missing.

20. D. In option A, colors of the triangles at the edges have interchanged; in option B, 2 blue semicircles are missing and in option C orange and purple colors in the triangles have interchanged.

21. D. In option A, there are 6 black dots and 1 triangle instead of 7; in option B the colors of triangles at the bottom are light pink instead of dark pink and in option C the colors of green and pink triangles have changed positions.

22. D. In option A, the colors of center triangles' have interchanged; in B, the colors of triangles on the outer side have interchanged and in C on the outer side, altogether there are only 8 pink triangles instead of 10.

23. B. In option A, positions of blue and violet triangles with black dots has interchanged; in option C the circle in the center has different colors and in option D the colors of semicircles outside have interchanged.

24. B. In A, positions of the green and orange triangles have interchanged; in C positions of blue and purple triangles have interchanged and positions of orange and green triangles have interchanged and in D the white center circle is replaced by a square.

COLOR PERCEPTION

1. C 2. B 3. C 4. D 5. C 6. C 7. D

8. B 9. D 10. B 11. B 12. D 13. A 14. A

15. B 16. D 17. A 18. B

19. A. In B & C color of the star has changed, in option D all the colors except the star and 2 circles have changed.

20. C. In A, purple ring is replaced by blue; in B, black circle is missing and in D, the white circle is replaced by a black circle.

21. D. In option A, the original white dot has become black; in B the lavender color is replaced by dark purple and in option C, the light yellow color has become bright yellow.`

22. C. In option A, pale yellow and orange colors have changed positions, in B, the white center dot of the oval is missing and in option D the light yellow and orange colors change positions.

23. B. In option A, white circle inside yellow circle is missing, in C, there is an additional shape on the 'ring-shape' at the center and in D the overlap of the circle and the pink shape has interchanged.

24. D. In option A, B & C the colors of the ovals, seen in the answer figures, has changed.

MATRIX

1. A 2. C 3. A 4. B 5. C 6. D 7. A

8. A 9. C 10. D 11. A 12. D 13. A 14. D

15. A 16. C 17. A 18. C

19. D. The colors of at least one of the rings in other 3 options has changed.

20. A. Either the color or the shape has changed in the other 3 options.

21. A. The colors have changed in the other 3 options.

22. B. The color of at least one 'diamond-like' shape has changed in the other 3 options.

23. C. The colors in the other 3 options has either changed or is missing.

24. B. The colors in the other 3 options have changed.

WORD POWER

1. Germ, Term, Team, Mine, Mean, Meat, Rain, Name, Tame, Mare, Gram, Tram, Mint, Rate, Mate, Grate, Greet, Giant, Great, Agent, Meter, Green, Grain, Train, Merge, Regent, Meager, Enrage, Remain, Germinate
2. Mart, Tape, Peer, Reap, Pear, Mere, Rear, Perm, Tram, Meat, Rate, Part, Term, Mate, Meet, Tear, Trap, Pram, Team, Ream, Meter, Parameter
3. Full, Fuel, Less, Clue, Useful, Successful
4. Nib, Bin, Bog, Boo, Big, Book, Boon, Booking
5. Cord, Bard, Dart, Drab, Road, Toad, Card, Broad, Board, Broadcast
6. Lie, Leg, Gel, Nil, Tile, Till, Tilt, Tell, Lent, Line, Glee, Nile, Elite, Glint, Linen, Little, Lentil, Intelligent
7. Brim, Ream, Mare, Mail, Berm, Lama, Mild, Dime, Meal, Mile, Beam, Lime, Male, Lame, Lamb, Balm, Limb, Dame, Maid, Mire, Drama, Amber, Realm, Dream, Blame, Marble, Ramble, Admire, Bedlam, Limber, Admirable
8. Yard, Dart, Damn, Darn, Data, Toad, Road, Drama, Dormant, Mandatory
9. Ice, Tie, Hen, Net, Ten, Cite, Nice, Kite, Neck, Cent, Then, Hike, Thicken
10. Cord, Core, Rote, Race, Card, Care, Tree, Rate, Dart, Cart, Dare, Tear, Read, Dear, Deer, Road, Trace, Erode, Cater, Decor, Trade, Erect, React, Crate, Create, Decorate
11. File, Fail, Life, Left, Felt, Flab, Flit, Fate, Flat, Fuel, Leaf, Feat, Flute, Fable, Fault, Futile, Beautiful
12. Pear, Peer, Pipe, Ripe, Cape, Nape, Deep, Pile, Clap, Peep, Leap, Pale, Pure, Pail, Pane, Pair, Reap, Pain, Carp, Clip, Drip, Pride, Drape, Plane, Paper, Prude, Upper, Prune, Caper, Pupil, Rapid, Pearl, Repel, Plain, Peril, Preen, Price, Creep, Apple, Repeal, Pauper, Dipper, Ripple, Diaper, Nipple, Ripper, Peculiar, Prudence, Perpendicular
13. Awe, Raw, War, Dew, Cow, Wad, Row, Ware, Wide, Ward, Wire, Crew, Crow, Draw, Wade, Wear, Weir, Word, Wider, Weird, Coward, Cowardice
14. Ale, Lay, Let, Tale, Teal, Halt, Late, Heal, Hale, Health, Healthy
15. Dim, Mind, Some, Mode, Dome, Mine, Dime, Monde, Demon, Dimension
16. Cake, Sake, Cook, Like, Cask, Poke, Soak, Look, Pack, Sack, Lack, Lake, Disk, Peak, Leak, Silk, Spook, Spoke, Cloak, Slack, Polka, Sickle, Pickle, Kaleidoscope
17. Aim, Gin, Gain, Mini, Main, Magic, Magician
18. Bus, Tub, Use, Sue, Out, But, Blue, Lout, Tube, Bout, Oust, Stub, Lust, Slut, Lute, Salute, About, Louse, Tousle, Blouse, Absolute
19. Cite, Cure, Curt, Care, Cart, Race, Rice, Cute, Cater, Trace, Carat, Crate, Trice, Crater, Carter, Caricature
20. Sit, Sun, Sue, Sag, Sir, Sin, Site, Sing, Suit, Sure, East, Sign, Seat, Nest, Rise, Sage, Stir, Sire, Rest, Stag, Stun, Star, Rust, Gust, Sane, Gist, Suite, Aster, Rinse, Singe, Stare, Stain, Siren, Sting, Stage, Stern, Grist, Resign, Satire, Singer, String, Strange, Signature
21. Helm, Meet, Mine, Time, Lime, Melt, Mint, Mile, Them, Emit, Might, Theme, Melee, Mitten, Helmet, Mettle, Element, Enlightenment
22. Near, Yarn, Sane, Nest, Rant, Rain, Tent, Tone, Stan, Rent, Stone, Taint, Stint, Saint, Train, Stain, Nasty, Arson, Ornate, Retain, Reason, Orient, Station, Senorita, Stationery
23. Rig, Tan, Tin, Ant, Rat, Tag, Ton, Not, Rot, Rain, Gain, Gait, Grit, Iron, Rant, Gnat, Riot, Train, Grain, Grant, Groin, Ration, Irrigation
24. Sour, Horn, Rose, , Core, Hire, Sore, Rice, Rise, Nice, Icon, Nose, Iron, Cine, Sure, Hose, Sire, Hour, Hero, Ruse, Cone, Soon, Rush, Corn, Shun, Coin, Siren, House, Ounce, Rouse, Noise, Rinse, Curse, Choir, Nurse, Heron, Croon, Horse, Crush, Shore, Ruins, Since, Honour, Course, Heroin, Cruise, Shrine, Chorus, Rhinoceros

SPACE PERCEPTION

1. B	2. B	3. A	4. C	5. E	6. A	7. B
8. C	9. D	10. B	11. A	12. C	13. B	14. D
15. C	16. D	17. B	18. A			

In the answer figures shown below, a particular part of the figure has been indicated as the base and top to facilitate the explanation. However, remember, that it is a three dimensional figure which can be rotated in any angle so as to arrive at the correct answer. Use the suggestion as a starting point and do not think of it as an absolute rule.

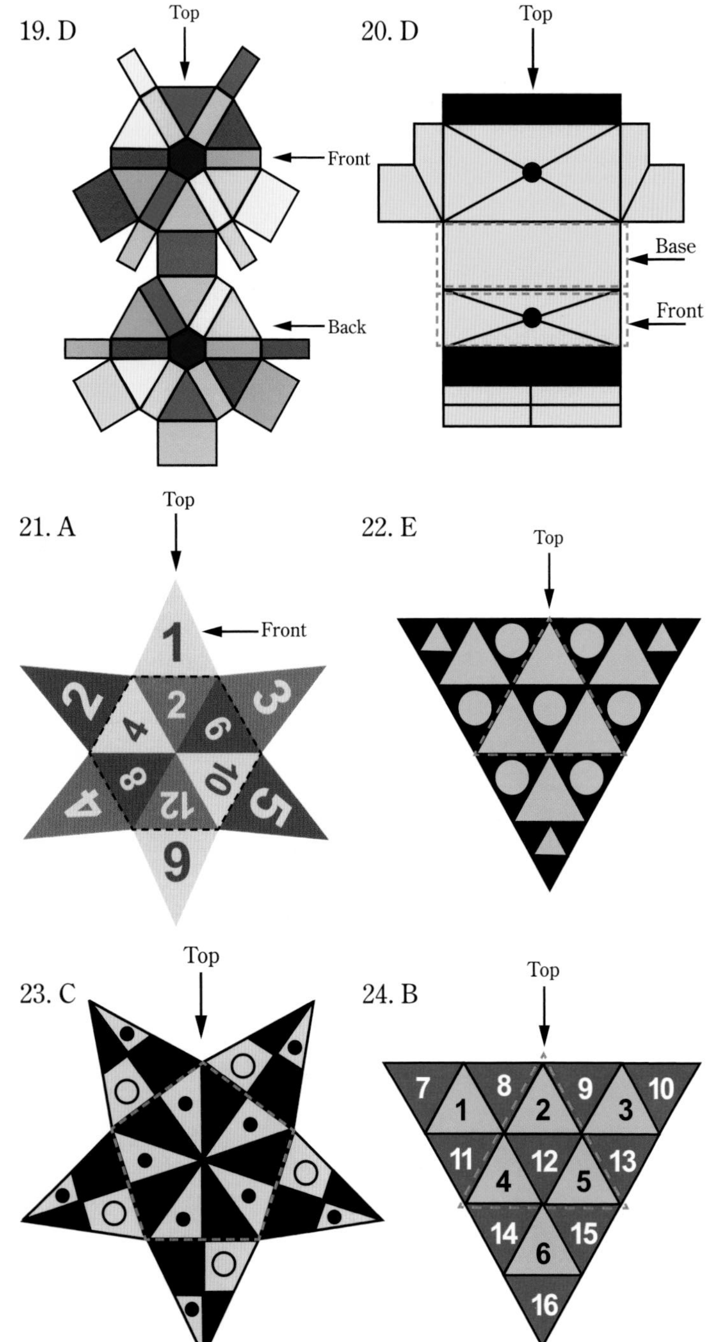

CLUSTER

1. A 2. C 3. A 4. A 5. D 6. C 7. D

8. A 9. D 10. A 11. D 12. B 13. B 14. A

15. B 16. D 17. D 18. B

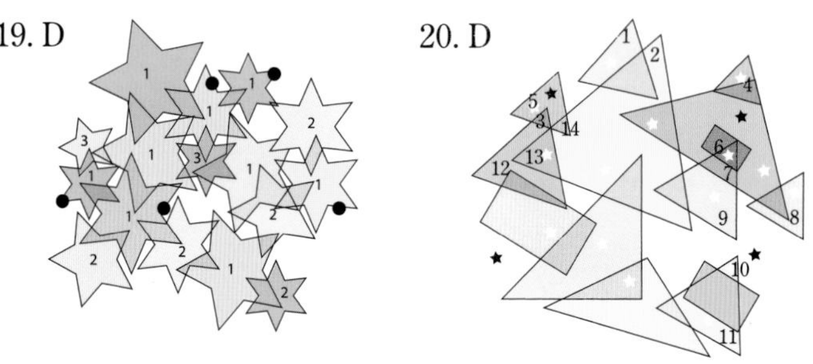

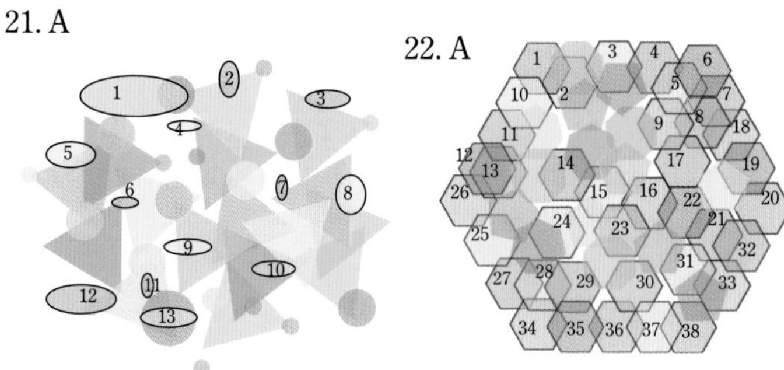

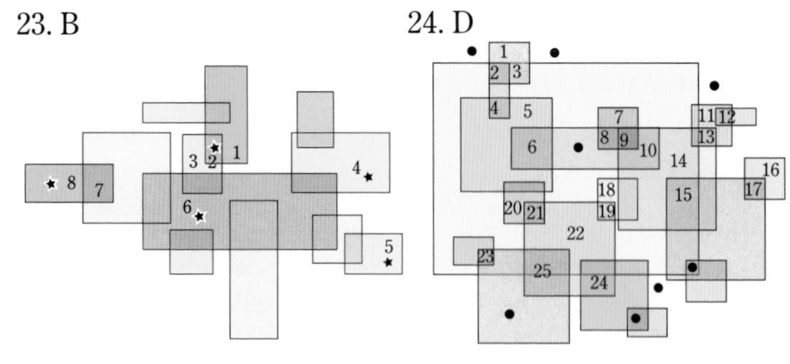

WORD FIND

1.

S	T	E	L	B	A	T
Y	E	S	E	D	S	M
R	D	E	A	E	N	N
J	E	E	D	L	E	U
K	N	A	E	D	R	R
U	S	Y	B	E	U	S
R	T	A	C	E	E	E
S	Y	R	I	N	G	E

2.

A	U	S	T	N	A	T	B	B	A	T
U	E	S	A	O	B	S	D	D	I	S
C	H	I	N	R	H	T	I	R	N	O
E	S	R	N	T	E	R	E	E	D	U
A	L	A	N	H	L	M	A	E	L	T
N	E	U	M	A	A	D	F	D	I	H
E	B	S	R	M	E	U	R	N	A	A
N	Y	T	G	E	R	G	I	E	I	M
A	E	I	L	R	A	I	C	L	M	E
F	P	P	A	I	B	S	A	D	R	R
R	O	D	G	C	T	R	E	A	A	I
Y	R	U	N	A	T	E	D	E	T	C
A	U	S	T	S	A	M	E	E	N	A
N	E	E	U	G	L	A	N	D	A	R
E	B	A	N	T	A	R	T	I	C	A
S	D	N	A	F	R	I	H	T	E	N

3.

C	H	O	C	Y	D	I	P	E	N
C	B	H	T	T	B	L	E	Z	T
K	E	A	A	R	E	T	S	Y	O
X	L	D	Q	W	H	A	L	E	T
V	A	O	C	T	O	P	U	S	J
Z	O	L	B	E	S	R	E	R	O
E	R	P	Q	S	J	L	W	E	V
H	J	H	O	D	T	D	A	O	R
G	C	I	N	T	N	E	Q	E	I
O	Y	N	O	E	Q	R	R	R	W
F	R	O	N	U	G	Q	R	O	O
A	M	K	R	S	H	A	R	K	U
E	I	P	D	F	V	P	U	W	Y
S	T	A	R	F	I	S	H	G	T

4.

O	P	H	F	X	V	D	S	K	T	U	N	K	F	S	Q
H	Q	V	T	M	N	Q	B	L	I	G	X	N	C	I	L
F	L	O	P	P	Y	X	Q	E	C	O	A	Z	R	C	W
Q	Z	D	I	O	S	N	S	H	W	X	G	C	W	M	G
W	E	T	I	R	S	Y	H	A	R	D	D	I	S	K	B
X	I	C	W	T	A	S	E	F	R	R	A	X	L	N	M
W	A	S	E	R	V	O	O	A	S	A	C	U	E	S	D
E	J	E	N	O	K	I	O	M	O	B	A	R	O	I	A
V	R	L	U	T	G	B	C	E	V	A	T	I	C	A	J
H	J	D	Q	X	Y	U	T	O	M	O	N	I	T	O	R
M	C	N	R	E	R	S	K	E	O	X	Q	R	T	L	D
C	U	R	K	S	G	S	A	S	U	B	A	N	H	L	R
J	E	O	S	U	H	N	S	O	S	M	N	P	E	R	N
R	M	U	R	C	A	M	C	D	E	T	B	I	B	K	T
O	I	P	D	F	V	J	A	W	F	X	W	H	H	J	G
P	L	C	O	M	P	A	C	T	D	I	S	C	K	C	B

5.

C	M	S	W	O	O	D	P	E	C	K	E	R	B
C	W	L	W	L	I	A	M	G	M	T	E	S	E
R	R	I	I	E	I	P	A	R	O	R	W	R	R
C	K	A	R	L	A	A	B	S	C	O	H	T	I
S	I	N	N	R	E	R	Y	P	K	S	I	W	A
T	W	M	R	E	E	A	D	A	I	L	I	N	R
O	J	A	I	E	C	K	I	R	N	K	D	U	C
P	S	C	N	S	R	E	B	R	G	S	L	O	U
L	F	L	A	M	R	E	E	O	B	L	V	S	R
A	U	A	R	U	A	T	N	W	I	E	E	T	N
T	U	R	K	E	Y	R	M	D	R	F	R	R	A
T	A	L	M	I	E	T	U	N	D	R	E	I	O
O	N	D	C	N	U	L	W	A	H	I	H	C	G
G	O	O	S	E	L	N	O	E	E	B	A	H	N
N	R	L	U	S	A	C	L	A	I	O	W	F	U
I	R	L	B	I	R	D	S	R	M	R	K	N	M
M	A	C	A	W	A	R	C	N	E	U	T	O	E
A	P	I	M	P	R	T	O	R	A	L	A	C	L
L	B	U	D	P	A	M	L	N	I	B	O	R	F
F	E	N	S	E	T	U	T	H	O	M	S	R	A

6.

A	T	E	L	B	A	T	B	B	A	T
U	E	S	E	D	B	S	D	D	Y	I
C	H	I	N	A	T	Y	N	N	T	N
E	R	R	N	E	E	R	A	E	E	D
R	L	A	N	D	L	M	E	E	L	I
N	E	N	M	D	R	D	F	D	A	A
E	B	D	Y	E	T	E	R	L	T	E
N	Y	R	G	E	R	G	A	E	O	A
A	L	E	L	I	A	I	N	B	A	M
J	A	P	A	N	B	S	C	D	B	E
S	T	D	G	D	T	Y	E	A	T	R
E	I	U	N	I	T	E	D	E	E	A
R	L	N	I	E	L	E	E	E	L	E
N	E	E	N	G	L	A	N	D	A	D
E	B	D	Y	L	T	E	L	L	T	E
S	D	N	A	L	R	E	H	T	E	N

7.

Y	A	S	T	R	O	N	O	M	E	R	I	B	T	P
U	P	E	S	A	O	D	A	N	S	E	U	S	E	E
U	P	H	O	L	S	T	E	R	E	R	O	G	O	D
P	H	P	U	B	L	I	S	H	E	R	R	E	U	I
A	A	H	C	O	U	N	T	A	N	C	Y	L	C	A
H	N	Y	U	G	A	R	C	H	I	V	I	S	T	T
E	G	S	S	N	R	E	B	M	U	L	P	A	S	R
J	N	I	T	I	C	R	G	H	E	I	A	I	T	I
A	A	C	I	S	H	A	I	A	L	M	I	M	I	C
G	M	I	D	I	I	I	N	E	D	R	H	R	D	I
R	H	S	T	A	T	I	S	T	I	C	I	A	N	A
Y	H	T	U	R	E	T	E	L	E	T	Y	T	P	N
G	A	U	S	E	C	A	M	O	E	N	S	N	Y	S
N	S	E	N	A	T	O	R	G	D	A	P	A	R	N
E	V	B	A	D	T	A	R	Y	I	C	A	C	A	A
C	O	M	M	U	N	I	T	Y	W	A	R	D	E	N

8.

C	F	M	S	E	R	O	L	I	V	C	R	W	S	J
H	W	P	S	L	G	L	O	R	G	H	B	I	I	O
R	I	R	D	I	E	I	P	N	A	U	R	L	R	H
I	L	I	U	Z	S	V	R	O	U	R	E	L	W	A
S	L	N	N	U	R	E	A	Y	T	C	S	I	I	N
T	I	T	S	A	I	L	U	N	A	B	L	A	N	N
O	I	E	D	I	E	C	W	I	M	I	L	M	S	E
P	J	S	U	R	W	R	I	U	B	L	S	S	T	S
H	R	S	N	I	A	O	H	E	U	L	L	H	O	G
E	O	D	E	S	S	A	F	N	D	C	I	A	N	U
R	O	I	D	A	M	W	R	L	D	L	E	K	C	T
C	S	A	C	M	I	E	E	A	H	I	W	E	H	E
O	H	N	E	C	N	L	Y	P	A	N	E	S	U	N
L	A	D	O	N	G	L	N	C	E	T	I	P	R	B
U	K	N	B	E	T	A	C	I	N	O	S	E	C	E
M	E	N	I	W	R	A	D	S	E	L	R	A	H	R
B	H	O	R	A	S	S	A	R	N	S	N	T	H	G
U	S	I	R	I	S	A	A	C	N	E	W	T	O	N
S	I	E	L	O	I	S	P	R	U	S	L	E	L	I
L	A	B	R	N	H	A	M	L	Q	N	C	O	L	N
A	L	B	E	R	T	E	I	N	S	T	E	I	N	N

9.

K	P	H	O	T	Q	D	A	A	Z	U	N	K	F	S
E	E	R	L	A	X	W	L	I	V	B	X	C	G	I
P	M	N	Y	B	A	L	P	S	C	D	D	C	B	E
A	V	D	M	I	C	K	I	S	O	U	G	C	B	E
C	Z	S	P	X	Z	Y	L	K	H	D	U	L	X	E
X	Z	U	I	Z	D	B	L	U	E	R	I	D	G	E
S	A	R	C	B	S	R	E	E	S	C	S	C	S	Y
S	I	U	M	Z	B	I	S	M	O	W	T	R	N	I
A	Y	A	U	L	N	E	C	E	N	X	K	T	S	R
Y	T	T	N	U	H	S	S	N	I	P	Q	Y	E	K
A	S	S	S	R	J	S	A	S	D	E	R	N	D	L
L	U	E	O	E	K	O	U	N	S	C	H	A	R	Z
A	B	T	H	W	K	I	R	I	D	X	R	D	V	F
M	B	N	W	G	L	K	Q	E	G	E	U	R	L	K
I	N	O	Q	F	N	Y	B	L	O	R	S	T	O	M
H	X	M	G	S	O	J	N	Y	G	R	R	Y	B	C

10.

F	M	S	E	R	O	L	I	V	C	R	W	S	S
W	P	S	L	G	L	O	R	G	H	B	I	I	H
I	R	D	I	E	I	P	N	B	U	R	L	R	I
L	I	U	Z	O	V	R	O	L	R	E	L	W	B
L	N	N	G	R	E	A	Y	N	C	S	I	I	E
I	C	S	S	G	R	H	D	H	B	L	A	N	N
I	E	D	I	E	C	W	I	T	I	L	M	S	J
A	S	U	R	W	R	I	N	E	L	S	S	T	A
R	S	N	I	A	O	N	E	B	L	L	H	O	M
O	D	E	S	S	M	F	N	A	C	I	A	N	I
O	I	D	A	H	W	R	L	Z	L	E	K	C	N
S	A	C	A	I	E	E	A	I	I	W	E	H	F
H	N	E	C	N	L	Y	P	L	N	E	S	U	R
A	A	O	N	G	L	N	C	E	T	I	P	R	A
K	N	B	E	T	A	C	I	N	O	S	E	C	N
E	N	I	W	R	A	D	S	E	L	R	A	H	C
T	N	N	T	N	N	U	O	E	L	L	R	I	L
I	E	L	O	I	S	P	R	U	S	L	E	L	I
A	B	R	N	H	A	M	L	Q	N	C	O	L	N
S	H	O	R	A	T	I	O	N	E	L	S	O	N

11.

A	S	G	T	B	U	O	D	F	O	W	O	D	A	H	S	X
E	M	P	N	O	C	I	R	P	A	C	R	E	D	N	U	R
S	R	F	S	L	A	R	T	U	U	E	Y	P	Z	N	E	I
G	I	E	F	Y	O	W	S	R	J	H	F	G	F	B	F	V
F	U	P	A	E	C	M	O	I	C	F	B	U	E	B	U	G
B	A	A	S	R	F	H	O	W	M	K	L	C	R	M	T	L
L	F	M	H	Y	W	R	O	P	E	H	C	X	N	G	D	E
B	A	H	I	U	L	I	E	C	E	A	L	E	Q	M	T	A
P	R	A	O	L	S	B	N	O	T	O	R	I	U	S	B	T
K	G	J	T	N	Y	T	L	D	M	I	M	W	D	S	O	D
H	F	U	L	T	E	P	E	K	O	S	D	E	B	P	B	V
A	F	G	H	A	N	T	L	A	M	W	O	W	A	S	U	D
A	S	G	F	G	O	W	S	O	J	H	F	Z	F	E	F	X
L	A	R	T	U	U	E	Y	P	T	N	R	C	Z	N	H	F
F	R	E	S	A	C	E	N	I	D	A	R	A	P	E	H	T

12.

R	O	M	E	O	A	N	D	J	U	L	I	E	T	Y	F	K
S	D	F	H	L	A	R	T	U	U	E	Y	P	Z	N	R	I
G	I	X	C	O	R	I	O	L	A	N	U	S	Z	A	G	N
U	R	P	P	E	K	M	O	I	C	F	B	U	X	B	U	G
B	A	H	A	M	L	E	T	U	M	K	L	M	M	M	T	L
L	F	H	H	Y	S	P	H	S	L	H	Z	X	N	G	D	E
B	A	H	F	U	L	T	E	C	E	K	L	E	Q	M	T	A
P	R	A	O	W	S	B	L	A	H	P	D	F	B	V	B	R
K	G	J	T	N	L	T	L	E	M	I	M	W	D	S	U	D
M	A	C	B	E	T	H	O	S	H	S	D	E	B	V	B	V
F	A	G	H	A	N	T	D	A	M	A	O	W	T	S	U	D
A	S	G	F	G	O	W	S	R	J	H	F	G	F	E	F	X
T	I	M	O	N	O	F	A	T	H	E	N	S	Z	N	H	F
F	R	S	U	C	I	N	O	R	D	N	A	S	U	T	I	T

13.

P	R	A	O	W	S	B	V	F	D	A	H	R	I	A	N	I
S	C	J	M	A	R	C	U	S	A	U	R	E	L	I	U	S
G	D	A	G	K	H	Q	D	T	I	B	E	R	I	U	S	X
J	S	I	L	R	O	J	O	D	F	I	F	G	I	Y	F	X
B	A	H	O	I	L	T	W	N	A	I	S	A	P	S	E	V
O	K	C	K	C	G	M	O	F	C	F	B	U	X	B	U	G
K	G	S	T	N	L	U	D	S	M	I	O	N	D	S	U	D
L	F	H	U	Y	S	E	L	F	L	H	A	X	N	G	N	M
B	N	H	F	I	L	T	T	A	K	I	L	E	Q	E	T	D
A	U	A	N	C	D	B	N	I	R	S	D	F	R	V	B	V
F	R	F	J	W	S	U	V	D	A	S	D	O	B	V	B	V
S	G	J	T	A	A	T	A	L	U	N	Y	P	Z	N	J	F
A	S	G	F	G	R	H	S	L	J	H	F	G	F	Y	F	X
S	H	U	W	K	V	T	D	S	C	A	O	W	D	S	U	D

14.

P	R	A	O	W	S	B	V	F	H	S	D	F	B	V	B	V
C	G	J	A	V	E	L	I	N	M	A	O	W	D	S	U	D
L	F	H	H	S	S	W	G	F	S	N	Z	X	N	G	D	M
J	S	A	R	R	O	W	S	G	F	H	F	G	F	Y	F	X
B	A	H	F	U	L	T	W	S	M	K	L	E	Q	M	T	D
A	C	E	G	I	K	M	O	F	C	F	W	O	X	B	U	G
S	G	J	T	U	L	T	R	L	U	E	Y	P	Z	N	J	F
G	I	X	G	K	H	Q	D	O	V	B	M	C	Z	I	G	X
H	G	J	T	U	R	T	S	L	F	H	H	S	S	W	M	F
F	S	N	Z	A	N	G	A	X	E	E	Y	P	Z	N	J	Z
P	R	F	E	W	S	B	V	F	H	S	D	F	B	V	B	V
B	W	P	F	U	L	T	R	U	M	P	E	T	E	R	U	D
J	S	G	F	G	C	L	U	B	J	H	F	G	F	Y	F	X
Q	B	O	W	T	S	W	G	F	S	N	Z	X	N	G	D	M

15.

A	N	N	T	K	U	R	N	I	K	O	S	G	T
G	N	S	A	D	B	S	D	D	B	S	E	R	H
R	E	D	J	N	T	Y	N	N	T	Y	R	E	E
A	R	U	M	E	E	R	N	E	E	U	E	A	G
N	N	N	A	K	U	R	N	I	H	O	N	T	R
D	N	S	H	D	B	S	D	C	B	S	G	P	E
C	E	D	A	N	T	Y	C	N	T	Y	E	Y	A
A	R	U	L	E	E	I	N	E	E	R	T	R	T
N	L	N	O	E	P	E	E	E	L	E	I	A	W
Y	E	E	G	U	A	D	D	D	A	T	M	M	A
O	A	D	H	L	Z	G	L	L	A	E	I	I	L
N	N	C	R	E	R	G	A	M	O	G	G	D	L
I	A	E	F	B	I	T	P	S	A	T	R	O	O
M	S	O	G	A	P	A	L	A	G	L	A	F	F
H	R	D	D	N	A	Y	G	N	A	I	T	G	C
O	P	U	E	S	I	R	N	N	E	R	I	I	H
R	A	N	R	E	N	E	O	E	L	E	O	Z	I
S	E	E	E	D	A	R	D	D	A	D	N	A	N
E	S	D	R	L	S	E	L	L	T	E	L	T	A
S	A	R	F	O	L	L	A	W	S	T	E	R	G

16.

B	P	H	F	X	V	D	S	A	M	U	N	K	F	V
D	E	R	R	T	M	S	B	I	L	E	X	C	O	O
P	A	N	A	F	S	O	C	S	C	B	D	S	B	S
A	P	O	L	L	O	N	S	H	H	U	K	C	W	T
N	E	T	I	C	Y	Y	H	A	E	H	X	X	X	O
A	L	C	A	L	U	E	E	F	O	C	A	X	A	K
S	T	E	G	N	Z	R	A	D	S	G	C	U	L	S
O	C	E	N	O	K	I	A	M	O	E	A	R	K	I
N	C	C	U	K	G	C	C	E	N	M	S	T	S	R
I	F	A	S	A	C	S	S	N	I	I	Q	Y	E	D
S	A	P	C	I	S	H	E	P	E	N	O	N	D	L
N	N	R	A	C	U	O	M	S	S	I	D	C	Y	D
U	F	O	S	U	H	N	S	I	C	X	R	D	V	F
X	M	E	R	C	U	R	Y	E	G	R	U	R	L	K
X	R	O	D	C	V	Y	A	L	O	R	O	T	O	M
C	I	M	S	F	V	J	G	Y	G	R	B	Y	R	C

17.

G	L	A	D	I	A	T	O	R	T	U	N	K	F	S
D	E	R	R	T	M	S	B	I	L	E	X	C	G	I
P	A	N	P	E	A	R	L	H	A	R	B	O	R	T
A	F	D	Q	X	S	N	S	H	H	U	G	C	W	M
N	E	T	I	C	S	Y	H	A	E	B	X	X	C	E
A	L	C	A	L	R	E	E	F	L	R	A	X	L	N
W	A	T	E	R	L	O	O	E	S	A	C	U	E	S
O	C	E	N	O	K	I	A	M	O	V	A	R	O	I
N	C	C	U	K	G	C	C	E	N	E	S	T	P	R
I	F	A	S	A	C	S	S	N	I	H	Q	Y	A	D
C	U	R	M	S	L	I	O	N	H	E	A	R	T	L
N	N	R	A	C	U	O	M	S	S	A	D	C	R	D
T	F	O	S	U	H	N	S	I	C	R	R	D	A	F
R	M	E	R	C	A	M	E	L	O	T	U	R	L	K
O	I	O	D	C	V	Y	A	L	O	R	O	T	O	M
Y	N	M	S	F	V	J	G	Y	G	R	B	Y	R	C

18.

J	I	S	B	D	F	G	H	D	E	N	B	A
A	R	G	A	T	N	A	N	A	F	C	J	F
W	G	A	F	R	S	A	V	M	U	N	I	C
S	P	O	R	G	L	A	G	K	L	V	D	G
T	K	G	A	G	R	D	X	B	X	R	I	E
D	R	Z	H	I	V	A	G	O	I	T	L	R
O	F	E	C	G	L	N	I	K	R	B	V	M
P	L	P	E	B	C	S	T	E	A	R	K	A
R	C	N	R	F	C	R	G	I	G	Z	G	N
P	O	R	U	H	D	N	L	A	N	I	Q	Y
D	H	J	F	L	I	H	Y	S	P	A	I	N
S	G	A	R	F	I	E	L	D	N	L	E	C
D	E	R	D	I	Y	L	F	F	F	T	E	O
A	A	L	I	Y	T	D	D	R	I	X	F	N
R	O	S	T	R	E	H	T	A	F	D	O	G
G	B	F	H	Y	I	H	F	Y	F	O	F	O

19.

A	L	B	E	R	T	O	S	A	U	R	U	S	H	S	X	M
P	L	E	S	I	O	S	A	U	R	U	S	U	D	S	U	A
S	R	L	S	L	A	R	T	U	U	E	Y	C	Z	R	E	I
G	I	E	O	Y	O	W	S	R	J	H	F	O	F	O	F	A
F	U	P	A	S	C	M	O	I	C	F	B	D	E	T	U	S
B	A	A	S	R	A	H	O	W	M	K	L	O	R	P	T	A
L	F	M	H	Y	W	U	O	P	E	H	C	L	N	A	D	U
B	A	H	I	U	L	I	R	C	E	A	L	P	Q	R	T	R
P	R	A	O	L	S	B	N	U	T	O	R	I	U	I	B	U
K	G	J	T	N	Y	T	L	D	S	I	M	D	D	C	O	S
H	P	R	O	T	O	C	E	R	A	T	O	P	S	O	B	V
K	I	N	E	T	O	S	A	U	R	S	W	O	W	L	S	U
A	S	G	F	G	A	R	C	H	A	E	O	P	T	E	Y	X
H	A	D	R	O	S	A	U	R	U	S	G	J	K	V	H	F

20.

K	G	J	T	N	Y	T	L	D	S	I	M
P	O	U	N	D	E	L	B	U	R	U	S
E	A	H	I	O	L	I	R	C	U	A	L
S	I	W	E	L	O	S	A	U	P	S	W
O	U	A	A	L	C	M	O	I	E	F	B
B	A	N	S	A	A	H	O	W	E	K	L
T	F	M	H	R	A	H	O	M	E	H	C
A	R	F	S	L	I	R	T	U	D	E	Y
E	R	R	L	L	S	A	N	U	I	O	R
L	L	A	E	O	T	O	L	A	N	R	U
H	A	N	R	O	R	A	U	R	A	S	G
G	I	C	O	Y	O	I	S	R	R	H	F
A	S	G	F	G	A	R	N	H	A	E	O
M	A	H	R	I	D	C	E	R	A	T	O

21.

a	S	K	E	L	E	T	O	N
b	S	P	I	T	T	O	O	N
c	P	L	A	S	T	R	A	L
d	W	I	N	N	O	W	E	D
e	F	U	M	I	G	A	T	E
f	O	C	T	U	P	L	E	T
g	M	I	S	C	H	I	E	F
h	L	U	M	B	E	R	E	D

22.

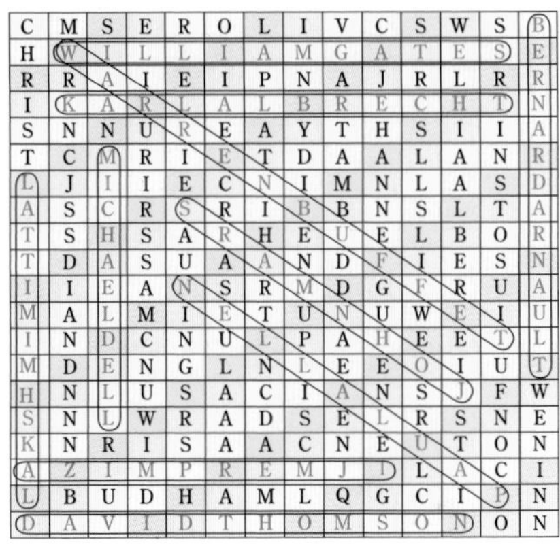

C	M	S	E	R	O	L	I	V	C	S	W	S	B
H	W	I	L	L	I	A	M	G	A	T	E	S	E
R	R	A	I	E	I	P	N	A	J	R	L	R	R
I	K	A	R	L	A	L	B	R	E	C	H	T	N
S	N	N	U	R	E	A	Y	T	H	S	I	I	A
T	C	M	R	I	E	T	D	A	A	L	A	N	R
L	J	I	I	E	C	N	I	M	N	L	A	S	D
A	S	C	R	S	R	I	B	B	N	S	L	T	A
T	S	H	S	A	R	H	E	U	E	L	B	O	R
T	D	A	S	U	A	A	N	D	F	I	E	S	N
I	I	E	A	N	S	R	M	D	G	F	R	U	A
M	A	L	M	I	E	T	U	N	U	W	E	I	U
I	N	D	C	N	U	L	P	A	H	E	E	T	L
M	D	E	N	G	L	N	L	E	E	O	I	U	T
H	N	L	U	S	A	C	I	A	N	S	J	F	W
S	N	L	W	R	A	D	S	E	L	R	S	N	E
K	N	R	I	S	A	A	C	N	E	U	T	O	N
A	Z	I	M	P	R	E	M	J	I	L	A	C	I
L	B	U	D	H	A	M	L	Q	G	C	I	P	N
D	A	V	I	D	T	H	O	M	S	O	N	O	N

23.

W	I	L	B	U	R	W	R	I	G	H	T	G	T
G	B	S	A	D	S	S	D	D	B	O	E	R	S
E	E	D	J	I	T	Y	N	N	T	R	R	E	I
N	N	U	T	E	E	R	N	E	E	V	E	A	R
R	J	O	H	N	D	E	E	R	E	I	N	T	I
I	A	S	E	D	B	E	D	C	B	L	G	P	S
C	M	D	N	N	E	D	I	S	T	L	E	T	A
O	I	U	R	E	N	I	N	L	L	E	T	H	A
F	N	N	Y	E	J	S	E	E	L	W	I	O	C
E	F	E	F	U	A	D	R	O	A	R	E	M	N
R	R	D	O	L	Z	G	L	L	A	I	I	A	E
M	A	C	R	E	R	G	A	M	R	G	G	S	W
I	N	E	D	B	I	T	P	U	A	H	R	E	T
M	K	O	G	A	P	A	C	A	G	T	A	D	O
A	L	B	E	R	T	E	I	N	S	T	E	I	N
O	I	U	E	S	I	R	N	N	E	R	I	S	H
R	N	N	R	R	N	E	O	E	L	E	O	O	I
S	E	E	A	D	A	H	E	N	R	D	N	N	N
E	S	M	R	L	S	E	L	L	T	E	L	T	A
S	A	R	F	L	L	E	B	M	A	H	A	R	G

24.

O	P	H	F	X	V	D	S	K	T	U	N	K	F	S	R
H	P	V	T	M	N	Q	B	L	I	G	X	N	C	I	O
P	C	U	P	E	A	Y	T	E	M	P	L	A	R	C	B
Q	Z	D	S	X	S	N	S	H	A	X	G	C	W	M	E
W	E	T	I	D	S	Y	U	A	R	Z	Y	X	C	E	R
X	I	C	W	L	E	S	E	F	Y	R	A	X	L	N	T
W	A	S	E	R	V	I	O	E	S	A	C	U	E	S	L
E	J	E	N	O	K	I	A	M	O	V	A	R	O	I	A
V	R	L	U	T	G	C	C	E	V	A	T	I	C	A	N
H	O	L	Y	G	R	A	I	L	I	H	M	Y	A	D	G
M	C	N	R	W	R	S	K	E	H	X	Q	R	T	L	D
C	U	R	M	S	G	S	A	S	D	B	A	N	H	L	O
J	E	O	S	U	H	N	S	I	S	D	R	D	A	F	N
R	M	U	R	C	A	M	C	L	O	T	B	O	B	K	T
O	I	O	D	F	V	J	A	A	O	X	W	Q	H	J	G
P	R	I	O	R	Y	O	F	S	I	O	N	Y	K	C	B

25.

W	A	S	E	R	E	T	R	E	H	T	O	M	S
G	B	S	A	D	S	S	D	D	B	O	E	I	H
E	E	D	J	I	W	R	N	N	T	R	R	K	I
N	N	U	T	E	A	I	N	E	E	V	K	H	R
T	E	N	Z	I	N	G	Y	A	T	S	O	A	I
I	L	S	E	D	G	O	D	C	B	L	F	I	N
C	S	D	D	N	A	B	I	S	T	L	I	L	E
O	O	U	A	E	R	E	N	L	L	E	A	G	B
R	N	N	L	E	I	R	E	N	L	L	N	O	A
E	M	E	A	U	M	T	R	E	A	I	N	R	D
T	A	D	I	L	A	A	L	L	A	E	A	B	I
R	N	C	L	E	A	M	A	S	R	W	N	A	W
A	D	E	A	B	T	E	P	U	A	E	R	C	T
C	E	O	M	A	H	N	C	A	G	I	A	H	O
Y	L	B	A	R	A	C	I	N	S	S	E	E	N
M	A	U	E	S	I	H	N	N	E	E	I	V	H
M	N	N	R	R	N	U	O	E	L	L	O	O	I
I	E	M	A	N	D	H	E	N	R	D	N	N	N
J	O	S	E	P	H	R	O	T	B	L	A	T	A
S	A	R	F	E	B	L	L	M	A	H	G	R	A

26.

F	M	S	E	R	E	T	R	I	T	R	A	M	S
R	A	S	A	G	E	O	R	G	E	B	U	S	H
A	R	D	J	E	W	P	N	B	I	R	R	K	I
N	T	U	T	O	A	R	O	L	S	E	O	H	B
K	I	N	G	R	N	A	Y	N	T	S	N	A	E
L	N	S	E	G	G	H	D	J	B	L	A	I	N
I	L	D	O	E	A	W	I	S	I	L	L	L	J
N	U	U	R	W	R	I	N	L	L	E	D	G	A
R	T	N	L	A	I	N	E	I	L	L	R	O	M
O	H	E	A	S	M	F	N	E	C	I	E	R	I
O	E	D	I	H	A	R	L	N	L	E	A	B	N
S	R	C	L	I	A	E	A	S	I	W	G	A	F
E	K	E	A	N	T	Y	P	U	N	E	A	C	R
V	I	O	M	G	H	N	C	A	T	I	N	H	A
E	N	B	A	T	A	C	I	N	O	S	E	E	N
L	G	U	E	O	I	H	N	N	N	E	I	V	K
T	N	N	R	N	N	U	O	E	L	L	O	O	L
I	E	L	V	I	S	P	R	E	S	L	E	Y	I
A	B	R	A	H	A	M	L	I	N	C	O	L	N
S	A	W	A	S	H	I	N	C	A	T	O	N	G

REPOSITION

1.

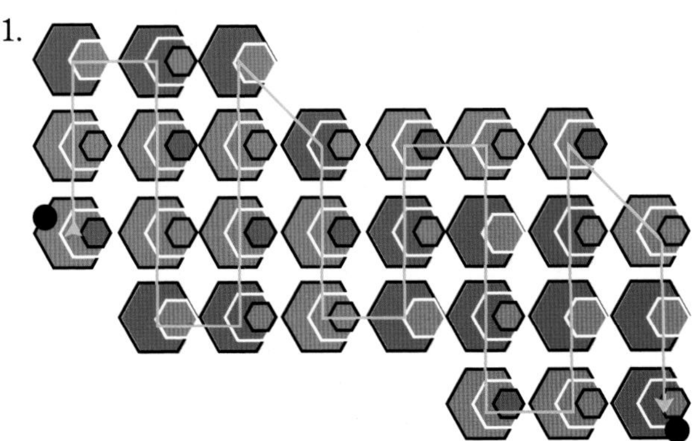

2.

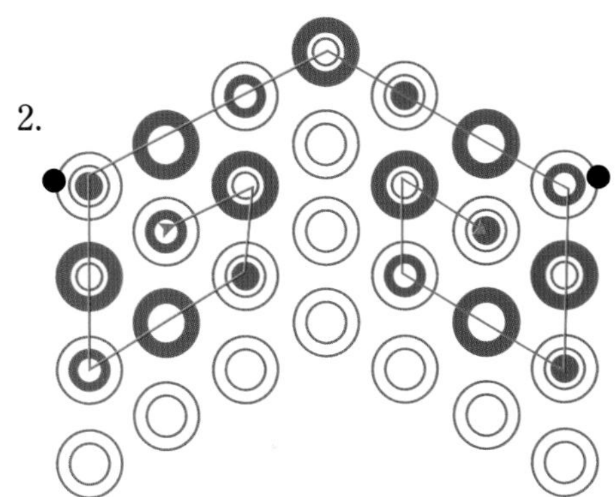

3.

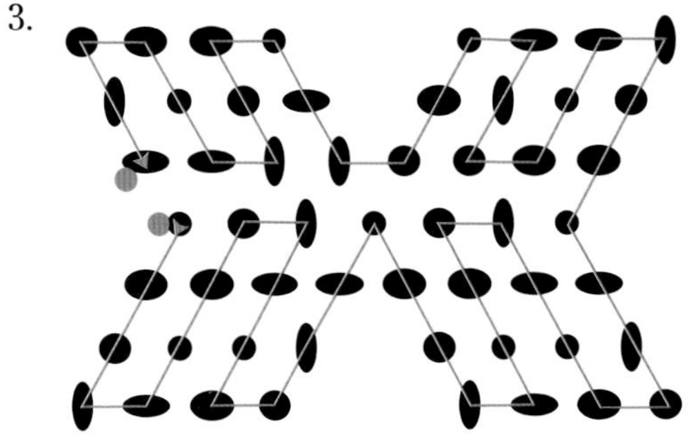

4.

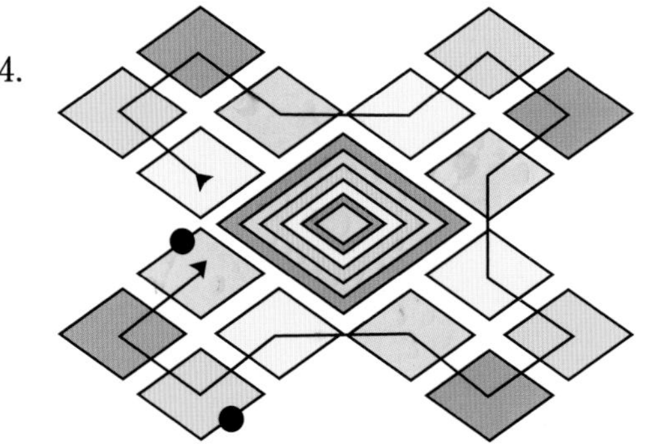

5.

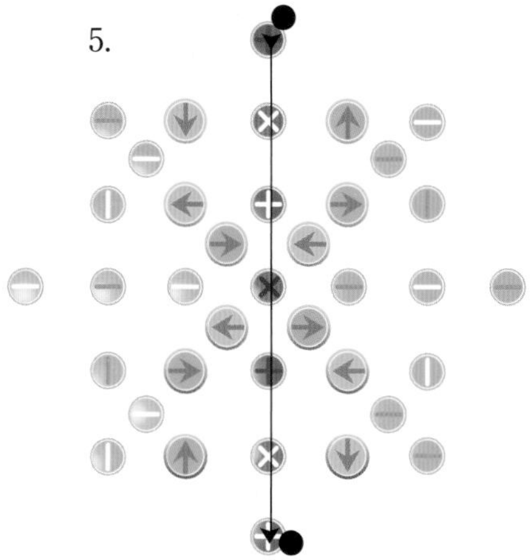

6.

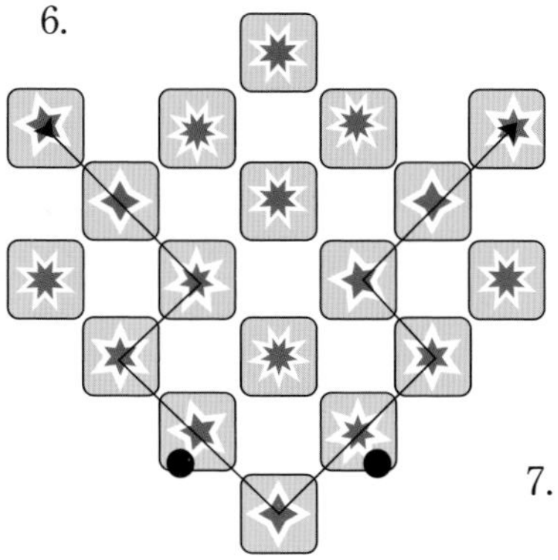

7.

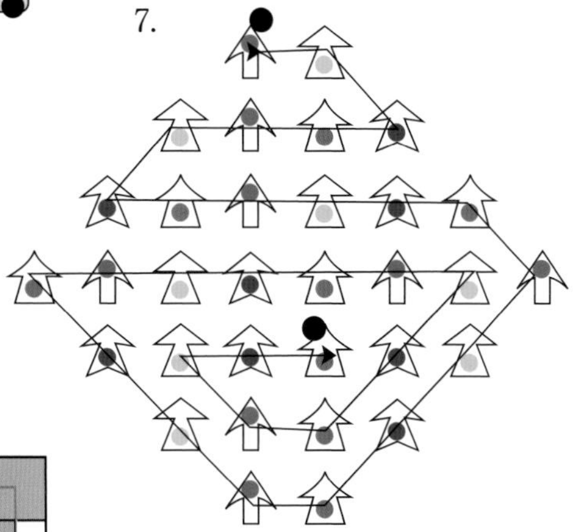

8.

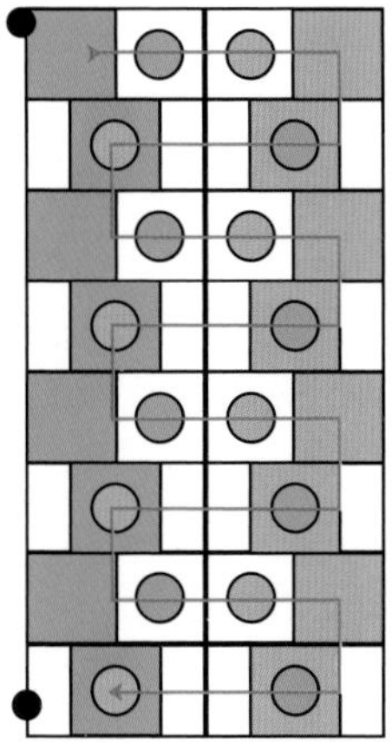

9.

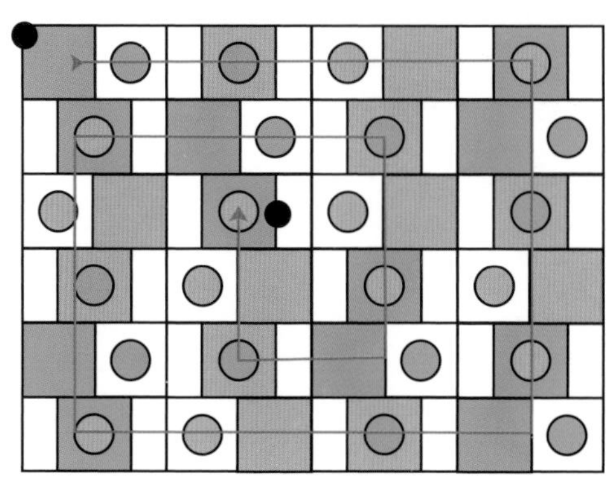

10.

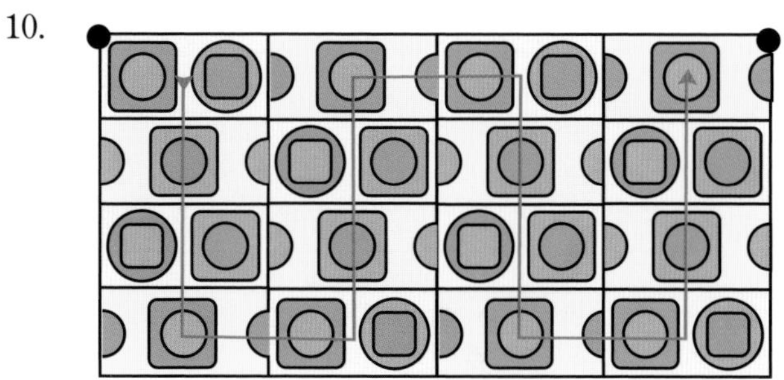

11.

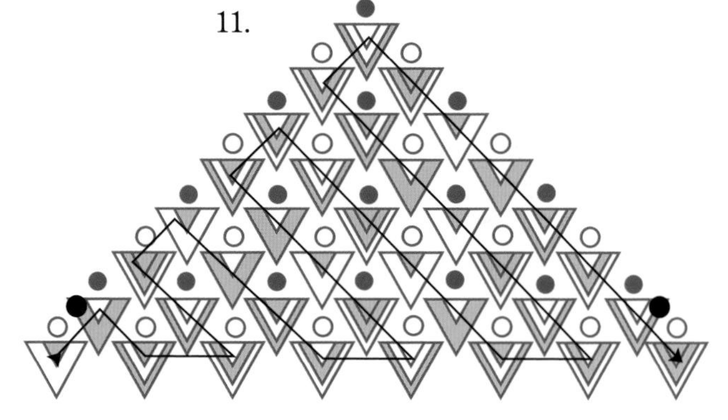

12.

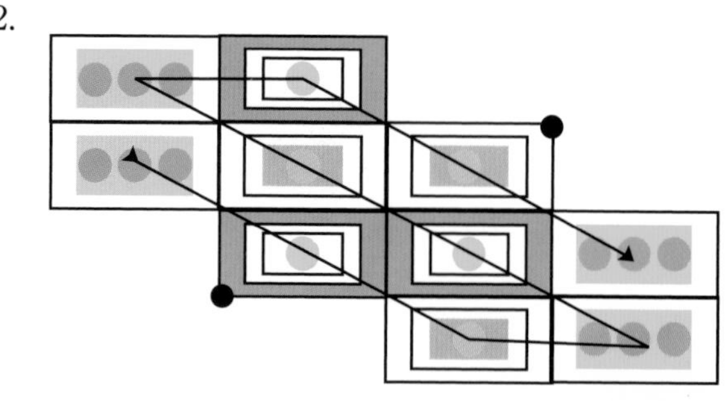

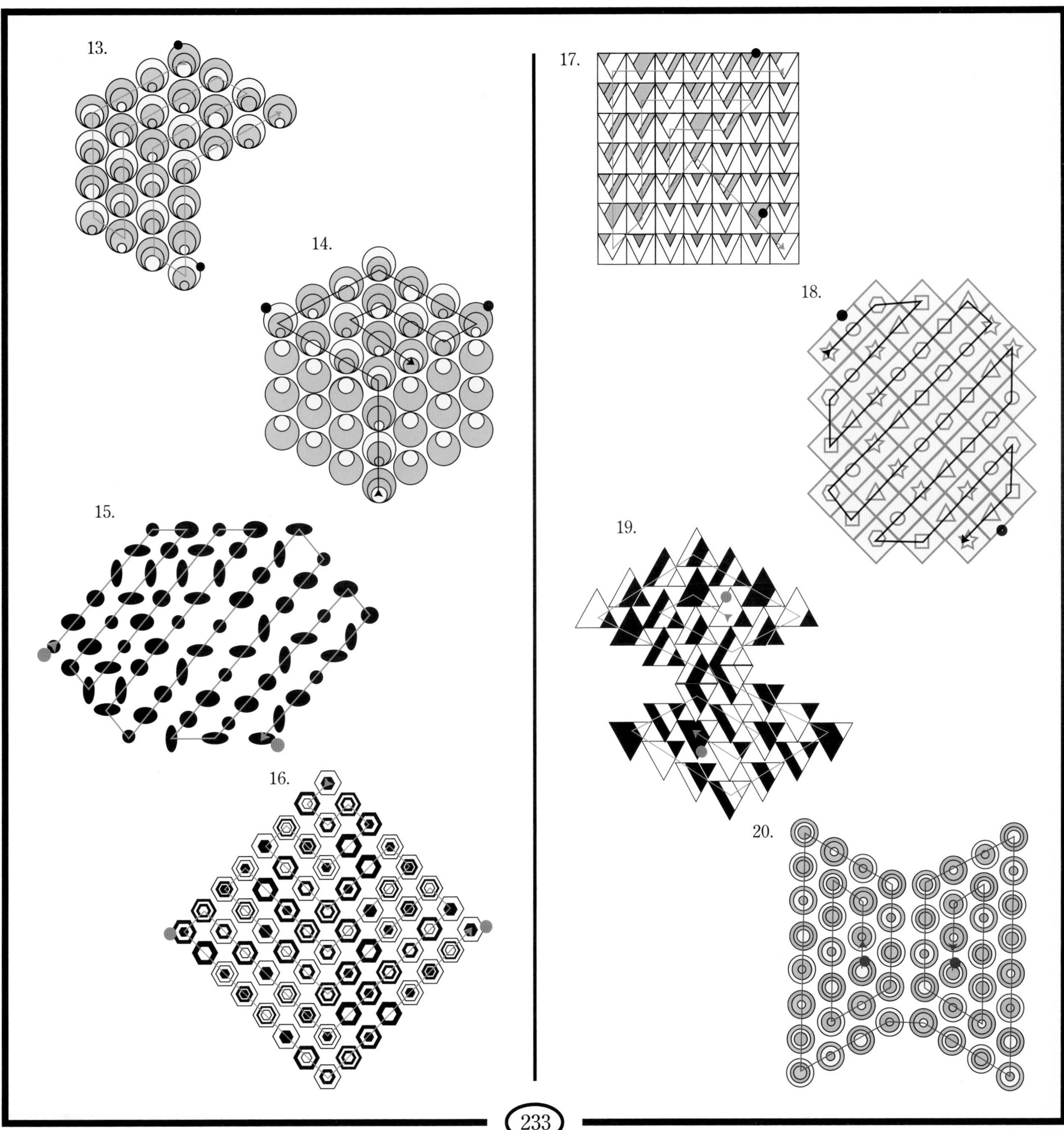
13.
14.
15.
16.
17.
18.
19.
20.

21.

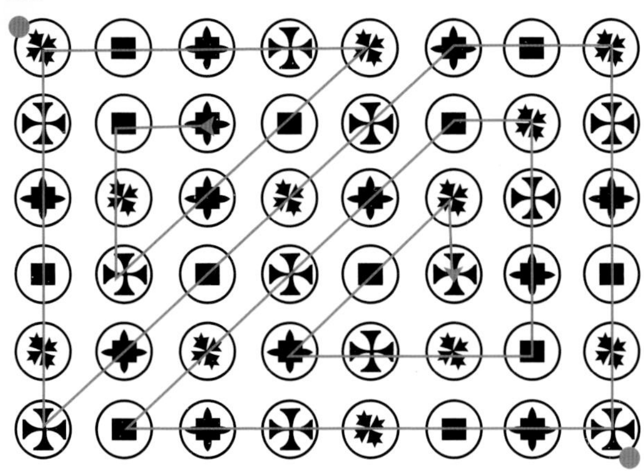

22.

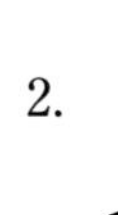

23.

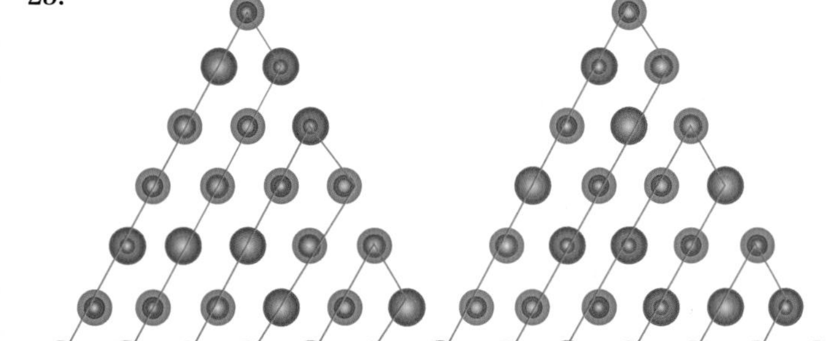

24.

PERFECT CUT

1.

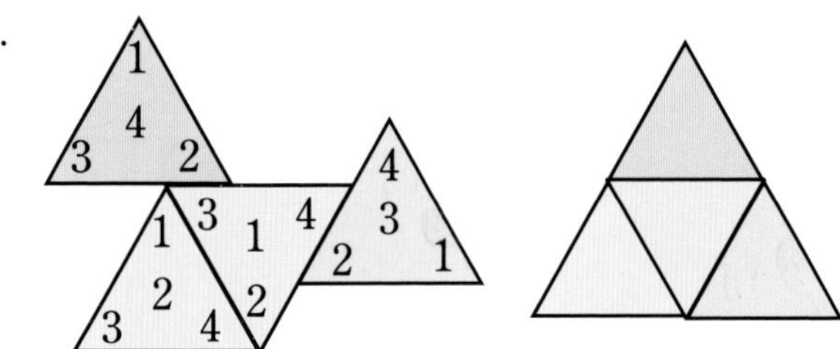

2.

3.

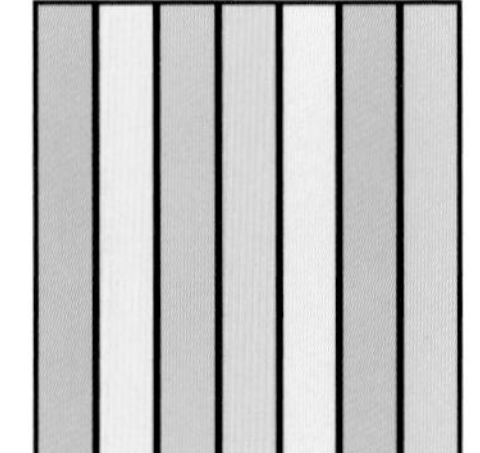

4.

5.

6.

7.

8.

9.

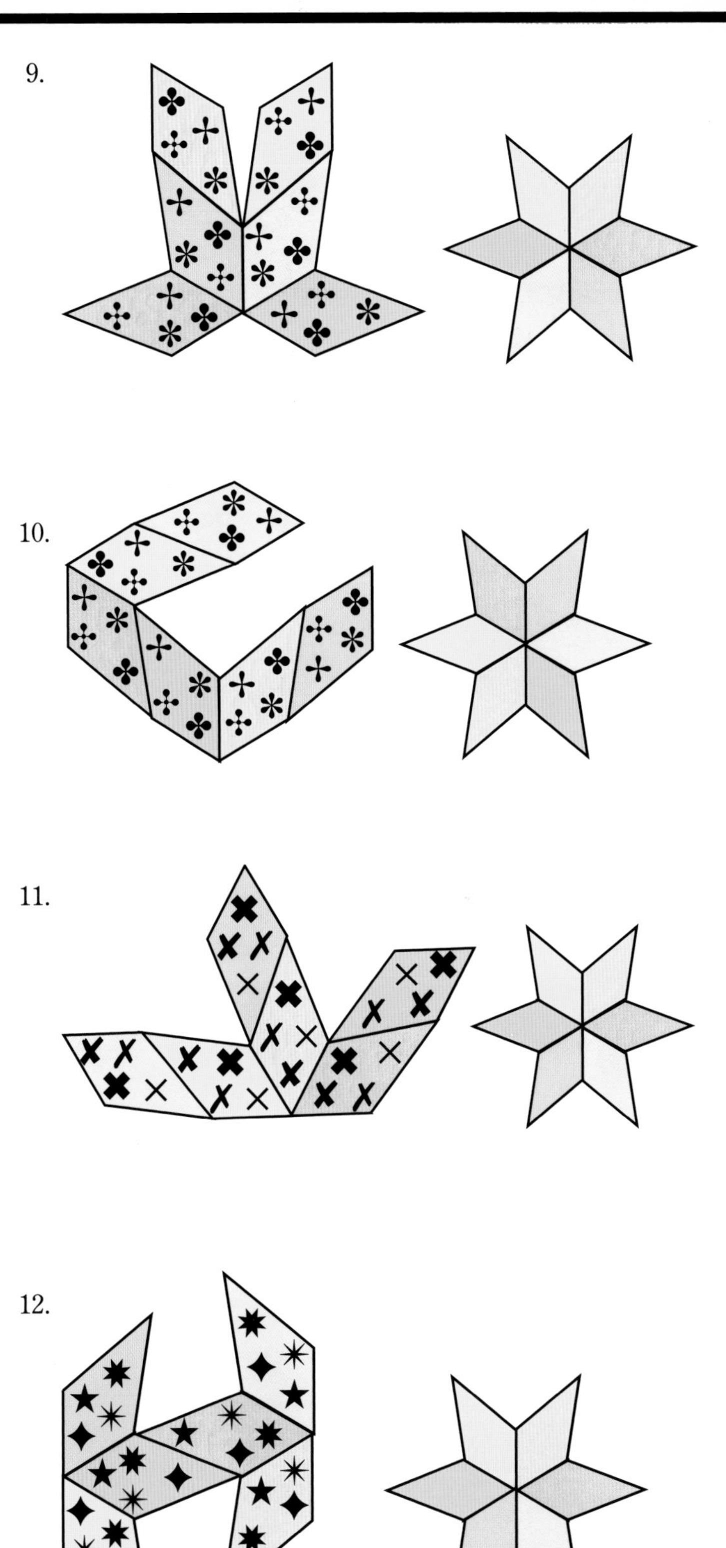

10.

11.

12.

13.

14.

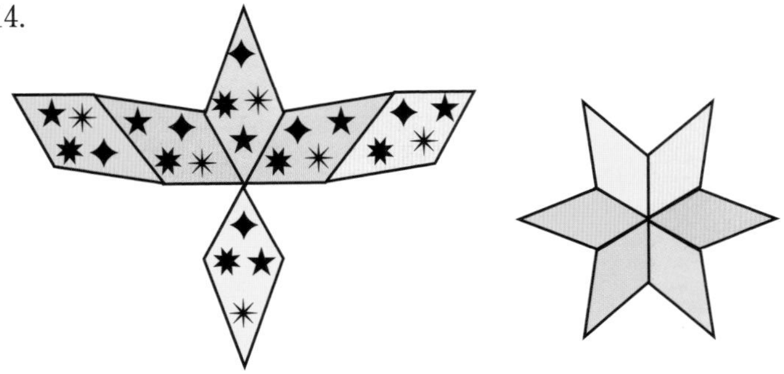

15.

16.

17.

18.

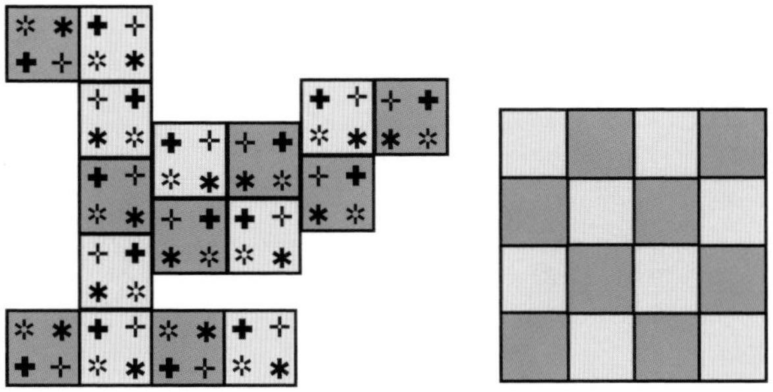

19.

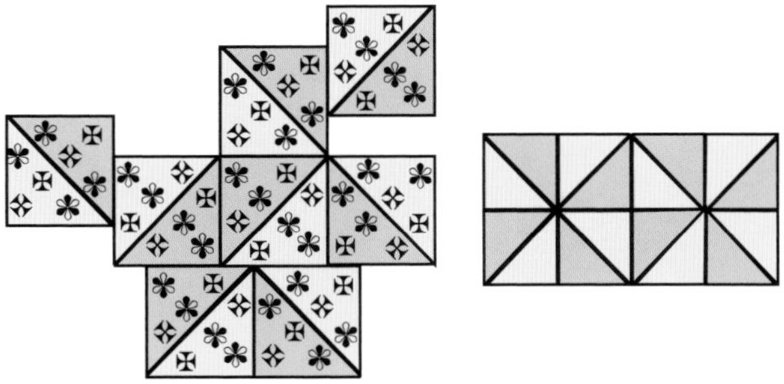

20.

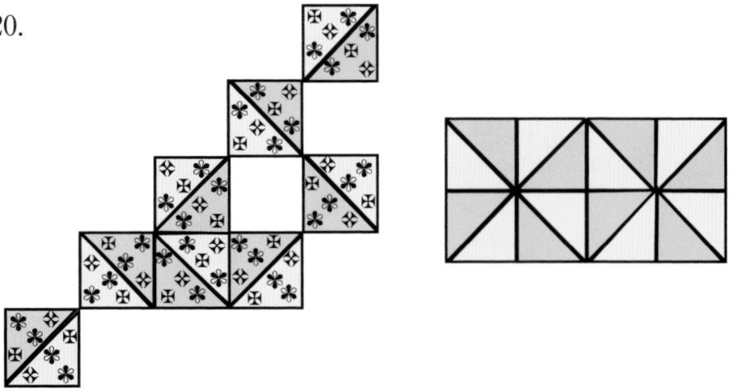

21.

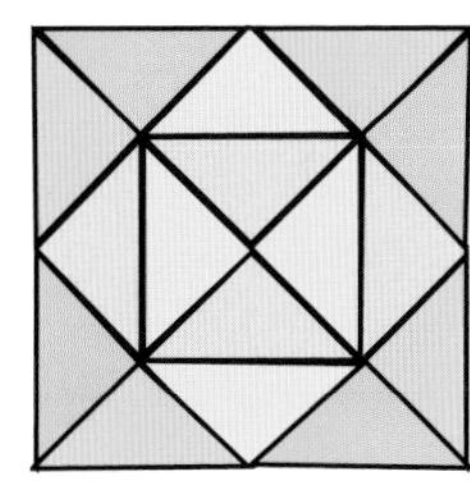

22.

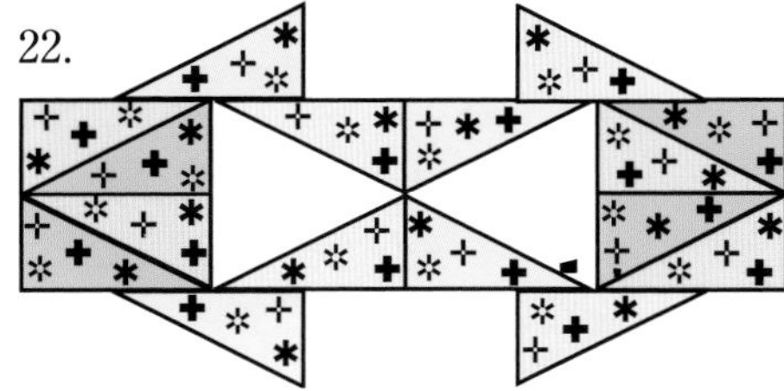

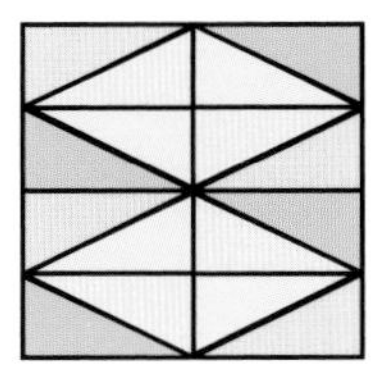

23.

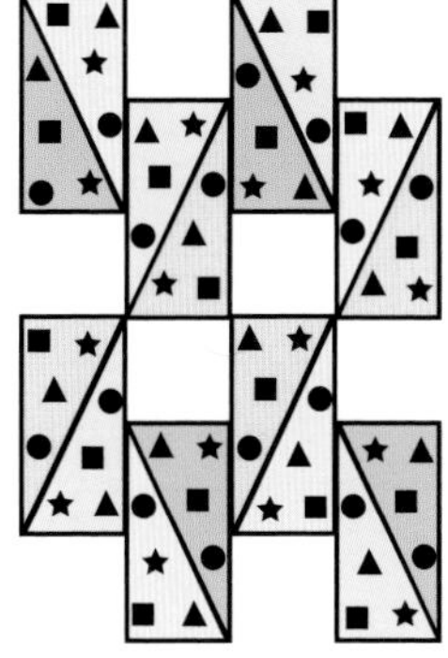

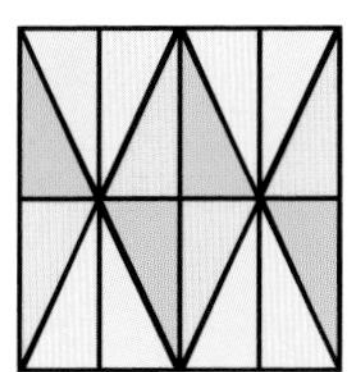

24.

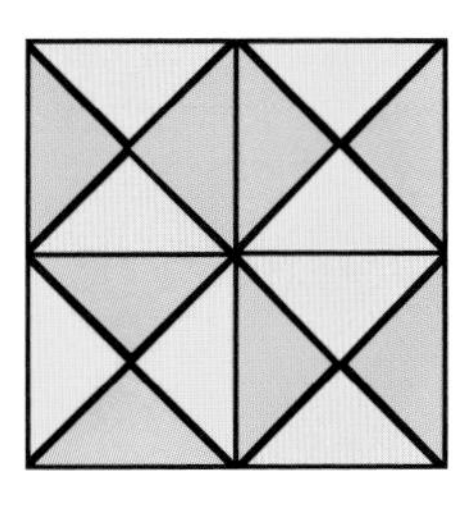

SUDOKU

1.

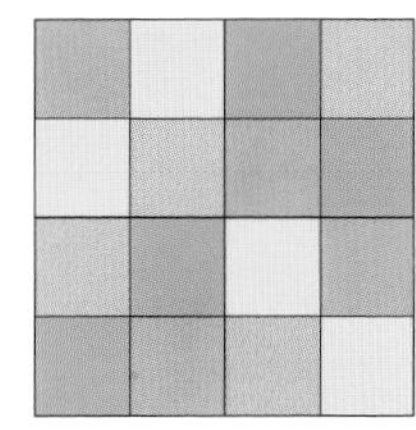

2.

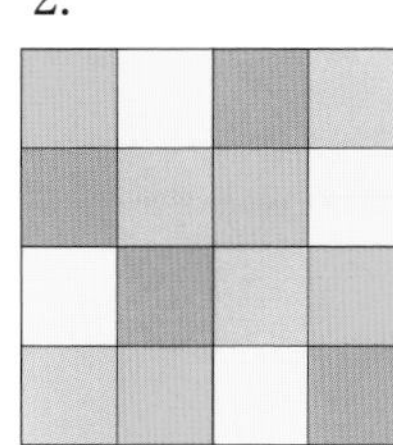

3.

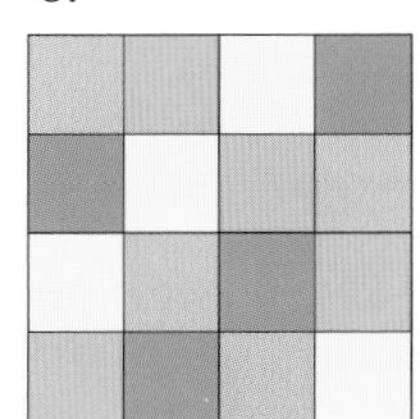

4.

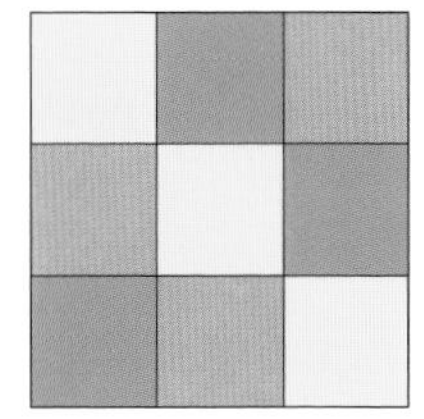

5.

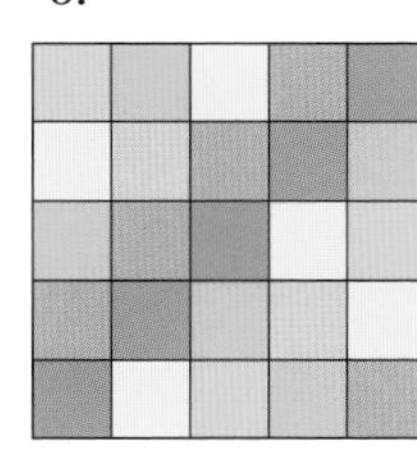

6.

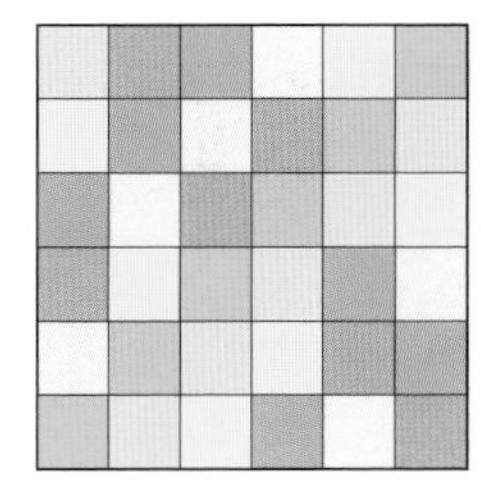

7.

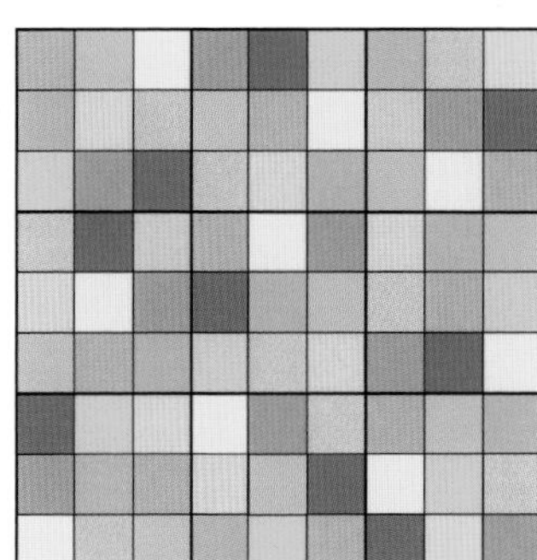

8.

9.

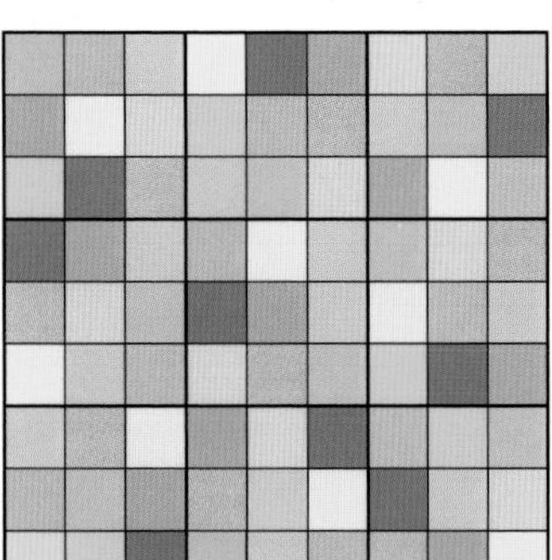

10.

11.

Δ	□	√	◇	O	×	Ω	☆	+
Ω	+	☆	□	Δ	√	O	◇	×
◇	×	O	Ω	+	☆	√	□	Δ
☆	Δ	◇	√	Ω	+	×	O	□
O	Ω	□	×	☆	Δ	+	√	◇
×	√	+	O	◇	□	☆	Δ	Ω
√	◇	×	+	□	O	Δ	Ω	☆
+	☆	Ω	Δ	√	◇	□	×	O
□	O	Δ	☆	×	Ω	◇	+	√

12.

O	☆	×	◇	√	Ω	□	Δ	+
Ω	□	◇	+	Δ	O	√	☆	×
Δ	√	+	☆	□	×	Ω	◇	O
◇	Ω	O	×	+	□	☆	√	Δ
□	+	Δ	Ω	☆	√	×	O	◇
☆	×	√	O	◇	Δ	+	Ω	□
√	Δ	Ω	□	×	◇	O	+	☆
×	◇	☆	√	O	+	Δ	□	Ω
+	O	□	Δ	Ω	☆	◇	×	√

13.

+	Δ	Ω	□	×	☆	√	◇	O
O	×	◇	√	+	Ω	Δ	☆	□
□	☆	√	Δ	O	◇	×	+	Ω
Δ	Ω	+	◇	☆	×	O	□	√
◇	√	☆	Ω	□	O	+	×	Δ
×	□	O	+	Δ	√	◇	Ω	☆
√	◇	□	O	Ω	+	☆	Δ	×
☆	O	Δ	×	◇	□	Ω	√	+
Ω	+	×	☆	√	Δ	□	O	◇

14.

×	Ω	□	+	◇	☆	O	Δ	√
☆	√	O	×	Δ	□	Ω	+	◇
+	Δ	◇	Ω	O	√	□	×	☆
◇	×	Ω	O	□	+	☆	√	Δ
Δ	□	√	☆	Ω	×	◇	O	+
O	+	☆	Δ	√	◇	×	Ω	□
Ω	◇	+	□	×	Δ	√	☆	O
√	☆	×	◇	+	O	Δ	□	Ω
□	O	Δ	√	☆	Ω	+	◇	×

15.

Δ	◇	Ω	+	×	☆	□	O	√
√	☆	□	O	Δ	Ω	+	◇	×
+	×	O	√	□	◇	Ω	Δ	☆
Ω	Δ	◇	□	+	×	☆	√	O
☆	O	+	Ω	√	Δ	◇	×	□
□	√	×	◇	☆	O	Δ	Ω	+
×	□	☆	Δ	◇	√	O	+	Ω
O	+	Δ	×	Ω	□	√	☆	◇
◇	Ω	√	☆	O	+	×	□	Δ

16.

×	Ω	+	□	◇	O	☆	√	Δ
☆	O	Δ	√	Ω	×	□	+	◇
◇	√	□	☆	+	Δ	Ω	O	×
Δ	+	◇	Ω	√	□	×	☆	O
O	×	√	Δ	☆	+	◇	Ω	□
Ω	□	☆	O	×	◇	√	Δ	+
+	☆	O	×	□	Ω	Δ	◇	√
□	◇	Ω	+	Δ	√	O	×	☆
√	Δ	×	◇	O	☆	+	□	Ω

17.

Δ	Ω	□	☆	√	O	◇	+	×
×	+	√	Ω	◇	Δ	☆	O	□
☆	O	◇	+	□	×	√	Δ	Ω
□	×	+	◇	O	☆	Ω	√	Δ
√	☆	Δ	□	×	Ω	+	◇	O
O	◇	Ω	√	Δ	+	×	□	☆
Ω	√	×	Δ	+	□	O	☆	◇
◇	□	☆	O	Ω	√	Δ	×	+
+	Δ	O	×	☆	◇	□	Ω	√

18.

O	√	+	☆	×	Ω	Δ	□	◇
Δ	◇	□	√	O	+	Ω	☆	×
Ω	☆	×	□	◇	Δ	√	+	O
□	×	Ω	O	+	☆	◇	Δ	√
◇	+	☆	×	Δ	√	□	O	Ω
√	O	Δ	Ω	□	◇	☆	×	+
×	Ω	◇	+	☆	□	O	√	Δ
☆	Δ	O	◇	√	×	+	Ω	□
+	□	√	Δ	Ω	O	×	◇	☆

19.

□	☆	◇	+	×	√	Ω	O	Δ
Ω	O	Δ	☆	□	◇	×	√	+
+	×	√	Δ	Ω	O	□	☆	◇
O	√	×	□	Δ	☆	◇	+	Ω
☆	+	Ω	◇	O	×	√	Δ	□
Δ	◇	□	√	+	Ω	☆	×	O
√	□	+	×	◇	Δ	O	Ω	☆
×	Δ	O	Ω	☆	□	+	◇	√
◇	Ω	☆	O	√	+	Δ	□	×

20.

Ω	√	□	Δ	◇	☆	+	O	×
×	+	O	□	Ω	√	☆	◇	Δ
☆	◇	Δ	+	O	×	□	Ω	√
√	☆	◇	O	□	Δ	×	+	Ω
□	O	Ω	☆	×	+	Δ	√	◇
Δ	×	+	Ω	√	◇	O	□	☆
+	Ω	×	√	Δ	O	◇	☆	□
◇	□	☆	×	+	Ω	√	Δ	O
O	Δ	√	◇	☆	□	Ω	×	+

21.

√	+	◇	×	□	Δ	Ω	O	☆
☆	Ω	×	+	O	√	□	Δ	◇
O	Δ	□	☆	Ω	◇	+	√	×
Δ	√	+	□	◇	☆	O	×	Ω
◇	□	O	Ω	×	+	Δ	☆	√
Ω	×	☆	Δ	√	O	◇	+	□
+	O	Ω	◇	☆	×	√	□	Δ
×	◇	Δ	√	+	□	☆	Ω	O
□	☆	√	O	Δ	Ω	×	◇	+

22.

O	√	+	☆	×	Ω	Δ	□	◇
Δ	◇	□	√	O	+	Ω	☆	×
Ω	☆	×	□	◇	Δ	√	+	O
□	×	Ω	O	+	☆	◇	Δ	√
◇	+	☆	×	Δ	√	□	O	Ω
√	O	Δ	Ω	□	◇	☆	×	+
×	Ω	◇	+	☆	□	O	√	Δ
☆	Δ	O	◇	√	×	+	Ω	□
+	□	√	Δ	Ω	O	×	◇	☆

23.

☆	◇	Ω	×	√	+	□	O	Δ
O	×	Δ	□	Ω	◇	+	√	☆
+	√	□	O	☆	Δ	◇	Ω	×
√	Ω	◇	Δ	□	☆	O	×	+
□	☆	O	+	×	Ω	√	Δ	◇
×	Δ	+	√	◇	O	☆	□	Ω
◇	O	×	☆	Δ	□	Ω	+	√
Ω	+	√	◇	O	×	Δ	☆	□
Δ	□	☆	Ω	+	√	×	◇	O

24.

O	☆	×	◇	√	Ω	□	Δ	+
Ω	□	◇	+	Δ	O	√	☆	×
Δ	√	+	☆	□	×	Ω	◇	O
◇	Ω	O	×	+	□	☆	√	Δ
□	+	Δ	Ω	☆	√	×	O	◇
☆	×	√	O	◇	Δ	+	Ω	□
√	Δ	Ω	□	×	◇	O	+	☆
×	◇	☆	√	O	+	Δ	□	Ω
+	O	□	Δ	Ω	☆	◇	×	√

25.

O	□	+	×	☆	Ω	◇	√	Δ
Δ	Ω	√	+	◇	□	O	×	☆
◇	×	☆	O	√	Δ	□	+	Ω
×	Δ	◇	√	□	☆	+	Ω	O
□	+	O	Δ	Ω	×	√	☆	◇
√	☆	Ω	◇	+	O	Δ	□	×
☆	√	×	□	O	◇	Ω	Δ	+
Ω	O	□	☆	Δ	+	×	◇	√
+	◇	Δ	Ω	×	√	☆	O	□

26.

Ω	+	□	√	☆	×	◇	Δ	O
Δ	☆	◇	□	Ω	O	+	×	√
√	O	×	Δ	+	◇	Ω	□	☆
□	Δ	+	◇	√	Ω	O	☆	×
×	√	Ω	☆	O	+	Δ	◇	□
O	◇	☆	×	Δ	□	√	Ω	+
+	×	Δ	Ω	□	√	☆	O	◇
☆	□	O	+	◇	Δ	×	√	Ω
◇	Ω	√	O	×	☆	□	+	Δ